CANADIAN CULTURE

AN INTRODUCTORY READER

EDITED BY ELSPETH CAMERON

CANADIAN SCHOLARS' PRESS · TORONTO · 1997

First published in 1997 by Canadian Scholars' Press Inc.
180 Bloor Street West, Ste 402
Toronto, Ontario M5S 2V6

Canadian Cataloguing in Publication Data

Main entry under title:

Canadian culture: an introductory reader

ISBN 1-55130-090-7

1. Canada – Intellectual life. 2. Arts – Canada.
3. Humanities – Canada.   I. Cameron, Elspeth, 1943-   .

FC95.C34 1997   971   C96-931463-9
F1021.C35 1997

PRINTED AND BOUND IN CANADA

CONTENTS

Introduction • 7

INTRODUCTION

What does it mean to be Canadian? What sort of people are we, and what values are typically ours? If current social theory is valid and such values are "constructed" by the societies we inhabit, which values are "Canadian?" And how are they imbedded, encoded or expressed in our culture?

This collection of readings approaches answers to these questions in a number of ways. First, historically — a stance that may in itself signal a Canadian way of understanding the world. For a country that has never had a revolution, never fought a civil war, and — more important — has frequently defined itself *against* other nations which have done so — evolution is preferable to abrupt change. To understand what it means to be Canadian, a Canadian is likely to ask next what it *meant* to be Canadian. To comprehend the present, take a look at the past.

This book is no exception. Although selections are not arranged in strict chronological order, these readings pre-date Canada's Confederation in 1867, touch on the surge of nationalism that accompanied the Centennial celebrations in 1967, but mainly address the vital shifts and re-constructions of national cultural self-image that have occurred since.

The thematic sections into which these "historical" excerpts are arranged is a structure deliberately intended to emphasize a few salient themes in Canadian culture. It must be admitted at once that this structural emphasis is artificial. Many readings on closer examination will reveal characteristics that might just as well have resulted in their inclusion elsewhere. The winter setting in Timothy Findley's story "Foxes," for example, qualifies it for inclusion in the section on "The North," or — since it also features definite aspects of the city of Toronto — it could have been defined as an example of "Regionalism," typical in many ways of central Canada or, more precisely, southern Ontario. Similarly, the "season" in the life of Marie-Claire Blais' Emmanuel is winter. And historian Sylvia Van Kirk's description of Indian women in the fur trade is both expressive of "Regionalism," since it studies a Western phenomenon, and a poignant example of "Beautiful Losers." Such overlapping characteristics, however, serve to confirm a closely meshed cultural fabric. I have isolated important threads, but they are meant to catch the light of other threads with an iridescent effect.

More important, these arbitrary categories seem — and indeed often *are* — mutually exclusive. How can a strong sense of "Nationalism" coexist with a strong sense of "*Inter*nationalism?" And how can "Regionalism" find a place next either? This paradox, too, betrays a Canadian characteristic. Many have observed that there never was, and certainly currently is, no one way of being Canadian. As the popular joke goes, it is possible to say "as American as apple pie," but there is no Canadian equivalent. We can say only the tentative and self-deprecating "as Canadian as might be expected under the circumstances." These readings and my categories intentionally suggest that Canadians are comfortable in what might be called an ideological limbo. Holding in suspension two or more mutually exclusive sets of values and finding irony or wry humour in the situation is a confusing, but characteristic, Canadian stance.

So, these selections are historical, arbitrary, inter-related and sometimes mutually exclusive. Behind them lies one basic assumption: the way people in a particular society relate to reality — or rather *invent*, then collude in, a collective "reality" — can be located not only in its political and economic systems but also in patterns of intellectual or cultural expression. Such patterns are demonstrated directly in the choice of subjects cultural theorists and artists address — that is, in content — and indirectly through the ways in which those subjects are treated or expressed. What do Canadians chose to write or sing about, paint or study? If such choices involve human subjects, what are these people like? What issues intrigue them? What point of view is taken? What atmosphere is created? What assumptions are made? Some answers at least can be located in popular as well as elitist works of art or essays on cultural and social matters, also in music and film.

Ideally this book would contain excerpts from music and film. It was possible to print song lyrics, but readers are urged to listen and look at the tapes and videos mentioned wherever they are available (and given new library and art gallery technologies as well as NFB distribution networks they *are* widely available). Similarly, colour reproductions and slides of paintings — or, better still, the paintings

ELSPETH CAMERON

themselves — say more than the black-and-white representations necessarily offered here.

These selections begin where Canada began — or rather *didn't* begin, for the colonial state evolved gradually, arrogantly imposing its ideologies and customs on the aboriginal cultures which were deeply rooted across the country. That early colonial state is well-expressed in Voltaire's dismissive and ignorant description of New France as "quelques arpents de neige." Today it lingers in such nominal political positions as the Queen's representative, the Governor General, in Quebec's attachment to a global Francophonie and other vague traces of fellow-feeling and symbolic links abroad.

Early immigrants (or, more accurately, *emigrants*) — like Susanna Moodie — tended to back into Canada, their eyes firmly fixed on what they were losing. That included specifically a long-standing culture elsewhere. It still does. Though the dynamic affecting immigrants is much more complex than I am suggesting here, sociologist John Porter's concept of the "vertical mosaic" is useful in that it acknowledges a nation composed of a variety of ethnic groups, and a national predisposition not to interfere with the customs, beliefs and rights of those different from oneself.

From the earliest records in Canada — the journals and diaries of explorers, missionaries and settlers, and, long before that, the artifacts of aboriginal groups — there is a keen sense of being marginal. As literary critic Northrop Frye succinctly put it in the NFB film, which documents his personal understanding of what it means to be Canadian, *Journey Without Arrival*, "Head Office is somewhere else."

Much in the Canadian identity is tied to the land itself. For this reason, despite the fact that this collection focuses on culture rather than the social sciences, I have opened with economic historian Harold Innis' classic statement in his "Conclusion" to *The Fur Trade in Canada* of the way in which Canada emerged "not in spite of geography, but because of it." The physical shape of Canada, the east-west thrust of the fur trade that signalled Canada's role as a marginal source furnishing European markets, the way — as Frye puts it — that the experience of entering Canada as early explorers and settlers did from the east into the deep gulf of the St. Lawrence River is like being swallowed, literally engulfed. We are — and always were — a marginal people. And we have seen to it that the indigenous peoples who were the only hope for a culture deeply rooted in place were marginalized too. The NFB film *The Other*

Side of the Ledger: An Indian View of the Hudson's Bay Company, art historian Dennis Reid's description of painter Paul Kane's "records" of Indian life, Sylvia Van Kirk's study of the central social role of Indian women in the fur trade (a conscious revision of Innis's theories) and Daniel Francis's thoughts on the white European appropriation and stereotyping of the image of the Indian, all go far in explaining this travesty.

The Canadian conviction of marginal status was confirmed and deepened by the ascendency of the American industrial empire, notably in the 1950s, when technologies honed to meet wartime needs were turned to peacetime uses. As intellectual historian Carl Berger has shown in his essay "The True North Strong and Free," much of the rhetoric in Canada during the American Civil War — the years that led up to Confederation — defined Canadians as marginal, but superior to Americans. Though the term "anti-American" would not appear until much later, such "American" characteristics as decadence, a predilection for violence, immorality and a chaotic "me-first" democracy amounted to a Canadian denigration of American values and a determination not to be taken over by the larger, stronger, wealthier country to the south. As journalist and popular historian Pierre Berton shows in *Hollywood's Canada*, and as the Heritage Minute films on Sam Steele of the Northwest Mounted Police and Indian chief Sitting Bull also demonstrate, Canadians still tend to turn their marginality *vis-à-vis* the United States into a smug sense of moral superiority. In part sour grapes, this sensitivity to the suspicion that powerful "others" may deliberately or — worse — inadvertently try to take us over (politically, economically, culturally) is essentially the defensive stance of the vulnerable. The English version of our national anthem expresses this in the repeated line "O, Canada, we stand on guard for thee;" and in the French version, the line — also repeated — "Protegera nos foyers et nos droits."

This defensive orientation to a larger world where "Head Office is somewhere else," has predisposed minority groups in Canada — of which there are many — to be suspicious even of the stronger groups *within* the country. French Canada cannot stomach the *maudit Anglais*. Native peoples rebel against centuries of unfair treatment. There is considerable resentment in the West and Maritimes towards central Canada. Even *within* minority groups with such grievances, there exist sub-groups who feel marginalized. The debates at Meech Lake in 1991, for instance, made clear that aboriginal women's groups harboured serious complaints against the men in control of their societies. And historian Robin W. Winks concludes from his examination (including on-site interviews) of blacks in Canada, that "the common mistake of whites — liberals as well as conservatives — [is] of viewing blacks as a monolith."

Not surprisingly, the feminism of the last half of the century meshed with the Canadian tendency to feel marginalized to produce a special and powerful dynamic that might be called national-feminism or feminist-nationalism: an ideological combination usually thought to be mutually exclusive. Margaret Atwood's work is a clear example of this phenomenon. There has long been a tendency to envisage Canada as female in relation to the patriarchal U.S., and a corresponding tendency to see Quebec as female in relation to English Canada. Analogies to the wife, the mistress, the kept woman abound in commentary at all levels about Canada. In "'Shape Shifters': Canadian Women Writers and the Tradition," literary critic Linda Hutcheon draws this same analogy, claiming that Canada's essential literary voice is the voice of a woman. As soon as there is a "tradition," it becomes, for Canadians, "Head Office;" and there follows a suspicion of power and a repositioning that brings margins to the fore. This same pattern can be seen in art historian Maria Tippett's endeavour to restore balance to a patriarchal canon of Canadian art. Florence McGillivray and Henrietta Mabel May, exact contemporaries of Tom Thomson and the Group of Seven painters, is one of the many female artists Tippett rescues from second-rate status in *By A Lady* and lauds them as producing vital work equal to that of their male counterparts. Revisionist work such as Tippett's or Van Kirk's or Daniel Francis's — and Giorgio di Ciccio's "Male Rage Poem," a cry from the male margin in a feminist world — is profoundly Canadian.

Perhaps this discomfort with the loss of marginality through the location of a tradition, a mainstream or a centre explains something about the Canadian taste for self-deprecating satire such as Stephen Leacock's *My Financial Career*, Robert Service's *The Cremation of Sam McGee*, Paul Hiebert's *Sarah Binks*, numerous Heritage Minute films, such as *Joe Naismith*, the Canadian who invented basketball, and the NFB film on how the beaver came to be our national symbol, *The Canadian Scream*.

It is partly *because* the north is the most marginal area of our marginal country that it has always been a significant repository for Canadians' sense of themselves. It is, by analogy, the blank white sheet upon which we project many of our characteristics. For white European immigrants in the nineteenth century — as Carl Berger has shown — it conveniently symbolized such virtues (largely Christian) as purity, moral strength, chastity, good health, freedom and spirituality. For Lawren Harris, a mystic, the exquisite northern landscapes that attracted him (including the northern landscapes of Norwegian painter Harald Sohlberg whose work inspired him) evoked powerful "psychic vibrations." The notion of Canadians as a "northern" people (i.e., from northern Europe) formed a stark symbolic contrast with the darker, hedonistic, immoral races that were seen as sullying the American society to the south.

This concept was not only a distortion of immigration patterns, which were varied and complex, it was also unmistakably racist. Founded on the then-popular notions of Darwin's concepts of "survival of the fittest" and Kiplingesque bravado about the glory of the British Empire as it imposed its "superior" traditions and genes on the colonies, Canadians attributed to their northern geography (much of which few Canadians then or now actually experienced first-hand) moral, physical and spiritual virtues. That this was an imaginative construct is obvious in the virtual absence of reference to the *real* northern inhabitants who for generations had certainly proved they were fit to survive a harsh climate, the Inuit and others who were neither white nor European.

Snowy landscapes, blizzards, igloos, icebergs, ice-sculpture, northern lights, snowmen, snowbirds, snow angels, polar bears — and, in popular culture, the Abominable Snowman, Jack Frost and Ookpik — weave in and out of Canadian artistic productions like a keen white thread. As Quebecois poet and musician Gilles Vigneault wrote in his poignant, classic waltz: "Mon pays, ce n'est pas un pays, c'est l'hiver." Whether humourously rendered as in Dawson City poet Robert Service's quintessestial and popular verse "The Cremation of Sam McGee" or seriously represented as in Group of Seven painter Lawren Harris's snowscapes and icebergs, composer Harry Somers's eerie arching violins and pianist Glenn Gould's carefully researched and emotionally profound Centennial CBC-radio programme "The Idea of North," the equation of "Canadian" and "northern" is an enduring one. Bob and Doug Mackenzie's comic Canadian version of the English carol "The Twelve Days of Christmas" from their album *The Great White North* pokes fun at the irrelevance of British tradition for Canadians as well as at the stereotypical image non-Canadians have

ELSPETH CAMERON

of us as illiterate beer-drinking louts clad in lumberjack coats and tuques against the cold.

The conviction that there is more than one way to be Canadian is not just the result of groups and sub-groups struggling to define themselves against colonialism, whether that colonialism was British political control or, later, American economic control, or, yet later, central Canadian — or whatever other internal — control. Nor does it stem simply from a consequent sensitivity to a sort of filling of the vacuum felt in the absence of some important and powerful centrality. Typically, it was a decision made *outside* the country that made it as Canadian to be French-speaking, Roman Catholic, governed by the Napoleonic Code of law as it was to be English-speaking, Protestant, and governed by the British Constitution. Depending on whether the view is English or French, Britain acquired New France as a result of "The Conquest of New France" or "The *Cession* of New France" in 1760 within a year after the famous Battle on the Plains of Abraham in Quebec City on 13 September 1759 between Wolfe and Montcalm. It was Britain's decision to grant New France continued rights of religion, language and legal system within British North America in the Quebec Act of 1774. In other words, the bi-national, bi-lingual, bi-cultural — and indeed bi-religious and bi-legal — nature of Canada is fundamental to this nation's identity.

Hugh MacLennan's intentionally nationalistic and ground-breaking novel *Two Solitudes* was written to illustrate the *superiority* of Canada's political and social arrangement of the peaceful coexistence of profoundly different groups to the European nations at war in 1945. Ironically, the title became a catch-phrase for the irreconcilable differences between the two "nations" and has been used whenever the extremely volatile emotions on both sides have been stirred. Today, MacLennan's novel seems heavy-handed. And his rosy conclusion in which intermarriage between French and English mollify both sides through love proved off-target, as he recognized in his essay "Two Solitudes Thirty-three Years Later." It is not his own prophecies he sees coming to pass with the election of the first Separatiste provincial government under René Levesque in 1976, but those in the much bleaker conclusion of a novel by his French Canadian contemporary, Gabrielle Roy's *Bonheur d'occasion* (translated into English as *The Tin Flute*) (1945).

The issues MacLennan explored are still with us. When push comes to shove, as it did during the Conscription crisis depicted by

MacLennan in the excerpt from his novel printed here, English and French Canadians differ dramatically in their priorities. And, as MacLennan also makes clear, there is a tendency for all groups to reduce other groups to stereotypes, a tendency that was a blind spot for MacLennan himself. The portrait of rural life in Quebec depicted in Marie-Claire Blais's *A Season in the Life of Emmanuel* — a portrait painted from the inside — is radically different from MacLennan's happy farm folk, his nun-like Marie-Adele, Quebec M.P. Athanase Tallard's first wife, or his benign, idealistic priest, Father Beaubien. Blais uses black humour to observe the rank poverty, inadequate education, religious corruption and general demoralization of a people. In other words, given MacLennan's *Two Solitudes*, Blais's novel twenty years later could be seen as inadvertently revisionist fiction.

If a nation is fundamentally — as in "founded upon" — two nations that are as decidedly different as English and French Canada, the *principle* of "difference within sameness" is established. The choice has been made *not* to assimilate the other, but to coexist with that other. On *principle*, then, the way is open for other "differences" to be included. If there can be two solitudes, there is no reason why there cannot be more. This is the implication of Michael Greenstein's study of Jewish-Canadian Literature, *Third Solitudes*, a particularly apt concept since the Jewish population in Quebec since the beginning of this century was certainly large and important enough not to have been overlooked by MacLennan or other cultural theorists. The idea of a third solitude begs the question of the native peoples who predated both the English and the French. The NFB film, *The Other Side of the Ledger* (1972) takes a second look at the formation of the Hudson's Bay Company, not from the point of view of the traders and factors described by Innis and assumed to be carrying on the great work of expanding the British Empire and economy, but from the point of view of the Indians whose labour was exploited and whose land was "bought" to their great disadvantage. Like Marie-Claire Blais's picture of rural Quebec from the inside, this film strips away colonial hypocrisy and exposes the self-defeating attitudes of the oppressed that mesh tragically with circumstances. Looking at the same problem from a completely different perspective in *The Imaginary Indian*, Daniel Francis demonstrates the ways in which the most serious exploitation of Canadian native peoples occurred: the appropriation of their very identity through image-making. For this

ELSPETH CAMERON

reason, Francis's work echoes Pierre Berton's *Hollywood's Canada*; just as Berton showed how Hollywood imposed a distorted image of Canada and Canadians on us as a nation, Francis shows how immigrant European settlers appropriated and twisted beyond recognition the voices and customs of aboriginal peoples. From this proliferation of ethnic solitudes out of the original two solitudes, many, many other solitudes based on race, class, ethnicity or gender — or various combinations of these social constructions — have found their voices. The NFB film *Forbidden Love*, for example, illustrates vividly the marginal and persecuted lives of lesbian Canadians during the mid-twentieth century.

It might well be asked how such a plural society — a "group of groups" as it is sometimes called — could possibly experience nationalism. How could a society whose tendency on finding a centre or locating power and success prefer to turn its attention to a different margin? In fact, Canada has experienced nationalism, notably at three specific points in our history. First, at Confederation, when poets and painters were urged, or felt inspired, to compose works such as Sir Charles G.D. Roberts's jingoistic poem "Canada" or Lucien O'Brien's collection of paintings commissioned for *Picturesque Canada* (1882) in imitation of the American record of national landscapes *Picturesque America* a few years earlier. During the First World War, partly as a result of serving overseas with Canadians from other parts of Canada, but particularly after the success of Canadian troops at Vimy Ridge, Canadians felt pride in nationhood and expressed it in such works as the paintings of the Group of Seven (some of whom served as military artists overseas) and John McCrae's classic poem "In Flanders Field."

The strongest upsurge of nationalism occurred around the national celebration of the Centennial in 1967. Expo '67 in Montreal brought together many Canadian cultural figures, numerous books on Canada were published and eagerly bought — including the first encyclopedic literary history of Canada, the popularity of the strongly federalist Pierre Elliott Trudeau inspired enthusiasm for a strongly united nation. Throughout our history, the strongest and most vivid symbol of Canadian nationalism has been the railway. It is a clear example of the east-west thrust described by Innis as stemming from our specific geography and the infrastructure needed for our early staples economy. The image of Donald Smith driving in the last spike at Craigellachie, B.C. in 1885 has stood for the triumph of human will over natural obstacles, as well as for the linking of disparate communities and landscapes that emphsizes closure and unity rather than the fragmentation of two or more solitudes. E.J. Pratt's poem "Towards the Last Spike" is one of many celebrations of this national enterprise (frequently referred to as "The National Dream" of our first prime minister, Sir John A. Macdonald), but it exhibits also Pratt's imaginative grasp of Canada's inexorable geography in ways that reinforce Innis's theories and Berger's analysis of Canada's "northern" temperament.

Both internationalism and regionalism are more congenial "isms" than nationalism to a nation that distrusts "isms" in the first place. Since immigrants to Canada have often maintained strong links to their homelands, and since assimilation on arrival is not expected because no homogeneous society ever took shape here, an ongoing interest in the "global village," as Canadian communications theorist Marshall McLuhan called it, is hardly surprising. In other words, Canada might be described as a group of groups that represents in microcosm the larger world of nations. To some idealists, it seems to be what MacLennan hoped to demonstrate in *Two Solitudes*: a mini-United Nations or a successful national experiment in peaceful coexistence.

The notion of Canada as peace broker for other nations (as in the Heritage Minute film on Lester Pearson's peace-keeping mission in the Suez) arises from this perception. For some intellectuals and artists, especially those such as civil rights activist F.R. Scott and poet Earle Birney who saw the destructive effects of nationalism in the Second World War, internationalism was a positive concept. Both these men, like Mavis Gallant who left Montreal for Paris in 1950 where she has lived since, spent considerable portions of their lives outside Canada without ever feeling that this made them any less Canadian. For others, like Pier Giorgio di Cicco, the choice of a subject in a work like "Male Rage Poem" addresses males far beyond Canadian borders. The subject is universal.

The flip side of Canadians' ease in international settings — the ways in which others outside Canada see us — is important. Because "Head Office" is assumed to be somewhere else, Canadian culture for a long time was not just partly shaped from outside, but artists often looked to international markets for approval before being convinced of success. As novelist Robertson Davies once wryly observed, Canadian audiences won't applaud a play unless a British or American audience already applauded it. Because

Canada is not a world power, and because our society is complex, outsiders know little about us. In her poem "At the Tourist Centre in Boston," Margaret Atwood satirizes some of the misconceptions others have of us, misconceptions similar to those treated elsewhere in Berton's *Hollywood's Canada*.

Defining the regions of Canada is a game Canadians like to play. No one can win. The most common definition involves east-to-west blocks of provinces based on geographical common denominators. The Maritimes (Nova Scotia, New Brunswick, Prince Edward Island, Newfoundland); Central Canada (Quebec and Ontario); the Prairies (Manitoba, Saskatchewan, Alberta); the West Coast (British Columbia). For obvious reasons, though, Ontario and Quebec are often seen as separate regions. Central Canada tends to see itself not as a region at all, but as *the* economic and political centre against which the more "rural" regions are defined. Newfoundland, which entered Confederation only in 1949, is usually considered a separate entity, complete with a set of Newfie jokes. The north is sometimes considered a region, but at other times is split into more than one region as northern extensions of the provinces. Albertans, with their foothills and Rocky Mountains, do not appreciate being lumped in with the true prairie provinces. And, finally, there exist within the traditional regions of Canada a number of smaller regions which emphasize the connection between place and ethnicity — such as the Acadians in Nova Scotia and New Brunswick (extending into New England in the U.S.), or the Doukabours in B.C., or the Oka in Quebec; or, indeed, the French populations of Manitoba and New Brunswick, who claim significant, separate status.

To complicate matters, regionalism also has a historical dimension. The early painters and writers in Canada, for example, often saw themselves as doing descriptive work. Much like photographic journalists or television crews today, they tried to capture the specific characteristics of landscape and social custom for audiences elsewhere — usually the home country where audiences, publishers, galleries and markets were located. In answering such questions as "What does it look like there?" or "How do people live in that climate?" for markets abroad, they demonstrated that in the arts too, Canada was a margin related to "Head Offices" elsewhere. The result was to lengthen the period of cultural colonialism through what Russell Harper in his *Painting in Canada* calls "surface realism."

After the First World War, regionalism in Canada took on deeper meaning as a more intimate search for meaning in immediate surroundings. This stage — and it was merely a stage — in the arts in Canada represented the first tentative statements *by* Canadians, and *for* Canadians, of the nature of life in specific locations. Although the 1920s paintings of the Group of Seven are usually construed as nationalistic, they can also be seen as a visual exploration of the landscape of the Canadian Shield. For western Canadians, whose landscape does not include the brilliant fall maples so often the subject of the Group's paintings, their works do not read as national statements. E.J. Pratt's "Newfoundland" broke new ground in 1923 as the first significant attempt in verse to capture the harsh sounds and pounding rhythms of life lived in bleak conditions next an intractable sea — the entry, it could be argued, of Canadian poetry into the modern period. The "high realism" paintings of Maritime artist Alex Colville, such as *Boy, Dog and the St. John River* (1958), or *Church and Horse* (1964) are lovingly detailed records of local landscapes and customs in the daily lives of ordinary people. Colville captures the essence of this type of regionalism when he describes himself as having "a fantastic and deep emotional attachment to the Maritime Provinces." Though what artists and critics call "realism" is always to some extent an aesthetic construction, W.O. Mitchell's "A Boy's Prairie," Frederick Philip Grove's "Snow" and William Kurelek's documentary paintings do for the prairie what Colville did for the Maritimes. A.M. Klein's poem, "Montreal," is a playful and witty attempt to reflect in often-invented language the intertextuality of a city in which English, French, Jewish and aboriginal cultures and languages jostle for attention. In this poem, Montreal is seen as a specific region in itself, unlike any other in Quebec. The carvings and prints of the Inuit represent not only habits and a habitat, but also a coherent world view that underlies both. As most of these examples demonstrate, universal themes and truths can be conveyed through intensely specific settings and communities.

The well-known engagement of Emily Carr with the landscape and totems of the Haida Indians reflects the west coast landscape but also raises important questions about appropriation of culture and voice. Can someone from *outside* a culture give true expression to it? Or are the Haida alone entitled or qualified to do so? This is an important cultural issue in Canada, where marginal groups abound, for the argument is often made that *any* experience of

ELSPETH CAMERON

marginality suffices to induce empathy for all other marginalized people. This issue is complex and subtle, but from the outside, Canada's regions will for the time being continue to be seen in the simple, frequently inaccurate stereotypes imposed from the 1920s on by Hollywood and perpetuated in such mass media representations as the comic series "Veronica in Canada."

In the 1940s, when the pressure on Canadian artists to produce pan-Canadian nationalistic works was intense, regionalism was disdained. Artists generally did their best to avoid the ultimate put-downs "provincial" or "regional." These terms at that time meant "narrow," "superficial" or "trivial." Artists whose work was condemned by these labels were assumed to be culturally limited, if not illiterate. For some, such as Earle Birney or Mavis Gallant, avoiding regionalism meant eliminating descriptions that could betray a specific place in Canada and addressing an international audience. F.R. Scott's poem "Creed," is the quintessential statement of this identification with the human race, rather than with any specific region. For others, like Hugh MacLennan, it meant focusing on issues that were pertinent to the country as a whole.

It is because regionalism was regarded as amateurish art from a culturally illiterate hinterland that satire such as Paul Hiebert's *Sarah Binks* was so apt in the late 1940s. In documenting the life of Sarah, "The Sweet Songstress of Saskatchewan" (an entirely imaginary person), Hiebert mocked the poet-as-hick in a misogynist tour-de-force.

Sarah Binks is also one of a long line of beautiful losers typical of Canadian heroes. If a culture is marginal, if "Head Office" is somewhere else, if even the tentative establishment of a tradition inspires revisionist art and counter-movements rather than consolidation. If a culture is plural, it is not surprising that Canadians — as Charles Taylor argues in *Six Journeys* — do not particularly like heroes. Unlike the larger-than-life characters who predominate in the arts elsewhere, Canadian protagonists — a term which is more accurate than "hero" for Canadian subjects — tend to be ordinary. To paraphrase Harold Innis, they succeed not in spite of failure, but because of it. They are, in the phrase Leonard Cohen invented for the title to his second novel, *Beautiful Losers*. As Margaret Atwood argues in "Animals and Other Victims" from *Survival*, Canadians characteristically position themselves imaginatively as if they were animals on the verge of extinction. This contrasts vividly with the British representation of animals as social beings and with the

American identification with the hunter who pursues, then kills, his quarry. Atwood's theory, which was expressed also in Alec Lucas's chapter on Canadian writers of animal stories in the *Literary History of Canada* and in Frye's collection of cultural essays *The Bush Garden* (1965), is a useful concept.

As early as 1895, humourist Stephen Leacock portrayed a kind of self-effacement, an identification with the vulnerable little man, that struck a peculiarly Canadian note. "My Financial Career" encapsulates this stance. Much the same feeling about the relation of Canadians to their world can be observed in Timothy Findley's enigmatic short story "Foxes," where a man fantasizes about becoming a fox after trying on animal masks at a museum, and in Al Purdy's poignant "Lament for the Dorsets," a sympathetic tribute to an extinct northern tribe. The NFB film *Richard Cardinal: Cry from a Diary of a Metis Child* documents the tragic life of a much-marginalized boy who commits suicide at sixteen. Typically, the film emphasizes the good that resulted from this loss: the ways in which Richard was a beautiful loser.

Although the tendency in the arts in Canada is to explore either loss or the beauty of loss, the notion of the loser also invites satire. Bob and Doug Mackenzie, the fictitious brothers invented to pad out the percentage of "Canadian content" mandatory on Canadian radio and television networks, epitomize the ordinariness of Canadian protagonists, emphasize their marginality, illiteracy and naivety, and delight in them as losers who live their lives happily on the lowest possible level. The contrast between the elegant English Christmas carol "The Twelve Days of Christmas" and the Mackenzie brother's "Canadian" version pokes droll fun at our colonial status.

It is unlikely that Canadians will ever develop a homogeneous society expressed in an elegant and coherent artistic vision at all. As the last section of the famous Report of the Federal Committee on Bilingualism and Biculturalism pointed out in 1965, many Canadians interviewed for the Report made it clear that they considered themselves neither French nor English, but essentially from some other culture. Thus Book IV of the Report was titled "Multiculturalism." Almost simultaneously, the ten years of research of sociologist John Porter was published in his landmark study *The Vertical Mosaic*. Attention to multiculturalism within Canada has deepened and widened since them. Within each new wave of immigration comes new members to strengthen established communities, such as the Chinese or Ukrainians, or members of communities relatively new to Canada, such as the Vietnamese or Iranians. The so-called mosaic has not — and probably will not — settle into any definite mosaic.

It is only recently that some groups, such as the Japanese, have recorded their experiences in their voices. Joy Kogawa's *Obasan* (1981), based on the persecution of her family and her own letters during the deportation of what the Canadian government termed "enemy aliens," raises serious questions about the common notion that Canada is a place of tolerance and peace. More recently, Trinidadian writer Marlene Nourbese Philip has raised questions of the importance of language to culture in such works as *Harriet's Daughter* (1988), a novel for adolescents modelled on L.M. Montgomery's *Anne of Green Gables* (1908), which traces the difficult transplantation of a West Indian family into Toronto. Much academic study, such as Robin W. Winks' conclusion "The Black Tile in the Mosaic" from *The Blacks in Canada* (1971), has unearthed the facts and figures of a huge range of ethnic groups. In the visual arts, too, immigrants and established ethnic communities themselves have documented not only the facts but also the feelings undergone in adapting to a new place in which there is little pressure to assimilate.

Perhaps there is no better place to observe the cultural ideology of a nation than in its symbols. Canada is unique in having chosen its own flag very late in its history. The excerpts from the 1965 parliamentary debate that preceded that choice, the journalistic cartoons that highlighted the more ludicrous aspects of the endeavour and a sampling of some of the designs that were seriously discussed are reprinted here from John Ross Matheson's *Canada's Flag* (1980). They throw much light on how Canadians saw themselves. The fact that there *was* a debate — and a lengthy and heated one at that — is itself telling. Only a country without a consensus or strong central identity would entertain such an exercise. And the symbols and issues that surfaced and about which Canadians felt passionately — one way or the other — indicate essential values. Similarly, the NFB film documenting the process by which a number of artists, cultural figures and thinkers worked out suitable contributions to the fiftieth anniversary issue of Canada's only national cultural magazine is revealing. The title is all too Canadian, a phrase coined by

Northrop Frye in his conclusion to the *Literary History of Canada*: *Where Is Here?* More recently since 1991, Canadians have been widely exposed to the popular "Heritage Minutes," a series of one-minute historical moments intended to inspire national pride. Anyone who views this series of forty episodes will touch on the essence of Canadian culture, history and sociology. And finally, since our national symbol — the lowly beaver — is surely one of nature's more ridiculous animals, the NFB spoof on the National Dream — *The National Scream* about how the beaver came to be chosen to represent our nation — combines many of the themes and issues raised in these readings.

PART ONE:
MARGINS & CENTRES

Harold A. Innis

From "Conclusion"
The Fur Trade in Canada:
An Introduction to Canadian
Economic History

The methods by which the cultural traits of a civilization may persist with the least possible depreciation involve an appreciable dependence on the peoples of the homeland. The migrant is not in a position immediately to supply all his needs and to maintain the same standard of living as that to which he has been accustomed, even with the assistance of Indians, an extremely fertile imagination, and a benevolent Providence such as would serve Robinson Crusoe or the Swiss Family Robinson on a tropical island. If those needs are to be supplied he will be forced to rely on goods which are obtainable from the mother country.

These goods were obtained from the homeland by direct transportation as in the movement of settlers' effects and household goods, involving no direct transfer of ownership, or through gifts and missionary supplies, but the most important device was trade. Goods were produced as rapidly as possible to be sold at the most advantageous price in the home market in order to purchase other goods essential to the maintenance and improvement of the current standard of living. In other words these goods supplied by the home country enabled the migrant to maintain his standard of living and to make his adjustments to the new environment without serious loss.

The migrant was consequently in search of goods which could be carried over long distances by small and expensive sailboats and which were in such demand in the home country as to yield the largest profit. These goods were essentially those in demand for the manufacture of luxuries, or goods which were not produced, or produced to a slight extent, in the home country as in the case of gold and of furs and fish. The latter was in some sense a luxury under the primitive conditions of agriculture in Europe and the demands of Catholic peoples. The importance of metropolitan centres in which luxury goods were in most demand was crucial to the development of colonial North America. In these centres goods were manufactured for the consumption of colonials and in these centres goods produced in the colonies were sold at the highest price. The number of goods produced in a north temperate climate in an area dominated by Pre-Cambrian formations, to be obtained with little difficulty in sufficient quantity and disposed of satisfactorily in the home market under prevailing transport conditions, was limited.

The most promising source of early trade was found in the abundance of fish, especially cod, to be caught off the Grand Banks of Newfoundland and in the territory adjacent to the Gulf of St. Lawrence. The abundance of cod led the peoples concerned to direct all their available energy to the prosecution of the fishing industry which developed extensively. In the interior, trade with the Indians offered the largest returns in the commodity which was available on a large scale and which yielded substantial profits, namely furs and especially beaver. With the disappearance of beaver in more accessible territory, lumber became the product which brought the largest returns. In British Columbia gold became the product following the fur trade but eventually lumber and fish came into prominence. The lumber industry has been supplemented by the development of the pulp and paper industry with its chief reliance on spruce. Agricultural products — as in the case of wheat — and later minerals — gold, nickel, and other metals — have followed the inroads of machine industry.

The economic history of Canada has been dominated by the discrepancy between the centre and the margin of western civilization. Energy has been directed toward the exploitation of staple products and the tendency has been cumulative. The raw material supplied to the mother country stimulated manufactures of the finished product and also of the products which were in demand in the colony. Large-scale production of raw materials was encouraged by improvement of technique of production, of marketing, and of transport as well as by improvement in the manufacture of the finished product. As a consequence, energy in the colony was drawn into the production of the staple commodity both directly and indirectly. Population was involved directly in the production of the staple and indirectly in the production of facilities promoting production. Agriculture, industry, transportation, trade, finance, and government activities tend to become subordinate to the production of the staple for a more highly specialized manufacturing community. These general tendencies may be strengthened by governmental policy as in the mercantile system but the importance of these policies varies in particular industries. Canada remained British in spite of free trade and chiefly because she continued as an exporter of staples to a progressively industrialized mother country.

The general tendencies in the industrial areas of western civilization, especially in the United States and Great Britain, have had a pronounced effect on Canada's export of staples. In these areas machine industry spread with rapidity through the accessibility of the all-year-round ocean ports and the existence of ample supplies of coal and iron. In Great Britain the nineteenth century was characterized by increasing industrialization[1] with greater dependence on the staple products of new countries for raw material and on the population of these countries for a market. Lumber, wheat, cotton, wool, and meat may be cited as examples of staple imports. In the United States[2] the Civil War and railroad construction gave a direct stimulus to the iron and steel industry and hastened industrial and capitalistic growth. These two areas began to draw increasingly on outside areas for staples and even continental United States has found it necessary with the disappearance of free land, the decline of natural resources, and the demand for new industrial materials, notably rubber, to rely on outside areas as shown in her imperialistic policy of the twentieth century. Canada has participated in the industrial growth of the United States, becoming the gateway of that country to the markets of the British Empire. She has continued, however, chiefly as a producer of staples for the industrial centres of the United States even more than of Great Britain making her own contribution to the Industrial Revolution of North America and Europe and being in turn tremendously influenced thereby.

...

The early history of the fur trade is essentially a history of the trade in beaver fur. The beaver was found in larger numbers throughout the northern half of North America. The better grades of fur came from the more northerly forested regions of North America and were obtained during the winter season when the fur was prime. A vast north temperate land area with a pronounced seasonal climate was a prerequisite to an extensive development of the trade. The animal was not highly reproductive and it was not a migrant. Its destruction in any locality necessitated the movement of hunters to new areas.

The existence of the animal in large numbers assumed a relatively scant population. It assumed an area in which population could not be increased by resort to agriculture. Limitations of geological formation, and climate and a cultural background dependent on these limitations precluded a dense population with consequent destruction of animal life. The culture was dependent on indigenous flora and fauna and the latter was of prime importance. Moose, caribou, beaver, rabbit or hare, and fish furnished the chief supplies of food and clothing. This culture assumed a thorough knowledge of animal habits and the ability of the peoples concerned to move over wide areas in pursuit of a supply of food. The devices which had been elaborated included the snowshoe and the toboggan for the winter and the birch-bark canoe for the summer. This wide area contained numerous lakes and difficult connecting waterways, to which the canoe was adapted for extensive travel. Movement over this area occasioned an extended knowledge of geography and a widespread similarity of cultural traits such as language.

The area which was crucial to the development of the fur trade was the Pre-Cambrian shield of the northern half of the North American continent. It extended northwesterly across the continent to the mouth of the Mackenzie River and was bounded on the north by the northwesterly isothermal lines which determined the limits of the northern forests and especially of the canoe birch (*B. papyrifera*). The fur trade followed the waterways along the southern edge of this formation from the St. Lawrence to the Mackenzie River. In its full bloom it spread beyond this area to the Pacific drainage basin.

The history of the fur trade is the history of contact between two civilizations, the European and the North American, with especial reference to the northern portion of the continent. The limited cultural background of the North American hunting peoples provided an insatiable demand for the products of the more elaborate cultural development of Europeans. The supply of European goods, the product of a more advanced and specialized technology, enabled the Indians to gain a livelihood more easily — to obtain their supply of food, as in the case of moose, more quickly, and to hunt the beaver more effectively. Unfortunately the rapid destruction of the food supply and the revolution in the methods of living accompanied by the increasing attention to the fur trade by which these products were secured, disturbed the balance which had grown up previous to the coming of the European. The new technology with its radical innovations brought about such a rapid shift in the prevailing Indian culture as to lead to wholesale destruction of the peoples concerned by warfare and disease. The disappearance of the beaver and of the Indians necessitated the extension of European organization to the interior. New tribes demanded European goods in increasingly large amounts. The fur trade was the means by which this demand of the peoples of a more limited cultural development was met. Furs were the chief product suitable to European demands by which the North American peoples could secure European goods.

Notes

1   C.R. Fay, *Great Britain: An Economic and Social Survey from Adam Smith to the Present Day.*

2   See Chas. A. and Mary R. Beard, *The Rise of American Civilization.*

DENNIS REID

CORNELIUS KRIEGHOFF: 1845-1865

Little is known of Krieghoff's early life, although it has been established that he was born in Amsterdam of a German father and a Dutch mother. He is supposed to have spent most of his childhood in Dusseldorf and to have lived for two years near Schweinfurt, Bavaria. He was trained as a painter and possibly as a musician. About 1833 he left home to wander about Europe, living a bohemian existence on the returns from his painting and music. He arrived in New York City early in 1837 with his brother Ernest. Barbeau says it was likely there that he met Louise Gautier *dite* Saint-Germain, a young girl from Longueuil, a small town across the St Lawrence River from Montreal. His brother soon joined the United States Navy and Cornelius, on July 5, 1837, enlisted in the U.S. Army. Possibly he worked as a documentary artist, although he gave his occupation as 'clerk' upon enlisting.

For the next three years he was in Florida fighting in the Seminole Wars, but by May 1840 we find him at the other end of the country — in Burlington, Vermont. There he was discharged. But he re-enlisted as a topographical artist and then, mysteriously, deserted later the same day! Whether Louise Gautier had anything to do with this strange behaviour is not known, but about ten days later she gave birth to a boy they named Henry. (This first child lived little more than a year, but the parents' grief at his death would have been somewhat softened by the birth of a daughter, Emily, probably that same year.) Burlington is about seventy miles from Longueuil. Given its proximity, Krieghoff and Louise could simply have crossed the border. (Louise did in fact cross into Canada, alone, to have her son baptized.) But Barbeau suggests that, since they hadn't formalized their marriage — they seem never to have done so — they may not have wanted to settle near Louise's parents so soon. One story has it that Cornelius set up a studio in Rochester, N.Y., and there worked up canvases based on his Seminole sketches for the U.S. Government. That would seem very unlikely, given his service record. A more plausible story is that his brother Ernest, who had also deserted, made his way on foot to Buffalo and there met Cornelius. They both would have stayed there briefly before crossing the border and going on the hundred miles or so to Toronto. Ernest set up in the cabinet-making business and Cornelius presumably found a studio. This would have been about 1840-1.

The Krieghoffs eventually did move to Longueuil to live with Louise's parents, but there is no record of when they arrived. Henry Jackson, the grandfather of A.Y. Jackson of the Group of Seven, was a neighbour and friend of Louise's family and it is known that he bought three canvases from Krieghoff, probably in 1847. There are few works that can be dated convincingly before then, though from the evidence of the one known Jackson picture we can be sure that he had been painting for some time. It is the highly successful *The Ice Bridge at Longueuil* (NGC). Doubtless drawn from life, it is nonetheless closely related to the genre painting then very popular in the United States and Europe, which in turn was based on the works of Dutch seventeenth-century minor masters that Krieghoff would also have known at first hand.

The *Ice Bridge* and similar works of this period must have caused a considerable stir among artists in the Montreal region. There were no other painters then working there who were able to paint in oils with Krieghoff's precision of detail, to say nothing of achieving as well his breadth of sky and snowy ground. The exact rendering of the distinctive sleighs and clothing of the local habitants must have excited Krieghoff's Canadian admirers. He was almost immediately accepted as a man of ability by his painter colleagues and in 1847 was invited to join with some of them to form the Montreal Society of Artists. The Montreal group included the portraitist William Sawyer (1820-89), James Duncan, and Martin Somerville (active 1839-56), who from 1847 to 1850 taught painting with Krieghoff at the Misses Plimsoll's School. Somerville's specialty was the small souvenir genre scene of an old Indian woman selling mocassins or baskets in the snow. Variations on these were very popular with tourists and soldiers and Krieghoff soon caught on and turned out these 'pot-boilers' by the hundreds himself.

Krieghoff, Louise, and their daughter moved across the river to Montreal in 1849. In that year he painted a *Winter Landscape* (NGC), one of his most ambitious canvases — it is more than four feet wide. He wasn't able to sell it until four years later in Québec, however, as Montreal was then arid ground for a painter. This was a difficult period in Krieghoff's career, but he tried the usual ways

DENNIS REID

CORNELIUS KREIGHOFF (1815-1872) *Coming Storm at the Portage*, 1859, oil on canvas, 33.7 x 45.7 cm (13 1/4 x 18 in). Gift of Dr. and Mrs. Matthew Boylen. The Beaverbrook Art Gallery, Fredericton, NB.

to make money from his art. Besides teaching, he and Duncan planned a 'panorama of Canada' for commercial viewing (this was a popular entertainment of the time); under the patronage of Lord Elgin, the governor-general, he published a set of prints. His works were eminently saleable and he seems to have sold many small paintings as souvenirs. But the larger, more ambitious canvases that would support him both creatively and financially could not be sold. Montreal businessmen were not yet ready to collect art. Finally, in 1851, Krieghoff almost stopped painting.

In this discouraging situation it is a wonder that he stayed in Canada. He did have a Canadian wife, however, and presumably arrest for desertion was awaiting him in the United States. Shortly after arriving in Longueuil Krieghoff had met an auctioneer from Québec City named John Budden, who bought a few pictures. Early in 1853 they met again and Budden made Krieghoff a proposition. If he would move to Québec, where he was certain there was a market for Krieghoff's work, Budden would act as his agent. Krieghoff accepted the offer and he, Louise, and Emily relocated there. They even moved in with Budden.

Québec, which is a good deal further north than Montreal, is well into the Laurentians; the land is more hilly and rugged and the autumn colour more intense and pervasive. A surprising number of new themes came off Krieghoff's easel in the summer and fall of 1853 and the spring of 1854. In the obligatory *Montmorency Falls in Winter* and his first pure landscapes he responded to his new surroundings with directness and freshness. He still painted the habitant scenes that had attracted John Budden to him. But now he increased the amount of observed local detail and generally enriched the anecdotal qualities. Indian subjects became more common. There should not be any confusion with the intention behind Kane's work, however. Krieghoff was not involved in any systematic program. He simply sought out picturesque genre subjects with local flavour. Canadian peasants and Canadian aborigines equally well fulfilled the requirement.

Krieghoff's clientele in Québec was drawn almost exclusively from the English-speaking governing classes and the garrison. Some businessmen, like John Budden and James Gibb, were his closest friends and supporters. They all admired his scenes of Indian hunters and rollicking habitants and encouraged him to paint richer and richer images of the simple but jolly life they imagined the

DENNIS REID

local folk led. The French-speaking bourgeoisie, however, did not buy his pictures.

Barbeau suggests a basic difference in the cultural aspirations of the two races. He claims that francophone Quebeckers insisted on the classical hierarchy in the arts in which genre scenes were the 'lowest' form of painting. There was doubtless something in this, but there must equally have been embarrassment for educated Quebeckers in Krieghoff's patronizing view of the jolly habitant as the typical native of the province. Be that as it may, Barbeau seems convinced that it was French-speaking friends in Québec who talked Krieghoff into returning to Europe. They believed that he needed a refresher course in the noble aims of the art of painting. He and Louise left for London in the spring of 1854. It is not known how long they stayed — probably between six months and a year. They were definitely back by the summer of 1855.

From London they went to Paris, where Krieghoff copied in the Louvre, and then on to Germany. They spent most of their time at Dusseldorf, which then was enjoying a great reputation as the seat of a vigorous school of grand-scale landscape and genre painting. Krieghoff painted copies of Old Masters to sell in Canada and very soon after his return — while still on the boat, Barbeau contends — he painted the *Self-portrait* that is now in the National Gallery. Fresh from Europe, he would have wanted to demonstrate his assured grasp of the current modes, and in this painting he has presented himself as a dark, brooding figure, the very image of the romantic artist. Barbeau sees the first of Krieghoff's elaborate canvases to depict the Jolifou Inn — *After the Ball, chez Jolifou* (private collection) of 1856 — as a renewed commitment to the native scene and a rejection of Continental 'airs'. However, this type of 'stage-set' genre scene with many figures had been developed at Dusseldorf and was currently popular across Europe and in the United States.

This period (1856-c.1862) was Krieghoff's most fruitful, and the bulk of his finest snow scenes dates from it. The years before 1862 also saw a further exploration of the theme of autumn; he responded warmly, with rich, intense colour. During the late fifties and early sixties he travelled extensively around the province — as far west as the Ottawa River, south to the Eastern Townships, and north up the Saint-Maurice River to Shawinigan Falls. The year 1859 was a creative peak in his career. His *Owl's Head, Lake Memphremagog* and *Coming Storm at the Portage* both date from that year. Both are dramatic, rich in detail, thoughtfully composed, and unified in mood and emotional thrust. Technically superb, they are also works of art of considerable force. Krieghoff continued to turn out souvenir 'pot-boilers' for sale to tourists and the garrison throughout these years, but this necessity seems not to have impinged on his creativity.

In 1860 he produced a painting that was the culmination of one of his most popular themes: the all-night revel at the country inn. *Merrymaking* is not only one of his largest works — four feet wide — but is one of his most pleasing. He lavished great attention on all the tiny figures — there are more in this work than in any other — and yet through a masterly use of arrangement, colour, and atmosphere he retained a unified whole.

Pierre Berton

Hollywood's Canada:
The Americanization of Our
National Image

God's Country and other euphemisms

Canada was never Hollywood's favourite word. In fact the moviemakers went out of their way *not* to use it. In scores of cases, the only way you knew a movie was about Canada was when a Mountie or a French-Canadian trapper hove into view.

Take a look at the titles: the words Canada and Canadian scarcely ever appeared. Instead, every possible euphemism was used to get around those dreadful words. But everybody knew, when a picture came out using code words like Northwest or Big Snows or Great Woods, that the setting was north of the border. More than 170 movies bore that kind of code in their titles; only eight dared to use Canada or Canadian.

Code Word	Number of Titles
North, Northwest	
Northern, Northwoods	79
Wild, Wilderness, or Trail	50
Mounties or Mounted	37
Klondike or Yukon	18
Snow	11

Even best-selling Canadian classics were carefully de-Canadianized by the moviemakers. It's been largely forgotten that there was a period in Canadian literary history when certain Canadian novels were in furious demand by an international audience and therefore by the movies. Of the five best-selling Canadian authors of all time, four have had their classic novels transferred to the screen by Hollywood. They are: Ralph Connor, Mazo de la Roche, L. M. Montgomery, and Robert W. Service. Only the work of Stephen Leacock, perhaps the biggest seller of them all, has never been given feature film treatment.

These best sellers were all unmistakably Canadian — a fact that in no sense conspired against their popularity. The first American printing of Ralph Connor's novel *The Sky Pilot*, for instance, was 250,000 copies. The novel's eventual sales exceeded one million copies.* Hollywood bought it, of course, but then proceeded to de-Canadianize it. The only Canadian reference in the entire picture is to the fact that the Sky Pilot comes from Montreal. Presumably the setting is the Canadian Rockies; but the movie was shot on location at Truckee, California, and the saloons, gun-fights, and even the costumes are those of the American wild west. The major trade reviews didn't even mention the story's Canadian origin but praised the picture as "an exceedingly good western"[1] with a "collection of thrilling punches."[2]

The other big best sellers were given a similar laundering. Service's novel, *The Trail of '98*, is all about the Klondike gold rush but the only evidence of any Canadian location in the movie is a fleeting shot of a British flag at the summit of the Chilkoot Pass.

The picture made from Mazo de la Roche's prize-winning novel, *Jalna*, had only three direct references to Canada and a few indirect ones. The characters were shown speaking with English accents, living in a panelled English manor, dressed in English tweeds, indulging in English upper-class slang (meself, old gel) and being waited on by jovial Cockney servants, all of whom knew their place.

The movie version of L.M. Montgomery's classic novel, *Anne of Green Gables*, did have a few references to Prince Edward Island and an opening scene or two showing the gentle island landscape, but its sequel, *Anne of Windy Poplars*, was not identifiably Canadian. Except for a single reference to Charlottetown it could just as easily have been made in the American midwest, and there were undoubtedly thousands of moviegoers who thought it was.

The situation has not changed. When Margaret Laurence's important Canadian novel, *A Jest of God*, was made into the film

---

*   A later Connor novel, *The Man from Glengarry*, sold five million copies.

Rachel, Rachel, the location was changed, for no very good reason, from Manitoba to Maine.

It's a curious kind of attitude, when you think about it: make use of the Canadian classic novels; make use of the Canadian background; make use of the mounted police; but try not to mention Canada. As far as I can tell, ours is the only country that Hollywood treated in this fashion. But then it wasn't as easy to take a novel set in the African jungle or the China seas or the English countryside or a Graustarkian palace and camouflage it to the point where it might have taken place somewhere in America.

Actually, in the very beginning, some pioneer moviemakers exploited the name of Canada in their advertising. There was a kind of vogue for Canadian picture before the Great War. The country, to most Americans, was almost unknown and therefore exotic.[3] With an entrepreneurial zeal unmatched in later generations, the Canadian Pacific Railway, through its subsidiary, the Canadian Pacific Irrigation Colonization Company, seized on this curiosity about Canada to commission the Edison Company to cross the nation and make a series of movies calculated to encourage immigration. To this end, a special train was placed at the company's disposal to carry the entire cast and technical crew across Canada from Montreal to Victoria, with a side trip on the Sault line. The purpose was:

> ...to show to the struggling farmer through the medium of the moving picture the premium that western Canada offers for home-making and independence to the man of energy, ambition and small capital; to picture the range cattle, fat and happy, roaming the foothills of the mighty Rockies; to tell the piscatorial enthusiast of cool retreats beside rushing streams where the salmon and trout lurk beneath the rock's overhanging shade; to whisper to the sportsman and the hunter of the big and little game skulking the plains or roaming the mountainsides, waiting his coming; to depict to the tourist and traveller the beauties of mountain, wood and valley, prairie, crag and torrent, and the comfort and luxury of modern hotel, train, boat and steamer; to tempt the Alpine climber to further prowess on the great glaciers of central British Columbia...[4]

It was the kind of crazy scheme that could either be an unqualified success or a magnificent bust. This one was a success. The

Edison Company ground out thirteen one-reel movies about Canada, using locations that ran the gamut from the open prairie to a CPR Princess boat in the Gulf of Georgia. Although the stories are farcical by today's standards, these films, two of which still exist, were among the most authentic made about the Canadian west. The Canadian prairie, for instance, was scarcely ever again shown in a Hollywood movie. The Columbia valley was never to be seen again, either, because Oregon with its big trees was closer to the border. And who has ever bothered to go on location in Strathmore, Alberta, since 1910?

...After 1914 the moviemakers' view of Canada became more cynical. When the Kalem Company went on location to the Island of Orleans in the St. Lawrence River that year to make an historical movie about Wolfe's conquest of French Canada, some Canadian newspapers claimed that it was actually a German company, using the device of a movie production to establish a secret store of arms and build concealed gunpits. Whether or not that helped to discourage production in Canada I don't know, but the filming of authentic Canadian themes dried up.[5]

Hollywood preferred to stick to that vast, mythical region, never geographically defined, which it invented and called the Northwoods. That was the leading euphemism for Canada in the advertisements, the press sheets, and the reviews of the silent pictures.[6] It wasn't necessary to mention Canada at all if you talked about the Woods, the Northwoods, the Northwest Woods, or the Great Woods. In *The Confession*, the bearded villain who enters a Montana saloon is easily tagged as a Canadian because he says: "I come from the Northwoods." In *God's Country and the Law*, the subtitle tells us "a hunted man came out of the night into the bar of McQueen's Tavern on the edge of the Great Woods."

The phrase instantly conjures up a vision of a vast and virtually impenetrable forest, mysterious and almost enchanted, stretching back forever into the mists of the Unknown. The phrase didn't die with the silent pictures but kept turning up again and again. When Nelson Eddy reported for duty in *Rose Marie*, his superior officer knew what to do with him. "I'm sending you back to the woods," he said.

It was always the woods and never the plains that formed the setting for Hollywood's Mountie movies. The woods were wild; the plains had been tamed by the plough. The plains were American; it

PIERRE BERTON

was the woods and the forests that related to Canada. One reviewer wrote about "that paradise of the storyteller — the Northwoods"[7] almost as if the Northwoods was a nation unto itself, inhabited by what one piece of promotional literature called "forest people" and "the simple people of the woods."[8] One gets an impression of strange, elfin creatures, flitting among the trees and never emerging into the sunlight.

The "woods story," as it was called, became a distinctive Hollywood genre just after the Great War — "a Canadian woods story...the kind that never fails to take well with the public,"[9] as one writer remarked of a 1919 feature. The name stuck. In 1934 one of the first fan letters to reach the mother of the Dionne Quintuplets was addressed simply: "Mrs. Oliva Dionne...Northwoods, Canada."

Two other code words for Canada were Northwest and Big Snows. The Northwest could be anywhere in Canada — ranching country in one picture, the St. Lawrence lowlands in another.[10] The Big Snows formed an equally vague geographical entity. The principal characters in *The Courage of Marge O'Doone*, for instance, were described as "people who live up in the big snows."[11] In the eyes of the moviegoing public, Canada seemed to be covered by a kind of perpetual blanket of white — an unbelievably vast drift that almost began at the border and through which Big Snow People plodded.

Happy-go-lucky rogues in tuques

The impression still persists in some parts of the world and, indeed, in some parts of neighbouring United States, that almost every Canadian speaks French. I have even met, in the course of various travels, some people — again including Americans — who assume that French, and *only* French, is the mother tongue of Canada. (Others, equally misinformed, believe that Canada is actually a part of the United States. That view is especially prevalent in eastern Europe, where little distinction is made between the two countries.)

That idea could come from one medium only: the movies. In Hollywood's Canada the forest people were almost always French-Canadians, although they weren't confined to Quebec. Actually there appear to have been more French-Canadians *outside* of Quebec than in the ancient province. As we'll see, Hollywood made several pictures set in Quebec which are remarkable for the absence of French-speaking Canadians. But elsewhere, from southern British Columbia to northern Manitoba, from the Yukon border to the Cypress Hills, they turned up in picture after picture, speaking a kind of pidgin tongue ("Dees Canada, she's lak beeg woo-*man!*"), sporting their colourful tuques and sashes, smoking their clay pipes, indulging in broad gestures, grimacing and capering, seducing willing women, raping unwilling ones, filching deeds for lost gold mines or simply sitting around in the virgin wilderness scraping away on fiddles.

There were only four classes of forest dwellers who were *not* French-Canadians: prospectors, mounted policemen, lumbermen, and Hudson's Bay Company factors.

The prospectors were usually Americans, invading Canada in order to strike it rich before retreating to warmer climes. Most were amateurs, such as Clark Gable in *The Call of the Wild*, while others were really cowboys, like Randolph Scott in *The Cariboo Trail* or James Stewart in *The Far Country*.

The mounted policemen tended to be Irish, with names like Moran, Callaghan, O'Rourke, and Shaughnessy. Eleven of the twenty names of policemen which appear in motion-picture titles, for instance, are Irish. O'Malley of the Mounted turns up three times.

The lumbermen were mostly Anglo-Saxons and they came in two models: the Roistering Lumberjack and the Villainous Timber Magnate. The roistering image was indelibly established in 1918 by William S. Hart, the pioneer western star, in the title role of *Blue Blazes Rawden*, a man with an apparently hollow leg and a legendary reputation ("The boss one time he keel a bear weeth hees hands!").

"Going to hit that Hell hole, Timber Cove, like a blaze of glory!" Rawden shouts at the beginning of the picture as he and his men, firing their pistols into the air, advance upon the little lumber town for an evening of sport. In the saloon Rawden swallows his liquor neat, smashes the empty glasses on the floor, beats up the bartender, one La Barge ("the best rough and tumble fighter in the Cove"), calls for more booze ("Whisky, you frog- eater or I'll swab your own bar with you"), guzzles it straight from the bottle, plucks a half-breed girl, Babette DuFresne, from the arms of the monocled proprietor, Ladyfingers Hilgard, and finally in a *mano a mano* gunfight shoots Hilgard dead.

It is an exhausting movie — almost as exhausting for the audience as it must have been for Hart, who appears to be engaged in calisthenics to the very end of the picture when, stricken by remorse (and also by a bullet), he stumbles off into the storm to Die Alone. No one, certainly not George Brent or even Barton MacLane, who were pitted against each other two decades later in another hard-fisted lumbering yarn, *God's Country and the Woman*, equalled Hart's portrayal.

I suspect that Hollywood preferred the Villainous Timber Magnate — men like J. Van Dyke Parker, millionaire lumberman, whose plotting and dynamite drive his partner into bankruptcy in *The Knockout*; or Hurd, the powerful lumber baron of *The Ancient Highway*, who has sworn to ruin his beautiful Canadian rival, Antoinette St. Ives, unless she marries him (more dynamite); or Garne, general manager of a Rocky Mountain timber firm who in *Forest Havoc* treacherously diverts valuable logs into a secret pond for his own use. Such tycoons outnumbered the logger heroes in the movies.

The Scots were given one role only in Hollywood's Canada. They were, naturally enough, factors of Hudson's Bay trading posts and they were almost all cruel or at the very least domineering.[1] These fur-trading pictures were set mostly in the twentieth century but, as in other Hollywood offerings about Canada, the mores were those of the eighteenth. There were undoubtedly tens of thousands of moviegoers who believed that in the Canadian north, factors held "absolute sway"[2] over their underlings, like The Eagle in *The Law of the North* or Hal Sinclair, "whose word was Law"[3] in *The Law of the Great Northwest*. And why wouldn't they believe it when the critics themselves appeared to? An American reviewer, Matthew A. Taylor, reporting on a re-make of *The Call of the North* in 1921, told his readers of "the tyranny of the Factors of the Hudson Bay Company...who even today in the more remote sections are practically absolute."[4] Three years later The Bioscope, reviewing Tom Mix's *North of the Yukon* (as it was titled in England), explained that "apparently there is a law in the North that, if a man commits murder, or helps one who has committed murder, the guilty party shall be driven off into the snow and deprived of food, fuel or weapons until he dies."[5]

This hardy Hollywood myth of La Longue Traverse or Journey of Death had its genesis in the original version of *The Call of the*

North, an early DeMille opus. It kept turning up in later films and was apparently swallowed whole by a generation of moviegoers. In the Mix version the wicked factor, Cameron MacDonald, is shown to be The Law, even though in one shot the director apparently couldn't resist showing a mounted policeman in full-dress uniform. The redcoat is produced like a rabbit out a hat and then conveniently vanishes, leaving MacDonald to run the court according to his personal whim. Since he wants to get his hands on the rich ore that Mix's dead brother has discovered, he swiftly sends the cowboy hero off on the Journey of Death. There is a nice touch at this point: before Tom Mix takes the long walk, the ever-present Roman Catholic priest blesses him.

When *The Call of the North* was re-made in 1921 the Hudson's Bay Company decided that enough was enough. The movie showed HBC factors attacking free-traders, burning down their shacks and generally breaking the law in a twentieth-century setting. The company filed a damage suit in London against the Famous Players-Lasky Corporation and won.[6] The court held that the movie distorted conditions in Canada as they existed after 1870 and ordered that the objectionable portions of the picture be revised. After that Hollywood was more careful about identifying its factors as Hudson's Bay men.[7]

By the mid-twenties, with the Mountie craze at its height, the all-powerful factor was obsolete. The French-Canadian trapper/guide farmer/habitant, however, was a key figure from the very beginning to the very end of the cycle of Canadian-content movies. The French-Canadian was to the northerns what the Mexican was to the westerns — an exotic primitive, adaptable as a chameleon to play a hero or a heavy.

In the early pictures there were two distinct French-Canadian stereotypes. On the one hand there was the Diabolical French-Canadian, a fiendish and often lecherous killer and thief. On the other there was the Happy-Go-Lucky French-Canadian, so cheerful, so humane, so fond of his fellow men that he was too good to be true. In the silent days, the devils outnumbered the saints by about two to one. Then, when the talkies arrived and screenwriters started putting some shading into their characters, the stereotypes began to blend and a kind of mutant appeared on the screen — the happy-go-lucky rogue, who couldn't be all bad. Gilbert Roland, John Carroll, Fernando Lamas, Paul Muni, and Stewart Granger all took a turn at playing this role which, with its Gallic shrugs, broad

PIERRE BERTON

gestures, and eye-rolling, was easily adaptable and had been so ever since Lou Chaney first created it in 1920.

Good or bad, almost all of these French-Canadians were presented as untutored children of the forest. One child of the forest who had some tutoring was Jean Courteau, the beast-hero of *The Snowbird*. A character in the story clearly had Courteau's number when he described him as "the type of bold French-Canadian with a good education, *which makes him shrewd and cunning* [my italics]."

The first French-Canadian characters to appear in a Hollywood movie turned up in 1908 in Griffith's *A Woman's Way*, a print of which has been preserved in the Library of Congress in Washington. The heavy is easily identified as a French-Canadian because he wears a tuque and a sash, sports a shaggy Louis-Napoleon moustache and beard, and is clearly a sex maniac. The hero is easily recognizable, too. He wears pure white buckskins and a coon cap. Other French-Canadians in the background wear tuques and sashes and smoke clay pipes. There is little time for plot development: the gesturing Quebecker simply seizes the heroine, who has been hugging a tree, and makes off with her; pistols are produced and fired; the hero gives chase and the rascal is bested.

From this point on, some combination of tuque, sash, and pipe were considered mandatory for actors playing French-Canadians in the movies. Occasionally, French-Canadians were shown wearing enormous fur hats or peaked habitant caps; but if they didn't wear a tuque, then the sash appeared. Fashions changed over the years: skirts grew shorter, bobbed hair came and went, the New Look appeared on the screen, fedora brims grew wider, then narrower, even cowboy hats changed in style, but the tuque held its own. Jan LaRose wears a tuque in *The Strength of Men* (1913). Gabriel Dupré wears a tuque in *Where the North Begins* (1923). Louis the Fox wears a tuque in *Men of the North* (1930). Pierre wears a tuque in *Pierre of the Plains* (1942). Jules Vincent wears a tuque in *The Wild North* (1951). And the women wear tuques, too. In *The Far Country* (1954) Corrine Calvet never removes her tuque: she wears it summer and winter, indoors and out, in Skagway, in Dawson, in the mountains, in the saloons, in the mining claim and, presumably, also in bed.

Of all the major stars who have played French-Canadian women, Miss Calvet was perhaps the least tempestuous. Joan Crawford, in the silent version of *Rose-Marie*, was praised for her ability to change her character with a vengeance, "flinging herself fiercely into the wildcat passion of the role of the French-Canadian girl and also into the purring cuteness it called for."[8] Renée Adorée, who was often given French-Canadian roles, was at her most ebullient in *The Eternal Struggle*, leaping up and down in the middle of the street and egging on two fellow French-Canadians to fight over her with knives. And, of course, Lupe Velez, the so-called Mexican Spitfire, fitted easily into the title role of *Tiger Rose*, "The tempestuous French-Canadian ward of Hector McCollins of the Hudson's Bay Company."[9] Mexican spitfires and French-Canadian wildcats have been practically interchangeable down through the years. In *Quebec* Nikki Duval was "the untamed spitfire of the Canadian woods."[10]

In Hollywood's Canada, all French-Canadians had brutally simple first names: none of your Jean-Pauls or Jean-Jacques for the movies. By far the most popular Hollywood name, I blush to say, was Pierre. Most of the Pierres were scoundrels: I've counted at least seventeen, including Pierre, the trapper who beats up his wife in *A Pack of Cards*; Pierre Ledoux, another trapper who acts as triggerman for a group of thieves in *North of the Yukon*; a third trapper named Pierre in *Blind Circumstances* who is hired by a brutal skipper to murder the fiancé of the girl he loves. There is also Pierre the Bully in *The Trap* and Bad Pierre in *White Hell*. I have been able to find only two innocuous Pierres. It's obvious that Hollywood found the bad Pierres much more interesting.

Hollywood's other favourite names, in order of popularity, are Jacques, Jean, Jules, Gaspard, Louis, Raoul, 'Poleon, and Baptiste or Bateese. In the B movies, faceless villains tended to have last names only and these fell into two alliterative families: Dumont, Durand, Duval, Dubec, and Duclos; and Larue, LeBeau, LeClerc, and LaFarge.

Most of the French-Canadian villains in the early silents were devoid of any socially redeeming qualities. They were, in fact, unspeakable blackguards, consistently unfaithful to their wives whom they beat unmercifully in movie after movie.[11] "Unkempt" is almost too mild a word to describe them. Loup, the wicked and lustful trapper in *North of Hudson Bay*, was a wild man — all hair and beard — with a half-crazy look in his eyes. Joseph Dumont, the murderer in *The Confession*, had a black beard, long greasy hair, and a swarthy complexion. Jean LaFarge, a minor reprobate in *The Calgary Stampede*, was shown as an evil- looking, suspicious man "who guards his daughter and his herds with the same fierce jealousy." In place of a tangled mass of hair, LaFarge sported a drooping moustache and a goatee. He could not be made to look too shaggy, since Hoot Gibson was fated to marry his daughter at the end of the picture.[12]

The latter-day knaves were less interesting. By the late fifties they had lost all personality. The accents vanished along with the Christian names and all that was left were trunk-tag characters, easily interchangeable — LeRoux in *Yukon Vengeance*, LeBeau in *Northwest Territory*, Duval and LeClerc in *Yukon Manhunt*. Hollywood had long since dumped the bestial, wife-beating, sex-mad French-Canadian blackguard for the happy-go-lucky rogue.

At first, the motion picture industry tended to idealize its good French-Canadians,[13] all of whom were carefully barbered — their hair short, slickly groomed, and parted in the middle after the wet-head fashion of the day. They rarely had beards but almost all had small moustaches, turned up at the ends to emphasize their incredible good nature. All had flashing, pearly teeth, which were in constant view. Happy and carefree, they capered through movie after movie, slapping friends and even enemies on the back and giving constant thanks to Le Bon Dieu for their existence.[14] Several of them played the fiddle incessantly, like 'Poleon in *God's Country and the Law*, "with a heart as light as the tunes he plays." In that picture, 'Poleon somehow managed to drive a horse and buggy and a cow home and to play the fiddle at the same time. And while the Wicked Half-Breed, Jacques Doré was forcing his unwelcome attentions on 'Poleon's daughter inside her own home, 'Poleon was shown prancing about on the road outside, a pack on his back and his fiddle under his chin, oblivious to all marauders.

We can, I think, give Lon Chaney, "the man of a thousand faces," the credit for inventing the stereotype of the happy-go-lucky French-Canadian. He developed it first in 1920 in *Nomads of the North* and perfected it two years later in *The Trap*. In the latter film, Fritz Tidden commented, Chaney "employs 667 of his reported one thousand facial expressions,"[15] possibly because he had been given a role that allowed him to play both hero and heavy.

At the opening of the picture, a print of which has been preserved, Chaney is Gaspard the Good. There he stands in the doorway of his simple cabin, the compulsory tuque crowning his head, hands on hips, head thrown back, laughing uproariously at his good fortune in being alive. The subtitles have him speaking pidgin English to the ever-present priest: "Good fath-aire, I so happy I

would geev thanks to Heem who made thees world so beauti-fool."
When Gaspard climbs a nearby mountain to his mine, he cannot
help kissing his hands and flinging his arms wide as he drinks in the
beauty around him.

Alas, the idyll is abruptly ended when Benson, a man from the
city (played by a young Alan Hale) steals his mine and his girl.
Gaspard the Good becomes Gaspard the Bad, plotting revenge. As
the years pass, "lighted only by the never-dimming fires of an all-
consuming hate," Chaney gives an animated performance of a Bad
French-Canadian trying to act like a Happy-Go-Lucky French-
Canadian, in order to dupe his enemy and savour sweet revenge. It
was all there for those who followed in his footsteps to study — the
malicious grin, the sneaky eyes, the hunched shoulders, the flaring
nostrils — and it was put to good use in the years that followed.
Nobody, however, outdid Chaney for expansiveness of gesture until
Paul Muni hammed his way through the role of Pierre Radisson in
Hudson's Bay in 1940.

Anyone who examines all of these major French-Canadian performances, from Lon Chaney in 1920 to Stewart Granger in 1951,
cannot help but be struck by a similarity of style and gesture. It is
as if none of these stars had ever met a French-Canadian, which
may very well be true. Lon Chaney and John Carroll were both
Americans, Gilbert Roland was a Mexican; Paul Muni was a Jew of
middle-European parentage; Stewart Granger was an Englishman;
(and J. Carroll Naish, who played the unwashed French-Canadian
guide in *Saskatchewan* — with a comic Indian wife, eternally preg-
nant — was Irish). Some of the best actors in Canada come from
the province of Quebec but they have never gone to Hollywood.

Charles Boyer, who has appeared as a French-Canadian in two
picture, *The Happy Time* and *The Thirteenth Letter*, never bothered with an authentic characterization. In both movies he
remained a Frenchman with a Parisian accent. This was not the only
inconsistency and it brings up a curious Hollywood blindness about
French-Canadians in general and the province of Quebec in particular. For years the movies populated Canada with men and women
who spoke with French-Canadian accents, confessed to Roman
Catholic priests, raised their eyes to Le Bon Dieu and uttered exple-
tives like "By Gar!" The Northwoods were crammed with such people, from Dawson City to Labrador. In *Pierre of the Plains* the
screenwriters made the mayor of a Rocky Mountain village a
French-Canadian — a comic figure in a wing collar, striped

trousers, and a bowler, who was addressed as Your Honour, in the American fashion. But when it came to placing French-Canadians in their own province Hollywood was clearly confused.

The Thirteenth Letter, for instance, produced by Otto Preminger on location in Quebec, must be baffling to any native because, in the small Quebec town of the story so many of the characters — the chief of police, the postman, all the doctors in the hospital, and most of the hospital personnel — are Anglo-Saxons.

Similarly in Alfred Hitchcock's *I Confess*, shot on location in Quebec City, the chief of police, the judge, many of the court officials, and leading detectives are Anglo-Saxons. In *The Scarlet Claw*, one of the movies in the Basil Rathbone/Nigel Bruce Sherlock Holmes series, all the hotel clerks in Quebec City seem to have English accents; the policeman in charge of the case has a Scottish burr; and the postman arrives at the hotel singing, of all things, The British Grenadiers. And then there is Jules, the French-Canadian youth from the Quebec village in *The Heart of Humanity*, who, dying of wartime wounds, utters a typically Québécois request: "Tell Mumsy I love her!" he whispers as he expires.

In *The Happy Time*, which supposedly deals with the tight French-Canadian community in the Ottawa of the twenties, there is a mixture of accents within the same family. Two of the younger generation don't appear to have anything more than rudimentary French. One, in fact, speaks English with a Harvard accent!

The most curious exhibit of all, however, is again provided by *The Country Doctor*, the over-praised picture about the Dionne Quintuplets. The French-Canadian locale, it will be remembered, was moved from Ontario to Quebec, somewhere north of Montreal. Where, then, are the French-Canadians in *The Country Doctor*? There just aren't any. Slim Summerville plays the town cop with an American drawl. John Qualen plays the quintuplets' father with his usual hick accent. Jean Hersholt, the doctor, speaks with a Scandinavian lilt. The action moves briefly to Montreal where again we hear no French — only the clipped British accents of Montague Love. In fact in the entire picture there is not one soul with a French-Canadian name; even the high Catholic prelates who come to bless the quints' new hospital are Anglo-Saxon. All those trappers and traders and guides, with their tuques and their sashes and their exotic way of speaking, have miraculously vanished and remain hidden away in the chill isolation of the Great Woods.

Peace and fishing, billions of pine trees, frozen waste

If there had been no Hollywood, might there have been a home-grown motion picture industry? And if there had been a home-grown industry, would it have projected a more accurate version of Canada to Canadians and to the world?

There are unanswerable questions. We do know that as long as Hollywood made movies about Canada, Canadians made very few movies about themselves. We also know that when Hollywood stopped making movies about Canada, Canadians began to make movies of quite a different kind for the international market — movies such as *Mon Oncle Antoine, Goin' Down the Road, Kamouraska,* and *The Apprenticeship of Duddy Kravitz.* These films spring out of a different kind of Canadian experience, one which has nothing to do with the foreign mythology of the Great Woods. But it is not possible here to suggest a causal relationship between the end of one era and the beginning of another. There are too many complicating factors (such as the Canadian Film Development Corporation).

Hollywood ceased being interested in Canadian subjects because movies changed. The subjects of the films became interesting subjects because movies changed. The movies changed because the audience changed and became fragmented. The backbone of Canadian-subject features was for many years the B picture, and that was killed by television. So was the old-fashioned melodrama, with the Bad Guys easily distinguishable from the Good Guys by speech, mannerisms, and costume.

Hollywood's version of the old west began to change in the 1950s and the Hollywood western reflected this new maturity; but the northerns never changed: the attitudes and the stereotypes were frozen into place in the early silents; the clichés of the twenties were still around in the postwar era. The Canadian myth was never debunked, as the western myth was; it was simply discarded. Except for *The Canadians,* three Walt Disney animal pictures, a soft-core sex movie, *Vixen,* and an excellent film about the Eskimos, *The White Dawn,* Hollywood stopped making movies about Canada after 1960.

Given the theatrical distribution system in Canada and the United States, controlled for most of this period by the major studios, the climate for presenting independently produced Canadian films to the world was certainly unfriendly. The Hollywood film companies weren't interested in helping to fund independent Canadian producers. On the other hand, the old cry that the world market would not accept films with a Canadian setting was so much balderdash. The world market accepted close to six hundred of them over a period of half a century. Some of them could have been vastly superior if they had been made by people with greater knowledge and understanding of the country they were supposed to portray.

I don't think there's much doubt that if Canada had persevered, if the government had insisted that the American film makers use some of their Canadian profits to back Canadian productions, or if we had encouraged a native film industry through public subsidy, the movies coming out of Canada would have matured to become more faithful to the Canadian experience than foreign-made movies. Certainly they could not have been more spurious than the ones Hollywood presented.

But it is fruitless to speculate about what might have been. What we do know is that, for one reason or another, for most of the century this country was blind to the potential of the feature film as a medium of propaganda or education. It was not the National Film Board that gave us our image of ourselves and it was not the National Film Board that gave the rest of the world its image of Canada. It was Hollywood.

The image is still there, as I discovered for myself during the winter of 1969-70 in the course of preparing a nightly interview program for television that took me to various parts of the world. That year I decided to ask some of my better-known guests about their image of Canada and Canadians. Their answers — the answers of literate, well-travelled men and women of above-average intelligence and ability — suggest the extent of Hollywood's influence on the world's view of this country.

Nanette Fabray, American comedienne: "Canada? ...One vast wonderland of lakes and clear skies and beautiful picturesque small towns that have hanging baskets of flowers on every lamp post, and quaint, lovely old buildings....You don't have smog, you don't have pollution, you don't have any problems...."

Tony Randall, American actor: "I just see billions of pine trees. Am I right?"

Gore Vidal, American novelist: "...one thinks of the Queen and cowboys...."

Jack Lemmon, American actor: "Peace and Fishing....Peace is being able to get away from the smog, out of the madness, the suicidal drive that makes us all collect like ants in an ant hill....Peace: to be in the woods and to live there where hopefully pollution is not rampant...."

Dyan Cannon, American actress: "My image of Canada? I don't know...blinking cold, cold weather...[I see] Canadians in a healthy, outdoor way."

Ron Moody, British actor: "I think of frozen waste...ice, big spaces. I think of tremendous space — freshness....It's not developed yet, is it?"

The Earl of Litchfield, portrait photographer: "I think largely of lakes and I think of trees...."

Arthur Treacher, British actor: "It seems to me you've got to be a pretty virile bloke to live there, don't you?"

Ann Todd, British actress: "You always see Canada with lovely space. I adore space. And *snow*. Snow and dark woods and things against it."

Britt Ekland, European actress: "Mounted police...the snow... the wilderness and the cold...."

Hermione Gingold, British comedienne: "When I went there I had the image of vast snow everywhere, gorgeous-looking men dressed in furs, riding on sleighs. I got very excited about going. I just saw this wild, virile country — and wolves stalking you and all the rest of it. After I'd been there I found it wasn't like that at all."

Thus did a British musical comedy star, born at the dawn of the motion picture era and exposed for all of her life to the flickering image of a country she had not yet seen, echo the words of Papa

Dionne. Like others of her era, her vision of Canada was a confused montage of old plot-lines, scraps of dialogue, screaming advertisements, screen images of snow and pine trees, and marquee posters. How quaint that dialogue seems today; how campy the silent subtitles; how corny the advertising slogans:

THRILL AND THROB AMONG THE SNOW-CLAD MOUNTAINS AND SKIIS AND DOG SLEDS AMONG THE NORTHERN FORESTS, THE HAUNT OF FURRY GAME AND THE TREACHEROUS CHILCOTT INDIAN...."I took an oath when I entered this service. I swore to obey all lawful orders without fear, favour, or affection toward any person."...*But who can blame Malloy that the bright eye of Marie LaFarge had made him forget his quest?*... "Looks like war on a big scale, Sir; signal fires are burning and the tribes are gathering from every spot in the West."...A MOUNTIE'S ROARING GUNS! A DOG'S VENGEFUL FANGS!...*Under the spell of Edith's witchery Annesley throws discretion aside....* "It looks like the whole Cree nation is on the march!...NOW...AS THE STRANGER WITH A GUN...DRIVEN BY RESTLESS LONGINGS, CHALLENGING THE KLONDIKE'S SNOW AND SIN AND GREED. WHERE GOLD WAS THE LURE AND THE FANCIEST WOMAN IN DAWSON HIS FOR THE TAKING!... "Some of these thieving Indians can smell liquor for ten miles on a clear night."...*and so the rugged spirit of the North locks arms with human kindness....* "The Redcoats have murdered one of my braves and now they must die!"...DEATH STRUGGLE WITH THE WOLVES! A FIGHT FOR LIFE AGAINST THE FURY OF FANGS AND CLAWS!... "Oh, André, they are feet for a Queen." — "Oui, ma Chérie, that ees who I buy dem for — my Queen."...*Never again will Joe La Barge be called the best slugger in Timber Cove....* "W'y all you men want to mak' merry wid me?"...THUNDERING TERROR OF THE AVALANCHE! A MOUNTAIN MOVES AND THREATENS TO BURY BEAST AND MEN FOREVER!... "The Athabascans won't take this lying down. I wouldn't want to be in your shoes for a minute."...*The Far North, where men pit brain and brawn against the cunning of the Silver Fox whose pelts are worth more than their weight in gold....* "Toto, the devil wolf have returned. I weel trap heem."...MAD GAMBLE WITH RAGING RAPIDS! A FRAIL CANOE SHOOTS TO THE BRINK OF DESTRUCTION!... "White Spirit call all day, all night. Must go!"... "My time has come to take the Lone Trail, Joe, and I'm going —

Alone."... "The Beeg Trapper got me by de t'roat!"

Did we really fall for this hokum? Were we actually glued to our seats when redcoated riders dashed past on the screen? Did we feel a thrill of apprehension when the Blackfoot tied their victims to the stake? Did our eyes mist up when the White Spirit called and the Flawed hero hit the Lone Trail and the Beeg Trapper got Akim Tamiroff by the throat? You bet we did. We *all* did. We loved it and the box-office figures prove it. It never occurred to us, or at least not to very many of us, that an entire culture, our own, was being held up to the world to view through a distorted glass. Now it is all over. Hollywood's Canada no longer exists on the silver screen — only on the late, late shows and in the memory boxes of everyone who made their weekly pilgrimage to the movies, in the days before they were called films.

Notes

The Great Woods and the Big Snows

1. *New York Mail,* quoted MPW, 25 May 1921.
2. Unidentified review quoted MPW, 7 May 1921.
3. D.W. Griffith advertised his *A Woman's Way* as "A Romance of the Canadian Woods." The Kalem company went on location in Canada for several films before World War One, including *The Girl Scout,* a story of the Lord Strathcona Horse in the Boer War (which used actual members of that famous Canadian group of roughriders): *The Cattle Thieves,* featuring real, live Mounties; *The Canadian Moonshiners;* and *Fighting the Iroquois in Canada.* Vitagraph made *Foraging,* also billed as a story of Canadian action in the Boer War. Canada's part in the Boer War got as much attention from the pioneer moviemakers as her much larger contribution to the two world wars that followed.
4. *Man to Man Magazine,* vols. 6 and 7, Jan. - June 1991, pp. 935-940.
5. MPW, Oct. 1, 1910.
6. Ibid., 12 December 1914.
7. 'Northwoods' became a popular phrase in movie vernacular as early as 1912. Moving Picture World that year referred to 'the Royal Mounted Police of the Northwest woods" (carefully omitting the word Canadian) and two one-reelers used the phrase that year in their titles. In *The Man Who Died* (1915), the action was described

as centring around the village of Grand Pierre 'in the Northwest woods.' The locale did not need to be identified. Twenty-one years later *The Hollywood Reporter,* reviewing *The Country Beyond,* simply described it as a story of 'the Mounties in the great north-woods,' never once mentioning Canada.

8. Robert C. McElravy, reviewing *Nine Tenths of the Law,* 4 May 1918.
9. *The Old Code,* MPW, 9 January 1915.
10. MMA *Photoplay* clipping file re: *Paid in Advance,* n.d.
11. In *Gene of the Northland,* the heroine and her brother are described as living alone 'in the great Northwestern country' (MPW, 1 May 1915). It was not thought necessary to identify the locale further. In *Blood is Thicker than Water* (1912) the Northwest was western ranch country but in *A Leap for Life* (1910) it was clearly French Canada. In *Mounted Fury,* made twenty-one years later, the code word was still being used. Because the Northwest was mentioned, *Variety's* reviewer explained that 'the audience is supposed to guess it is Canada.'
12. Advertisements for *A Hero of the Big Snows* (1926) merely said the story took place among trappers 'in the snow country.' *The Law of the North* was described as 'a dramatic story of hearty, red-blooded life in the snow-clad North' (MPW, 20 April 1912). Again it wasn't necessary to identify the locale.

Happy-go-lucky rogues in tuques

1. *Bioscope,* 29 May 1919.
2. MPW, 20 April 1918.
3. MMA, *Photoplay* file, unidentified clipping.
4. *Bioscope,* 14 February 1924.
5. CMPD, 15 December 1922.
6. Factors were also shown as seducers. Chad Galloway, villain of *Where the North Begins* 'has long cast a covetous eye on Felice, the daughter of McTavish, his storekeeper.' The strangest of these Romeos was the Right Honourable Reginald Annesley (an Englishman for once) who ran the Keewatin post in *The Law of the North* and was shown dressing for dinner every night, being served by a turbanned East Indian, and ordering fresh flowers sent up all the way from Winnipeg to lavish upon the heroine.
7. Quoted in J. Quirk, "The Films of Joan Crawford", (Toronto: St. Paul Pioneer Press, 1968), p. 57.
8. AFI, p. 813.

9. Paramount press sheet.

10. Larue in *One Day* was 'a typical ignorant man of the brute type and his treatment of his wife is such that one would accord to a dog' (MPW, 14 December 1912). Raoul LaFane of *The Northern Code* was 'a drunken Canadian trapper [who] attacks his young wife' (AFI Catalogue, p. 553). François LeFevre in *Out of the Night* is 'fickle as well as faithless' (MPW, 9 May 1914).

11. The one exception to the stereotype was Monroe Salisbury's portrayal of Rossignol, the mysterious outlaw in *The Man in the Moonlight* who is dressed as a South American gaucho in a flat black hat, black poncho, open shirt, and beads. To complete the characterization Salisbury kept a cigarette dangling constantly from his lips.

12. *In the Northland* told of 'the intense love and wonderful heroism of a stout-hearted French-Canadian, whose wife is on the point of deserting him for a cowardly city weakling' (MPW, 16 May 1914). The hero of *Hugon, the Mighty* was a 'vigourous woodsman respected for his physical strength and moral courage' (ibid., 26 October 1918. 'Poleon Dufresne in *The Lure of the Wild* 'loved the wild things of the forest too much to ever become rich as a trapper.'

13. For example: Baptiste, the 'jovial, hearty, light-hearted woodsman' of *Sons of the Northwoods* (ibid., 30 March 1912); Jacques, the 'happy-go-lucky Canuk trapper' of *Jacques of the Silver North* (ibid., 14 June 1919); Hilair Latour, the 'impulsive, warm-hearted trapper' of *Prisoner of the Pines* (ibid,. 14 September 1918); Jules, the 'high-spirited, laughing, whole-souled woodsman' of *Jules of the Strongheart* (MMA *Photoplay* file, unidentified); and another Jacques of *Wild Sumac,* 'a happy-go-lucky French adventurer running over with the wine of life, with zest, humour and complete fidelity' (MPW, 17 October 1917).

14. MPW, 13 May 1922.

15. Ralph E. Friar and Natasha A. Friar, "The Only Good Indian ... The Hollywood Gospel" (New York, 1972), p. 81: *'The Cattle Rustlers* used that classic character of the dime novel: the dirty, no-good half-breed....'

Sylvia Van Kirk

"Many Tender Ties"
Women in Fur-Trade Society in
Western Canada, 1670-1870

"There is indeed no living with comfort in this country until a person has forgot the great world and has his tastes and character formed on the current standard of the stage...habit makes it familiar to us, softened as it is by the many tender ties, which find a way to the heart."

James Douglas, Fort Vancouver, March 1842

Introduction

In 1840 on the occasion of his marriage to a Scottish lady, Chief Trader James Hargrave was warmly congratulated by his colleagues throughout the Hudson's Bay Company's vast western territories. His friend James Douglas took the opportunity to muse upon the changing pattern of fur-trade marriages:

> There is a strange revolution in the manners of the country; Indian wives were at one time the vogue, the half-breed supplanted these, and now we have the lovely tender exotic torn from its parent bed to pine and languish in the desert.[1]

This book, which derived its initial inspiration from Douglas's intriguing observation, examines the role played by Indian, mixed-blood and white women in the development of fur-trade society in what is today Western Canada. Such an approach provides valuable insights into the nature of the society which evolved and permits the reconstruction of the complex, human dimension of the fur trade which has been little appreciated.

The fur trade forms the basis of recorded history in Western Canada. For almost two hundred years, beginning with the founding of the Hudson's Bay Company in 1670, the fur trade dominated western development. Although the English laid claim to the huge drainage basin of Hudson Bay known as Rupert's Land, initially they did not venture inland. Instead, they established a line of strategic posts on the shores of the Bay and relied upon the Indians to bring their rich catches of furs down to trade. Soon the English faced relentless competition from French traders with headquarters in Montreal, who pushed west to take their goods to the Indians. By the early eighteenth century, French-Canadian voyageurs had pioneered the vital canoe links through the rock and morass of the Canadian Shield to Lake Winnipeg. At mid-century, French posts were astride the Saskatchewan River, effectively diverting the Indians from trading on the Bay.

The British conquest of Quebec in 1759 shattered the French colonial fur trade, yet the Hudson's Bay Company enjoyed only a brief respite. British-American traders quickly re-organized the Montreal trade and were soon offering such formidable competition that, in 1774, the Hudson's Bay Company was forced to extend its operations inland. For many years, however, the English Company remained completely overshadowed by its powerful Canadian rival, the North West Company, a partnership of traders which emerged under the leadership of Simon McTavish in 1783. It was the intrepid Nor'Westers who first crossed the Rocky Mountains and established posts on the Pacific Slope, creating Canada's first transcontinental economic enterprise. Yet in 1821, the Hudson's Bay Company, largely because of its superior geographical position, finally won the long struggle for the control of the western fur trade. For the next fifty years, this vast region, including the Pacific Slope as far south as the Columbia River, was united under the aegis of the Hudson's Bay Company. Posts were linked by the mighty rivers of the Saskatchewan, the Mackenzie and the Fraser, creating pockets of European habitation throughout the West. It was also with the support of the Company that the earliest colonization ventures in Western Canada were undertaken at Red River and on Vancouver Island.

Detailed accounts of the events sketched above are provided in the works of Harold Innis, A.S. Morton and E.E. Rich, but the rich social history of the fur trade has been ignored until recently.[2] This neglect has marred our understanding of the dynamics of the fur trade because it was not simply as economic activity, but a social and cultural complex that was to survive for nearly two centuries.[3] Like most of the staple industries which characterized the economic development of pre-Confederation Canada, the fur trade generated a distinctive regional way of life; this was reflected in patterns of work, family life, modes of transport, and items of food and clothing. One important difference between the fur trade and other staple indus-

SYLVIA VAN KIRK

tries was that it was the only one which was based on a commodity exchange between two divergent groups of people. The growth of a mutual dependency between Indian and European trader at the economic level could not help but engender a significant cultural exchange as well. As a result, a unique society emerged which derived from both Indian and European customs and technology.

In seeking to discover the norms of fur-trade society, one is immediately confronted with the enormous complexity of the social interaction between Indian and white. The broad categories "Indian" and "white" must be differentiated. While it is convenient to speak in general term of "the Indian," the traders actually encountered many different tribes with varying languages, customs, and standards of living. In the Shield region, the traders came in contact with bands of Cree and Ojibwa, members of the widespread Algonkian linguistic group. On the prairies were the Plains Cree, the Assiniboine and the populous Blackfoot confederacy. To the north were the Athapaskan tribes, the most important being the Chipewyan, who were drawn into the trading orbit of the Hudson's Bay Company in the early eighteenth century. The Nor'Westers were the first to encounter the numerous tribes which inhabited the Pacific Slope. Significant among these were the turbulent Carrier Indians of the northern interior of British Columbia and the sophisticated, class-conscious Chinook who inhabited the lower reaches of the Columbia River.[4]

As for the traders, it is misleading to think of them as a single group; within the fur trade, the Hudson's Bay Company and the North West Company were two distinct entities with differing social policies and practices. In examining the role played by women in the fur trade, it is important to differentiate their experience within the context of the two companies.

Traditionally the Western Canadian fur trade has been regarded as a totally male sphere. I have often been met with the bemused query, "What women were there in the fur trade?" This study reveals that there were many women in the West who played an essential role in the development of fur-trade society. It is true that for many decades there was a virtual ban on all European women in the West, and this fact in itself is of the utmost importance. Contrary to what might be anticipated, the Canadian trader did not conform to the image of the "womanless frontiersman." Fundamental to the growth of a fur-trade society was widespread intermarriage between the traders and Indian women. This phenomenon has been remarked upon in previous works, but the nature and extent of these unions have not been subject to detailed scrutiny.[5] A major concern of the present study is to show that the norm for sexual relationships in fur-trade society was not casual, promiscuous encounters but the development of marital unions which gave rise to distinct family units. There were differences in attitude and practice between the men of the two companies; yet fur-trade society developed its own marriage rite, marriage á la façon du pays, which combined both Indian and European marriage customs. In this, the fur-trade society of Western Canada appears to have been exceptional. In most other areas of the world, sexual contact between European men and native women has usually been illicit in nature and essentially peripheral to the white man's trading or colonizing ventures.[6] In the Canadian West, however, alliances with Indian women were the central social aspect of the fur traders' progress across the country.

An explanation for this phenomenon can be found in the nature of the fur trade itself. Both the attitudes of the Indians and the needs of the traders dictated an important social and economic role for the native woman that militated against her being simply an object of sexual exploitation. Fur-trade society, as in both Indian and pre-industrial European societies, allowed women an integral socio-economic role because there was little division between the "public" and "private" spheres, between the spheres of work and home.[7] The marriage of a fur trader and an Indian woman was not just a "private" affair; the bond thus created helped to advance trade relations with a new tribe, placing the Indian wife in the role of cultural liaison between the traders and her kin. In Indian societies, the division of labour was such that the women had an essential economic role to play. This role, although somewhat modified, was carried over into the fur trade where the work of native women constituted an important contribution to the functioning of the trade.

An analysis of the evolution in the choice of marriage partners among the traders provides insights into the changing nature of fur-trade society. Indian wives were "the vogue" during the initial stages of the fur trade when the traders were dependent upon the Indians for survival. The important economic role of the Indian wife reflected the extent to which the traders adopted a native way of life. Nevertheless, fur-trade society was not Indian; rather it combined both European and Indian elements to produce a distinctive, self-perpetuating community. This process was symbolized by the emergence of a large number of mixed-blood children.[8] The replacement of the Indian wife by the mixed-blood wife resulted in a widespread

SYLVIA VAN KIRK

and complex pattern of inter-marriage among fur-trade families. It produced a close-knit society in which family life was highly valued. James Douglas echoed the sentiments of many of his colleagues when he declared that without "the many tender ties" of family, the monotonous life of a fur trader would be unbearable. Fur-trade society was not static and the shifting influence of its dual cultural roots was mirrored in the experience of successive generations of mixed-blood girls. Initially Indian influences were strong, but there was a noticeable tendency, particularly on the part of Company officers, to wean their daughters away from their Indian heritage and to encourage them to emulate the style of European ladies. After an absence of over a century, the actual appearance of white women in the Canadian West was to have serious repercussions, particularly upon the fur-trade elite. Their coming underscored the increasing class and racial distinctions which characterized fur-trade society in the nineteenth century. In the Rupert's Land of the 1830s, a genteel British wife was a conspicuous status symbol for a Hudson's Bay Company officer, but, ironically, the white wife also presaged the ultimate decline of the fur trade. Her presence was most visible in the Red River Settlement, where, like the missionary, she symbolized the coming of a settled, agrarian order. This would be a world in which native women would have little role to play.

This study supports the claims of theorists in women's history that sex roles should constitute a category of historical investigation. Traditionally the experience of women has differed substantially from that of their male counterparts; the lives of both sexes and how they interact must be examined if we are to fully understand the dynamics of social change.[9] Much has been said about the impact of the fur trade upon the Indian, yet little has been done to differentiate this in terms of the sexes. It appears that even more than the men, Indian women welcomed the advent of European technology. Items such as kettles, knives, awls and woolen cloth considerably alleviated their onerous domestic duties. The notable instances that can be cited of the Indian woman acting as ally or peacemaker to advance the cause of the trader suggests that it was in the woman's interest to do so. Anthropological studies in other parts of the world have documented native women playing an active, even leading, role in promoting the economic change brought about by European technology.[10] Furthermore, because of her sex, the Indian woman could be absorbed into fur-trade society in a way not open to the Indian man. To become the wife of a fur trader offered the Indian woman the prospect of an alternative way of life that was easier physically and richer in material ways. An analysis of fur-trade society from the women's perspective also extends our knowledge of the role of women in race relations. The existence of numerous harmonious mixed unions suggests that on an individual level many traders were able to overcome the racial prejudice of their parent society. A sharp rise in the expression of racist sentiments emerges, however, when European women appear upon the scene, a phenomenon which has parallels in the meeting of races in other parts of the world.[11]

In reconstructing the role of women in the fur trade, the paucity of sources, in particular those written by native women, presents a difficult challenge. One is forced to piece together snippets of information from the extensive collections of traders' journals, letters and wills which have survived. Although a substantial body of evidence can be amassed in this way, it is understandably coloured by the male perspective. As is often the case in the history of women, an analysis of this material reveals that there is a significant disparity between the traders' perception of the women's position and the reality of their actual lives. The implications of this important paradox are examined throughout this book as it applies to all three groups of women. With regard to Indian women, most of the fur traders believed that women occupied a degraded position within western Indian societies; the Indian women in their view had everything to gain by becoming the wife of the "superior" trader. In reality the Indian woman may have enjoyed an easier existence at the fur-trade post, but she sacrificed considerable personal autonomy, being forced to adjust to the traders' patriarchal views on the ordering of home and family. In the final analysis, it is debatable whether the lot of an Indian woman in marrying a European was improved to the extent that the fur traders claimed.

Similarly, many fur-trade fathers sincerely believed that it was in their daughters' best interests to acculturate them to British standards of womanhood. In many cases, this process simply rendered mixed-blood girls helpless and vulnerable in a society which was becoming increasingly racist and sexist toward native women. Finally, nineteenth-century fur-trade society presents a fascinating microcosm for the study of the Victorian concept of "the lady." The officers of the Hudson's Bay Company fell into genuine rapture over the charms and accomplishments of the few British ladies who set foot in Rupert's Land. But in this wilderness situation, the impracticality and artificiality of this "ideal" of womanhood was sharply etched. Ironically, the very qualities for which these women

SYLVIA VAN KIRK

were so much extolled made it almost impossible for them to adapt to the rigours of fur-trade life. The "lovely tender exotics" did indeed "pine and languish in the desert."

In examining the experience of women within the male-dominated world of the fur trade, there is a temptation to place the woman ultimately in the role of passive victim. This would accord well with the common stereotype of the Indian being the exploited victim of the greedy, rapacious trader.[12] In both cases, within the fur-trade period, emphasis on the concept of victimization leads to an over-simplification of the dynamics of social and economic interaction. Recently several important revisionist works have appeared which delineate an active role for the Indian in the fur trade, showing that his responses were dictated by his own needs and interests.[13] It is necessary to extend this concept of "active agent" to the women, even though their roles within fur-trade society were restricted. Women's roles were defined in terms of their relationships to men: wife, mother, daughter or worker. Nevertheless, within these spheres, women did act to make the most of the opportunities available to them. There is considerable evidence that it was not uncommon for Indian women to take the initiative in seeking to become the wives of traders, and for a while at least, they were able to utilize their position as "women in between" two groups of men to improve their status. Mixed-blood wives anxiously sought to preserve their place within the hierarchy, and if white women emerged as agents of racism, this was largely because they felt forced to protect their social status. In a society where marriage defined a woman's position, white women felt threatened by the presence of acculturated native women against whom they might have to compete for husbands. Investigators of women's history are discovering that the view of women as "active agents," instead of the simplistic view of women as "passive victims," promises to provide the key to understanding women's motivations and actions.[14] In this instance, it is believed that the examination of the role played by women as actors upon the fur-trade stage is essential to a full understanding of the complexities of what was an unusual society in early Western Canada.

References

1   G. P. deT Glazebrook, ed., *The Hargrave Correspondence 1821-1843* (Toronto: Champlain Society, XXIV), 310-311.
2   See Harold A. Innis, *The Fur Trade in Canada* (Toronto, 1962); A. S.

Morton, *A History of the Canadian West to 1870-71* (London, 1939); and E. E. Rich, *The History of the Hudson's Bay Company, 1670-1870*, 2 vols. (London: H.B.R.S., XXI and XXII).

3   John Foster, "Rupert's Land and the Red River Settlement, 1820-1870" in L. G. Thomas, ed., *The Prairie West to 1905* (Toronto, 1975), p. 21.

4   For a good general discussion of the Indian tribes of Canada, see Diamond Jenness, *The Indians of Canada* (Ottawa, 1955).

5   The only published work on this subject is a popular work by Walter O'Meara, *Daughters the Country: The Women of the Fur Traders and Mountain Men* (New York, 1968). In Lewis Saum's *The Fur Trader and the Indian* (Seattle, 1965), there is only a brief, superficial mention of this important aspect of Indian-white relations. Marcel Giraud, however, lays useful groundwork in his massive study *Le Métis Canadien* (Paris, 1945).

6   For a useful overview of the process of miscegenation in India, Africa and the Americas, see Fernando Henriques, *Children of Caliban: Miscegenation* (London, 1974).

7   For a discussion of women's role in pre-industrial society, see Alice Clark, *Working Life of Women in the Seventeenth Century* (London, 1919).

8   In this study, the term "mixed blood" will be used to descibe people of Indian-European origin. Like the French word "Métis", it accommodates all gradations of racial mixture and does not carry the pejorative connotation of the word "half-breed". For a discussion of both contemporary and modern terms and the problems connected with their usage, see Jennifer Brown, "Linguistic Solitudes in the Fur Trade: Some Changing Social Categories and their Implications" in C. M. Judd and A. J. Ray, eds., Old Trails and New Directions: Papers of the Third North American Fur Trade Conference (Toronto, 1980).

9   Joan Kelly-Gadol, "The Social Relation of the Sexes; Methodological Implications of Women's History", *Signs*, I, 4 (1976):809-824.

10 See particularly Yolanda and R. F. Murphy, Women of the Forest (New York, 1974).

11 See Henriques, *Children of Caliban*.

12 This view is again articulated in a recent important text by R. C. Harris and John Warkentin, *Canada Before Confederation* (Toronto, 1974), 245.

13 See Arthur J. Ray, *Indians in the Fur Trade. 1660-1870* (Toronto, 1974) and Robin Fisher, *Contact and Conflict, Indian-European Relations in British Columbia, 1774-1890* (Vancouver, 1977).

14 Sheila Johansson, "'Herstory' as History: A New Field or Another Fad" in Berenice Carroll, ed., Liberating Women's History, 400-430.

LINDA HUTCHEON

THE CANADIAN POSTMODERN

Introduction

A number of critics lately[1] have noted the relationship between the national search for a cultural identity and the feminist seeking for a distinctive gender identity in terms of the paradoxical (and I would say, postmodern) recognition and combatting of 'colonial' positions toward the power of dominating cultures. They have pointed to shared themes of powerlessness, victimization, and alienation, as well as to a certain ambivalence or ambiguity that makes both Canadians and women open, tolerant, accepting, yet also at times angry and resentful. Lorna Irvine believes that the female voice 'politically and culturally personifies Canada.'[2] On a national level, male aggression is usually associated, by analogy, with the United States, while Britain represents the stifling force of colonial tradition. As Mavis Gallant ironically put it, 'The father in Canada seemed no more than an apostle transmitting a paternal message from the Father in England — the Father of us all.'[3] Unlike Quebec women writers, who practise a more overtly radical subversion, those writing in English (like their male counterparts, in many cases) use a more disguised form of subversion, which only implicitly questions the prevailing authority. In so doing they also challenge related liberal-humanist notions of art as original and unique, notions that are tied up with (male) notions of individual subjectivity. And they often do so by means of parody: by first recalling the (male; British/American) canonical texts of our culture, both 'high' and popular, and then challenging them by undoing their status and power. The frequent use of verbal irony and word play in the work of Kroetsch, Atwood, and Thomas, for example, is another way in which the ex-centrics, be they Canadians, women, or both, can subvert the authority of language, language seen as having a single and final meaning. Not surprisingly, language has been called the major issue in the general history of decolonialization,[4] whether in terms of gender or of nationality.

Parody and irony, then, become major forms of both formal and ideological critique in feminist and Canadian fiction alike. The reason is, I think, that they allow writers to speak to their culture, from within, but without being totally co-opted by that culture. The irony and distance implied by parody allow for *separation* at the same time that the doubled structure of both (the superimposition of two meanings or texts) demands recognition of *complicity*. Parody both asserts and undercuts that which it contests. For example, many critics — from Northrop Frye to D.G. Jones — have argued for the importance of the Bible and biblical structures in Canadian literature, but novels such as Cohen's *Beautiful Losers* or Findley's *Not Wanted on the Voyage* parody those structures and narratives in a typically postmodern way, both exploiting and subverting their undeniable cultural authority. Kroetsch's novels assert the male myths of the quest journey (that of Odysseus, Orpheus, Conrad's Marlow, the knight errant, and so on) in order to show the male (and female) cultural roles as fictions, as constructed by culture rather than as 'natural' in any sense of the word. in *Badlands* both the male will to knowledge (and power) and its undermining are parodically presented through Kroetsch's deliberate conjunction of male story and female first-person narration.[5]

Atwood's *The Handmaid's Tale* uses parody with similar ideological and political intent. Her play with the narrative form and details of Yevgeny Zamyatin's *We*[6] (the police state; the secret agents; the subversion of authority by love; the escape; the state-regulated sexuality) is both underlined and undermined, for here women are the victims of a right-wing feminism that supports male authority in return for certain privileges. The conjunction of this kind of feminism with religious fundamentalism points to another parody (rooted in earlier New England puritanism), that of Hawthorne's *The Scarlet Letter*. Its setting, what we might call its colour-coding, and its frame narrative, which suggests historical verification through documentation, are all present, but are also all made ironic in context: the 'Custom-House' genesis (and foreword) of Hawthorne's novel is here inverted into Atwood's epilogue, with its sexist and academic interpretations by male experts; the embodiment of shame (the illegitimate child) becomes the aim of all sex (reproduction by surrogate mothers of sorts).

Parody is a typical postmodern paradoxical form because it uses and abuses the texts and conventions of the tradition. It also contests both the authority of that tradition and the claims of art to originality.

Chapter 6: 'Shape Shifters': Canadian Women Writers and the Tradition

In the first chapter of this book I mentioned the temporal conjunction of postmodernism and feminism, but stressed that they could in no way be equated, mostly because the particular political agenda of feminism makes it substantially different in intent from the more complicitous questioning of the political (that is, usually without any final answers) that characterizes postmodernism. I should also say that I think we can no longer talk of feminism in the singular, but must talk of feminisms in the plural, for there are as many kinds of feminism as there are kinds of women: white, black, Asian, Indian; Anglo- or French, native, 'ethnic'; lesbian, heterosexual. Those ex-centrics outside the 'mainstream' (white, Anglo /French, heterosexual) have often been the ones whose split identities — as Japanese- or Italo-Canadians, for instance — have made them feel closer to the postmodern concerns for difference and multiplicity rather than sameness and single identity. These women writers live as well as write their doubled sense of self. So too do native women, doubly colonized by history and by gender.[1] Their own cultural traditions (mostly oral) and their personal past often become the focus of works that cannot escape that postmodern irony we saw in Chapter 3, because they are in fact written, not oral. These writers also tell us as much about their people as themselves. History, autobiography, and metafictional self-reflexivity meet, for instance, in the opening of Maria Campbell's *Halfbreed*:

> I am not very old, so perhaps some day, when I too am a grannie, I will write more. I write this for all of you, to tell you what it is like to be a Halfbreed woman in our country. I want to tell you about the joys and sorrows, the oppressing poverty, the frustrations and the dreams.[2]

The fact that postmodernism values difference and ex-centricity is due in great part to the fact that feminisms (along with studies of postcolonial racism, Marxist class analysis, and gay theory, of course) pushed it in that direction. Feminists noticed that, in theory at least, poststructuralist challenges to the bastions of liberal humanism, especially to the notion of universal 'Man,' had not necessarily led to the discovery of Woman, as we have seen. The modernist avant-garde too, for all its aesthetic radicalism and political utopianism, had not been very ideologically aware of its representations of women. Postmodernism, thanks to feminisms, now is.

These two forces have come together today in their related challenges to the canon (to the 'eternal' 'beauty' and 'truth' of the 'universally' agreed-upon 'great tradition') and to the borders that conventionally divide fiction from non-fictional forms. They both try to offer reasons to rethink the notion of 'definitive' inscriptions of identity, especially the ex-centric, 'minoritarian' identity: Big Bear, Riel...women! In general, both feminisms and postmodernism 'situate' themselves and the literature they study in historical, social, and cultural (as well as literary) contexts, challenging conventions that are presumed to be literary 'universals,' but can in fact be shown to embody the values of a very particular group of people — of a certain class, race, gender, and sexual orientation.

But this contestation is operating not just on the level of theory: women writers too have done much to challenge systems that 'totalize' — that unify with an eye to power and control, with an eye to obliterating traces of difference. They too have worked to replace 'universal' 'Truth' with particular truths. The techniques they have chosen make their work overlap with what I have been calling the postmodern: in their challenges to form, as well as in their ideological critique, these are postmodern writers — but they are also feminist writers, and the difference of agenda must be respected.

Two of the major 'universals' contested by both postmodernism and feminism are the notions of authority (in its various forms) and originality. One of the most common means of contesting used by writers of both persuasions is intertextuality in general, and parody in particular. Parody, in a sense, is a use and abuse of convention. By definition it is not fully original: it is borrowed or stolen — and only then altered. Like all forms of intertextual borrowing, it is ostentatiously not a single, unique utterance of an original genius. Herein lies the implicit critique of those liberal humanist 'universals.' If anything, intertextuality and parody signal a kind of textual collectivity, as well as a textual history: they deliberately recall other texts. They undercut the notion that authorial authority rests on a single meaning, fixed in the past, by materially reminding us

LINDA HUTCHEON

of the process of re-interpretation that we call the act of reading. To re-present or re-narrate (parodically or otherwise) is always to re-conceptualize the possibilities of meaning: *Beautiful Losers* desacralizes the authority of the male, French, Jesuit inscription of the identity of the female, Indian saint Catherine Tekakwitha, by means of rather irreverent parody. And as I mentioned in Chapter 1, writers as different as Robert Kroetsch and Audrey Thomas translate or trans-code male narrative patterns (like the quest) into significantly different female forms, thereby demystifying their presumed 'universal' attributes and re-en-gendering them.

In much postmodern fiction it is the conventions of narrative in particular that get rethought, especially the so-called 'transparency' of stories and story-telling, whether in novels or in history-writing. As Marjorie Perloff has put it, postmodern story 'is no longer the full-fledged *mythos* of Aristotle...but a point of reference, a way of alluding, a source...of parody. To tell a story is to find a way — sometimes the only way — of *knowing* one's world.'[3] While my focus in this chapter will be on novelistic intertextuality and parody, a few things must be clarified. First, these are in no way the only means at the disposal of writers to de-form and challenge literary 'universals.'[4] Second, novels are clearly not the only generic form in which they work their challenges.[5] Third, parody in particular can exist on other levels than that of genre. Any coded form of communication or behaviour can be parodied. For instance, in *Lives of Girls and Women* Alice Munro parodies our cultural codes regarding the loss of female virginity (the need for the show of blood) through Del's provocative allegorical lie about the tom cat and the bird told to mother: it both calls attention to and explains the presence of (her) blood on the flowers by the house. Or, to offer one further example, many feminist novels parody certain theoretical notions: those of Nicole Brossard and Louky Bersianik take on the Lacanian psychoanalytic theories about the feminization of the child's relation to the parents.[6]

Parody — or intertextuality in general — plays an important role in much women's fiction today, as it seeks a feminine literary space while still acknowledging (however grudgingly) the power of the (male/'universal') space in which it cannot avoid, to some extent, operating. This enforced complicity does not diminish the impact of its protest, but it does set up the conditions within which it will exist. The representations of women in so-called 'universal' conventions are still being contested. In Smaro Kamboureli's terms:

Whether [women writers] adhere to a radical or non-radical feminist ideology, or whether they choose forms and structures that conform to the literary tradition or depart from it, they all take exception to the anemic double of the feminine body that male language and mythology have constructed. They do so by deconstructing the culture that has hosted them as parasites.[7]

Notes

Introduction

1. See Lorna Irvine, *Sub/version: Canadian Fictions by Women* (Toronto: ECW Press, 1986) and Coral Ann Howells, *Private and Fictional Words: Canadian Women Novelists of the 1970s and 1980s* (London and New York: Methuen, 1987).
2. Irvine, p. 11.
3. *Home Truths: Selected Canadian Stories* (Toronto: Macmillan, 1981), p. 269.
4. Elaine Showalter, "Feminist Criticism in the Wilderness", *Critical Inquiry* vol. 8, no. 2 (1981), p. 192.
5. See Kroetsch in Shirley Neuman and Robert Wilson, *Labyrinths of Voice: Conversations with Robert Kroetsch* (Edmonton: NeWest Press, 1982), p. 97.
6. See Glen Deer, 'Rhetoric, Ideology, and Authority: Narrative Strategies in Six Innovative Canadian Novels', Ph.D. Dissertation, York University, 1987, pp. 182-3.

Chapter 6: Shape Shifters: Canadian Women Writers and the Tradition

1. For a study of the problems of native and ethnic women, see section II ('Writing Against Double Colonization') in *In the Feminine: Women and Words/Les Femmes et les mots* (Conference proceedings 1983), ed. Ann Dybikowski, Victoria Freeman, Daphne

Marlatt, Barbara Pulling, Betsy Warland (Edmonton: Longspoon Press, 1983), pp. 53-74.

2. Maria Campbell, *Halfbreed* (Halifax: Goodread Biographies, 1973), p. 2.

3. Marjorie Perloff, *The Dance of the Intellect: Studies in the Poetry of the Pound Tradition* (Cambridge: Cambridge University Press, 1985), p. 161. Perloff's focus is American postmodern narrative poetry, but her point is valid not only for the Canadian long poem, but for much Canadian postmodern prose fiction.

4. See Smaro Kamboureli, 'Dialogue with the Other: The Use of Myth in Canadian Women's Poetry' (in *In the Feminine*, pp 105-9), on how women poets deform and demythologize myths and stereotypes of the feminine that act as 'paradigmatic models for reality' through a variety of deconstructive and dialogic strategies — of which parody is one.

5. For example, from the same volume, on poetry see Daphne Marlatt's 'musing with mothertongue', pp. 171-4; on short fiction see Gail Scott's 'Shaping a Vehicle for Her Use: Women and the Short Story', pp. 184-92; on drama see Pol Pelletier's 'Myth and Women's Theatre', pp. 110-13 and Solange Collin, 'An Alternative to the Traditional Theatre in Québec', pp. 219-23.

6. See Carolyn Hlus, 'Writing Womanly: Theory and Practice', in *A Mazing Space: Writing Canadian/Women Writing* (Edmonton: Longspoon/NeWest Press, 1986), pp. 295-7.

7. Smaro Kamboureli, 'The Body as Audience and Performance in the Writing of Alice Munro', in *A Mazing Space*, pp. 31-2.

Maria Tippett

By a Lady:
Celebrating Three Centuries of
Art by Canadian Women

Introduction

During the nineteenth century, the work of Canadian women artists seldom received the attention it deserved. Hence the title of this book, *By a Lady*. This generic attribution automatically placed art made by women in a sub-category of its own. Women's names, it seemed, were as irrelevant as their work. This book celebrates the achievements of Canadian women artists; their recognition is long overdue.

Through three centuries of art-making in Canada, women artists have been ignored, forgotten and marginalized. It is not surprising, then, that with very few exceptions, they have been omitted from books dealing with Canadian art.

This book seeks to set the record straight.

Women have been forced to produce art under conditions and social constraints that frequently contradict their experience. Historians and critics have typically considered their work in terms of their gender and weighed it against the star system of male art. Above all, they have measured women's success by the number of their works collected by and displayed in public repositories, illustrated in art magazines, placed on the auction block and hung on the walls of commercial galleries.

Given that these institutions have been largely dominated by men, it is hardly surprising that women have received fewer government grants, exhibited less frequently in public galleries, sat on fewer juries and panels and earned lower sums from the sale of their work than their male contemporaries. In a society that measures artistic success in economic terms, how can women hope to be viewed as anything other than second rate?

Before I began my research for *By a Lady,* I frankly was not sure what I would find. I had no wish to scrape the barrel by dealing with inferior works just to give Canadian women their own art history. I knew that the most recent study devoted to Canadian painting, Dennis Reid's *Concise History of Canadian Painting,* had, like the histories before it, paid almost no attention to women. It illustrates the work of only five women. This meant that any attempt to suggest that there were more women worthy of inclusion in a survey of Canadian art would be challenging the canon, upsetting the apple cart.

From my earlier studies of landscape painting in British Columbia and of Emily Carr, I knew that many women had produced paintings of quality equal to their male peers throughout that province's short history. This was later confirmed when I looked beyond British Columbia to the paintings and sculptures that women contributed to the First and Second World War art programs. But it was only when I embarked on this book that I discovered, with great joy, just how many women had painted, sculpted, and created works of art in other media. Indeed, by the end of my research I had collected the names of so many women artists that I was forced to select one among many in order to illustrate a point, style, or an idea. Sometimes my choice was influenced by the willingness of living artists, their heirs or the owners of their work to release copyright permission for illustration. My own aesthetic "gaze" played a part in the decision-making, too.

Not only did I find that many women artists had been at work since the final decades of the seventeenth century; I realized that women had also been active art teachers, curators, critics, private gallery dealers, and art society organizers, playing important roles in giving women a variety of forums for their work.

What impressed me was not simply the sheer number of women who had consistently produced works of art since the settlement of New France, but the wide range of their work. Fine paintings like Susanna Moodie's mines, Frances Anne Hopkins' voyageurs and Lady Hariot Dufferin's native villages on the Queen Charlotte Islands helped dispel the notion that nineteenth century women artists produced only delicate botanical watercolour paintings. The work of Paraskeva Clark, Frances Loring, Wanda Koop, Marian Scott, Ghitta Caiserman-Roth and Shirley Wiitasalo during this century attested to women's ability to respond to social and political issues. Jori Smith, Suzanne Duquet and Prudence Heward demonstrated that they, along with other women figurative painters, had the courage to part with the overwhelmingly popular genre of landscape painting during the interwar period. Edna Taçon, Rita Letendre, Marcelle Ferron, Marion Nicoll, Alexandra Luke and Milly Ristvedt proved that women were capable of using a "male" art form — in this case, non-objective art — to express their distinct voice. And those women who elected to produce gender-based work — from the early nineteenth-century genre paintings of Jane Ellice, the *maternité* of Mary Bell Eastlake and Sophie Pemberton, and the carvings of Lucy Tasseor to the feminist canvases of Susan Scott, Thérèse Joyce-Gagnon, and Hilda Woolnough — made clear the need for a female-centred art in our society.

By a Lady challenges the all-too-common view that women artists are second-rate, scaled-down versions of their male contemporaries, producing derivative and diluted examples of work in genres dominated by male excellence. Indeed, despite economic, social and commercial restraints, women have produced a diverse and vital body of work. By celebrating it, we can help these women and their successors take their rightful place in the canon of Canada's art history, and in the consciousness of Canadians.

Laying the Foundations

Women artists not only came home from study abroad with larger reputations and new styles for which they frequently received criticism. Some — like Florence McGillivray, Henrietta Mabel May (1884-1971), and Emily Carr — returned to a new way of portraying the Canadian landscape and the native Indians who inhabited it.

Florence McGillivray, a Toronto painter, was one of the artists to discover the aesthetic possibilities of the northern Ontario landscape. Members of the Toronto Art Students' League had painted northern Ontario wilderness landscape motifs on their calendars from 1893 to 1904. And Mary E. Wrinch (1877-1969) and a handful of other men and women had been painting Lake Muskoka and other parts of northern Ontario from their Toronto base since 1906. But it was McGillivray who approached the northern wilderness in a distinct way. Study in Paris under Lucien Simon and Emile René Ménard, travel in Brittany where she drew and painted the landscape in the manner of Paul Gauguin, Maurice Denis and other

EMILY CARR, *Yan Mortuary Poles*, c. 1928-29, oil on canvas, 85.5 x 61.0 cm. Collection of the Art Gallery of Windsor. Purchased by public subscription and a grant from the Ontario Arts Council, 1964.

MARIA TIPPETT

artists of the Pont-Aven school, and the acceptance of her work at the 1913 Salon des Beaux-Arts in Paris sent her home to Canada in 1914 a committed Fauve. The patchwork effect created by the palette knife, the juxtaposition of intense colour and the use of a thick black outline to enclose her forms, all characteristic of Fauve painting, enabled her to inject the northern Canadian landscape with unprecedented luminosity. Works such as *Afterglow* (c. 1914) predate the now conventional and familiar views of northern Ontario that would soon be familiar in the oil sketches of Tom Thomson, an artist to whom McGillivray reputedly gave "some helpful hints," and in the work of the emerging Ontario Group of Seven.[1] Thus McGillivray belongs to the small group of artists whose pre-First World War landscape paintings linked two visions of the land: the romantic-realist view of the railway artists of the 1880s and 1890s and the heroic view of the landscape that characterized the mature work of the Group of Seven and their adherents following the Great War.

Working out of her St Catherine Street studio in Montreal, Henrietta Mabel May demonstrated how far ahead she was of many of her Canadian contemporaries. The flat areas of Fauve colour in *Indian Woman, Oka, 1917* (1917) along with the strong modelling and impersonal rendering of the native woman, the two-dimensional sense of space and the order applied to every element in the work had all been acquired during May's 1912 visit to Europe with fellow artist Emily Coonan.

Emily Carr, who returned from study in France the same year, applied some of these same Post-Impressionist techniques to the West Coast Indian motif. In her watercolour painting *Tanoo* (1912) Carr chose bright colours and enclosed every object in a bold thick line, dramatically discarding her earlier penchant for detail and exactitude. The canvases which resulted from the same trip to northern British Columbia were not only rich in vivid daubs of pigment but had grown to immense proportions, too. Though her style would alter considerably over the years to come, it was in France that, by her own admission, her "seeing had broadened," and there that she had first taken her rightful place among like-minded artists during the 1911 Salon d'Automne exhibit.[2]

By the outbreak of the First World War, then, several Canadian women artists were working to international standards and applying their modernists styles to Canadian and foreign subjects. Yet women continued to be either totally ignored by the critics or written about according to gender-based criteria. If a woman happened to be interviewed in her studio, the critic paid more attention to the exotic environment in which she worked than to what she was producing on canvas and paper or in bronze.[3] If a woman stepped outside the boundaries of conventional art, as did Emily Carr, for example, she was harshly criticized.[4]

The continued bias against women artists owed a great deal to the lingering belief that they were dabblers, that they simply could not tackle important subjects. The fact that by the end of the nineteenth century women were mounting group exhibitions seemed to make no difference. Sometimes they showed with societies such as the Women's Art Association. At other times they contributed to small group shows, such as Mary Hiester Reid and Mary Wrinch's 1912 exhibition at Toronto's Art Metropole, or Claire Fauteux, Berthe Le Moyne (active 1890s-1920) and Rita Mount's (1888-1967) show at Montreal's Bibliothèque Saint-Sulpice in 1917. Although women had become prominent in many areas of the visual arts, had traded their tight bodices and cumbersome bustles for separate shirtwaists and divided skirts, the rhetorical question asked in the mid-1890s in *Massey's Magazine* continued to be posed: "But where is women's realm more unquestioned, more secure, than in the home?"[5]

The idea than women artists belonged solely in the home was challenged suddenly during the Great War. In 1916 the Canadian government founded the Canadian War Memorials Fund expressly to hire artists to record events on the home and war fronts in paintings, prints and sculptures. The first artists commissioned by the war artists' program organizers were British. After some artists complained, A. Y. Jackson, Maurice Cullen, F. H. Varley and other male Canadian artists were sent to the front. But the program organizers, Lords Beaverbrook and Rothermere, were committed to doing more than making a record of the war zone. Indeed, the director of the National Gallery of Canada, Eric Brown, another organizer, stated that the home front "had vastly more pictorial possibilities than front line trenches."[6]

Recognition of the home front as valid subject matter for the war artist meant that women were involved in the program in a modest way. They were not commissioned as official war artists. Mabel May was sent to the Northern Electric Plant in Montreal to record scenes of the female workers who had replaced conscripted soldiers.[7] Florence Carlyle of London, Ontario, was commissioned to paint the portrait of the head of the Canadian Red Cross, Lady Julia Drummond.[8] ("I have been a great swell lately," she wrote home from Drummond's palatial residence near Westminster Abbey while completing the commission, "dining at nine o'clock in full dress."[9]) Caroline Armington spent the war in France. She was commissioned to make an etching of the Canadian General Hospital in St Cloud.[10] And two American newcomers to Toronto, Frances Loring (1887-1968) and Florence Wyle (1881-1968), followed Mabel May into the munitions factories with their sketchbooks....

Notes

1. Colin S. MacDonald, *Dictionary of Canadian Artists,* Vol. 4 (Ottawa, 1968), p. 1022.

2. Emily Carr, *Growing Pains* (Toronto, 1966; first published 1946). The work she completed before travelling to France was *War Canoes* (1908), held by the Montreal Museum of Fine Arts.

3. See, for example, Margaret Wade, "Miss Eva Bradshaw: Artist," *Echo* (Dec. 1920), p. 5, along with the series of fifteen articles devoted to Canadian female artists which appeared in *Sunday World* (Toronto) from 25 May 1924 to 14 Sept. 1924.

4. Tippet, *Emily Carr: A Biography* (Toronto, 1979), especially Ch. 6, "Vancouver and the North, 1911-1913."

5. "Woman's Realm," *Massey's Magazine,* Vol. 1, No. 1 (Jan. 1896), p. 51.

6. Brown cited in Maria Tippett, *Art at the Service of War: Canada, Art and the Great War* (Toronto, 1984), p. 51.

7. Henrietta Mabel May, *Women Making Shells* (c. 1918), Canadian War Museum.

8. Florence Carlyle, *Portrait of Lady Drummond* (c. 1918), Canadian War Museum.

9. Woodstock Public Library and Art Gallery, Woodstock, Ontario, Florence Carlyle to Russell Carlyle (3 April 1918).

10. Caroline Armington, *No. 8, Canadian General Hospital, St Cloud France* (c. 1919), Canadian War Museum.

PART TWO:
THE NORTH

CARL BERGER

THE TRUE NORTH STRONG AND FREE

Hail! Rugged monarch, Northern Winter, hail!
Come! Great Physician, vitalize the gale;
Dispense the ozone thou has purified,
With Frost and Fire, where Health and age reside,—
Where Northern Lights electrify the soul
Of Mother Earth, whose throne is near the Pole.

Why should the children of the North deny
The sanitary virtues of the sky?
Why should they fear the cold, or dread the snow,
When ruddier blood thro' their hot pulses flow?
...
We have the Viking blood, and Celtic bone,
The Saxons' muscled flesh, and scorn to groan,
Because we do not bask in Ceylon's Isle,
Where Heber said, that "only man is vile".
...
But we, as laymen, must get down to earth,
And praise the clime which gave our nation birth.
Kind Winter is our theme.

> William Henry Taylor,
> *Canadian Seasons. Spring: Summer:*
> *Autumn: Winter: with a Medley of*
> *Reveries in Verse and Prose and*
> *Other Curios,*
> Toronto, 1913, pp. 63-64.

Everybody talks about the weather and the climate: seldom have these been exalted as major attributes of nationality. Yet from the days of the French explorers, who often remarked that the future inhabitants of northern America must necessarily be as hardy as their environment, to John Diefenbaker's invocation of the northern destiny of the nation, detached observers and patriotic spokesmen alike have fixed upon the northern character of Canada as one of the chief attributes of her nationality. Canadian national feeling, like the nationalist impulse in other countries, has expressed itself in myths and legends about the past and anticipations of noble mission in the future, as well as in distinctive economic and international policies. Such myths and symbols nourish and sustain the emotional taproot of nationalism, and impart to it an intellectual content which itself has an attractive power. The purpose of this paper is to describe the elements and savour the texture of one such recurrent theme in Canadian nationalist thought which flowered in the half century after Confederation and which is, in muted form, still with us — the idea that Canada's unique character derived from her northern location, her severe winters and her heritage of 'northern races.'

The True North, Strong and Free

In the rhetoric of the day, Canada was the "Britain of the North," "this northern kingdom," the "True North" in Tennyson's phrase, the "Lady of the Snows" in Kipling's. "Canada is a young, fair and stalwart maiden of the north."[1] "The very atmosphere of her northern latitude, the breath of life that rose from lake and forest, prairie and mountain, was fast developing a race of men with bodies enduring as iron and minds as highly tempered as steel."[2] Canada was the "Young giant nation of the North", the "Young scion of the northern zone"; her people, "Our hardy northern race"; her location, those "Stern latitudes."[3] These images denote not merely geographical location or climatic condition but the combination of both, moulding racial character. The result of life in the northern latitudes was the creation and sustenance of self-reliance, strength, hardness — in short, all the attributes of a dominant race. "Northern nations always excel southern ones in energy and stamina, which accounts for their prevailing power."[4] In the north "the race is compelled by nature to maintain its robust attributes, mental and physical, whereas in more sunny countries like Africa and

CARL BERGER

Australia the tendency of the climate is toward deterioration."[5] "A constitution nursed upon the oxygen of our bright winter atmosphere,"[6] exclaimed Governor General Dufferin, "makes its owner feel as though he could toss about the pine trees in his glee..." Just as "northern" was synonymous with strength and self-reliance, so "southern" was equated with degeneration, decay and effeminacy. Our "bracing northern winters," declared the *Globe* in 1869, "will preserve us from the effeminacy which naturally steals over the most vigorous races when long under the relaxing influence of tropical or even generally mild and genial skies."[7] Moreover, it was believed that liberty originated among the tribes of northern Europe and was dependent upon those very characteristics which the northern environment called forth. Canada, then, was not only the true north, but also strong and free.

In origin, ideas about the relationship between climate and the character of "races" and their institutions were rooted in myths and stereotypes in classical, medieval and renaissance Europe, most of which viewed the southern Mediterranean peoples as gay, lively and individualistic, and the northerners as stupid and dull barbarians.[8] The first coherent Canadian statement of the idea of the northern race came from an associate of the Canada First Movement who was also a Fellow of the Royal Society of Northern Antiquaries of Copenhagen, Robert Grant Haliburton. Lamenting the fact that Confederation had been created with as little excitement among the masses as if a joint-stock company had been formed, he asked, "Can the generous flame of national spirit be kindled and blaze in the icy bosom of the frozen north?" Convinced that the indispensable attribute of a nation, a "national spirit," was the product of slow growth unless stimulated by a violent struggle, the memory of a glorious past, or the anticipation of a bright future, Haliburton added to the Canada First spirit the contention that Canada's future as a dominant nation was secure because of its northern character. *"We are the Northmen of the New World,"* his lecture to the Montreal Literary Club in 1869 on the men of the north and their place in history was the seedbed of the northern race idea. Ironically, Haliburton's poor health compelled him to spend his winters in tropical climates, where he devoted himself to ethnological and anthropological investigations. In 1887 he discovered the existence of a race of pigmies in North Africa.

Haliburton's declaration that Canadians were a northern race was expressed in the language of science and the rich imagery of romantic history. "Our corn fields, rich though they are, cannot compare with the fertile prairies of the West, and our long winters are a drain on the profits of business, but may not our snow and frost give us what is of more value than gold or silver, a healthy, hardy, virtuous, dominant race?" The peculiar characteristic of the new Dominion, he asserted, "must ever be that it is a Northern country inhabited by the descendants of Northern races." This claim to dominance rested on two assumptions: firstly, the hardy northern races of Europe are attracted to Canada. The British people themselves are "but a fusion of many northern elements which are here again meeting and mingling, and blending together to form a new nationality." This new nationality must comprise at once "the Celtic, the Teutonic, and the Scandinavian elements, and embrace the Celt, the Norman French, the Saxon and the Swede." Secondly, to Haliburton, the climate itself was a creative force. "Is it climate that produces varieties in our race or must we adopt the views of some eminent authorities of science, who hold that the striking diversies now apparent in the languages, temperament, and capacities of nations, must have existed *ab initio*? The Mosaic chronology must be rejected and the period of man's life on earth must be extended to millions of years." "If climate has not had the effect of moulding races, how is it that southern nations have almost invariably been inferior to and subjugated by the men of the north?"

The stern climate would preserve in their pristine vigour the characteristics of the northern races and ensure that Canada would share the destiny of the northmen of the old world, who destroyed Rome after it "had become essentially Southern in its characteristics." Those northmen were not barbarians but the carriers of the germ of liberty. "On investigating the history of our laws and of the rise of civil and political liberty in Europe," Haliburton found them rooted in the elemental institutions of the northmen. "Almost all the Northern nations had similar systems of regulating the rights of property and the remedies of wrongs. Their laws were traditions called by them their *customs*, an unwritten code which still exists in England where it is known as the Common law,....(and) it is a remarkable fact that wherever these unwritten laws have been preserved, civil and political liberty has also survived." In Canada, "the cold north wind that rocked the cradle of our race, still blows through our forests, and breathes the spirit of liberty into our hearts."[9] Thus, because of the climate and because Canadians are sprung from these men of the north — the "Aryan" family, Canada must be a pre-eminent power, the home of a superior race, the heir of both the historical destiny of the ancient Scandinavians and their spirit of liberty.

In the exuberant optimism of Canada First nationalism, Haliburton took the Canadian climate — since the days of Voltaire's famous disparagement, the symbol of sterility, inhospitality and worthlessness — and turned it into the dynamic element of national greatness. Though he was to break with Haliburton over the issue of Canadian independence, to the end of his days the irrepressible Colonel Denison could boast that "We are the Northmen of the new world."[10] Charles Mair, too, thought that "whilst the south is in a great measure a region of effeminacy and disease, the north-west is a decided recuperator of decayed function and wasted tissue."[11] And William Foster, in his address on the new nationality in 1871, said that "The old Norse mythology, with its Thor hammers and Thor hammerings, appeals to us, — for we are a Northern people, — as the true out-crop of human nature, more manly, more real, than the weak marrow-bones superstition of an effeminate South."[12] It is no accident that members of this youthful and intellectual nationalist group should appeal to what Mair, in his poem on Foster's death, called "the unconquered North," that they should extol Alexander Morris' vision of "the Great Britannic Empire of the North," or that they should be remembered a generation later as exponents of the northern destiny of Canada. Their most practical achievement in politics was the agitation for Canadian acquisition of the north-west territory, the importance of which they contended had been obscured by tales of ice and snow falsely broadcast by Hudson Bay Company officials to protect their fur domain from settlement.

Climatic or Racial Determinism?

While Haliburton's address included much that was to receive progressive elaboration by others, such as the notion that both French and English were, in racial terms, one people, it contained an ambivalence that was to become more obvious as the idea of the northern race became enmeshed in a popularized Darwinism. This dichotomy was simply between an optimistic, idealistic meliorism which took climate as moulding desirable qualities irrespective of the racial origins of the people, and a scientific determinism which saw racial capacities as fixed, or changeable only to a limited degree. Haliburton avoided such subtleties by implying that all future immigration into Canada would consist of those races already inured and adapted to the northern environment. Later, more pessimistic writers were to see the climate as a "barrier" to certain kinds of immigrants, rather than as an agency for totally transforming them. This dualism can be best illustrated by considering two different versions of the idea.

A most forceful statement of the view that assumed the complete malleability of character was made in 1877 by another Nova Scotian, Charles R. Tuttle. A self-educated school teacher who later made a career of journalism in Winnipeg and the United States, Tuttle produced a large number of now forgotten books including an imposing two-volume history of Canada. In this history he expressed the optimistic opinion that the institutions, soil and climate of Canada would determine the character of the people. The immigrant, he wrote, come from the monarchical countries of Europe, "ignorant, rude, and unmannerly," but their character is transformed, they become self-reliant, and exhibit a "manly independence," under the influence of British institutions and the "broad rivers, boundless prairies, high mountains, and pathless woods."[13]

In Tuttle, a romantic ruralism was mixed with the conviction that man's capacity for improvement was infinite and, in a favourable environment, inevitable. Where he saw the "ignorant, rude, and unmannerly" being formed into independent and hardy yeomen by the natural features of the country and British institutions, more pessimistic observers, while not denying the potent influence of environment, nevertheless emphasized rather the inherent and unchangeable aptitudes of the "northern races." That the northern climate constituted a national blessing because it excluded "weaker" races was the persistent theme of the writings and orations of the Canadian imperialist George Parkin. A native of New Brunswick, Parkin was one of the most forceful and idealistic spokesmen of the Imperial Federation League, Principal of Upper Canada College during the late 1890s, and subsequently one of the organizers of the Cecil Rhodes scholarship trust. Heavily influenced by the social Darwinism of the time, and acknowledging his debt to the historian Buckle for the idea of climatic influence upon the life of nations, Parkin called the Canadian climate "one of our greatest blessings." The "severe winter climate of Canada," he said,

CARL BERGER

"is perhaps the most valuable asset that the country has." A temperature of twenty degrees below zero which he found at Winnipeg "seemed to give an added activity to peoples' steps and a buoyancy to their spirits." The climate necessitates vigorous effort; "it teaches foresight; it cures or kills the shiftless and improvident; history shows that in the long run it has made strong races."

Where Tuttle viewed the capacity for self-government as the product of the environment, Parkin contended that fitness for self-government was itself the inherent function of the northern races. Without race vanity, he asserted, we may attribute to the Anglo-Saxon race a unique aptitude for self-government. The special importance of the Canadian climate, therefore, was not merely that it sustained the hardy character of the stronger races, but that it also constituted, in Darwinian terms, "a persistent process of natural selection." The northern winters ensured that Canada would have no negro problem, "which weighs like a troublesome nightmare upon the civilization of the United States"; and it seemed that nature itself had decreed that Canada would have no cities "like New York, St. Louis, Cincinnati, or New Orleans which attract even the vagrant population of Italy and other countries of Southern Europe." "Canada," Parkin emphasized, "will belong to the sturdy races of the North-Saxon, and Celt, Scandinavian, Dane and Northern German, fighting their way under conditions sometimes rather more severe than those to which they have been accustomed in their old homes." The climate "is certain, in short, to secure for the Dominion and perpetuate there the vigour of the best northern races."[14]

The Advantages of Northernness

To recapitulate and detail the elements of this concept is to indicate the basis of its credibility and the nature of its appeal. First of all, the very fact of northernness connoted strength and hardihood, vigour and purity. "Strength and power," ran the familiar refrain, "have ever been with the Northern peoples."[15] In the struggle for existence, the northern conditions called forth the virtues of self-reliance and strength: only the fittest survived. On the other hand, the "south" conjured up the image of enervation, of abundance stifling the Victorian values of self-help, work and thrift, or effeminacy, of voluptuous living and consequently of the decay and degeneration of character.

A whole series of desirable national characteristics were derived from Canada's northern location. It was implied that northern peoples expressed their hard individualism in an individualistic religion, stripped of the gorgeous luxuries congenial to southern Catholicism. The climate, said Parkin, imparts "a Puritan turn of mind which gives moral strenuousness."[16] A Methodist clergyman and editor, who attended the American centennial exhibition in 1876 and saw a representative collection of European paintings, reported his disgust with the Catholic art of the south, a reaction he attributed to the lax morals of the "Latin" races. "I must," he wrote, "record my protest against the sensuous character of many of the foreign paintings, especially of France, Austria, and Spain. In this respect they are in striking contrast with the almost universal chaste and modest character of the English and American pictures, and those of Rothern (*sic*, Northern) Europe. I attribute this difference partly to the only partial moral restraints of the Roman Catholic religion, and partly to a survival, in the old Latin races, of the ancient pagan characteristics which created the odious art and literature, and social corruptions of the effete and dying Roman Empire."[17] These impurities, of course, were due to much else besides climate, but the clear, cold and frosty air itself seemed an insulation against lax morality. Another clergyman found in the Canadian winter the impulse to cultural and mental improvement. The winter "is prophetic...of a race, in mind and body and moral culture, of the highest type." Applying to Canada the remarks that Sir Charles Dilke had made in reference to Scotland, Reverend Wightman cited with approval the opinion that the "'long winters cultivate thrift, energy and fore-thought, without which civilization would perish, and at the same time give leisure for reading and study. So the Scottish, the Icelanders, the Swedes, and the northern races generally, are much better educated than the Latin and southern races.'"[18]

The Canadian winter was not only considered to be conducive to mental improvement: in maintaining physical health and stimulating robustness, according to one of the foremost Canadian physicians of the day, it was unsurpassed. A belief in the healthful qualities of the climate was expressed in much of the literature on the northern theme, but it was left to a surgeon at the Hôtel-Dieu in Montreal to impart to this idea the authority of medical knowledge and statistical proof. William Hales Hingston had studied medicine at McGill and Edinburgh, as well as Berlin, Heidelberg and Vienna;

CARL BERGER

in 1854 he began practice in Montreal and was for many years surgeon at the largest hospital in Canada and a professor of clinical surgery at the Montreal School of Medicine. In 1884 Hingston published a series of papers under the title, *The Climate of Canada and its relation to Life and Health*. Employing statistics provided by the surgeons at British and American army stations, he ascertained that as one passed northward the salubrity of the climate increased, that the ratios of mortality from digestive, respiratory and nervous disorders decreased in a northward progression. After considering practically every known malady from diarrhoea to dysentery, consumption to cataract, he emphasized that there are no diseases indigenous to the country. The dry air and cold winter, moreover, are decided recuperators of disease. "Indeed," he concluded, "in considering the few diseases which here afflict humanity relatively to elsewhere, we have great reason to be thankful to the All-powerful Controller of the seasons as of our fate,...He keeps us in health, comfort and safety." If only such pernicious social habits as intemperance could be avoided, the climate was most "favourable to the highest development of a hardy, long-lived, intelligent people"; the tendency "is unmistakably in favour of increased muscular development"; "the future occupants of the soil will be taller, straighter, leaner people — hair darker and drier and coarser; muscles more tendinous and prominent and less cushioned..." These future occupants of the soil will be, emphatically, a "*Canadian* people," for the distinct nationalities of Europe will blend here into a homogeneous race, the predominating characteristics of which will be determined "after the fashion described by Darwin as the struggle for existence." To this people "will belong the privilege, the great privilege, of aiding in erecting, in what was so lately a wilderness, a monument of liberty and civilization, broader, deeper, firmer, than has ever yet been raised by the hand of man."[19] There was much in Hingston's book — a description of the variety of the climate, reflections on social habits, and the straight-faced observation that those frozen to death display on their visages a look of contentment achieved only by successful religious mystics — but its central burden was that the northern location will breed a distinctive, superior and healthy people.

It seemed that scarcely any advantages accruing to Canada from the winter season went unnoticed or unsung. The winter snow covers and protects fall crops; the frost acts as a solvent on the soil, ploughing the ground and leaving it in springtime "completely pulverized"; the cold freezes newly-killed livestock and preserves them for market. It makes possible the commercial activity of lumbering for the "frost makes bridges without a cent of cost; the snow provides the best roads," "the whole face of the country being literally Macadamized by nature." Winter makes possible sleighing, tobogganing, snowshoeing and skating. "Jack Frost effectually and gratuitously guards us on three thousand miles of our northern coast, and in this he does us a distinct service, greatly relieving national expenditure and contributing much to our sense of security."[20]

A Rationale for Anti-Americanism

The Canadian people were thus not only collectively a superior race, but their "northernness" was constantly compared to the "southernness" of the United States. The third use of the idea was a vigorous statement of the separateness of the two countries. When the annexationists asked "why should the schism which divided our race on this continent 100 years ago, be perpetuated?...What do we gain by remaining apart?" and answered their own question by saying that "Union would be the means of ultimately cementing the Anglo-Saxon race throughout the world,"[21] the usual retort was to deny that the Republic was an Anglo-Saxon country and to elaborate Canadian virtues derived from its northernness against the degeneration of "the south." While the northern climate of Canada was both moulding the northern elements and rejecting weaker, southern immigration, thus creating a homogeneous race, the southern climate of the United States was sapping the energies of even those descendants of vigorous races at the same time that it was attracting multitudes of the weaker races from Southern Europe, in addition to providing a hospitable home to the large negro element. This destruction of the homogeneity of the Republic was regarded as "diluting" its strength, as a species of "deterioration." This was because the southern immigrants were neither formed by a hardy climate in their homeland nor forced to adapt to one in the States. In Canada, Principal Falconer of the University of Toronto reassured his readers, "the rigour of the northern climate has been, and will continue to be, a deterrent for the peoples of Southern Europe."[22] Our climate, contended Parkin, excludes the lower races, "squeezed out by that 30 or 40 degrees below zero." Canada attracts "the stronger people of the northern lands. That is the tendency to squeeze out the undesirable and

CARL BERGER

pump in, as Kipling says,...the strong and desirable." "We have an advantage, this northern race, of a stern nature which makes us struggle for existence." The "submerged tenth," the weaker members of even the stronger races, are also excluded, and hence Canada does not suffer from the American labour troubles. Labour problems are unknown in Canada partly because of the abundance of land and partly because the "Canadian winter exercises upon the tramp a silent but well-nigh irresistible persuasion to shift to a warmer latitude." The United States itself thus serves as a "safety-valve" for labour questions in the Dominion. The climate "is a fundamental political and social advantage which the Dominion enjoys over the United States." It ensures stability and ordered development as well as superiority.[23]

Northernness and Liberty

The notion of strength and superiority inhering in the quality of northernness included a fourth, and perhaps the most important, element of the general idea. Expressed in the words of Emerson, it was that "Wherever snow falls, there is usually civil freedom."[24] Not only did the northern climate foster exactly those characteristics without which self-government could not work, but it was held that, historically, the "germs" of the institutions of liberty originated among the northern peoples and that northern races, inured by centuries of struggles with the elements and acquaintance with these institutions of self-government, enjoyed a superior capacity for governing themselves. Liberty itself depended upon self-reliance, a rugged independence, instilled by the struggle for existence. Thus to the equation of "northern" with strength and the strenuous virtues, against "southern" with degeneration and effeminacy, was added the identification of the former with liberty and the latter with tyranny.

Because "liberty" was itself somehow the major stimulant to "progress," the comparison was often made in terms of progress and regression. In a book review, the editor of the *Canadian Methodist Magazine* contrasted the result of Anglo-Saxon development in North America with that of the Latin races in South America. "On the one side," he wrote, "a forward motion of society and the greatest development of agriculture, commerce and industry; on the other, society thrown backward and plunged to grovel in a morass of idle, unproductive town life, and given up to officialism and political revolutions. In the North we have the rising of the future, in the South the crumbling and decaying past."[25] Wherein, asked a pamphleteer, lies the secret of such marvellous progress? "It springs largely from the fact that the country was people by the Anglo-Saxon race,...When Rome was overshadowing the nations of Southern and Central Europe with its greatness, in the cheerless, uninviting north, a people was undergoing hardy discipline, on land and sea, in constant strife and endless foray, which produced a nobler type of manhood than Rome...It is from these fearless freemen of North Germany, England is indebted in a large measure for her political liberties."[26]

The idea that it was in the north "that the liberties of the world had their birth" was sustained by the political science of the day. Influenced by the "comparative politics" of E.A. Freeman in England and H.B. Adams in the United States, the constitutional and political writings of George Bourinot detailed the operations of the Teutonic germ theory in Canada. In biological analogy, freedom was a "seed," a "germ," which originated in the tribal assemblies of the ancient Scandinavians, was transplanted to England and subsequently to New England and then to Canada by the migration of descendants of these Teutonic races. Wherever the favoured race appeared, its early institutional life was repeated and amplified because "freedom" was in "the blood." Conversely, southern non-Teutonic peoples were either "untutored" in self-government but were educable, or were incapable of governing themselves altogether. In the bracing climate of the north, so resembling freedom's original home, liberty, it was thought, would flourish in a purer form.[27]

It was this identification of liberty with northernness that gave such force to the anti-American emotion that Canadian, or "British," liberty, was far superior to the uproarious democracy of the United States. It was a charge taken directly from pessimistic American racists. The "new immigration" coming from southern and south-eastern Europe became the object of concern and then dread in the late 1880s, partly because it coincided with political and social disturbances arising from the transition from an agrarian to an industrial civilization. It was thought that this immigration not only destroyed the homogeneity of the American people, but also threatened the very existence of Anglo-Saxon leadership and Anglo-Saxon values. Commenting editorially on an article by

CARL BERGER

Henry Cabot Lodge, the chief immigration restrictionist in the Senate, the *Empire* agreed that the old-stock families in the United States were losing their hold, that immigration and the multiplication of "the dregs of the old world population" were increasing too rapidly for assimilation. "The Anglo-Saxon element, the real strength of the nation, is not proportionally as influential now as it once was."[28] Even earlier, Goldwin Smith feared that "the Anglo-American race is declining in numbers;...The question is whether its remaining stock of vitality is sufficient to enable it, before it loses its tutelary ascendancy, to complete the political education of the other races."[29] What Smith viewed with apprehension, others relished in the conviction that Canada was preserved from such a fate. "Take the fact that one million two hundred thousand people passed through Ellis Island into the port of New York last year. Who were they," asked Parkin, "Italians, Greeks, Armenians, Bulgarians, the Latin races of the South. People unaccustomed to political freedom, unaccustomed to self-government, pouring in...They did not come to Canada."[30] In Canada, because of the climate, there were no Haymarket riots, no lynchings, no assassinations of public men. "The United States" declared the *Dominion Illustrated* in 1891, "are welcome to the Hungarians, Poles, Italians and others of that class; they are, as a rule, wretchedly poor, make very poor settlers, and bring with them many of the vices and socialistic tendencies which have caused much trouble to their hosts already. Renewed efforts should...be made by our government to induce more of the hardy German and Norwegian races to remain here...."[31]

The Northern Myth in Canadian Art

The image of Canada as a northern country with a strenuous and masterful people was reinforced and sustained in the novels, travelogues, and works of scientific exploration that abounded in the period. The adventure stories centering on life in the isolated Hudson Bay posts and the exploits of the lonely trapper had long been the staple themes of the novels of Robert M. Ballantyne and the boys' books of J. Macdonald Oxley. But after 1896, when the north-west became the locus of immigration and investment, imaginative writers found in that region not only a picturesque setting and indigenous historical incidents and themes; but also an area which a large number of their readers had never experienced. Certainly it is significant that a number of the best-selling writers in the decade before the First World War, Ralph Connor, Robert Service and William Fraser, not only set their works in the northerly setting but also lived there.

The very titles of these books are indicative of their focus: Agnes Laut's story of the fur trader, *Lords of the North* (1900), and her history, — *Canada, Empire of the North* (1909); Gilbert Parker's *An Adventure of the North* (1905); H.A. Cody's life of Bishop Bompas, *An Apostle of the North* (1905); Ralph Connor's many manly novels set in the north-west, like *Corporal Cameron* (1912) with its inevitable blizzard; travelogues like Agnes D. Cameron's description of her journey through the Athabaska and Mackenzie River region to the Arctic, *The New North* (1909); chronicles of exploration, J.W. Tyrell's *Across the Sub-Arctic of Canada* (1897), and Vilhjalmur Stefansson's *My Life with the Eskimo* (1913). In 1926, a literary critic complained that the "whole of Canada has come to be identified with her northernmost reaches," and in "modern folk-geography Canada means the North."[32]

This image was strengthened by the paintings of the "national movement" in Canadian art, the Group of Seven. While some of the most characteristic work of men like A.Y. Jackson and J.E.H. Macdonald was done in the post-war decades, it was during the years before 1913 that their group was formed, their nationalism inspired, and their determination made to express the essence of Canada through her landscape. Some of them were directly influenced by a Scandinavian art exhibition in 1912 which "impressed them as an example of what other northern countries could do in art." A member of the group admitted that in their minds Canada was "a long, thin strip of civilization on the southern fringe of a vast expanse of immensely varied, virgin land reaching into the remote north. Our whole country is cleansed by the pristine and replenishing air which sweeps out of that great hinterland. It was the discovery of this great northern area as a field of art which enticed and inspired these painters." But the north — with its sparkling clear air and sharp outlines which could never be apprehended with the techniques of Old World art — was much more than a field of art: it was the mirror of national character. After a trip into the Arctic with A.Y. Jackson, Lawren Harris reported that "We came to know that it is only through the deep and vital experience of its total environment that a people identifies itself with its land and gradually a deep and satisfying awareness develops. We were convinced that no virile people could remain subservient to, and dependent upon the creations in art of other peoples...To us there was also the strange brooding sense of another nature fostering a new race and a new age." Though they displayed a variety of personal styles and attitudes, the group was united in the effort to portray the rugged terrain of the Canadian shield and the changing seasons in the northern woods. While present in J.E.H. Macdonald's *The Solemn Land* (1921) and other early works, the theme of northernness culminated in A.Y. Jackson's *The North Shore of Baffin Island* (c. 1929) and Lawren Harris' *Bylot Island* (1930) both of which literally exude the crystalline cold and seem themselves to be a part of the stark northern wastes.[33]

The Northern Theme in Retrospect

In retrospect, the northern theme, as it was expressed in the first half century after Confederation, must be regarded as a myth, for not only did the observations it exalted conflict with objective appraisal, but its primary, intellectual assumptions became suspect. While it rested on the truism, confirmed by modern human geography, that certain climates are stimulating to human exertion, it too frequently glossed over the variety of climatic regions within Canada, and it tended to identify the whole country with that region of it which contained the fewest of her people. It was related and sustained, moreover, by the ebullient faith in the progress of the north-west, in the lusty but mistaken hopes of the wheat-boom years that the northern zone would become the home of millions of happy yeomen. The northern theme also assumed a racist aspect, holding that the capacity for freedom and progress were inherent in the blood of northern races. Not only was this belief progressively undermined by modern anthropological scholarship, but the identification of the Teutonic race with the spirit of liberty appeared especially specious after the First World War. In addition, the appeal of the northern race idea was limited in the post-war period because its main usefulness had been to underline the differences between Canada and the United States. In the 1920s the focus of nationalist thought shifted, and one of its dominant preoccupations came to be the definition of Canadian character in terms of North American experience, to emphasize the similarities between Canada and the United States.

Intellectual styles change but the permanent facts they seek to interpret and render meaningful do not. As long as there exists a nationalist impulse in Canada the imagination of men will be challenged by the very existence of the fascinating north. Though racism and crude environmentalism have now largely been discredited, the effort to explain Canadian uniqueness in terms of the north has not. As late as 1948, Vincent Massey found several differences between the United States and Canada, such as "the air of moderation in Canadian habits" to be derived from climate and race:

> Climate plays a great part in giving us our special character, different from that of our southern neighbours. Quite apart from the huge annual bill our winter imposes on us in terms of building construction and clothing and fuel, it influences our mentality, produces a sober temperament. Our racial composition — and this is partly because of our climate — is different, too. A small percentage of our people comes from central or southern Europe. The vast majority springs either from the British Isles or Northern France, a good many, too, from Scandinavia and Germany, and it is in northwestern Europe that one finds the elements of human stability highly developed. Nothing is more characteristic of Canadians than the inclination to be moderate.[34]

Apart from the muted tone, these observations do not really differ in substance from the remarks made in ringing rhetoric and with scientific certainty in the late nineteenth century by George Parkin, who was, incidentally, Massey's father-in-law.

Very different, however, and of high political potency, was the emotional appeal to the Canadian northern mission evoked by John Diefenbaker in the election of 1958. Seizing upon a theme which his native northwest had inspired in poets and nationalists since Confederation, he declared, suitably enough at Winnipeg, that "I see a new Canada" — not orientated east and west, but looking northward, responding to the challenges of that hinterland, its energies focused on the exploration and exploitation of the Arctic — "A CANADA OF THE NORTH!" To this compelling theme, which runs so persistently through Canadian nationalist thought since the days of D'Arcy McGee, Canadians responded eagerly and with conviction.[35]

CARL BERGER

On a more sober and scholarly plane, but not less pungent and appealing, is another recent exposition of the northern theme articulated by a president of the Canadian Historical Association, W.L. Morton, also a native of the north-west. In an address delivered in 1960, Professor Morton fixed upon Canada's "northern character," her origins in the expansion of a northern, maritime frontier, and her possession of a distinctive, staple economy, as factors which explained a substantial aspect of her development, her historical dependence upon Britain and the United States, the character of her literature, even the seasonal rhythm of Canadian life.[36]

The concept of Canada as a northern nation, like the idea that the unique character of the United States was shaped by the westward movement, is as important for understanding the intellectual content and emotional appeal of nationalism as it is for explaining the objective determinants of historical development. From the time of Benjamin Franklin, Americans saw 'the west' not so much as a geographical fact but as a symbol, around which they grouped the leading tenets of their nationalist faith — that its movement westward was carrying the American further and further away from effete Europe, that 'the garden' would become the home of an independent yeomanry in which alone reposed true Republican virtue, that the frontier was a safety valve which kept social conditions in the new world from ever approximating those in decadent, classridden Europe. Like the American symbol of the west, the Canadian symbol of the north subsumed a whole series of beliefs about the exalted past, the national character and the certain future. Unlike the American frontier of free land, however, the north itself was inexhaustible: as A.R.M. Lower has recently reminded us, it is a perpetual breath of fresh air.

If Canadian nationalism is to be understood, its meaning must be sought and apprehended not simply in the sphere of political decisions, but also in myths, legends and symbols like these. For while some might think that Canadians have happily been immune to the wilder manifestations of the nationalist impulse and rhetoric, it seems that they too have had their utopian dreamers, and that they are not totally innocent of a tradition of racism and a falsified but glorious past, tendencies which have always been the invariable by-products of nationalism. For by its very nature, nationalism must seize upon objective dissimilarities and tendencies and invest them in the language of religion, mission and destiny.

Notes

1. William Pitmann Lett, *Annexation and British Connection, Address to Brother Jonathan,* Ottawa, 1889, p. 10.

2. Walter R. Nursey, *The Story of Isaac Brock,* Toronto, 1909, p. 173.

3. Joseph Pope, *The Tour of Their Royal Highnesses the Duke and Duchess of Cornwall and York through the Dominion of Canada in the Year 1901,* Ottawa, 1903, p. 259; Hon. George W. Ross, *The Historical Significance of the Plains of Abraham, Address Delivered Before the Canadian Club of Hamilton, April 27th, 1908* (n.p., n.d.) p. 18; *The Canadian Military Gazette* XV (January 2, 1900) p. 15; Silas Alward, *An Anglo-American Alliance,* St. John, N.B., 1911.

4. G.D. Griffin, *Canada Past, Present, Future, and New System of Government* (n.p.) 1884, p. ii.

5. George Parkin, address to the Canadian Club and Board of Trade in St. John, N.B., reported in *The Daily Telegraph,* St. John, N.B., 6 March 1907. Clipping in *Parkin Papers,* vol. 82 (Public Archives of Canada, hereinafter P.A.C.).

6. William Leggo, *History of the Administration of the Earl of Dufferin in Canada,* Toronto, 1878, p. 599.

7. *Weekly Globe,* 2 April 1869.

8. For a fascinating sketch of these myths see J.W. Johnson, "'Of Differing Ages and Climes,'" *Journal of the History of Ideas* XXI (Oct. - Dec., 1960) pp. 465-480.

9. R.G. Haliburton, *The Men of the North and their place in history. A lecture delivered before the Montreal Literary Club, March 31st, 1869,* Montreal, 1869, pp. 2, 8, 16.

10. Clipping from *The Globe,* 8 December 1904 in *Denison Scrapbook 1897-1915,* p. 167, *Denison Papers* (P.A.C.)

11. Charles Mair, "The New Canada: Its natural features and climate," *Canadian Monthly Magazine* VIII (July, 1875) p. 5.

12. *Canada First: A Memorial of the late William A. Foster,* Toronto 1890, p. 25.

13. Charles R. Tuttle, *Popular History of the Dominion of Canada,* 2 vols., Boston, 1877 and 1879, vol. 1, p. 28.

14. G. R. Parkin, *The Great Dominion, Studies of Canada,* London, 1895, pp. 25, 211-215; "The Railway Development of Canada", *The Scottish Geographical Magazine* (May, 1909) p. 249, reprint in *Parkin Papers,* vol. 66 (P.A.C.), address to Canadian Club and Board of Trade in St. John, New Brunswick, reported in *The Daily*

Telegraph, 6 March 1907. Clipping in *Parkin Papers,* vol. 82 (P.A.C.)

15. Edward Harris, *Canada, The Making of a Nation,* (n.p., ca. 1907) p. 7.

16. G.R. Parkin, *The Great Dominion,* p. 216.

17. W.H. Withrow, "Notes of a Visit to the Centennial Exhibition," *Canadian Methodist Magazine* IV (December, 1876) p. 530.

18. Rev. F.A. Wightman, *Our Canadian Heritage, Its Resources and Possibilities,* Toronto, 1905, p. 46.

19. W. H. Hingston, *The Climate of Canada and its Relation to Life and Health,* Montreal, 1884, pp. xviii, 94, 126-27, 260, 263, 265-66.

20. Wightman, *Our Canadian Heritage,* pp. 280, 44-45; J. Sheridan Hogan, *Canada, An Essay: to which was awarded the first prize by the Paris Exhibition Committee of Canada,* Montreal, 1855, pp. 53-54.

21. F. B. Cumberland, "Introduction", *Maple Leaves: being the papers read before the National Club of Toronto at the "National Evenings," during the Winter 1890-1891,* Toronto, 1891, pp. vii-viii.

22. Wightman, as cited, p. 221.

23. Benjamin Suite, *Origin of the French Canadian. Read before the British Association, Toronto, August, 1897,* Ottawa, 1897, p. 14. See also his essay of 1897, "Défense de nos Origines" in *Mélanges Historiques,* compiled by Gérard Malchelosse, vol. 17, Montreal, 1930.

24. *The Storied Province of Quebec, Past and Present,* W. Wood, (ed.), vol. 1, Toronto, 1931, p. 3.

25. G.M. Wrong, *The Two Races in Canada, a Lecture delivered before the Canadian Historical Association, Montreal, May 21st, 1925,* Montreal, 1925, pp. 4-5.

26. Abbé Arthur Maheux, *Canadian Unity: What Keeps Us Apart,* Quebec, 1944, pp. 22, 23, 25.

27. *Canada's Future! Political Union With the U.S. Desirable,* 1891, pp. 2-3.

28. Principal R. A. Falconer, "The Unification of Canada," *University Magazine* VII (February, 1908) pp. 4-5.

29. George Parkin, "Canada and the United States on the American Continent," reported in Yarmouth Herald, March 3, 1908. Clipping in *Parkin Papers,* vol 84, (P.A.C.); *The Great Dominion,* p. 214.

30. Cited in Charles and Mary Beard, *The American Spirit, A Study of the Civilization in the United States,* New York, 1962, p. 173.

31. *Canadian Methodist Magazine,* LXVIII (December, 1908) pp. 566-567.

32. Silas Alward, as cited, pp. 8-10.

33. See especially, J. G. Bourinot, *Canadian Studies in Comparative Politics*, Montreal, 1890.
34. *The Empire*, January 24, 1891.
35. *The Week*, January 1, 1885.
36. G. Parkin, in *Yarmouth Herald*, March 3, 1908.

CARL BERGER

ROBERT SERVICE

THE CREMATION OF SAM MCGEE

There are strange things done in the midnight sun
*   By the men who moil for gold;*
The Arctic trails have their secret tales
*   That would make your blood run cold;*
The Northern Lights have seen queer sights,
*   But the queerest they ever did see*
Was that night on the marge of Lake Lebarge
*   I cremated Sam McGee.*

Now Sam McGee was from Tennessee, where the cotton blooms
    and blows.
Why he left his home in the South to roam 'round the Pole, God
    only knows.
He was always cold, but the land of gold seemed to hold him like
    a spell;
Though he'd often say in his homely way that 'he'd sooner live in
    hell.'

On a Christmas Day we were mushing our way over the Dawson
    trail.
Talk of your cold! through the parka's fold it stabbed like a driven
    nail.
If our eyes we'd close, then the lashes froze till sometimes we
    couldn't see;
It wasn't much fun, but the only one to whimper was Sam
    McGee.

And that very night, as we lay packed tight in our robes beneath
    the snow,
And the dogs were fed, and the stars o'erhead were dancing heel
    and toe,
He turned to me, and 'Cap', says he, 'I'll cash in this trip, I guess;
And if I do, I'm asking that you won't refuse my last request.'

Well, he seemed so low that I couldn't say no; then he says with a
    sort of moan:
'It's the cursed cold, and it's got right hold till I'm chilled clean
    through to the bone.
Yet 'tain't being dead — it's my awful dread of the icy grave that
    pains;
So I want you to swear that, foul or fair, you'll cremate my last
    remains.'

A pal's last need is a thing to heed, so I swore I would not fail;
And we started on at the streak of dawn; but God! he looked
    ghastly pale.
He crouched on the sleigh, and he raved all day of his home in
    Tennessee;
And before nightfall a corpse was all that was left of Sam McGee.

There wasn't a breath in that land of death, and I hurried,
    horror-driven,
With a corpse half hid that I couldn't get rid, because of a promise
    given;
It was lashed to the sleigh, and it seemed to say: 'You may tax
    your brawn and brains,
But you promised true, and it's up to you to cremate those last
    remains.'

Now a promise made is a debt unpaid, and the trail has its own
    stern code.
In the days to come, though my lips were dumb, in my heart how
    I cursed that load.
In the long, long night, by the lone firelight, while the huskies,
    round in a ring,
Howled out their woes to the homeless snows — O God! how I
    loathed the thing.

And every day that quiet clay seemed to heavy and heavier grow;
And on I went, though the dogs were spent and the grub was
    getting low;
The trail was bad, and I felt half mad, but I swore I would not
    give in;
And I'd often sing to the hateful thing, and it hearkened with a
    grin.

Till I came to the marge of Lake Lebarge, and a derelict there lay;
It was jammed in the ice, but I saw in a trice it was called the
    'Alice May'.
And I looked at it, and I thought a bit, and I looked at my frozen
    chum;
Then 'Here', said I, with a sudden cry, 'is my cre-ma-tor-eum.'

Some planks I tore from the cabin floor, and I lit the boiler fire;
Some coal I found that was lying around, and I heaped the fuel
    higher;
The flames just soared, and the furnace roared — such a blaze you
    seldom see;
And I burrowed a hole in the glowing coal, and I stuffed in Sam
    McGee.

Then I made a hike, for I didn't like to hear him sizzle so;
And the heavens scowled, and the huskies howled, and the wind
    began to blow.
It was icy cold, but the hot sweat rolled down my cheeks, and I
    don't know why;
And the greasy smoke in an inky cloak went streaking down the
    sky.

I do not know how long in the snow I wrestled with grisly fear;
But the stars came out and they danced about ere again I ventured
    near;
I was sick with dread, but I bravely said: 'I'll just take a peep
    inside.
I guess he's cooked, and it's time I looked';...then the door I
    opened wide.

And there sat Sam, looking cool and calm, in the heart of the
     furnace roar;
And he wore a smile you could see a mile, and he said: 'Please
     close that door.
It's fine in here, but I greatly fear you'll let in the cold and
     storm—
Since I left Plumtree, down in Tennessee, it's the first time I've
     been warm.'

There are strange things done in the midnight sun
     By the men who moil for gold;
The Arctic trails have their secret tales
     That would make your blood run cold;
The Northern Lights have seen queer sights,
     But the queerest they ever did see
Was that night on the marge of Lake Lebarge
     I cremated Sam McGee.

Ann Davis

The Logic of Ecstasy:
Canadian Mystical Painting
1920-1940

III

Lawren Harris was probably as imbued with Whitman as was Carr. In 1925, in notes for a play, Bertram Brooker developed a character, Manchee, based on Lawren Harris. There is no reason to believe Brooker was not documenting Harris as he saw him. On 26 August 1925 Brooker wrote:

> Manchee: Something like Harris...Under forty, supremely confident of his art and...rather self-centred, rather wanting to be courtiered, especially in his own studio...
>
> As a Canadian almost ferociously patriotic, with a great feeling for the country, which has been greatly bolstered by Whitman, hesitating to go to Europe or even New York for fear of being seduced from his utterly native viewpoint. Everything new is going to happen in this country.
>
> As a mystic he also believes that things are going to happen in this country, indeed are happening. He feels himself in the vanguard of the movement and is looking for every sign. Unless people show some sign of it he is impatient with [them]. He hates Europe and is impatient with slavish admiration of anything that comes from there. He quotes Whitman a great deal.[1]

This sketch is interesting for several reasons. The two references to Whitman, the only authority noted, are surely telling. Brooker also, without dissimulating, called Harris a mystic. The overriding theme, however, is Harris's 'ferocious' patriotism. How these three, potentially conflicting, characteristics are blended into one person is the subject to hand now.

The earliest reference Harris made to Whitman is found in his 1910-14 notebook. Here, among other recorded quotations (including numerous by the Irish mystic A.E. [George Russell]). Harris noted Whitman's admonition:

I say no man has ever yet been half devote enough,
None has ever yet adored or worship'd half enough.[2]

Coming as he did from a religious family, Harris seemed to take this statement to heart and, for the rest of his life, devoted a great deal of energy and discipline to his adoration and worship. If Harris's method was henceforth a devotional one, it was also one predicated on exploration and change. As Whitman expressed so convincingly in 'Song of the Open Road,' the challenge was the 'profound lesson of reception.' The individual must be ready and able to receive the joy and the sorrow, the beautiful and the ugly. In the 1920s Harris discussed his methods in his notebook:

We live only when we adventure and give expression to the results of our adventure. We should understand then and never forget that we permit all rules, conventions, institutions and prohibitions to become stable only that we may thereby have a base from which to venture further, a working place wherein we can give form to our findings and a haven where we can rest and recuperate from past strain and effort and acquire energy for further adventure. And we should recognize and never forget that with every least increase of vision the known means are going to be modified, changed, enlarged, the rules the learned make strained, broken or forgotten and to the exact extent of the increase of vision. And we should recognize and never forget that all pioneering is the advance guard of our adventure into the unknown where greater and greater amplitude of life awaits us. And we should further know that any pioneer in any pursuit is going to discover something new, untoward, strange and perhaps unpleasant to our grooved ways of life, and to the exact extent in which he does so is he of value to us.[3]

Given this transcendental attitude, Harris determined to adventure into the unknown, fully aware that his discoveries might prove strange and even frightening.

From the North Shore, Lake Superior exposes the duality characteristic of transcendentalism. Whitman believed that nature is formed and informed by the spirit, that every tree or mountain is a symbol of a greater spiritual reality, that God not only created nature but is *in* nature as well. Transcendentalists saw the physical world as both fact and symbol. Harris did too. In his notebook of the 1920s, he explained that 'visible nature is but a distorted reflection of a more perfect world and the creative individual viewing her is inspired to perceive within and behind her many garments that which is timeless and entirely beautiful.'[4] In *From the North Shore, Lake Superior* Harris worked both fact and symbol. The title refers to a specific spot. The headland and island are carefully delineated. The texture of the water is precisely rendered, suggesting specific weather conditions. Concrete facts abound. Yet the ideal is also clearly present. The viewer is placed above and well away from the foreground hills, so that distance is created between viewer and scene, access is difficult, and penetration impossible. Unnatural clouds and unexpected light make the section more exalted, more beautiful. Perhaps, as Roger Mesley suggests, these cloud-like forms are flower petals unfolding beneath a mystical light.[5] This light, as Emerson would have it, causes the universe to become 'transparent, and the light of higher laws than its own'[6] to shine through it. For Emerson the soul of man 'is not an organ...not a faculty, but light...From within or from behind, a light shines through us upon things and makes us aware that we are nothing, but the light is all.'[7] If the view below the horizon seems based on concrete fact, that above the horizon line seems composed of mystic organisms. Nature here is not a setting for human activity or habitation, but a primeval place, uncontaminated by history or civilization. It is vast, solitary, alive, and timeless.

An important factor in this painting is a person's place within such a system. Harris believed that individuality, personality, was detrimental. Rather what he sought was the individual union with the greater self, with that which is also timeless and beautiful. The personal is to be transcended. Harris wrote that 'each of us here as a personality is but a reflection of a greater self that abides eternally in a greater world and ever seeks to inform us here of that perfect world.'[8] Through meditation and thought Harris believed that the individual could venture on the avenue of 'the high impersonal great soul of man.' Subsequently, great art might result. Harris summarized his beliefs about an individual's position, abilities, methods, and artistic potential: 'All great art is impersonal[,] achieved by a sublimation of the personal in ecstasy.'[9] The easiest place to see that greater, perfect world is in nature. Many of these aspirations were, in Harris's case, simply that: while he penned universal and democratic ideals, he practised individual and patrician art.

Whitman was similarly inclined. His sublimation of individuality is less apparent, however, because of his democratic style, which was partly adumbrated by writing in the first person. For Whitman the poet should not be an alienated genius but a democratic writer having a deep affinity with the spirit and literary tastes of the common people. In the 1855 preface to *Leaves of Grass* he stressed that the American poet fails 'if he be not himself the age transfigured.' Furthermore, in describing his own reform principles, in writing seemingly contradictory poems against and for free love, or prostitutes, or evil, or corrupt people and things, Whitman admitted prizing unsullied reform principles, not particular reform policies. The leaders of reform interested him not for their individual politics but rather for their fiery passion. 'We want,' he wrote in 1863, 'no *reforms*, no *institutions*, no *parties* — We want a living principle as nature has, under which nothing can go wrong.'[10] Yet at the same time that Whitman was promoting the common and the average, he was promulgating the great and heroic, of whom he was a prime example.

Characteristics were ascribed not only to man but also to nature. The prime characteristic Harris identified in nature — vast, solitary, alive, and timeless — is one that Whitman explored in *Leaves of Grass*. Here Whitman linked divinity and roughness, a concept vital for a real understanding of Canadian landscape painting in the 1920s.

> The earth never tires;
> The earth is made silent, incomprehensible at first —
> Nature is rude and incomprehensible at first;
> Be not discouraged — keep on — there are divine things,
> well envelop'd;
> I swear to you there are divine things more beautiful
> than words can tell.[11]

ANN DAVIS

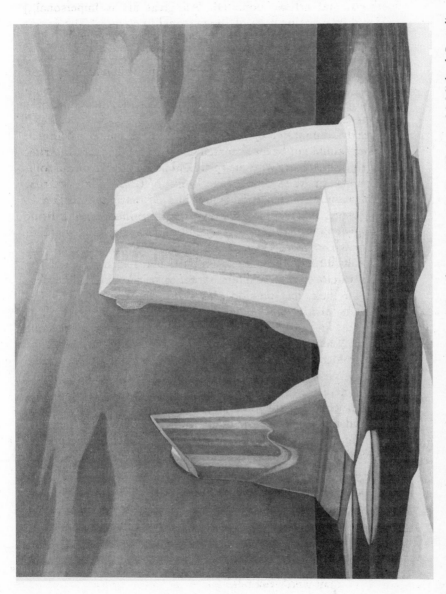

LAWREN S. HARRIS, 1885-1970, *Icebergs, Davis Straits*, 1930, oil on canvas, 121.9 x 152.4 cm. McMichael Canadian Art Collection. Gift of Mr. and Mrs. H. Spencer Clark 1971.17

This concept of nature being both rude and incomprehensible on the one hand and divine on the other is the same concept Emily Carr struggled with when she tried to apprehend her mountain.

Whitman went further. He understood that nature, the elemental force, can be a serious threat to man's self-confidence. In his poetry, therefore, he attempted to arrange an accommodation, a reconciliation of man and nature through the medium of spirit. In 'Passage to India' Whitman specifically describes the poet's primary task as giving a humanly intelligible voice to 'this cool, impassive, voiceless earth.' The poet's responsibility is to reintegrate the natural and human orders, so the 'Nature and Man shall be disjoin'd and diffused no more.'[12] In this light it is obvious that Whitman's optimism was a brave front to the realities of an uncompromising American continent. In raising this problem of the human relationship with environment, Whitman was touching on social concerns, on the structural features of the new capitalist economy. He, however, never inquired too closely into the underlying economic assumptions of his society, preferring to accept a fundamental distinction between society and government and to identify the villain as government. In short, he found government, and the primary political circumstances that promoted it, to be the reason for what was unsatisfactory about American life.[13]

Harris had to wrestle with similar concerns, for he too knew that nature could be vast and inimical to people. Like Whitman, he decided to attack institutions rather than the society that engendered those institutions, or nature herself. Like Whitman,[14] again Harris coped with the physical world by gradually dismissing its outward aspect and then readmitting it on different terms. Harris explained in the 1928-9 *Yearbook of the Arts in Canada*:

So the Canadian artist was drawn north, and there at first devoted himself to Nature's outward aspect...at first more or less literally copying a great variety of her motives...Then followed a period of decorative treatment of her great wealth of material...Then followed an intensification of mood that simplified into deeper meaning and was more rigorously selective and sought to have no element in the work which did not contribute to a unified intense expression. The next step was a utilization of elements of the North in depth, in three dimen-

ANN DAVIS

sions, giving a fuller meaning, a more real sense of the presence of the informing spirit...

Today the artist moves towards purer creative expression, wherein he changes the outward aspect of Nature, alters colours, and, by changing and reshaping forms, intensifies the austerity and beauty of formal relationships, and so creates a somewhat new world from the aspect of the world we commonly see; and thus he comes appreciably nearer a pure work of art and the expression of new spiritual values. The evolution from the love of the outward aspect of Nature and a more or less realistic rendering of her to the sense of the indwelling spirit and a more austere spiritual expression has been a steady, slow and natural growth through much work, much inner eliciting experience.[15]

However, the problem does not end here. If Harris could find a way to remake nature in spiritual terms to satisfy his optimistic prognostications — even if in his remake few read optimism — he still had to find a way to cope with the linking of art and nature. Along with Carr and many other painters of his generation, Harris had to deal with the problem of the dialectic between art and nature, especially a nature that seemed rough and rude. In Europe, Kandinsky, Picasso, and Klee all had to confront the problem; in the United States, Dove, O'Keeffe, and Hartley were equally concerned. Three solutions appeared: obviate the tension between art and nature, as the Symbolists did, by making them separate and autonomous; emphasize the tension, as the Cubists did, by visual puns and spatial ambiguities; or reconcile the tension, as did the five Canadians examined here, by perceiving art and nature as based on the same laws.

We have already seen how Emily Carr propounded this aesthetic belief, one that derives directly from German romantic philosophy and American transcendentalism. Harris was similarly moved. Agreeing with Housser and Whitman, he felt that the artist, seeing more clearly than other people, has a special duty. In his 1926 article 'Revelation of Art in Canada,' Harris forcefully commented that 'any change of outlook, increase of vision and deepening of conviction in a people shows itself first through some form of art, art being both a clarifying and objectifying process.'[16] In the 1928-9 *Yearbook of the Arts in Canada*, edited by Bertram Brooker, Harris denounced the theory that art is based on art. Rather, Harris wrote, in his famous statement: 'The source of our art then is not in the achievements of other artists in other days and lands, although it has learned a great deal from these. Our art is founded on a long and growing love and understanding of the North in an ever clearer experience of oneness with the informing spirit of the whole land and a strange brooding sense of Mother Nature fostering a new race and a new age.'[17]

Harris reverted to this idea of art and nature being based on the same laws on many occasions. Lauding Whitman's 'prophetic insight,' his ability to integrate (reminiscent of Bucke's praise for Whitman's integration and balance), Harris explained that 'in the golden age of a people as in ancient Egypt, in Greece and in a few of the Italian cities of the renaissance we get moments of harmony when life and the arts fuse and flourish in terms of unity of the soul.'[18] Concluding the same paper, Harris wrote: 'All great art is in one sense a rebirth, a recreation, an extrication by intensity, by penetration of vision, of intrinsic and timeless beauty from the infinitely changing appearances of nature and the processes of time in humanity.'[19]

For Harris in the mid-1920s, art based on the same laws as nature must respond to and be directed by what was characteristic of local nature, the North. Time and again Harris referred to Canada simply as the North, often employing a capital letter. He saw the North as having specific mystical and pictorial characteristics:

The Canadian artist serves the spirit of his land and people. He is aware of the spiritual flow from the replenishing North and believes that this should ever shed clarity into the growing race of America and that this, working in creative individuals, will give rise to an art quite different from that of any European people. He believes in the power and the glory, for the North to him is a single, simple vision of high things and can, through its transmuting agency, shape our souls into its own spiritual expressiveness. He believes that this will create a new sense and use of design, a new feeling for space and light and formal relationships.[20]

In developing these thoughts Harris was following a well-worn transcendental path, one that Emerson had been instrumental in adumbrating. Emerson, a creature of his time, viewed the arts pri-

ANN DAVIS

marily from a literary point of view, as the artist's expression of his moral insight, rather than from any concern with intrinsic, formal qualities. Emerson saw art's 'highest value' '*as history*,' and believed that art was simply a different mode of expressing historical, poetical, or philosophical ideas.[21] Moreover, Emerson believed that the fine arts sprang from indigenous sources. 'We have listened too long to the courtly muses of Europe,' he proclaimed in 1836. American culture must be domesticated. An art that embodied and conveyed the essential ideas of American nationality was an art eminently worthy of encouragement.[22] Harris, for whom Emerson was a constant companion while in Germany, followed these precepts at this stage.

Harris, and his friends in the Group of Seven, found further sources of support for their nationalistic painting. One was an exhibition of contemporary Scandinavian art, hung in the Albright Art Gallery in Buffalo in January 1913. Harris, along with J.E.H. MacDonald, saw this show and bought the catalogue. Many of their attitudes towards the exhibition seem to have come directly from the introductory catalogue essay, written by the Swedish-American art critic Christian Brinton. Brinton proposed a nationalistic interpretation of modern Scandinavian art, and tied this nationalism of the ordinary people firmly to the land. In 1931 MacDonald lectured on Scandinavian art and revealed Brinton's philosophic influence. But the influences went further. Since the natural aspects of Scandinavia and Canada are parallel in numerous respects, MacDonald suggested that 'except in minor points, the pictures might all have been Canadian.' Harris and MacDonald felt that 'this is what we want to do with Canada.'[23] Both philosophically and iconographically the Scandinavian show encouraged Harris to pursue nationalistic, land-based painting.

At the same time Harris and his friends found considerable support for their romantic northern nationalism closer to home. Right in Canada there was an important contemporary movement promoting the idea that Canada's unique character derived from her northern location, her severe winters, and her population of 'northern races.' For Tennyson Canada was the 'True North,' for Kipling the 'Lady of the Snows.' Ideas about the importance of geography, climate, and the character of 'races,' debated for centuries, surfaced in Canada soon after Confederation and were promoted by associates of the Canada First Movement and the Imperialists. An early proponent of these ideas, Robert Grant Haliburton, claimed

Canada's future as a dominant nation was secure because of its northern character. He proclaimed the northern race idea in a lecture of 1869 entitled 'We are the Northmen of the New World,' suggesting dominance of this race because of the attraction of Canada to hardy northern European immigrants, and because of the creative force of a northern climate. Nor, as Carl Berger has demonstrated, did these ideas dissipate.[24] Propelled as he was by transcendental nationalism, Scandinavian romanticism, and contemporary Canadian geographic determinism, it is little wonder that Harris should trumpet Canadian northern nationalism so loudly.

These nationalistic and idealistic concerns found pictorial expression in Harris's Lake Superior canvases, his Rocky Mountain works, and his Arctic landscapes. Seasonally and geographically they bespoke a northern country, where ice and snow, mountains, and icebergs were the norm. Katherine Dreier, Lawren Harris's American theosophical friend, explained that 'the greatest impression that was made on me when we saw something of each other [in the late 1920s], was your love and interest of the North. Your consciousness of the psychic vibrations which one finds there.'[25]

In *Icebergs, Davis Strait*, and in other similar works depicting Arctic scenes, Harris perhaps found his ultimate northern subject-matter. Using the format he had developed to such effect in his Lake Superior canvases, Harris delineates a narrow foreground, then places his main theme in a middle ground so demarcated that the viewer is both cut off from the subject and uncertain as to its precise location in space. Yet, recalling Whitman's 'Song of the Open Road,' the viewer is invited on a journey, one that will encompass barrenness, coldness, ice, nakedness, and pain as well as light and discovery. These spatial considerations notwithstanding, the work is still clearly focused in nature. (This canvas also certainly suggests further cosmic interpretation, but that is not the subject to hand.[26]) A few months before the trip to the Arctic that provided the material for *Icebergs, Davis Strait*, Harris, returning from Europe, wrote to Emily Carr about the centrality of nature: 'But I have an idea — confirmed by what I felt in Europe — that we here, in our own place, on new land, where a new race is forming[,] will find for the present and perhaps for some time to come, that the fullest life in art for us comes by way of nature, sharing and imbibing her life; her deep, deep intimations — and establishing ourselves by getting that into our art.'[27]

ANN DAVIS

Isolation Peak also exudes that very sense of northern power and climate, that tremendous faith based in nature. Here, more than in *Icebergs, Davis Strait*, are joined the real and the ideal mentioned above. Isolation Peak is a real mountain in the Canadian Rockies that Harris sketched. In his final canvas, however, the roughness and crudeness that he mentions as the properties of a forming country have been smoothed into compelling rhythms. He moulds and manipulates his volumes, building up his striated hills to climax in the forbidding mountain. Now the whole work is redolent of the ideal. The forms and colours of nature are only used as a point of departure in the ascent to a level of higher awareness.

The move from the particular to the general finds echo in the move from the real to the ideal. Time and again Harris understood the necessity of growth, of change. Always he recognized the importance of nature. Harris wrote about his move to the universal from the particular of the North:

> The artist moves slowly but surely through many transitions towards a deeper and more universal expression. From his particular love, and in the process of creating from it, he is led inevitably to universal qualities and toward a universal vision and understanding. These are the fruits of a natural growth having its roots deep in the soil of the land, its life in the pervading and replenishing spirit of the North, and its heart-beat one with the life of its people.[28]

Notes

1. Brooker Papers, diary, 26 Aug. 1925.
2. National Archives of Canada, Harris Papers, MG30, D208, vol. 2, notebook, n.d. cNatasha. 1910-14.
3. Harris Papers, notebook, n.d. [1920s], n.p.
4. Ibid.
5. Roger J. Mesley, "Lawren Harris' Mysticism: A Critical View," *Art Magazine* vol. 10, no. 41 (November/December 1978), p. 15.
6. Ralph Waldo Emerson, "Nature," in *The Selected Writings of Ralph Waldo Emerson,* ed. Brooks Atkinson (New York: Random House, Modern Library, 1950), p. 19.
7. "The Over-Soul," in *Selected Writings,* p. 263.
8. Harris Papers, notebook, n.d. [1920s], n.p.
9. Ibid.

10. Quoted in Reynolds, *Beneath the American Experience*, p. 111; from *Walt Whitman's Workshop: A Collection of Unpublished Prose Manuscripts,* ed. C.J. Furness (New York: Russell & Russell, 1964), p. 62.

11. *Leaves of Grass* (New York: Grosset and Dunlap, 1971), p. 111.

12. Scully Bradley et al., eds, *Leaves of Grass: A Textual Variorum,* 3 vols. (New York: New York University Press, 1980), vol. 3, p. 568.

13. M. Wynn Thomas, *The Lunar Light of Whitman's Poetry* (Cambridge, Mass.: Harvard University Press, 1987), pp. 23-7.

14. Ibid., p. 37.

15. "Creative Art and Canada", in *The Yearbook of the Arts in Canada,* ed. Bertram Brooker (Toronto: Macmillan, 1929), p. 185.

16. "Revelation of Art in Canada," *Canadian Theosophist* vol. 7, no. 5., (1926), p. 85.

17. "Creative Art and Canada", p. 185.

18. Harris Papers, vol. 5, "The Creative Individual and a New Order," n.d., p. 5.

19. Ibid., 12-13; see also vol. 6, "Science and Art," p. 9.

20. "Creative Art and Canada", p. 184.

21. Lilian B. Miller, *Patrons and Patriotism: The Encouragement of the Fine Arts in the United States 1790-1860* (Chicago and London: University of Chicago Press, 1961), p. 25.

22. Ibid., pp. 25-6.

23. Art Gallery of Ontario, J.E.H. MacDonald Papers, lecture delivered 17 April 1931; see also Ann Davis, "An Apprehended Vision: The Philosophy of the Group of Seven" (unpublished PhD Thesis, York University, 1973), pp. 230-2; and Roald Naasgard, *The Mystic North: Symbolist Landscape Painting in Northern Europe and North America 1890-1940* (Toronto: University of Toronto Press, exhibition catalogue, 1984), pp. 158-61.

24. "The True North Strong and Free."

25. Yale University, Société Anonyme Papers, Katherine Dreier to Lawren Harris, 25 July 1949.

26. For a good analysis of how Ouspensky's concept of dualities influenced this work see Mesley, "Lawren Harris' Mysticism," p. 16.

27. National Archives of Canada, Carr Papers, Harris to Carr, June [1930].

28. Bess Harris and R.G.P. Colgrove, *Lawren Harris* (Toronto: Macmillan, 1969), p. 39. After Harris returned to Canada in 1940, he became more political, like Whitman. Like Whitman, and Brooker after him, Harris professed great interest in the common

man. Like all transcendentalists, Harris railed against material power in favour of things of the spirit. In "Democracy and the Arts" (an undated typescript, presumably a speech, National Archives of Canada, Harris Papers, vol. 5, 9) Harris wrote: 'And we are becoming convinced that the only standard we can apply if we are to serve not only the highest ends but the mere preservation of our society, as a thing of the spirit...

'I think we all see that the present vast struggle is one between those forces which would control the world for the sake of material power — and this always means tyranny in some form — and those forces which would release the great resources of the world, both material and cultural, for the benefit of all people, those forces which are guided by the principles of the spirit.

'We are all aware that the things of the spirit are a sense of over-all justice, veracity, rightness and appropriateness, and the primary, the basic feeling and concern for the welfare of all our fellows.'

FREDERICK PHILIP GROVE

SNOW

Towards the morning the blizzard had died down, though it was still far from daylight. Stars without number blazed in the dark blue sky which presented that brilliant and uncompromising appearance always characterizing, on the northern plains of America, those nights in the dead of winter when the thermometer dips to its lowest levels.

In the west Orion was sinking to the horizon. It was between five and six o'clock.

In the bush-fringe of the Big Marsh, sheltered by thick but bare bluffs of aspens, stood a large house, built of logs, whitewashed, solid — such as a settler who is still single would put up only when he thinks of getting married. It, too, looked ice-cold, frozen in the night. Not a breath stirred where it stood; a thin thread of whitish smoke, reaching up to the level of the tree-tops, seemed to be suspended into the chimney rather than to issue from it.

Through the deep snow of the yard, newly packed, a man was fighting his way to the door. Arrived there, he knocked and knocked, first tapping with his knuckles, then hammering with his fists.

Two, three minutes passed. Then a sound awoke in the house, as of somebody stirring, getting out of bed.

The figure on the door-slab — a medium-sized, slim man in sheepskin and high rubber boots into which his trousers were tucked, with the ear-flaps of his cap pulled down — stood and waited, bent over, hands thrust into the pockets of the short coat, as if he wished to shrink into the smallest possible space so as to offer the smallest possible surface to the attack of the cold. In order to get rid of the dry, powdery snow which filled every crease of his foot-gear and trousers, he stamped his feet. His chin was drawn deep into the turned-up collar on whose points his breath had settled in the form of a thick layer of hoarfrost.

At last a bolt was withdrawn inside.

The face of a man peered out, just discernible in the starlight.

Then the door was opened; in the ominous silence the figure from the outside entered, still stamping its feet.

Not a word was spoken till the door had been closed. Then a voice sounded through the cold and dreary darkness of the room.

'Redcliff hasn't come home. He went to town about noon and expected to get back by midnight. We're afraid he's lost.'

The other man, quite invisible in the dark, had listened, his teeth chattering with the cold. 'Are you sure he started out from town?'

'Well,' the new-comer answered hesitatingly, 'one of the horses came to the yard.'

'One of his horses?'

'Yes. One of those he drove. The woman worked her way to my place to get help.'

The owner of the house did not speak again. He went, in the dark, to the door in the rear and opened it. There, he groped about for matches and, finding them, lighted a lamp. In the room stood a big stove, a coal-stove of the self-feeder type; but the fuel used was wood. He opened the drafts and shook the grate clear of ashes; there were two big blocks of spruce in the fire-box, smouldering away for the night. In less than a minute they blazed up.

The new-comer entered, blinking in the light of the lamp, and looked on. Before many minutes the heat from the stove began to tell.

'I'll call Bill,' the owner of the house said. He was himself of medium height or only slightly above it, but of enormous breadth of shoulder: a figure built for lifting loads. By his side the other man looked small, weakly, dwarfed.

He left the room and, returning through the cold, bare hall in front, went upstairs.

A few minutes later a tall, slender, well-built youth bolted into the room where the new-comer was waiting. Bill, Carroll's hired man, was in his underwear and carried his clothes, thrown in a heap over his arm. Without loss of time, but jumping, stamping, swinging his arms, he began at once to dress.

He greeted the visitor. 'Hello, Mike! What's that Abe tells me? Redcliff got lost?'

'Seems that way,' said Mike listlessly.

'By gringo,' Bill went on, 'I shouldn't wonder. In that storm! I'd have waited in town! Wouldn't catch me going out in that kind of weather!'

FREDERICK PHILIP GROVE

'Didn't start till late in the afternoon,' Mike Sobotski said in his shivering way.

'No. And didn't last long either,' Bill agreed while he shouldered into his overalls. 'But while she lasted...'

At this moment Abe Carroll, the owner of the farm, re-entered, with sheepskin, fur cap, and long woollen scarf on his arm. His deeply lined, striking, square face bore a settled frown while he held the inside of his sheepskin to the stove, to warm it up. Then, without saying a word, he got deliberately into it.

Mike Sobotski still stood bent over, shivering, though he had opened his coat and, on his side of the stove, was catching all the heat it afforded.

Abe, with the least motion needed to complete dressing, made for the door. In passing Bill, he flung out an elbow which touched the young man's arm. 'Come on,' he said; and to the other, pointing to the stove, 'Close the drafts.'

A few minutes later a noise as of rearing and snorting horses in front of the house....

Mike, buttoning up his coat and pulling his mitts over his hands, went out.

They mounted three unsaddled horses. Abe leading, they dashed through the new drifts in the yard and out through the gate to the road. Here, where the shelter of the bluffs screening the house was no longer effective, a light but freshening breeze from the northwest made itself felt as if fine little knives were cutting into the flesh of their faces.

Abe dug his heels into the flank of his rearing mount. The horse was unwilling to obey his guidance, for Abe wanted to leave the road and to cut across wild land to the south-west.

The darkness was still inky black, though here and there, where the slope of the drifts slanted in the right direction, starlight was dimly reflected from the snow. The drifts were six, eight, in places ten feet high; and the snow was once more crawling up their flanks, it was so light and fine. It would fill the tracks in half an hour. As the horses plunged through, the crystals dusted up in clouds, flying aloft over horses and riders.

In less than half an hour they came to a group of two little buildings, of logs, that seemed to squat on their haunches in the snow. Having entered the yard through a gate, they passed one of the buildings and made for the other, a little stable; their horses snorting, they stopped in its lee.

Mike dismounted, throwing the halter-shank of his horse to Bill. He went to the house, which stood a hundred feet or so away. The shack was even smaller than the stable, twelve by fifteen feet perhaps. From its flue-pipe a thick, white plume of smoke blew to the south-east.

Mike returned with a lantern; the other two sprang to the ground; and they opened the door to examine the horse which the woman had allowed to enter.

The horse was there, still excited, snorting at the leaping light and shadows from the lantern, its eyes wild, its nostrils dilated. It was covered with white frost and fully harnessed, though its traces were tied up to the back-band.

'He let him go,' said Mike, taking in these signs. 'Must have stopped and unhitched him.'

'Must have been stuck in a drift,' Bill said, assenting.

'And tried to walk it,' Abe added.

For a minute or so they stood silent, each following his own gloomy thoughts. Weird, luminous little clouds issued fitfully from the nostrils of the horse inside.

'I'll get the cutter,' Abe said at last.

'I'll get it,' Bill volunteered. 'I'll take the drivers along. We'll leave the filly here in the stable.'

'All right.'

Bill remounted, leading Abe's horse. He disappeared into the night.

Abe and Mike, having tied the filly and the other horse in their stalls, went out, closed the door, and turned to the house.

There, by the light of a little coal-oil lamp, they saw the woman sitting at the stove, pale, shivering, her teeth achatter, trying to warm her hands, which were cold with fever, and looking with lack-lustre eyes at the men as they entered.

The children were sleeping; the oldest, a girl, on the floor, wrapped in a blanket and curled up like a dog; four others in one narrow bed, with hay for a mattress, two at the head, two at the foot; the baby on, rather than in, a sort of cradle made of a wide board slung by thin ropes to the pole-roof of the shack.

The other bed was empty and unmade. The air was stifling from a night of exhalations.

'We're going to hunt for him,' Mike said quietly. 'We've sent for a cutter. He must have tried to walk.'

The woman did not answer. She sat and shivered

'We'll take some blankets,' Mike went on. 'And some whisky if you've got any in the house.'

He and Abe were standing by the stove, opposite the woman, and warming their hands, their mitts held under their armpits.

The woman pointed with a look to a home-made little cupboard nailed to the wall and apathetically turned back to the stove. Mike went, opened the door of the cupboard, took a bottle from it, and slipped it into the pocket of his sheepskin. Then he raised the blankets from the empty bed, rolled them roughly into a bundle, dropped it, and returned to the stove where, with stiff fingers, he fell to rolling a cigarette.

Thus they stood for an hour or so.

Abe's eye was fastened on the woman. He would have liked to say a word of comfort, of hope. What was there to be said?

She was the daughter of a German settler in the bush, some six or seven miles north-east of Abe's place. Her father, an oldish, unctuous, bearded man, had, some ten years ago, got tired of the hard life in the bush where work meant clearing, picking stones, and digging stumps. He had sold his homestead and bought a prairie-farm, half a section, on crop-payments, giving notes for the equipment which he needed to handle the place. He had not been able to make it a 'go.' His bush farm had fallen back on his hands; he had lost his all and returned to the place. He had been counting on the help of his two boys — big, strapping young fellows — who were to clear much land and to raise crops which would lift the debt. But the boys had refused to go back to the bush; they could get easy work in town. Ready money would help. But the ready money had melted away in their hands. Redcliff, the old people's son-in-law, had been their last hope. They were on the point of losing even their bush farm. Here they might perhaps still have found a refuge for their old age — though Redcliff's homestead lay on the sandflats bordering on the marsh where the soil was thin, dreadfully thin; it drifted when the scrub-brush was cleared off. Still, with Redcliff living, this place had been a hope. What were they to do if he was gone? And this woman, hardly more than a girl, in spite of her six children!

The two tiny, square windows of the shack began to turn grey.

At last Abe, thinking he had heard a sound, went to the door and stepped out. Bill was there; the horses were shaking the snow out of their pelts; one of them was pawing the ground.

Once more Abe opened the door and gave Mike a look for a signal. Mike gathered the bundle of blankets into his arms, pulled on his mitts, and came out.

Abe reached for the lines, but Bill objected.

'No. Let me drive. I found something.'

And as soon as the two older men had climbed in, squeezing into the scant space on the seat, he clicked his tongue.

'Get up there!' he shouted, hitting the horses' backs with his lines. And with a leap they darted away.

Bill turned, heading back to the Carroll farm. The horses plunged, reared, snorted, and then, throwing their heads, shot along in a gallop, scattering snow-slabs right and left and throwing wing-waves of the fresh, powdery snow, especially on the lee side. Repeatedly they tried to turn into the wind, which they were cutting at right angles. But Bill plied the whip and guided them expertly.

Nothing was visible anywhere; nothing but the snow in the first grey of dawn. Then, like enormous ghosts, or like evanescent apparitions, the trees of the bluff were adumbrated behind the lingering veils of the night.

Bill turned to the south, along the straight trail which bordered Abe Carroll's farm. He kept looking out sharply to the right and left. But after awhile he drew his galloping horses in.

'Whoa!' he shouted, tearing at the lines in a seesaw fashion. And when the rearing horses came to a stop, excited and breathless, he added, 'I've missed it.' He turned.

'What is it?' Abe asked.

'The other horse,' Bill answered. 'It must have had the scent of our yard. It's dead...frozen stiff.'

A few minutes later he pointed to a huge white mound on top of a drift to the left. 'That's it,' he said, turned the horses into the wind, and stopped.

To the right, the bluffs of the farm slowly outlined themselves in the morning greyness.

The two older men alighted and, with their hands, shovelled the snow away. There lay the horse, stiff and cold, frozen into a rock-like mass.

'Must have been here a long while,' Abe said.

Mike nodded. 'Five, six hours.' Then he added, 'Couldn't have had the smell of the yard. Unless the wind has turned.'

'It has,' Abe answered, and pointed to a fold in the flank of the

FREDERICK PHILIP GROVE

snow-drift which indicated that the present drift had been superimposed on a lower one whose longitudinal axis ran to the north-east.

For a moment longer they stood and pondered.

Then Abe went back to the cutter and reached for the lines. 'I'll drive,' he said.

Mike climbed in.

Abe took his bearings, looking for landmarks. They were only two or three hundred feet from his fence. That enabled him to estimate the exact direction of the breeze. He clicked his tongue. 'Get up!'

And the horses, catching the infection of a dull excitement, shot away. They went straight into the desert of drifts to the west, plunging ahead without any trail, without any landmark in front to guide them.

They went for half an hour, an hour, and longer.

None of the three said a word. Abe knew the sand-flats better than any other; Abe reasoned better than they. If anyone could find the missing man, it was Abe.

Abe's thought ran thus. The horse had gone against the wind. It would never have done so without good reason; that reason could have been no other than a scent to follow. If that was so, however, it would have gone in as straight a line as it could. The sand-flats stretched away to the south-west for sixteen miles with not a settlement, not a farm but Redcliff's. If Abe managed to strike that line of scent, it must take him to the point whence the horses had started.

Clear and glaring, with an almost indifferent air, the sun rose to their left.

And suddenly they saw the wagon-box of the sleigh sticking out of the snow ahead of them.

Abe stopped, handed Bill the lines, and got out. Mike followed. Nobody said a word.

The two men dug the tongue of the vehicle out of the snow and tried it. This was part of the old, burnt-over bush land south of the sand-flats. The sleigh was tightly wedged in between several charred stumps which stuck up through the snow. That was the reason why the man had unhitched the horses and turned them loose. What else, indeed, could he have done?

The box was filled with a drift which, toward the tail-gate, was piled high, for there three bags of flour were standing on end and leaning against a barrel half-filled with small parcels, the interstices between which were packed with mealy snow.

Abe waded all around the sleigh, reconnoitring; and as he did so, wading at the height of the upper-edge of the wagon-box, the snow suddenly gave way beneath him; he broke in; the drift was hollow.

A suspicion took hold of him; with a few quick reaches of his arm he demolished the roof of the drift all about.

And there, in the hollow, lay the man's body as if he were sleeping, a quiet expression, as of painless rest, on his face. His eyes were closed; a couple of bags were wrapped about his shoulders. Apparently he had not even tried to walk! Already chilled to the bone, he had given in to that desire for rest, for shelter at any price, which overcomes him who is doomed to freeze.

Without a word the two men carried him to the cutter and laid him down on the snow.

Bill, meanwhile, had unhitched the horses and was hooking them to the tongue of the sleigh. The two others looked on in silence. Four times the horses sprang, excited because Bill tried to make them pull with a sudden twist. The sleigh did not stir.

'Here is an axe,' Mike said at last, 'to cut the stumps. We'll get the sleigh later.'

Mike hitched up again and turned the cutter. The broken snow-drifts through which they had come gave direction.

Then they laid the stiff, dead body across the floor of their vehicle, leaving the side-doors open, for it protruded both ways. They themselves climbed up on the seat and crouched down, so as not to put their feet on the corpse.

Thus they returned to Abe Carroll's farm where, still in silence, they deposited the body in the granary.

That done, they stood for a moment as if in doubt. Then Bill unhitched the horses and took them to the stable to feed.

'I'll tell the woman,' said Mike. 'Will you go tell her father?'

Abe nodded. 'Wait for breakfast,' he added.

It was ten o'clock; and none of them had eaten since the previous night.

On the way to Altmann's place in the bush, drifts were no obstacles to driving. Drifts lay on the marsh, on the open sand-flats.

Every minute of the time Abe, as he drove along, thought of that woman in the shack: the woman, alone, with six children, and with the knowledge that her man was dead.

Altmann's place in the bush looked the picture of peace and comfort: a large log-house of two rooms. Window-frames and doors were painted green. A place to stay with, not to leave....

When Abe knocked, the woman, whom he had seen but once in his life, at the sale where they had lost their possessions, opened the door — an enormously fat woman, overflowing her clothes. The man, tall, broad, with a long, rolling beard, now grey, stood behind her, peering over her shoulder. A visit is an event in the bush!

'Come in,' he said cheerfully when he saw Abe. 'What a storm that was!'

Abe entered the kitchen which was also dining- and living-room. He sat down on the chair which was pushed forward for him and looked at the two old people, who remained standing.

Suddenly, from the expression of his face, they anticipated something of his message. No use dissembling.

'Redcliff is dead,' he said. 'He was frozen to death last night on his way home from town.'

The two old people also sat down; it looked as if their knees had given way beneath them. They stared at him, dumbly, a sudden expression of panic fright in their eyes.

'I thought you might want to go to your daughter,' Abe added sympathetically.

The man's big frame seemed to shrink as he sat there. All the unctuousness and the conceit of the handsome man dwindled out of his bearing. The woman's eyes had already filled with tears.

Thus they remained for two, three minutes.

Then the woman folded her fat, pudgy hands; her head sank low on her breast; and she sobbed, 'God's will be done!'

GILLES VIGNEAULT

MON PAYS

Mon pays ce n'est pas un pays c'est l'hiver
Mon jardin ce n'est pas un jardan c'est la plaine
Mon chemin ce n'est ne pas un chemin c'est la neige
Mon pays ce n'est pas un pays c'est l'hiver

Dans la blanche cérémonie
Où la neige au vent se marie
Dans ce pays de pouderie
Mon père a fait bâtir maison
Et je m'en vais être fidèle
A sa manièr à son modèle
La chambre d'amis sera telle
Qu'on viendra des autres saisons
Pour se bâtir à côté d'elle

Mon pays ce n'est pas un pays c'est l'hiver
Mon refrain ce n'est un refrain c'est rafale
Ma maison ce n'est pas ma maison c'est froidure
Mon pays ce n'est pas un pays c'est l'hiver

De mon grand pays solitaire
Je crie avant que de me taire
A tous les hommes de la terre
Ma maison c'est votre maison
Entre mes quatre murs de glace
Je mets mon temps et mon espace
A préparer le feu la place
Pour les humains de l'horizon
Et les humains son de ma race

Mon pays ce n'est pas un pays c'est l'hiver
Mon jardin ce n'est pas un jardin c'est la plaine
Mon chemin ce n'est ne pas un chemin c'est la neige
Mon pays ce n'est pas un pays c'est l'hiver

Mon pays ce n'est pas un pays c'est l'envers
D'un pays qui n'était ni pays ni patrie
Ma chanson ce n'est pas une chanson c'est ma vie
c'est pour toi que je veux posséder mes hivers...

GILLES VIGNEAULT

GENE MACLELLAN
SUNG BY ANNE MURRAY

SNOWBIRD

Beneath this snowy mantle cold and clean
the unborn grass lies waiting
for its coat to turn to green.
The Snowbird sings the song he always sings
and speaks to me of flowers
that will bloom again in spring.

When I was young my heart was young then too
any thing that it would tell me
that's the thing that I would do.
But now I feel such emptiness within
for the thing I want the most in
life is the thing that I can't win.

Spread your tiny wings and fly away
and take the snow back with you
where it came from on that day.
The one I love forever is untrue
and if I could you know that
I would fly away with you.

The breeze along the river seems to say
that he'll only break my heart again
should I decide to stay.
So little Snowbird take me with you when you go
to that land of gentle breezes
where the peaceful waters flow.
Yeah if I could you know that I would
fly away with you.

OTTO FRIEDRICH

THE IDEA OF NORTH

"What I have in mind, believe it or not," Glenn Gould wrote to a friend in San Francisco early in 1965, less than a year after his retirement, "is a trip to the Arctic. I have an enormous compulsion to look upon the Polar seas and I find that this is growing apace each year, so that I really must get it out of my system somehow."

Now that he was free to come and go as he pleased, he really did head north that June to fulfill his "enormous compulsion." To his admirer in Leningrad, Kitty Gvozdeva, he provided a few details: "I went to Hudson's Bay to a point just a few miles above the most northerly growth of forest in that area, which is for the moment the most northern point to which you can take a train in Canada.... This train, although it has one car with sleeping accommodations, is not really intended for tourists. Everyone seemed to think I was just slightly mad to be on it in the first place — and practically every member of its crew turned out to be fabulously gifted as a raconteur, in the way that people who have experienced great isolation tend to be. And so for approximately 1,000 miles and for two nights and a day (each way), I was able to see an aspect of Canada with which very few people concern themselves. And I have come away from it with an enthusiasm for the North which may even get me through another winter of city living which, as you know, I loathe...."

It was true, at least as of that time, that very few Canadians concerned themselves with the North. "We have administered these vast territories of the north in an almost continuing state of absence of mind," Prime Minister Louis St. Laurent said in 1953, when he first created the Department of Northern Affairs. Yet the North has long haunted the Canadian imagination, not just the Arctic territories themselves but the fundamental idea of North. The North is everything beyond the horizon, beyond the comfortable and the familiar, everything frozen and dark, treeless and windswept. It is a little like the American image of the western frontier, but unlike the compliant West, the hostile Arctic still presents an enormous wilderness. It has no San Diego, no Las Vegas, no Disneyland. "The North is always there," as André Siegfried once wrote. "It is the background of the picture without which Canada would not be Canada."

"It includes great, unrelieved stretches of snow and ice..." Barry Lopez wrote in *Arctic Dreams*. "But there are, too, surprising and riveting sights: Wilberforce Falls on the Hood River suddenly tumbles 160 feet into a wild canyon in the midst of the Canadian tundra, and its roar can be heard for miles.... The badlands of east-central Melville Island, an eroded country of desert oranges, of muted yellows and reds, reminds a traveler of canyons and arroyos in southern Utah. And there are places more exotic, like the Ruggles River, which flows out of Lake Hazen on Ellesmere Island in winter and runs 2,000 feet through the Stygian darkness, wreathed in frost smoke, before it disappears underneath its own ice...."

In an obscure way, the history of the North makes Canada's national origins older and quite different from those of the United States. "The ferment that led explorers to the Canadian frontier did not begin in the fifteenth-century courts of Lisbon and Madrid, or in the counting houses of London and Bristol," as R.A.J. Phillips wrote in *Canada's North*. "It started much earlier, in Scandinavia." Five centuries before Columbus set sail, Eric the Red had led the Vikings to Greenland. They built settlements there, and on the coast of Newfoundland, which they called Markland. They erected stone houses and barns, brought in farm animals, cut down forests. Throughout the Middle Ages, the Viking settlements in northern Canada were known in Europe as a source of two treasured animals: falcons and polar bears. Canada, then, was not an obstacle discovered during the search for a new route to the Indies but rather, as Phillips put it, "the frontier of northern Europe."

Yet even after the gold rush in the Klondike at the end of the nineteenth century, even after the building of roads and airfields during World War II, the North remained largely untouched. When the Canadian government recovered from its "absence of mind" and began a decade of building and development, the entire population of this vast region still amounted to no more than 25,000. In all the Northwest Territories, there were exactly eight doctors. Education was provided by Anglican and Catholic missionaries, administration by the Royal Canadian Mounted Police. Even today, when icebreakers can force their way through the legendary Northwest Passage, now known as Lancaster Sound, and when trash and garbage can be found littering the bare tundra, there remains a mysterious attraction.

"The towns and telephones, the sound of generators, the grinding of sewage trucks, the ugliness of oil tanks: all this human defilement has not robbed the North of its strange power," Phillips wrote. "When men live in the North, their values change.... They live a lifetime alone, and die when they emerge. They become citizens of a different kind of country, a country where nature is overwhelmingly stronger than man.... Northern travellers seem to have found an extraordinary fulfillment in this unlikeliest of lands and seas.... In success or failure, almost all become missionaries for their cause. When they could return, they did. When they could not return, they relived their northern voyagings throughout their days, the way other men have spent their lives experiencing over and over the trauma of wartime."

Gould, with his Scottish origins, felt an almost mystical sense of the Canadian North and of its connections to the rest of the northern world. If you look at the globe from the North Pole rather than the Equator, Canada joins Russia, Scandinavia, Britain, and Germany on the peripheries of that frozen Mare Nostrum. This international idea of North was never fully articulated in Gould's writings, but it is hardly accidental that he not only loved Bach and Beethoven and Wagner but also recorded less universally admired Scandinavian composers like Grieg and Sibelius and even performed the music of the reclusive and eccentric Norwegian atonalist Fartein Valen. He thoroughly disapproved of the French, Debussy and Ravel, and he seems to have known very little of the great Italian opera composers.

Typically enough, Gould never actually went to the Arctic North. Most of this frozen wilderness can be reached only by airplane, and nothing could now make Gould get into an airplane. The nearest to the Arctic that he ever ventured was that trip aboard the train known as the *Muskeg Express*, which ran and still runs from Winnipeg a thousand miles north to Churchill, on the southwestern shore of Hudson's Bay. The railroad ends there, and so does the highway system. From a southern perspective, Churchill is almost at the end of the world. But although the tree line ends here, this is barely the beginning of the Canadian North. There are about another 100 miles to the 60th parallel, the southern border of the Northwest Territories, another 200 miles beyond that to Repulse Bay, another 600 miles or so to Resolute Bay and Lancaster Sound and the Northwest Passage, and another 400 miles beyond that to the glaciers of Ellesmere Island. And only there lie the "polar seas" that Gould said he felt "an enormous compulsion to look upon." For an inhabitant of Toronto to describe one train trip to Churchill as a voyage to the North is a little like a Bostonian thinking (as any true Bostonian would think) of a visit to Washington as a journey south, or of a trip to Cleveland as the West.

Still, it was not the reality of the North that fascinated Gould, and he admitted as much, *en passant*, in the introduction to his extraordinary radio documentary, "The Idea of North": "I've been intrigued for quite a long time...by that incredible tapestry of tundra and taiga country, as they call it.... I've read about it, written about it occasionally, and even pulled up my parka once and gone there. But like all but a very few Canadians, I guess, I've had no direct confrontation with the northern third of our country. I've remained of necessity an outsider, and the north has remained for me a convenient place to dream about, spin tall tales about sometimes, and, in the end, avoid."

"He said, 'Let's go for an automobile ride, and I'll show you Toronto,'" Leonard Bernstein recalls. "So, well, what is there to see? It was cold, and it was getting dark, and I had sort of seen it the day before. So we went out, Glenn in his usual three coats and two hats, and I don't know how many pairs of gloves. We got into his car, which was a black sedan. He turned the heat up to maximum, and the radio volume up to maximum, and he got a station that was playing pop tunes, and Petula Clark was singing, and I said, 'Do you really want to hear this?' It was so hot in that car, I can't tell you, and the music was so loud, and there was nothing to see — it was growing dark — but we drove around for maybe half an hour, having a conversation by shouting over this radio full blast, and that was our tour of Toronto.

"One of the things we talked about was his new love affair with the Arctic. This man who was so afraid of cold, and so geared against it — and I mean literally, the gear he travelled with was immense — why would he seek it out, why would he seek out this enemy? Which was the enemy of his fingers, which were always getting cold at a recording session or a rehearsal, so that he had to have hot water, and many, many mittens. And he tried to answer it in — I don't know — without turning off the radio. It's very hard to tell you what was actually said, but what I came away with was a feeling of a kind of cosmic exploration. There was something spiritual about it. Elements of magic, having to do with the magnetic pole.

"I was terribly moved by it, because I'd have thought that the only explanation would be to seek out the thing that hurts you the most and confront it, in a sort of good old-fashioned Freudian way. The only way you can conquer your fear of elevators is to get into one and say, 'This is an elevator, I'm here, and everything's all right.' But it wasn't that. It was something much more magical and mystical."

"It was through me that Glenn encountered the concept of the radio documentary," says John Roberts of the CBC. "It was in sixty-one, I think — I produced a program called *Music by Royal Composers*, and it was just that, you know, all kinds of interesting people, in all varieties of monarchies of Britain, and it was an exploration of that area. Glenn was very fascinated. He asked me how it was put together, and I explained in immense detail, and he was very, very fascinated. He said, 'You know, I'd like to do that.' And then not long afterwards, he said to me, 'Look, I would like to try and put together a documentary on Schoenberg. Would you be interested?' And I said, 'Terribly interested.' And so, his first Schoenberg documentary was the result of that. And of course, having gone through all that, he was absolutely bitten by the bug, and he wanted to continue, and then other departments were interested in him and what he was doing, and so his scope widened...."

Gould himself recalled his involvement with documentary radio beginning much earlier, in 1945 or 1946. Indeed, there was something about the medium itself, something about hearing a disembodied voice trying to make a connection, that had attracted and delighted the lonely schoolboy. Radio brought him the outside world, and yet it did so without violating his strong sense of privacy. "It's always seemed to me," he wrote, "that when that first person heard that second person's voice by virtue of a crystal set, or whatever it was heart on, that they had not only the most unique experience in music — of music in the sense of voice as sound, obviously, but that they had the one true approach to radio. They were able to get at something quite special...that original human contact, that incredible, spine-tingling sense of awareness of some other human voice and persona."

Gould remembered his first documentary on Schoenberg with some dismay, however. "I was always dissatisfied with the kind of documentaries that radio seemed to decree," he said. "You know, they very often came out sounding... — okay, I'll borrow Mr. McLuhan's term — linear. They came out sounding 'Over to you, now back to our host, and here for the wrap-up is' — in a word, predictable. I wrote the script, for instance, for a program on Schoenberg in sixty-two...[and] it seemed that one had to accept a linear mold in order to pursue any kind of career in radio at that time. So I was very dissatisfied with the available techniques, and in 1967, for the first time, I got a chance to try my hand at producing something on my own."

This was to become "The Idea of North." "What I would most like to do," Gould wrote to a friend in the summer of 1967, "is to examine the effects of solitude and isolation upon those who have lived in the Arctic or Sub-Arctic. In some subtle way, the latitudinal factor does seem to have a modifying influence upon character, although I have no editorial axe to grind in the matter...." And to another friend: "My Arctic bluff has finally been called by Mother CBC, no less. They have suggested that I really do go ahead...."

Gould's plan was to interrogate a number of people who had lived and worked in the North. "Something really does happen to people who go into the north," Gould later wrote, "— they become...in effect, philosophers." Then, with razors and glue, he would see what he could make of their taped recollections. One of his first choices was Bob Phillips, who had worked in the Department of Northern Affairs and was now assistant secretary of the cabinet, Privy Council Office. He was also a perceptive and sympathetic observer whose new book on the North had undoubtedly attracted Gould's attention.

"I remember so vividly the first contact," says Phillips, a graying, craggy-faced man who now devotes much of his time to renovating old houses. "It was a Sunday evening when we happened to have guests in, and the phone rang, and it was somebody from — he identified himself as from CBC in Toronto, called Gould, and he said he was doing a series of programs on the North, and asked my help. A couple of years had gone by since I'd been professionally associated with the North, so I offered to introduce him to other people, authorities on the North, but he was very insistent. He said, no, it doesn't matter if you're not up-to-date — it isn't about being up-to-date. It's more philosophical.

"So since we had guests waiting, I finally took the line of least resistance and agreed to meet him at the CBC studios in a day or

OTTO FRIEDRICH

two, and that was that. Or then — I remember the next stage even more vividly because I think it was the greatest *gaffe* in my life. I met this strange character up on the seventh floor of the Château Laurier, and we first went through a *strange* performance, in which there were more microphones than I'd ever seen laid out before, and finally he said, 'Well, may we talk?' And then he asked really quite penetrating, interesting questions about the North, which required very long answers. And while I was answering, I was astonished at his attitude. He was sort of shaking his head, and smiling, and shaking his head some more, affirmatively, and he seemed to be sort of happy, and then at times it was almost as though he were direct-ing an orchestra, with his hands.

"And so it went, fairly intensely, for about an hour. I had no idea it was so long. And he said, 'Well, look, this is just absolutely mar-velous, just what I wanted. Now why don't we take a break? You must be tired.' And so the coffee was produced. And so, making conversation over the coffee, I asked him, I said, 'Excuse me, Mr. Gould, but are you related to the pianist?' And he then said that he *was* the pianist. Well, it seemed to me the most extraordinary thing. I had no idea...."

By some mysterious system of his own, Gould chose four other "participants" who had spent substantial amounts of time in the North. "We wanted," he said later, "an enthusiast, a cynic, a gov-ernment budget-watcher, as well as someone who could represent that limitless expectation and limitless capacity for disillusionment which inevitably affects the questing spirit of those who go north seeking their future." For these roles, he picked, in addition to Bob Phillips, Marianne Schroeder, a nurse; Frank Vallee, a professor of sociology in Ottawa; James Lotz, a British anthropologist; and W.V. (Wally) Maclean, an aged surveyor whom Gould had met on the *Muskeg Express*, and autodidact who loved to quote Shakespeare and to hold forth on the symbolic meanings of the North.

It was Maclean, in a way, who had given Gould the idea for "The Idea of North." A railroad steward had introduced them at the breakfast table, and after some talk about the prospects of the North, Maclean startled Gould by asking, "Are you aware, Mr. Gould, that both Thoreau and Kafka practiced my profession? That both were surveyors?" Gould confessed that he was not. Maclean went on to argue that "there's a real connection between surveying and literature." Gould was fascinated. "For me, to encounter this suddenly in the middle of nowhere was amazing," he later told an interviewer. "And we started an eight-hour conversation — we didn't rise from that table after mid-morning tea, after lunch, or afternoon tea, until four o'clock, by which time I had a headache from the weight of ideas.... That was the genesis of his participating."

As usual, though, Gould made of his characters what he imagined in himself. "I think he split his own psyche up into different parts to make the show," Jim Lotz recalls. "The nurturer (the nurse), the objective critic (university professor), the pontificator (the civil servant), and the antiestablishment adventurer (is that me, or am I the idealist?). Then he had the old man in the cave as the commentator. You must see what Glenn did in Jungian terms, not Freudian ones. We were not matched off against each other, but rather set up to complement each other. Glenn played me like a piano, and in fact the program should have been called 'The Idea of Glenn Gould.'"

Still, Gould organized "The Idea of North" by getting each of these people to talk about the North, about their own experiences of loneliness and isolation. Thus Nurse Schroeder: "I didn't have to go to somebody in Coral [Harbor] and say I'm lonesome or I'm depressed. I just had to go and visit them, play a game of chess, whatever they wanted to do, and right away there was a sense of sharing this life. One could realize the value of another human being. You're excluding the rest of the world that will never understand, and you've made your own world with these people, and probably what you'll never know, and what nobody else will ever know, is whether you're kidding yourself or not. Have you really made your peace with these other people...because the only alternative to peace is a kind of crackup?"

And Lotz: "I was in many respects solitary, but in a strange way the North has made me more sort of gregarious, because the North does show you exactly how much you rely on your fellow man. What the sense of community means in the North is a matter of life and death.... It's so big, it's so vast, it's so immense, it cares so little, and this sort of diminishes you. And then you think, 'My God, I am here. I've got here, I live here....'"

Such observations were reasonably interesting, reasonably perceptive, but they were still only raw material, reels of unedited tape, fodder. Once Gould had his interviews all recorded and transcribed in the south, he once again headed northward, on Route 17, a road that he loved, skirting the shores of Lake Superior. "No. 17 defines

OTTO FRIEDRICH

for much of its passage across Ontario the northernmost limit of agrarian settlement," he wrote some years later. "It is endowed with habitation, when at all, by fishing villages, mining camps, and timber towns that straddle the highway every fifty miles or so. Among these, names such as Michipicoten and Batchawana advertise the continuing segregation of the Canadian Indian; Rossport and Jackfish proclaim the no-nonsense mapmaking of the early white settlers; and Marathon and Terrace Bay...betray the postwar influx of American capital (Terrace is the Brasilia of Kimberly-Clark's Kleenex-Kotex operation in Ontario)."

While driving north, Gould heard on his car radio so many CBC renditions of Petula Clark singing "Who Am I?" that he decided to write an inquiry entitled "The Search for Petula Clark." But on this trip, the singer's question of "Who am I?" led Gould to a little coastal town named Wawa, where he enjoyed tramping along the lakefront piers built of giant timbers. "It's an extraordinary place..." he later said, "to sort out some thoughts and try to get some writing done."

"What did he do?" says Lorne Tulk, the skilled editor-engineer who worked with Gould on "The Idea of North." "He rented a motel room, and he sat in the motel room and wrote."

Q: What's up there, in Wawa?

A: Nothing.

Q: He just went up there for a visit?

A: No, he went to Wawa and wrote "North." He had all of his interviews transcribed, and he took all the transcripts with him, locked himself in a motel room in Wawa for two or three weeks, and came back with a program.

If the interviewing had been only a beginning, however, the writing was still only a beginning. In creating what he called "a documentary which thinks of itself as a drama," Gould had made a point of interviewing his five dramatis personae separately; they never met. He had originally planned these five separate interviews as five separate segments, perhaps even to be broadcast on five separate evenings. "And that remained true until something like six weeks prior to broadcast time," Gould later wrote, "which is pretty frightening when you come to think of it. *Five* weeks prior to broadcast time, I suddenly decided that that wasn't at all what I wanted to do — that, obviously, it had to be an integrated unit of some kind in which the texture, the tapestry of the words themselves would differentiate the characters and create dreamlike conjunctions within the documentary. These, of course, would have to be achieved through some rather prodigious editing, and I spent something like two to three weeks occupied with fine editing, still all the while being unsure as to the eventual form that the piece was going to take."

Since Gould had asked his chamber-music players roughly the same questions, he could organize his material into a half-dozen scenes, in which all the characters addressed themselves to the same general point. But when he had finished all this, he found that his hour-long show ran to nearly an hour and half. "So I thought, 'Well, obviously, one scene has got to go.' We had a scene on the Eskimo — couldn't lose that; we had a scene on isolation and its effects — that had to stay, obviously; we had our closing soliloquy, we had our opening trio and other indispensables — and I couldn't part with any of them.... I thought to myself, 'Look, we really could hear some of these people speaking simultaneously — there is no particular reason why not.'"

After telling this story, in "Radio as Music," Gould admitted that "perhaps I exaggerate ever so slightly," but that was essentially how he invented what he later took to calling "contrapuntal radio." Almost nothing, of course, is ever "invented" just like that. Frank Capra, for one, was experimenting with simultaneous dialogue in films as far back as the early 1930s, and all such experimenters were quite aware that even the most banal statements somehow sound, when juxtaposed against other banal statements, less banal. Gould was nonetheless the first professional musician to edit the tapes of spoken words as though they were the notes in a contrapuntal composition.

"The Idea of North" begins with Nurse Schroeder saying, somewhat wistfully: 'I was fascinated by the country as such. I flew north from Churchill to Coral Harbor...at the end of September. [Note how casually she names as her starting place the northernmost point that Gould ever reached.] Snow had begun to fall, and the country was partially covered by it. Some of the lakes were frozen around the edges, but towards the center of the lakes you could still see the clear, clear water...."

After about a minute of this, Professor Vallee's rather gruff voice begins speaking (Gould, for some reason, never specifically identified any speakers, or any music being played, in any of his radio documentaries): "I don't go — let me say this again — I don't go for this northmanship bit at all...." And so the duet continues:

Schroeder: We seemed to be going into nowhere, and the further north we went...

Vallee (simultaneously): I don't knock those people who do claim that they want to go farther and farther north, but...

These two people who have never met continue speaking simultaneously for a minute or so, and then, soon after Vallee says, "And the other fellow says, 'Well, I did one of thirty days,'" Bob Phillips's mellow voice starts saying, "And then for another eleven years, I served the North in various capacities...."

This may all seem rather commonplace, but Gould edited these taped observations with a meticulous sense of both meaning and sound. Nurse Schroeder's voice begins almost pianissimo, then very gradually gets louder, and each new voice in this spoken fugato comes in on a specific tangent. Gould described this as "a kind of trio sonata texture." Speaking of Vallee's entrance in the midst of Nurse Schroeder's monologue, he said, "By this time we have become aware of a gentleman who has started to speak and who upon the word 'further' says 'farther' — 'farther and farther north' is the context. At that moment, his voice takes precedence over hers in terms of dynamic emphasis. Shortly after, he uses the words 'thirty days,' and by this point we have become aware of a third voice which immediately after 'thirty days' says 'eleven years' — and another crossover point has been effected. The scene is built so that it has a kind of — I don't know if you have ever looked at the tone rows of Anton Webern as distinguished from those of Arnold Schoenberg, but it has a kind of Webern-like continuity-in-crossover in that motives which are similar but not identical are used for the exchange of instrumental ideas...."

It is a little difficult for an ordinary listener to accept Gould's assessment of "The Idea of North" as a musical composition. Granted that it is perfectly possible to treat the speaking voice as a musical instrument, granted that Gould edited his interview tapes just as skillfully and as imaginatively as he edited the tapes of his own performances on the piano, it nonetheless remains true that when Nurse Schroeder observes that "we seemed to be going into nowhere," these are neither abstract sounds being organized according to Gould's aesthetic plan nor are they Gould's words expressing Gould's ideas. Instead of composing a piece of verbal music, in other words, Gould was simply playing the role of editor, and succumbing, as editors often do, to the idea that what he had edited had become his own creation. A professional music critic like

William Littler of the *Toronto Star* can be more understanding. "It rather depends on how deeply you want to argue what composition consists of," he says. "If it means the ordering of materials, with a sense of structure, to produce an overall statement — yes, compositional principles were involved in 'The Idea of North.' He's working with words, so he's composing with words. Obviously, if you take it much further and try to analyze it in terms of sonata form, you can't do it. But the general principles of composition are there." Besides, in an era when John Cage composes an *Imaginary Landscape* that includes twelve radios simultaneously playing at random, in an era when Steve Reich takes a taped confession of an accused murderer and then reproduces one or two phrases in a googol of repetitions, how is one to define music, except that it is whatever a gifted musician says it is?

Gould himself indisputably believed that his radio documentaries were musical compositions. "Taking...an interview like this one into the studio after the fact," he said not long afterward, "chopping it up and splicing here and there and pulling on this phrase and accentuating that one, throwing some reverb in there and adding a compressor here and a filter there...it's unrealistic to think of that as anything but a composition.... And...it is the way of the future.... I think our whole notion of what music really is has forever merged with all the sounds around us, you know, everything our environment makes available." And when he learned in 1972 that a young student named Robert Skelton was planning to write a detailed analysis of his string quartet, he promptly sent him tapes of "The Idea of North" and its sequel, "The Latecomers." "There are...certain connecting links," Gould wrote, "which should, I think, be noted: perhaps, most obviously, a concentration on aspects of counterpoint...and perhaps, less obviously, a tendency in each case to celebrate, if not precisely a *fin de siècle* situation, then at least a philosophy which deliberately sought an isolated vantage-point in relation to its time and milieu.... There is a true fraternal link, both in subject matter and technique, between the vocal polyphony of 'The Idea of North'...and the chromatically constructed counterpoint of the quartet."

When all the theorizing has been done, a radio show depends on one man (or woman) who knows what he (or she) wants, and one who can carry out those wishes. In this case, Lorne Tulk saw his job as the translation into sound of anything that Gould could imagine. "My only function is to play the console, the way you play a piano," says Tulk, a short, stocky man, curly-haired, full of energy. "The difference is that instead of black and white keys, I have turntables and tape recorders.... You just say, 'I want something that sounds like—'"

Q: Like what? Can I say that I want it to sound like New York City? Or I want it to sound like blue?

A: Sure. Any of those things.

And so they set to work, night after night. Though Jessie Greig vividly remembers the young Gould playing the piano long after everyone else in the family had gone to bed, Tulk thinks that he was the one who introduced Gould to the rich possibilities of the night. "You can get more done in that time," he says, matter-of-factly. "There's less interruptions. The place is quiet. I don't think Glenn had ever thought in terms of working all night, but once he started doing it, he discovered he loved it. The only thing he didn't like, he didn't like to see the sun come up. So he'd try to get finished and get home before the sunrise."

Q: Like a vampire.

A: It's the one thing that for some reason he found depressing, to see the sun come up. I don't know why.

Q: Perhaps it just meant that the night was gone, and now he had to stop everything and go to bed.

A: I don't know. He just used to say that he didn't want to see the sun rise.

As the deadline approaches, as the opening night draws near, all attention must be focused on getting the job done. The *Star*'s Littler paid a visit to the CBC's Studio K on a pre-Christmas night in 1967 and found a scene of controlled chaos. "By 3 A.M., everyone in Studio K was beginning to look a little like last week's cut flowers," he wrote. "[Producer] Janet Somerville, leaning against the control room wall, stared blankly ahead. Lorne Tulk, bending over his knobs and dials, wore an equally expressionless gaze. And the man in charge, shoes off and shirt hanging out of his trousers, held his face in his hands. The man in charge was Glenn Gould. He had been sitting in CBC Studio K's control room since 6 P.M., drinking coffee, taking tranquilizers, and editing tapes...."

The show was supposed to be broadcast in a couple of days, but it was still far from finished. "You vant qvality, baby? It takes time," Gould offered in yet another of his ethnic impersonations. His listeners smiled weakly. Gould turned serious: "I started Thanksgiving Day, and except for my recording trips to New York, we've been working on this every night since then — last night until 2:30 A.M., the night before 3 A.M. I only regret we didn't start a week earlier to take the pressure off."

Gould then went back to work. Littler watched him and his crew labor over their four Ampex tape machines. "It was quite an operation to observe," he wrote. "Gould would sit up on the control panel, his script resting on a music stand, and cue Tulk with a vocabulary of gestures not unlike those of an orchestral conductor. They would talk together about crescendos and diminuendos, Gould would refer to a particular sequence as ternary or a particular voice as lyrical, and in general he seemed to be playing the role of composer-conductor.... Every now and then, when frustration threatened to erupt, he would break into an extravagant German-accented monologue or recall an anecdote associated with his research. His concentration was relentless. Each break would last only a minute or two, until the laughter died down. But he seemed to sense just when that break had to come. His coworkers never questioned him. They were there to help, to tell him what could be done, to activate his ideas. The ideas were almost invariably his."

Gould sustained these late-night sessions by his own enthusiasm, but there were limits. "Toward 5 A.M...." Littler reported, "Gould was still patient with his colleagues and they were still willing to go on as long as he wanted. But reactions were slowing and Gould's lack of sleep had already reduced his eyes to near-slits. 'It's beginning to catch up with me,' he smiled. 'I usually get by on seven or eight hours and can make out on four or five for a stretch. But I've stretched the stretch to the limit. Shall we call it a night?'"

Janet Somerville remembers those late-night editing sessions from a somewhat different perspective. "Lorne and Glenn loved each other, and so between them there was utter peace," she says. "It wasn't sick, it wasn't homosexual, it wasn't any of the things we put in a twentieth-century context. It was like a knight and a page, you know, on a great adventure. Lorne should have lived in the Middle Ages. I mean, he has that kind of loyal devotion, which was *the* human virtue of that relationship. And Lorne is just so rich in it. And Glenn found it all totally normal. I mean, he felt that of *course* people would feel that way about him."

A small white parrot suddenly flutters out of a corner of Miss Somerville's living room and swoops past her visitor. "Since it will go on doing that as long as you're here, I might as well put it away," she says, opening the door to the bird's cage and letting it take refuge. She remembers now that she had other work to do besides the Gould show. She was the producer on a nightly program called *Ideas*, of which "The Idea of North" was just one installment, and she was particularly engrossed at that point in taping Martin Luther King's Toronto lectures on nonviolence. But even after working all day, she felt an obligation to spend her nights in the nocturnal world of Glenn Gould. "I was a tired, very hardworking producer who was concerned with five hours a week of other programming at the same time," she says, "but still fascinated by the aesthetic elegance and technical precision of what Glenn was doing. And I enjoyed those all-night sessions, just watching the two of them.

"They would turn out the studio lights and just go by the lights from the console, which was — They were both sort of lit from beneath, and they both have lovely faces, with, you know, strong bone structures. And I would sit there, very tired, having been working all day, and being about to work all the next day, watching the light on their bones and their skin, and watching their fascination...."

Gould never played the piano for her, and now that he is dead, she can only watch him perform on television from time to time. "He looks beautiful," she says. "I mean, in a way, I sometimes feel a little embarrassed, as I sometimes did in watching him edit 'The Idea of North.' Because his physical reaction to beautiful sound, to making beautiful sound — or, in the case of editing, to *hearing* great sound — was so strong that I wanted to look away, sometimes. It was so autoerotic."

Q: Autoerotic?

A: Yes. I felt — you know, I felt sometimes that I was crossing that fine line of voyeurism. Because, I mean, *that's* where Glenn lived, you know, in that *total* response to what he had just created, and in its correspondence to what he had already previously heard in there, inside his head. And that was *so* much more important to him than personal relationships, or money, or, you know, the other things that we mortals get caught up in. That was — that was his *passion* in a very, very full sense.

The show did get done, and it got done just barely in time for Canada's celebration of its own centennial. It is sometimes a little difficult to remember how new the Canadian nation is. Not until well after the battle of Gettysburg, when Americans spent three days slaughtering each other in their struggle over the assertion of a national identity, was the Canadian federation born in 1867. And even then, the provinces of Manitoba and Saskatchewan did not yet exist, nor Alberta, nor British Columbia. So the centennial celebrations of 1967 were an important milestone in the Canadians' still evolving sense of their own identity. The Toronto *Telegram* printed a special magazine section that July 1, Canada Day, and asked various notables like Robertson Davies and Morley Callaghan to explain what it all meant. Gould's views were typically idiosyncratic: "Canada's a place to live comfortably, amicably, and with reasonable anonymity. And I think the latitudinal factor is important to me — the fact we're a northern people, cross-pollinated by influences from the south. But for the moment we're in danger of losing...something we Canadians could capitalize on: A synoptic view of the world we live in."

Gould said it all much better in "The Idea of North," which was finally broadcast at the very end of the anniversary year, on December 28. "I found myself listening at two levels simultaneously," Barbara Frum wrote in a clumsy but perceptive review in the *Toronto Star*, "— to the stream of ideas but just as compelling in this production, to the pattern of sounds Gould wove out of his speakers' voices. Using the hypnotic drone of moving train wheels as a bass, Gould wove the voices of the five persons he interviewed into a thick and moody line, fading the voices in and out, under and over each other.... There was no attempt to define a 'problem.' No urge to give climatic conditions, population statistics, recent history of the region.... Instead Gould used his interviews to create a sound composition about the loneliness, the idealism and the letdowns of those who go North." And the Ottawa *Citizen*: "A poetic and beautiful montage of the North emerged that...was more real and honest than the entire ten-foot shelf of standard clichés about Canada's northlands." And the Montreal *Star*: "The Gould broadcast...is likely to stand as the forerunner of a new radio art, a wonderfully imaginative striving for a new way to use the only half-explored possibilities of an established form."...

Before, during, and after the making of the Stokowski program, Gould was deeply involved in extending "The Idea of North" into a number of sequels. The first of these dealt with another remote region, Newfoundland, the land of the Viking settlements, which had joined the Canadian federation only in 1949. Gould called his program "The Latecomers." Newfoundland was considerably more accessible than the Arctic, and more inhabited. Gould actually went there in August of 1968 "in search of characters for a documentary, the subject of which was by no means clear to me."

The subject was, of course, perfectly clear. Once again, Gould was seeking to portray solitude, isolation. Though Newfoundland was less frozen than northern Ontario, it had the additional barrier of the ocean, which Gould used as an underlying *basso continuo* throughout his program. "The reality is in its separateness," he later wrote. "The very fact — the inconvenience — of distance is its great natural blessing. Through that fact, the Newfoundlander has received a few more years of grace — a few more years in which to calculate the odds for individuality in an increasingly coercive cultural milieu."

Gould used thirteen characters this time, and once again none of them ever met. By now, he was seeing in this separateness of his characters all kinds of opportunities. One of the unnamed men he interviewed, for example, compared Newfoundland to Thoreau's Walden and observed that "people who are removed from the center of a society are always able to see it more clearly." One woman, on the other hand, disliked the isolation and felt that she had to escape every once in a while. "I kept saying, 'But why?' and naïve things of that kind," Gould later recalled. "She kept repeating herself, essentially, though with infinite variations...and finally turned on me with a fine fury, stopped short of insult, but indicated that my line of questioning was foolish." By splicing these two interviews together, with the interviewer once again removing himself, Gould managed to suggest that the woman who was annoyed at him was actually annoyed at the other man, and that this scene "would appear to be taking place between, I suppose, a man and wife, certainly a lady and gentleman who are engaged in rather intimate conversation.... The dialogue represented in that scene never took place as dialogue, and yet I have a strange feeling that had they met, it would have."

Technology gave Gould an even more remarkable opportunity for "creative cheating" in the episode of the fake wave. Gould used the waves on the coast of Newfoundland much as he had used the clacking railroad in "The Idea of North," and since the ocean offers a far greater variety of sounds, Gould taped hours of possibilities, pounding waves, lapping waves, sighing waves, grinding waves. Only when he got back to the editing room in Toronto did he find, as he later confessed, that "there was one scene for which I just couldn't find the right surf sound; I tried everything, every tape of sound we'd recorded in Newfoundland, and nothing quite matched the mood of the voices in that particular scene."

Gould grumbled to someone at the studio about his problem, and so he learned that the CBC had other tapes of other waves beating on other shores. Specifically, he learned that a TV crew had recently returned from making a show about Charles Darwin's voyage aboard the S.S. *Beagle* to the Galápagos Islands off the coast of Ecuador. He couldn't resist listening. "So," he said, "we ended up borrowing a tape from someone who had just returned from the Galápagos, and that worked perfectly."

But what does it actually mean for something to "work perfectly"? One wave in the background may seem a very small point of contention, and yet all the traditions of history, scholarship, and even journalism dictate that every statement must at least try to be true, that the thing should be what it pretends to be. No matter how awkward or implausible it may sound, this is what happened. *"Wie es eigentlich gewesen,"* as Leopold von Ranke said of his history of Rome, "how it really was." So if we are to hear waves beating on the shores of Newfoundland, they are supposed to be waves actually recorded on the shores of Newfoundland. Whether the taped sounds "quite matched the mood of the voices" is quite secondary, tertiary. Indeed, there is no comparison. To "match the mood" of a Newfoundlander's voice with the sound of a wave breaking on the Galápagos Islands is almost a contradiction in terms, an absurdity.

One of the wonders of technology, though, is that it denies the very idea of historical truth. Since everything on tape is a simulation, and since everything can be dubbed, redubbed, overdubbed, what actually happened is of almost no importance. Just as Elisabeth Schwarzkopf could be employed to sing a certain high note that Kirsten Flagstad could no longer reach, and nobody could tell the difference. When this operatic event leaked out as gossip, purists complained that a Flagstad performance should not include a high note secretly sung by Schwarzkopf, but what were the alternatives? No Flagstad performance? A Flagstad performance with mangled high notes? To Gould, such arguments were antiquarian. The goal was not historical accuracy but artistic perfection, and while there might well be very different visions of perfection, Gould was determined to follow his own.

So were the Mennonites, those remarkable descendants of the sixteenth-century Anabaptists, who believed passionately that every injunction of the New Testament must be carried out exactly as

OTTO FRIEDRICH

written. Gould made these onetime heretics the subject of "Quiet in the Land" (1973), his second sequel to "The Idea of North." It is the most complicated and in some ways the most interesting of these three radio shows because the separateness of the Mennonites is spiritual rather than physical, and chosen rather than compelled.

And Gould's mastery of his medium had by now become overwhelming. The beginning of "Quiet in the Land" is one of the most beautiful things he ever did, first the slow tolling of a church bell, pianissimo, as though from a great distance; then faint chirpings, which sound vaguely like sea gulls but gradually reveal themselves to be the voices of children at play; then, with the church bell still tolling, a sound that resembles surf but is actually the rush of highway traffic; and then the jubilation of a Mennonite congregation singing a hymn.

"Let us bow for prayer," the minister declares. "Lord God, the Holy Ghost, in this accepted hour, as on the day of Pentecost, descend in Thy power...." And as the minister speaks those words, another voice is saying, "I think there is a conflict on the idea of Utopianism versus scattering into the world...." And as the earnest voices continue their explorations of these churchly matters, the music in the background keeps veering between a solo cello playing a reflective Bach saraband and Janis Joplin singing, "Oh, Lord, won't you buy me a Mercedes-Benz?"

Gould was by now possessed by the idea of pushing "contrapuntal radio" to its absolute limits, and beyond. "There's going to be a scene in there which will drive you crazy..." he said to a CBC "interviewer" in one of those promotional shows for which he now wrote out both questions and answers. "It's a scene in which nine characters...talk about the church's relationship to pacifism at what appears to be a church meeting. It's all hooked up from the eighttrack, of course. But it's going to make everything I've done up till the present seem like Gregorian chant by comparison."

It is a most impressive scene, about ten minutes long, and almost completely incomprehensible. At one point, for example, while one character says, "The Catholic Church takes a hard teaching like 'You shall not kill,'" a second character simultaneously says, "To me Christianity means unselfishness," and a third says, "When I am threatened as an individual, maybe then we had better reexamine how we have been doing things." Precisely because each of these speakers is saying something that requires concentration and reflection, the simultaneity of their words contradicts their purpose.

Gould acknowledged that in such scenes "not every word is going to be audible," but he argued that "by no means every syllable in the final fugue from Verdi's *Falstaff* is either," and "I do believe that most of us are capable of a much more substantial information intake than we give ourselves credit for." The analogy to Verdi is a very debatable one. It does not matter greatly whether we know that the cast of *Falstaff* is singing "Tutto nel mondo è burla" (The whole world is but a joke), for the music is telling us much the same thing, and the music is what we have come to hear. The voices of two or three Christians speaking seriously at cross-purposes is itself almost a *burla*, indeed almost diabolical in its reduction of spiritual statements into spiritual babble....

Since this is the age of television, somebody (possibly Gould himself) decided sometime in 1968 that "The Idea of North" should somehow be converted from "contrapuntal radio" into a television show. Gould was discussing this idea with a friend and producer at Columbia named Paul Myers, and Myers mentioned one of his friends, Judith Pearlman. She was just getting started in television, and she felt passionately about music in general and Gould's music in particular. So they all met and listened to a tape of "The Idea of North."

"That made me pretty nervous," Miss Pearlman recalls. "Because Gould was watching me like a hawk. And at the end, he said, 'Well, what do you think?' And I said, "I think it's very hard to come to a decision after just hearing it once, and I'd like to listen to it again for the next two weeks.' So that's what I did. I took the tape home and made it my matins and evensong, lauds and complines, for two weeks. As I listened, the patterns of sound became clearer, along with the personalities of the five characters. Then I wrote a treatment, and Glenn read that and liked it."

"At the core of the film is a train journey north to Hudson Bay," the treatment begins. "It is, of course, a real train on a scheduled run — yet also a train of mind and mythology, carrying men still seeking the last frontier as trial or escape...." Miss Pearlman barely realized that she had become a pawn in a complicated power struggle typical of television. The New York public broadcasting executives at WNET wanted to make a deal with the CBC for a series of ten coproduced shows, one of which would almost inevitably feature Glenn Gould, and the fact that Miss Pearlman had written a treatment that Gould had liked gave her a quasi-legal hold on "The Idea of North." It was a hold that was strong enough to survive sev-

OTTO FRIEDRICH

eral shifts and transfers among the executives who were supposed to decide things, and after nearly two years of negotiations and delays, she found herself in Ottawa, bargaining with the Canadian National Railways about what it would cost to rent a railroad car to carry a film crew from Winnipeg to Churchill.

Gould, who was busy making new recordings, elegantly removed himself from all these difficulties. While he sang the praises of technology, he liked to spend hours editing radio tapes with one technician in a studio but not in negotiating the price of a railroad car that would convert a fantasy of sound into a visual reality, or simulation of reality. "So I went over to talk to them, and they wanted five thousand dollars," Miss Pearlman recalls. "Well, my whole budget for such things was only eighteen thousand dollars, so we just kept on negotiating. They said we could have it for four thousand dollars, so I thought, We're making progress. And this went on for *days*. Finally, they said, 'Okay, you can have it for five hundred dollars.'

"So I went back to the CBC studio, and I could hear the producer shouting, the producer they had assigned to take charge of this project, and I knew he was drunk. He shouted that he would do all kinds of lascivious things to me. I was afraid of him, because of the way he talked, and because he was so big. He was about six feet four, and about two hundred fifty pounds. He had made his reputation producing sports events. So I got on the phone to New York, and I said, 'I don't think I can work with this guy.' And then I just held up the phone."

She demonstrates, holding her hand up over her head, holding up the telephone that carried the drunken bellowing of her assigned producer to the ears of supposedly protective coproducers in New York. "And the next Monday," she says, "I was told that he was off the show. Then they just left me on my own." This was not by any means the end of her social problems. She recalls that there was a certain amount of he-man drinking among the technicians, and that drinking repeatedly led to challenges to her authority. "Remember, I was a woman, one of the very few on an executive level at CBC," she says, "and I was from New York, and I was a Jew. I was everything you weren't supposed to be. It was not a good time to be in Canada, at least not for me."

But the work progressed. She hired an actor to play the homespun philosopher, Wally Maclean, and another to play the mute role of a symbolic young man going north for the first time. There had been no such character in the radio drama — he was just some-body Maclean talked about — but TV always needs to *show* every-thing that radio leaves to the imagination. And occasionally this has a miraculous effect. Miss Pearlman was determined to transfer Gould's whole opening "trio sonata" onto film, so when Nurse Schroeder started talking about the geese flying over Hudson Bay, Miss Pearlman showed us the geese in the air, and when Professor Vallee started grumbling about the North, she showed us the grum-bling in a clubby Toronto bar. When Phillips then began talking about the government's role in the North, the camera wandered into Ottawa's Department of Northern Affairs and showed us row on row of filing cabinets. And since Gould wanted his three characters talking simultaneously, Miss Pearlman very skillfully managed to get her three images on the screen simultaneously. Gould's trio sonata thus became a kind of sextet. When he saw it, he loved it. After looking at seven hours of unedited rushed, he pronounced them "absolutely remarkable."

Getting photographic material for such sequences was a lot more complicated than taping five interviews for radio. While Gould had made his one jaunt to Churchill in June, and later done his inter-views at his convenience, Miss Pearlman had to take her actors and her TV crew northward on her rented railway car in November. "It was forty-five degrees below zero when we got there," she recalls. "If you took off your glove, your hand began to feel burning. The only hotel was a Quonset hut, but there was a telegram waiting for me:

MAY WE RECOMMEND THE MONTEVIDEO EXCELSIOR — EIGHT PRESIDENTIAL SUITES, 3 BANQUET ROOMS, 2 SALT-WATER SWIMMING POOLS, SEASIDE DINER...FOR YOUR MID SEASON VACATION.

CORDIALLY,
G. GOULD, MANAGER

"Churchill was a town of about two thousand souls, and there was just one main street," Miss Pearlman says. "Beyond that, on the edge of town, there was a ring of shacks where the Indians lived, and many of them had no windows. I mean, they were open to the air, at forty-five below zero. I don't know how they survived. A lot of them were drunk all the time. I felt very bad. And another thing was that there were all these abandoned dogs up there. I remember one of them was a Great Dane, and Danes don't have the skin for that kind of weather. They were all scarred and starving and desperate. We were filming there for five days. I felt very bad."

Back in the semitropical metropolis of Toronto, Miss Pearlman found Gould "charming, nourishing, and supportive," but also very busy with his recordings. The language they had in common, while she worked on her film about solitude under his rather distant scrutiny, was not television but music. "It had to do with how lonely I was," she recalls. "I didn't know anyone in Toronto. He knew how I felt, not very happy." This was the occasion on which he played her *Die Frau ohne Schatten*, and the following week there occurred an even more remarkable scene.

Once again, Gould arranged for Miss Pearlman to use a piano in an empty CBC studio, looked in on her after his late-night recording session, and found her on the telephone to New York. Once again, he began to play, this time a Hindemith sonata. Once again, Miss Pearlman emerged from the control room. She happened to mention that she had heard that he had recently taped for the CBC something that nobody could imagine Gould playing, Chopin, the Sonata in B minor.

"Without saying anything, he started playing it," Miss Pearlman recalls. "Then all of a sudden, he got serious about it. It was like a switch being turned on. And he played the whole piece through from beginning to end. And it was the greatest performance I've ever heard in my life. I was more than stunned. At the end, he said, 'What do you think?' I said it was the best performance I'd ever heard. He said, 'Oh, it's not so good as the tape.' But I didn't agree. This was a live performance, and I told him that sometimes, even when he was recording, he should record a straight-through performance. Obviously, it made him acutely uncomfortable to play for a live audience. I remember going to his last performance of the Brahms concerto with Bernstein, and it was obvious that the person playing it was in great pain. But his playing for me now meant that he knew I was feeling awful. It was his gift to me, meaning, 'Hang in there.'"

The reviews in the summer of 1970 were generally favorable. The Toronto *Telegram*'s Kenneth Winters rightly judged that the television version was less daring than the radio original, but he added that it was "the first television production I have ever seen...which is a complete, organic and lyrical composition in sounds as well as a composition in pictures." But because television must show what it describes, the cameras showed the snow and ice that the radio had ignored, and this demonstration of what the fabled North actually looks like raised chauvinist hackles. "'The Idea of North' emerges as a foreigner's idea of Canada," the *Toronto Star* complained. "Still and icy landscapes stretch before the camera. Defensively dressed in hooded parkas and boots, inhabitants of shanty towns bustle along bleak streets. And it looks cold. So cold that you wouldn't want to live there...."

Such chamber-of-commerce carping overlooks the most important weakness in "The Idea of North" — and by implication in the whole "solitude trilogy" — which is that Gould never really told us what he thought about solitude. "I've always had some sort of intuition," he once said, "that for every hour that you spend in the company of other human beings you need X number of hours alone." And on another occasion, he declared that the basic theme of this whole trilogy was "that isolation is the indispensable component of human happiness." But how does solitude actually help or harm a man? How does it liberate him or cripple him? How does it enable him to see or prevent him from seeing? Is it a necessity or an accident? These would be difficult questions even if Gould were writing about them in the most straightforward way, but a radio drama spun out of other people's words was obviously the most ambiguous of approaches.

Janet Somerville astutely observed that Gould's passions concerned mainly the sounds that he heard inside his own head, and if this seems bizarre, it is only because we have all been trained in recent years to judge everyone in terms of his relations with other people. Anthony Storr, a lecturer in psychiatry at Oxford, argues that this is a major misconception, and he likes to cite Edward Gibbon's observation that "solitude is the school of genius." "It is widely believed that interpersonal relationships of an intimate kind are the chief, if not the only, source of human happiness," Storr wrote recently in *Solitude, A Return to the Self*. "Yet the lives of creative individuals often seem to run counter to this assumption. For example, many of the world's greatest thinkers have not reared families or formed close personal ties. This is true of Descartes, Newton, Locke, Pascal, Spinoza, Kant, Leibniz, Schopenhauer, Nietzsche, Kierkegaard and Wittgenstein." One could say much the same of Beethoven, Haydn, and Brahms, yet Gould never really

OTTO FRIEDRICH

tried to formulate or document any such theory, except as a personal preference of his own.

"I think for Gould the question of solitude must have been absolutely central," says Richard Sennett, the N.Y.U. sociology professor who has been working for several years on a book on the subject. "What solitude really does to people's sense of creativity — you can't really create difference without creating the sense of being alone. When you're in a community with other people, when what you express is what could be shared among all of them, that tends to be flat, tends to be ironed out. How does a person get the freedom to reflect, to be self-doubting without being self-indulgent? I suppose the writer who most resembles Gould is Wallace Stevens, with that notion of perfection in retreat. You also hear the silences of that kind of withdrawal in his poetry. Nothing escapes Stevens that isn't deeply, deeply considered. There's a kind of almost supernatural calm in his writing, and yet there's nothing studied about it. You just feel the lines flow one from the other, rather like what you sense in Gould's recording process...."

"Yes, it's very much me, in terms of what it says," Gould told one interviewer about his enigmatic explorations of the North, "— no matter how long Wally Maclean may take to say it — it's about as close to an autobiographical statement as I am likely to make at this stage of my life." As spoken, as broadcast, the aged surveyor's final peroration on the meaning of going north sounds shrewd and sagacious. And perhaps to prevent us from listening too closely, Gould suddenly dubbed in the Arctic strains of Sibelius's Fifth Symphony. But when one reads the actual words that Maclean was declaiming through all that Sibelius — supposedly representing Gould's "autobiographical statement" — they come perilously close to gibberish: "A few years back, certainly in human memory, people thought that this — well, what we call our North — presented a real challenge. Well, what form did they take? Hah! What form? As if everything must somehow have a form. This is hard, this is hard on you. He must notice that you're struggling a bit, eh? But what you're really saying then is something like this: That there was a time when the challenge was understandable. What challenge then? Oh, well, here you have to take it easy...." And so on.

In the way Gould presented "The Idea of North," he made it seem that these were his own ideas, his own creation. And yet he never signed the check. After Gould's brief opening statement, the listener never again hears him express any opinions whatever, never even hears him ask any questions. If anyone wants to take Wally Maclean's peroration as an expression of Gould's own views, all well and good, but Gould never committed himself to that. He remained offstage, the marionette-master, the magician. "Sure, he was a thinker, but very much a by-the-seat-of-the-pants thinker," says Littler of the *Star*. "He thought deeply, but he wasn't as worried by the contradictions in what he was saying as some people with more formal training in logical thought might be. There's an affinity between him and Marshall McLuhan, and I think he admired McLuhan's feeling that everything is provisional, that you make probes...." "What Glenn really thought about solitude, only Glenn knows," Miss Pearlman adds. "He designed his solitude to suit himself, like a pearly shell. He made it a work of art. He distanced himself from other people's emotions — and then he was brilliant."

Yet there were other people who could see through Gould's pearly shell, and read his invisible writings on the walls. More than a decade after making "The Idea of North," when Gould played a tape of it to Margaret Pacsu, who was collaborating with him on his jubilee record album, she began crying. "I suddenly understood what he was trying to do with these voices," she recalls. "It was a quartet of these beautifully balanced — there was a rhythm and a melody to it. Plus the underlying — Now careful, because I'm a good Hungarian-American here, and I will burst into tears in a minute. The sadness of this man was that he was unable to reach out and make a — a — an intimate, warm contact with anyone. That's why I found that devastating. Plus to be sitting there in front of the man and have this happen. He was — surprised, and quite pleased, and quite comforting — Excuse me —" Remembering that moment when she burst into tears while Gould played her "The Idea of North," she bursts into tears all over again.

OTTO FRIEDRICH

PART THREE:
TWO SOLITUDES,
OR MORE?

Hugh MacLennan

Two Solitudes

22

Marius sat on a log outside the sugar cabin and smoked his pipe in the dark. The air was warm, and the night throbbed with sound like the inside of a sea-shell. The hoarse noise of the falls underlay all other sounds, but he could hear crickets in the fields, and even the ringing of frogs floating up in slow waves from the marsh near the river. Somewhere in the village a dog's barks came in quick, broken volleys softened by distance as the animal barked at the moon. Marius looked down through the boles of the trees and saw the fields pale in the light of a first-quarter moon, the glimmer reflected from the church roof, and the wide path of light on the river beyond. The maple grove was a huge net of shadows suspended from the treetops with the open patches of ground whitened by the moon. As he looked down the ridge he saw the whole parish spread below him like a map. A little spit of land jutting out into the river was black with shadow on one side and white with moon-colour on the other. A thin spire of smoke rose from a single chimney in the Tallard house. He checked the chimneys off one by one and estimated that the fire was in the kitchen.

He did not move. His mind was tired from three months of worrying and scheming and dreaming of the things he would have to do if he were ever to appease the soreness within him. But tonight the peace and familiarity of the scene almost made him feel well again. He told himself that he was home. He would never go away from here if he could possibly stay. He had never wished to have this hatred in his life, this battle he was doomed to wage. He repeated that all he and his people had ever wished was to be let alone. And thinking this, he asked himself in sudden incredulity why he must wage a battle at all, why he had always been so wretched that a life's work would be too little to make up for it?

His right hand was in his pocket, and his moving fingers were crumpling the note his father had left in the cabin that morning. Words entered his mind: 'I will arise and go unto my father...' God knew he wanted to go home. His father had written in the note: 'This attitude you have, blaming everything you don't like on the English, is senseless. No one is harming you but yourself. If an Englishman heard you talking he'd think you were crazy. Come home and talk to me. You are only twenty-one and many things seem more important at that age than...'

In the darkness Marius' lips tightened. It was easy to say he was young; as easy as to say that the English had done him no harm. They had hounded him like a criminal for the past three months because he wished no part of their imperialism, that was all.

Normally, Marius would have let it go at that. But tonight he was not normal. The summer night and the sounds in the throbbing air had made him quiet. He asked himself if he really did hate the English, and why. By nature suspicious, he was suddenly suspicious even of himself. The face of Kathleen rose before his mind. But his hatred was caused by more than one woman alone. He had always hated them.

He got up and began slowly to walk among the maple trunks in the moonlight, his hands in his pockets and his head down. He felt he would become as empty as a broken bottle if he did not get an answer; that the sense would run out of everything unless he knew. His father's words returned: 'You are only twenty-one...' But perhaps that was just why he did see the truth, because he was too young to have sold out any part of himself? The English lessened him... that was it. Merely by their existence, they lessened a man. You could become great and powerful only if your own people were also great and powerful. But what could his people do when the English constantly choked them? What could the French do, alone against an entire continent, except breed children and hope?

He came back and sat on the log again, tapped out his pipe and refilled it. His father was fond of saying that the average Quebec farmer was not a nationalist; that he was the plainest, most decent land-worker in the world. But he, Marius, he was no average man. He could see the truth even if ignorant people couldn't. And the truth was that under the English a French-Canadian could not become great. You had to imitate the English or they refused to look at you. You had to do things their way. If you were different, they automatically regarded you as second-rate. If you wanted different

HUGH MACLENNAN

ends they called you backward. The Americans were just as bad. And all the time the English took what they wanted. They had the big business. They had the army, the railroads, the banks, they had everything. What was left to a man like himself but the Church, medicine, or the law? Father Arnaud at the seminary had said he was too personally ambitious to make a good priest. He set his teeth. Some day Father Arnaud... But now nothing was left but the law, for he knew he could never have the patience necessary to become a doctor. And in Quebec you could pick up lawyers at a dime a dozen.

He knocked out his pipe and rose, took a long look down the ridge and went back to the cabin. His nostrils caught the smell of dried-out lumber and the remaining reek of stale wood smoke. Inside the cabin the moonlight lay in a rectangle on the floor, preserving the cross made by the joints in the single window. He lit the candle, took off his boots and jacket and crawled into the sleeping bag with a sigh. He puffed out his cheeks and blew. The candle flickered; he blew again and it went out.

Marius was asleep when the English sergeant and the French plainclothesman flashed their electric torches on him. He tried to jump clear of the light. One light winked out, but the other followed him like a staring eye and his feet were caught in the sleeping bag and he knew he was helpless. He pulled himself half out of the bag and leaned back on his elbows.

A voice said in English, 'It's him, all right.'

Marius took a deep gulp of air and tried again to get his head free of the light; it was all he could see. The light followed him and he put his hand over his eyes.

The hidden voice spoke again, 'Get up!'

There was nothing else to do. He crawled out of the bag and rose without a word, sat on the bench and put on his shoes. A hand holding his jacket stretched out into the beam of the torch. 'You need this too. You're going places.'

He took the jacket. Then the light partially swung away from him, his pupils dilated in the semi-darkness and he was able to see the shadows of the men's forms. The one in uniform looked big and tough. He was the one with the light. He was leaning with his back to the closed door and the light revolved slowly as he played it from his wrist.

Marius straightened and put on his hat. 'What time is it?' he said.

He got no answer. He looked around and saw Labelle standing in the patch of moonlight thrown through the window.

'Don't make trouble and you won't be hurt,' Labelle said in French.

Marius stared at him. This was the last humiliation; one of his captors was French. When he reached the door the sergeant made a grab at his wrist, and before Marius knew what was happening, a handcuff was locked on it.

'God damn bastard!' Marius said.

He jerked his hand up to hit the sergeant, and the man's arm lifted with it. Then slowly, easily, the sergeant pressed his arm down again. Labelle came up on the other side and took his other arm and with his free hand pulled the door open. They jerked him outside, and the moonlight flowed over the three of them. They stood there in a clear patch in the maple grove, Marius panting softly as he strained with both arms locked by the men on either side of him, his chest expanded with air. Then, as the men jerked him forward, he stumbled and nearly fell.

'Come on,' Labelle said. 'You show some sense, eh?'

His eyes bright and angry in the moon, Marius scrambled to his feet. They walked through the shadows of the grove to the brink of the ridge, then down the path along the edge of the field. They were three tiny black smudges moving down the wide, moon-washed cloth of the hillside.

23

The next morning the whole parish knew that Marius had been arrested. Mme. Drouin had been wakened shortly after midnight by a Ford backfiring outside the store and had got out of bed and gone to the window to see what was happening. The sergeant and Labelle were driving away with another man between them, and she had recognized Marius by the set of his hat. One of the Bergerons also knew about it. He had been in the store playing checkers and had left when Drouin closed up. He had then got a lift into Sainte-Justine from François-Xavier Latulippe. In Sainte-Justine he knew a girl who worked in the station hotel, and when he was leaving the hotel by the back door he had seen the sergeant and Labelle drive up in the Ford and drag Marius out. Marius was handcuffed, and the police had kept him in a room in the hotel all night.

All morning people kept coming into Drouin's with more stories. A woman claimed she had heard a shot in the night and that Marius had been killed. When told he was not dead, she said he had certainly been wounded, because there was a bloodstain on the road near her house. Drouin said he didn't know for sure, but he wouldn't be surprised but what the surveyors had something to do about it. The surveyors were from the government, and nothing good ever happened when the government had anything to do with it. Then Frenette came in and said he had been speaking with Father Beaubien. The priest had told him only one thing: that he knew who had reported Marius' hiding place to the police.

When Athanase entered the store for his mail, just before noon, the men all glanced at each other and only Drouin spoke to him. He immediately guessed what had happened, and his face was sharp with anger as he took his letters and walked out. He climbed into his carriage and started the mare on her way home. Then he saw Father Beaubien coming down the road from the porch of his presbytery to speak to him.

Athanase reined in the mare and glanced over his shoulder. He saw that the men had all come out of the store and were now standing around the gasoline pump watching.

The priest's face was stern. 'You'd better come inside with me, Mr. Tallard.'

Athanase continued to hold the reins. 'I don't think that is necessary, Father.'

The priest walked to the side of the carriage and stood very erect, one hand on his pendant cross, the other at his side. 'I take it you know the police have arrested Marius? He was taken off your own land like a criminal.' A quiet intensity entered Father Beaubien's voice. 'That is what comes of your friendship with foreigners, Mr. Tallard. It was Mrs. Methuen who told the police where to find your son.'

Athanase flushed with anger. It seemed incredible. Then he remembered that the children had seen Marius up in the maple grove. They had probably seen him leave the sugar cabin.

'Do you need any more proof that I was right? You let Paul play with those English children, you make friends with them yourself. Now are you satisfied?'

Again Athanase glanced over his shoulders. There were nearly twenty people in front of the store now, all watching.

'I intend to protect my parish, Mr. Tallard,' the priest said slowly. 'The sort of things that happened last night — it is only one of many such examples we can look forward to if you have your way. Now then, I insist that you drop all plans for this factory. I insist that you come back to the Church and live like a Christian.'

Anger choked Athanase. 'I won't stand for this. Who do you think you are — giving orders to me?'

The priest's large knuckles whitened as he clenched his hand on the seat-rail of the carriage. 'All right, Mr. Tallard... I've done the best I could.' Without taking his eyes from Athanase's face, he nodded sideways. 'Those people there — my parishioners — they're watching us. They aren't fools. They know a lot more than you think they do. They're waiting to see what will happen.'

His lips a straight line, Athanase continued to stare at Father Beaubien's set face.

'On Sunday, without naming names,' the priest said steadily, 'I shall tell the people the truth about you. I shall tell them that you are no longer a good Catholic. I shall tell them that you are a bad man and a bad example. I shall warn them against having any further dealings with you. It will be known to every voter in your constituency that you no longer consent to receive the sacraments of their Church. They will know that God will not bless them if they elect a man like you to represent them. I think you know as well as I what this will mean to you, Mr. Tallard?' He stopped. 'Do you still want to take your choice?'

Athanase felt the blood rush to his head and his hand clenched on the whip-handle. 'I will not be talked to in this way!' he shouted. 'Not by anyone!'

He raised the whip and the watching men, seeing his shoulder rise with it, were appalled by the thought that he was going to strike the priest. Father Beaubien stood absolutely still, watching him. Then, still with the whip above his head, Athanase said between his teeth, 'No one has ever dared talk to a member of my family like this in our parish... not in more than two hundred years. You keep away from me! You keep out of my affairs, or by God...'

With a quick turning movement he swung around and brought the whip down with a crack on the mare's flank. The animal reared in the shafts and plunged wildly, then went down the road in a gallop, and Athanase bent forward holding the reins. By the time his gate was reached the mare had slowed to a trot. The welt made by the whip lay in a long, ugly line along her chestnut flank.

HUGH MACLENNAN

As Athanase took the harness off the mare he made up his mind. He would not remain in the position where anyone could presume to talk to him as Father Beaubien had talked to him this summer. Ever since the death of his first wife this moment had been coming. But he was finished with being between two stools now; he was finished with it for the rest of his life, and he would show the whole world that he was to be left alone.

MARIE-CLAIRE BLAIS

TRANSLATED BY DEREK COLTMAN

A SEASON IN THE LIFE OF EMMANUEL

I

Grand-mère Antoinette's feet dominated the room. They lay there like two quiet, watchful animals, scarcely twitching at all inside their black boots, always ready to spring into action; two feet bruised by long years of work in the fields (opening his eyes for the first time in the dusty morning light, he couldn't see them yet, was not yet aware of the hidden wound in the leg, beneath the woolen stocking, of the ankles swollen within their prisons of leather and laces...), two noble and pious feet (did they not make the journey to church once every morning, even in winter?), two feet brimming with life, and etching forever in the memories of those who saw them, even only once, their somber image of authority and patience.

Born without fuss, this winter morning, Emmanuel was listening to his grandmother's voice. Immense and all-powerful, she seemed to be ruling the whole world from her armchair. (Don't cry, what have you got to cry about? Your mother has gone back to work on the farm. Just you keep quiet till she gets home. Ah, you're already so selfish, already so wicked. Already in a temper!) He called for his mother. (You've picked a bad time to be born, we've never been so poor, it's a hard winter for everyone, the war, the food shortage, and you the sixteenth too...) She sat complaining to herself in a low voice, telling the beads of a gray rosary hanging from her waist. (I've got my rheumatism too, but no on ever mentions it. I have my troubles too. And besides I hate newborn babies; insects they are, crawling around in the dust! You'll behave just like the others, you'll be ignorant and cruel and bitter.... You didn't give a thought to all the worries you were bringing me, I have to think of everything, what name to give you, the christening...)

It was cold inside the house. There were faces all around him; figures kept appearing. He looked at them but didn't recognize them yet. Grand-mère Antoinette was so huge that he couldn't see all of her. He was afraid. He shrank into himself, closing up like a shell. (Enough of that, said the old woman, look around you, open your eyes, I'm here, I give the orders here! Look at me, properly, I am the only one here who is worthy of this house. I am the one who sleeps in the scented room, I store the soap under my bed...) "We shall have plenty of time," Grand-mère Antoinette said, "there is no hurry for today..."

(His grandmother had a vast bosom, he couldn't see her legs under the heavy skirts, dry sticks, cruel knees, such strange garments swaddling her body as it shivered in the cold.) He tried to hook his delicate fists onto her knees, to bury himself in the cave of her lap (for he was discovering that she was so thin beneath those mountains of cloth, those rough skirts, that for the first time he was not afraid of her.) But those woolen clothes still kept him at a distance from the icy bosom, from the breasts she was crushing into herself with one hand in a gesture of alarm or self-defense; for whenever you approached that body, stifled inside its austere dress, you felt that you were approaching some sleeping freshness within her, an ancient and proud desire that none had ever fulfilled — you wanted to go to sleep in her, as in some warm river, to lie and rest upon her heart. But she kept Emmanuel at a distance with that same gesture of the hand that had once rejected love, and punished man's desires.

"Oh Lord, another boy, what is to become of us?" But she quickly regained her confidence: "I am strong, child. You can give your life into my keeping. Put your trust in me."

He listened to her. Her voice rocked him with a monotonous, defeated chant. She wrapped him in her shawl, not fondling him but rather plunging him into the folds of cloth and into the smells of them as though into a bath. He held his breath. Sometimes, without meaning to, she scratched him slightly with her bent fingers; she held him aloft and shook him, and once more he called for his mother. (Bad boy, she said impatiently.) He dreamed of his mother's breast coming to appease his thirst and quiet his rebellious cries.

"Your mother is out working, as usual," Grand-mère Antoinette said. "Today is just a day like any other. You think only of yourself. I've got work to do too. Newborn babies are dirty. They disgust me.

MARIE-CLAIRE BLAIS

But you see, I'm good to you, I wash you, I take care of you, and you will be the first to be glad when I die..."

But Grand-mère Antoinette believed herself to be immortal. And her whole triumphant being was immortal for Emmanuel too, as he lay gazing up at her in astonishment. "Ah, my child, no one is listening to you, there is no use in crying. You will soon learn that you're alone in this world!"

"You too will be afraid..."

The beams of the sun shone in through the window. In the distance, the landscape was confused, unapproachable. Emmanuel could hear voices, steps all around him. (He trembled with cold as his grandmother washed him, or rather drowned him several times in icy water...) "There," she said, "it's all over. There's nothing to be afraid of. I'm here. One gets used to everything, you'll see."

She smiled. He felt the desire to respect her silence; he no longer dared to complain, for it seemed to him suddenly that he had already been familiar for a long while with cold, with hunger, and perhaps even with despair. In the cold sheets, in the cold room, he had suddenly been filled with a strange patience. The knowledge had come to him that all this misery would never end; but he had consented to live. Standing at the window, Grand-mère cried out, almost with joy:

"Here they are. I can feel them coming up the stairs, listen to their voices. Here they all are, the grandchildren, the children, the cousins, the nieces, and the nephews; you think they've been buried under the snow on their way to school, or else dead years ago, but they are always there, under the tables, under the beds, spying on me with their eyes shining in the dark. They are waiting for me to hand out lumps of sugar to them. There are always one or two around my armchair, or my rocking chair when I rock myself of an evening...

"They snigger, they play with my shoelaces. They run after me the whole time with that stupid sniggering of theirs, with that begging, hypocritical look in their eyes. I chase them away like flies, but they come back, they fasten themselves on me like a bunch of vermin, they gnaw at me..."

Grand-mère Antoinette was admirable as she tamed the tide of children roaring around her feet. (Where did they come from? Did they rise up out of the darkness, out of the black night? They smelled of the night, they spoke with the voice of the night, they crawled around the bed, and they had the familiar smell of poverty...)

"Ah, that's enough!" Grand-mère Antoinette said. "I don't want to hear another sound from any of you, out of my way all of you, go back to your beds... Vanish, I don't want to see any more of you, ah! heavens, what a smell!"

But then, accompanying the distribution with a few blows of her cane, she handed out the lumps of sugar they were waiting for with open mouths, panting with impatience and hunger, the sugar, the crumbs of chocolate, all the grimy treasures she had accumulated and now emptied out again from her skirts and from her strait-laced bodice. "Get away, get away," she cried.

She drove them off with an all-powerful hand (later, he was to see her walking in the same way through a host of chickens, and rabbits, and cows, sowing curses broadcast as she went, to recover some tearful baby that had fallen in the mud), she beat them back toward the staircase, still throwing them the lumps of sugar, which they scrabbled for as best they might, this flood of children, of animals, that later, once again, would emerge from their mysterious lair and come back, scratching at the door anew, to beg from their grandmother.

His mother came in. He recognized her. She didn't come over to him, not at first. He was ready to believe she had deserted him. He recognized her sad face, her drooping shoulders. She didn't seem to remember having brought him into the world that very morning. She was cold. He saw her hands clenching around the brimming milk pail. (He's over there, Grand-mère Antoinette said, he's hungry, he's been crying all day.) His mother was silent. She would always be silent. Some of his brothers were coming back from school and knocking the snow off their boots against the door. (Come here, Grand-mère said, but she hit out at them lightly with the tip of her cane when they passed under the lamp.) In the distance the sun was still red on the hill.

"And Number Seven, what have you done with Number Seven? As long as I live, you'll continue to go to school..."

His mother's waist was gently bellying out: she was bending over as she set down the second pail of milk.

"To think they've gone and lost Number Seven in the snow again," Grand-mère Antoinette said.

The bucket ran over. Little drops of milk rolled across the floor in the lamplight. Grand-mère was scolding, reprimanding, sometimes slapping a chapped cheek as it passed within her reach.

"You ought to thank me, ah! if I weren't here you'd never get to school, would you, eh?"

"Grand-mère," a man's voice said from the depths of the kitchen, "school isn't necessary."

The man's voice was merely a murmur. It faded, it disappeared. Standing leaning against the wall, her head tilted slightly onto one shoulder, his mother listened in silence. Perhaps she was asleep. Her dress was open, showing her pale, drooping breasts. Her sons looked at her in silence, and they too were waiting, waiting for night to fall on the hill.

"A hard winter," the man said, rubbing his hands together over the stove. "But perhaps it will be a good spring..."

He removed his snow-soaked clothes. He put them to dry on a chair near the fire. He took off his thick boots, then his socks. The smell of wet clothing spread through the house.

(He had taken everything from his mother's heart, he had drunk all her milk with an avid mouth, and now he pretended to be asleep...)

"There are orphanages too," the man's voice said.

"I prefer the Noviciat," Grand-mère Antoinette replied. "It doesn't cost anything, and they teach them how to behave."

"But I don't understand why they need all this schooling for," the father muttered into his beard.

"Ah! Men don't understand about these things," Grand-mère Antoinette said with a sigh. "But Grand-mère," the man's voice continued in the depths of the kitchen, while the flames flickered slowly up from the stove (and a little girl at the window looked out with boredom at the setting sun, hands clasped behind her back), "Grand-mère, I know more about life than you do, I know what my children are destined for!"

"For God!" Grand-mère Antoinette replied.

His mother took him in her arms. She was protecting him now with her fragile body, supporting his head so that he could feed and drink in peace; but Grand-mère's long silhouette was still keeping watch, very close, driven by some strange duty to find out what was happening in the hidden parts of his being, sometimes interrupting the insipid meal he was absorbing in a dream. (He was draining his mother, he was drinking up everything inside her!) She, his mother, said nothing, no longer answering, calm, deep, deserted perhaps. He was there, but she had forgotten him. He was producing no echo in her, either of joy or of desire. He slipped into her and lay there without hope.

"That child sees everything," Grand-mère Antoinette said, "you can't hide anything from him." (What shall we call him? David? Joseph? There have been too many Josephs in recent generations. They were weak men! The Emmanuels have all been strong, they took good care of their land.)

"Let us call him Emmanuel."

His mother listened solemnly. Sometimes she lifted her head in surprise, her lip trembled, and she seemed to want to say something, but she said nothing. They heard her sigh, then go to sleep.

"We must settle when is to be baptized," Grand-mère said.

The father spoke of waiting until spring. "Spring is a good time for baptisms," he said.

"Next Sunday," Grand-mère Antoinette said. "And I'll take him down to be baptized myself."

The mother bowed her head.

"My wife thinks Sunday will do very well too," the man said.

She sat there in her armchair, majestic and contented, and the dark spread little by little over the hill, veiling the white forest and the silent fields. (You should thank me for taking these decisions out of your hands, Grand-mère Antoinette thought in her armchair.)

The man yawned beside the fire. Grand-mère Antoinette was throwing him fleeting, sidelong glances. No, I shall not lift a finger to serve that man, she thought to herself. He thinks I shall do as my daughter does; but I won't bring him his bowl of warm water, or his clean clothes. No, no, I won't budge from my armchair. He is expecting a woman to come and wait on him. But I won't get up.

But something moved beneath the pointed toe of her boot, something shapeless that she tried to push away. Lord! a mouse, a squirrel, there's something under my dress...

"Go back to the school and bring back Number Seven, I'll teach him to dawdle about on the roads. Put on your boots, go on, you. You're not to go out, Jean-Le Maigre, you're coughing too much! Where were you just then? Were you reading under the table again?"

"I'll burn your book for you," the father's voice said. "I've told you, Grand-mère, we don't want books in this house."

"Jean-Le Maigre is talented; Monsieur le Curé said so," Grand-mère Antoinette replied.

"He's consumptive," the man said, "what good can it possibly do him to learn anything? I can't think what that Curé thinks he's about — there's nothing to be done with Jean-Le Maigre. He's got one lung rotting away!"

His mother listened. Tomorrow, at the same hour, they would say the same words all over again, and she would make that same slight movement of the head, that sign of silent protest in Jean-Le Maigre's defense, but, like today, she would merely listen, say nothing, perhaps feel astonishment that life should repeat itself with such precision, and she would think again: "How long the night's going to be." A strand of hair fell across her brow; she had already closed her eyes, and now she bent over her latest child, her face still gloomy and half asleep.

Standing on one leg, book in hand, Jean-Le Maigre gazed searchingly at the newborn infant with a moist gaze. "Who's he?" he asked, without interest. Without waiting for the reply, he coughed, sneezed, and disappeared again behind his book.

"I can see you, Jean-Le Maigre," Grand-mère said. "You think you're safe, but I can see you."

"You can't see me. No one can see me when I'm reading," Jean-Le Maigre answered.

"Watch out then; I'm going to make you drink your syrup soon," Grand-mère said.

"I'm not here," Jean-Le Maigre replied. "I'm dead."

"Perhaps you are," was Grand-mère's reply, "but I'm alive, and as long as I'm alive you'll drink your syrup."

"But what good can it possibly do?" the man's voice asked. The old woman thought of pronouncing one of the curses that the man beside the stove was calmly expecting; he was shrugging his shoulders, already feeling the pleasurable blow of her insult. But Grand-mère Antoinette, disdainfully smiling in her armchair, chose to remain silent — no, this time she would not say that word, she would remain proud and unapproachable. "Well," the man said, turning toward the stove, with its now dying fire, "you're right, Grand-mère, it's just as well they should get used to going to school in winter..."

Grand-mère Antoinette, speaking in a clipped, contemptuous tone, replied that she had known harder winters than any of them, and the man, dressing himself clumsily in the shadows, suddenly felt the familiar, daily sense of shame that only the presence of this woman could inspire in him. "Winters as black as death," Grand-mère Antoinette went on, with contempt for the man's body, watching him out of the corner of one eye. "Oh! It's not the first I've seen...."

"Yes, it's a gloomy evening," the man commented in weary tones. With his dirt-blackened nails, Jean-Le Maigre was gracefully turning the pages of his book. As happy as a prince in his tattered clothes, he was in a hurry to read it.

"Oh heavens, how funny it is," he exclaimed through a wild burst of laughter.

"I wouldn't laugh if I were you," the father said. "I might take that book of yours away from you."

Jean-Le Maigre shook his head, revealing the pale brow beneath his hair. "It's too late, I've read every page. You can't burn the pages I've read. They're all written here!"

For the first time, the man raised his eyes in a somber gaze toward the mother and child. Then he forgot them again immediately. He looked at the bowl of dirty water on the stove. He was beginning to feel more and more constricted in his waistcoat.

"It's stifling in here," he said.

The button suddenly burst off his shirt collar. "It's not going to be me who sews that button on," Grand-mère Antoinette said. "You know it'll be you," the man replied, "it is always you, Grand-mère!"

"Jean-Le Maigre," Grand-mère said, raising a triumphant head to look at her grandson, "listen, the Noviciat... There are infirmaries, warm dormitories.... You'd like it there..."

"Oh, Grand-mère," Jean-Le Maigre replied from behind his book, "let me read in peace and cough in peace, since I enjoy it."

Jean-Le Maigre coughed again. Oh Lord, it felt so good! He sneezed, he laughed, he wiped his nose on his dirty shirt.

"Grand-mère," he said, "I know this book by heart now."

"I'm going to give him a hiding, that Jean-Le Maigre of yours," the father's voice said.

"Come over by me," Grand-mère Antoinette said to Jean-Le Maigre. "No one can hurt you when you're near me."

Jean-Le Maigre scratched his nose, then his ears. "What is it now," Grand-mère Antoinette asked. "Nothing," Jean-Le Maigre replied. She pulled the ragged child against her, brushed the thin fringe of hair back from his forehead, and made a discovery that astounded no one.

"My God, his head is full of lice again!"

Michael Greenstein

Third Solitudes:
Tradition and Discontinuity in
Jewish-Canadian Literature

Introduction

From his outpost on the shores of Lake Ontario, that curious American onlooker Leslie Fiedler observes that the Jewish writer in Canada inhabits a "No-man's-Land, the Demilitarized Zone" where he is "invisible from South of the Border as well as from the Other Side of the Atlantic."[1] While Fiedler singles out Leonard Cohen and Mordecai Richler, he overlooks the founder of Jewish-Canadian literature, Abraham Moses Klein — an ironic oversight since Fiedler's first novel, *The Second Stone*, appeared a decade after Klein's *The Second Scroll* first appeared in 1951. Other names need to be added to those mentioned by Fiedler, for in the relatively brief period since World War II when mid-century modernism shades into *fin-de-siècle* postmodernism, Jewish writers have contributed significantly to Canadian literature. Irving Layton and Leonard Cohen in Montreal, Phyllis Gotlieb in Toronto, and Miriam Waddington and Eli Mandel on the prairies have all paid homage to Klein in their poetry. And if Klein has influenced his fellow poets, so too in fiction are Jewish-Canadian authors indebted to him, for Klein's seminal short novel, *The Second Scroll*, acts as a point of departure for short stories and novels by Mordecai Richler, Henry Kreisel, Adele Wiseman, Jack Ludwig, Norman Levine, Naim Kattan, Monique Bosco, and Matt Cohen. At first glance, such a diverse group of writers appears to have little in common, but closer scrutiny reveals their recurrent attempts to mediate between tradition and modernism, home and exile, Jewish-Canadian particularism and universal significance. To understand better the ambiguities of this mediation in the works of Klein and those who follow him, it is necessary to look south of the border and across the Atlantic, for other voices in the Diaspora....

...So much Jewish-Canadian fiction deals with the quests of anti-heroes, orphans, adolescents, and immigrants for their parents, their homeland, and a meaningful tradition. The story concludes with Klein's or Kreisel's final words to all exiled intermediaries: "It was impossible for me to see you... You wanted to ask me things. I have no answers. But you are in my heart. Let me be in your heart also. We had an almost meeting. Perhaps that is not much. And yet it is something. Remember me."[2] This understatement invites invisibility yet underscores an entire theory about anxiety of influence, including Klein's own wrestling with British and biblical traditions which beg to be remembered. Within a Jewish context, direct encounter seems impossible, forbidden in the anti-representational second commandment and forestalled in *The Second Scroll* where Klein's messianic Uncle Melech Davidson exceeds the diasporic reach of his nameless nephew. In addition to this aniconic, temporal agon, there appears a Buberesque dialogue, heart-to-heart, if not face-to-face; forever asking, these writers have memory, desire, and metaphor if not ultimate answers. Klein, through his disappearing double in *The Second Scroll*, foreshadows absence and exile in Jewish-Canadian literature, a cultural mediation that remembers its tradition....

...Henry Kreisel intuitively deconstructs the notion of marginality in a letter to Roy Daniells in 1968, one year after the appearance of Derrida's early essays:

> If something is "marginal," then it must be marginal to something. So that if the point of reference is a specific *Canadian historical experience*, then clearly my own novels, for instance, are marginal to it. And so is Klein's *Second Scroll*. But what about his *Rocking Chair*? I have even more problems with the image if I remove it from the Canadian context, applying a test I learned from you, but applying it in reverse... If you set Kafka beside Hasek, then Hasek is clearly more central to Czech experience, and Kafka is marginal. But what a margin!...I realize that your conception of the margin makes some provision for accommodating writers like Kafka, but at the same time the image of the "margin" doesn't stand by itself. It has to be explained, and that weakens its impact. On the other hand, I grant you that it has qualities of "teasing" us "out of thought."[3]

MICHAEL GREENSTEIN

With their reversals, displacements, and thoughtful teasings Kreisel's marginal comments move in a Derridean direction or Kafkaesque trajectory that seeks a *via negativa,* foregrounding *The Second Scroll* and subsequent Jewish writing in Canada.

A Canadian Derridean, Robert Kroetsch, traces margins, mazes, dislocations, irresolution, blurred photographs, and genealogical quest patterns in Canadian writing: "A.M. Klein, in *The Second Scroll* (1951), anticipates all these quests (a kind of reverse migration) with a quest that is religious and political and formal in its implications."[4] Indeed, Kroetsch's postmodern quest differs from Northrop Frye's earlier observations comparing Jewish and Canadian histories: "I use a Jewish metaphor because there is something Hebraic about the Canadian tendency to read its conquest of a promised land, its Maccabean victories of 1812, its struggle for the central fortress on the hill at Quebec, as oracles of a future. It is doubtless only an accident that the theme of one of the most passionate and intense of all Canadian novels, A.M. Klein's *The Second Scroll,* is Zionism."[5] But for Jewish writers the promised land may lie elsewhere, the sense of loss may override victories, the central fortress may be replaced by a decentred diaspora — not as oracles of a future, but of a past to be regained. Alternating between dystopia and utopia, the Diaspora's labyrinth frustrates Zion. Frye's question about Canadian identity — where is there? — becomes compounded by a Jewish question — where was there? Klein's nameless narrator, a no-name man in no-man's land, mediates the transformations between old and new worlds, old and new languages, Zion and Diaspora. With a Hebrew alphabet, written from right to left, and an historical pull to eastern ancestries, Jewish writers reverse migrations and revert to origins. What Klein's double or multiple exposure captures are Fiedler's sense of Canada's invisibility, the first scroll's aniconic injunction, the irresolution of negatives, Kreisel's almost meeting, and Derrida's trace.

Another of Derrida's key linguistic and philosophic concepts is *différance.* The modern Jewish writer in Canada experiences *différance* not only with respect to a majority gentile culture, but also in relation to his own religion from which he is alienated. This "dissemination" of traditional meaning and authority places the writer in a "decentred" system affording unlimited freedom that must somehow be restrained through the formal act of writing. Jewish-Canadian writers find themselves decentred in several ways:

they may look beyond the walls of their ghetto toward a Canadian vastness in nature or a gentile majority in society; they may look to the United States as a major centre of the Diaspora or they may look toward various European centres for their roots. To the Canadian sense of lonely long-distance runners probing a receding horizon, the Jewish perspective adds a belief that the answer to all quests and questions is always over the next horizon. But, there is never an answer. *Différance* is wandering — nomadic texts, mean(der)ings. Derrida also uses *différer* in the sense of "to defer." Just as spatial dimensions multiply and scatter, so time is deferred both through messianic rejection and backward through tracing of origins. Memory undermines the pragmatism of the present. In addition to spatial and temporal interference, religious and linguistic dissemination lead to a disorienting of identity, so that the marginal Jew fills absence with writing, revising a tradition from his own secular perspective. Mediation, displacement, deferment, exile, absence, equivocal meaning — these are the themes not only of Derridean interpretation, but of Jewish writing in Canada from Klein to the present....

...Leonard Cohen also shifts boundaries of the Diaspora in his departure from Klein's more central Torah, yet he too tries to capture its spirit in "Lines from my Grandfather's Journal":

> Doubting everything that I was made to write. My dictionaries groaning with lies. Driven back to Genesis. Doubting where every word began. What saint had shifted a meaning to illustrate a parable. Even beyond Genesis, until I stood outside my community, like the man who took too many steps on Sabbath. Faced a desolation which was unheroic, unbiblical, no dramatic beasts.
>
> The real deserts are outside tradition...
>
> Prayer makes speech a ceremony. To observe this ritual in the absence of arks, altars, a listening sky: this is a rich discipline.[6]

In his ritual of absence, Cohen's observant skepticism celebrates tradition and modern individual talent. Dictionaries lie because their definitions fail to capture metaphoric resonances of poetry, so Cohen traces language back to absent origins via parabolic drifts and shifting meanings. To revise family lines the Jewish secularist is driven back in memory even as he is driven forward through a modern Canadian landscape. Just as Kreisel's Hassid tells his secular counterpart to remember his grandfather, so Leonard Cohen — a postmodern Jew from Westmount — remembers his grandfather in strangely discontinuous songs that returned to a Hassidic past destroyed by Hitler. Cohen shares both the emptiness the Hassid had felt after the Holocaust and the mystical presence that later filled him in Montreal. These orphans and immigrants look for substitute fathers in their grandfathers' texts, and reject real uncles in favour of the mythical. Disciples of this rich anarchy step from the vanguard of postmodernism backward to Klein's grandfatherly journal and Kafka's parable: "Leopards break into the temple and drink the sacrificial chalices dry; this occurs repeatedly, again and again: finally it can be reckoned beforehand and becomes part of the ceremony."[7] Klein, Cohen, Kafka, and Derrida open the ceremony of the Diaspora where meanings shift, outsiders are admitted as insiders, and dramatic beasts exchange places with priests in a typically Jewish conflict with Jewry. The Torah procession may recede for these secular writers, but they retain just enough of the fervour of Hassidic joy on one side, and moral outrage or prophetic indignation on the other. In exile they write home.

Much of this equivocation in negative dialectics and deconstruction derives from the uncertainties and insecurities of exile. A classic modern statement on homelessness appears in Freud's essay on "The Uncanny" (1919) with its lengthy etymological opening equating *heimlich* and *unheimlich*, home and homelessness, canny and uncanny. After quoting extensively from dictionaries in several languages (including Hebrew), Freud concludes: "Thus *heimlich* is a word the meaning of which develops towards an ambivalence, until it finally coincides with its opposite, *unheimlich*."[8] If deconstructors mine this essay for its reversals of "uncanny," so too do modern Jewish hermeneuts, as Freud's essay masks his attitude to a Judaic past. As Charles Péguy has said of the Jews, "Being elsewhere [is] the great vice of this race, the great secret virtue, the great vocation of this race."[9] This "being elsewhere," this *différance*, constitutes the unresolved ambivalence of otherness in a ubiquitous diaspora from Europe to North America. Jewish-Canadian literature, in particular, turns back to a lost European tradition to help forge a new identity in its relatively unsettled Canadian homeland of vestigial ghettos.

In "Autobiographical" Klein proceeds "out of ghetto streets," wanders away from "home and the familiar" to seek a fabled city in "Space's vapours and Time's haze," but his passage from home is indeed a "dying off." Sensitized to exile, Klein pauses to observe the Indian Reserve at Caughnawaga, just outside of Montreal: "This is a grassy ghetto, and no home."[10] What for Klein has been a physical reality in his childhood, takes on figurative nuances in later writers. George Woodcock, for instance, relies on this metaphor to underline Canadian themes of isolation and division: "Jewish writers have also revealed with a peculiar force and sensitivity the tensions that are characteristic of Canadian life.... It might be a metaphorical exaggeration to describe Canada as a land of invisible ghettos, but certainly it is, both historically and geographically, a country of minorities that have never achieved assimilation."[11] Mordecai Richler delineates Montreal's invisible ghetto: the "ghetto of Montreal has no real walls and no true dimensions. The walls are the habits of atavism and the dimensions are an illusion. But the ghetto exists all the same."[12] Demonstrating that atavistic habits die hard, no less intrepid a *voyageur* than Irving Layton sketches his view of the Hochelaga: "In Montreal the dominant ethnic groups stare at one another balefully across their self-erected ghetto walls. Three solitudes. I remember this feeling of anxiety I had as a boy whenever I crossed St Denis Street. This street marked the border between Jewish and French-Canadian territories. East of St Denis was hostile Indian country densely populated with church-going Mohawks somewhat older than myself waiting to ambush me."[13]

At the very heart of Jewish-Canadian literature, this tension between erecting and destroying ghetto walls, between constructing boundaries and assimilating territories, between *voyageur* and blind *voyeur*, preoccupies the major poets and novelists who, for the most part, originate in Montreal's third solitude. They mediate between English and French solitudes, and Klein's "schizoid solitudes." Out of St Denis, St Dominique, and St Urbain, Layton, Bellow, Richler, and Klein dream pavement into Bible-land, combining street savvy with a transcending tradition where one-armed jugglers, tightrope walkers, pole-vaulters, dangling men, gymnasts of the spirit, and ambivalent acrobats defy gravity. From their intermediate vantage point, these writers and their ironic personae survey a Montreal which is at once both more and less than home, charged with more reality and human feelings than any other place.

Exile within Montreal's narrow ghetto may be carried over to the broader prairies, that other centre of Jewish-Canadian creativity. In

MICHAEL GREENSTEIN

"Driving Home," Miriam Waddington traverses prairie grain elevators and drives to the Volga on the world throughway to unearth ancestral roots. At the end of the Wandering Jew's peregrinations, the poet turns *schlemiel*, adopting a self-ironic persona in dispersed free verse:

> I am on my way home:
> home?
> Fool
> you *are* home
> you were home
> in the first place.[14]

But in tracing roots towards an origin, the displaced poet may discover that the first place is an illusion no longer retrievable, the nameless expanse of prairie and Diaspora. Waddington arrives at the same conclusion or unknown destination in "My travels" where she repeats that uncanny feeling of being at once lost and at home:

> I am homesick I
> am packing up
> I am going home
> but now I don't
> know anymore
> where home is.[15]

Home may be dispersed among the Promised Lands of America, Jerusalem, the *shtetlach* of Eastern Europe, or the capitals of Western Europe. If the modernist Jew perceives this century as a global ghetto, then he maps lines of demarcation, borders, boundaries, margins of discourse, and walls to contain his homelessness and childhood memories. In "Fortunes" Waddington is "untraditional, North American / Jewish, Russian, and rootless in all four," seeking "a homecoming / for my homeless half-and-half soul."[16] Culturally hyphenated in schizoid solitude, Jewish artists grapple with the paradoxes of ghetto cosmopolitanism or urban regionalism, of multiplicity and nothingness, rich sources and lack of status. Like Montreal's writers recapturing home, Waddington, Adele Wiseman, and Jack Ludwig travel across the prairies, the Atlantic, and Europe with an uncertain passport and burdensome baggage.

One of Richler's protagonists, another homeless half-and-half soul, thinks of himself as a guilty Diaspora Jew, carrying his double burden of the past and a copy of Maimonides' *Guide for the Perplexed*:

> Canadian-born, he sometimes felt as if he were condemned to lope slant-shouldered through this world that confused him. One shoulder sloping downwards, groaning under the weight of his Jewish heritage (burnings on the market square, crazed Cossacks on the rampage, gas chambers, as well as Moses, Rabbi Akiba, and Maimonides); the other thrust heavenwards, yearning for an inheritance, weightier than the construction of a transcontinental railway, a reputation for honest trading, good skiing conditions.[17]

More than just the shoulders of this Jewish-Canadian anti-hero are dislocated. As in Richler's dualistic confusions and cultural hyphenations (Canadian-born, slant-shouldered), and in response to an unstable inheritance, Jewish-Canadian literature mediates between marginal man and his discourse. Following Maimonides, authors of latter-day guides for the perplexed — Kafka, Derrida, Klein — advocate negatives, non-literal approaches to a modern diaspora, and a subversive resistance to closure. Their shoulders provide a unique slant or critical perspective on the dominant culture that articulates both an inside and outside view. In the absence of absolutes, their jeremiads and secular Hassidism offer an ethical and spiritual dimension that weighs them down and buoys them up. Breaking and joining with tradition, Jewish-Canadian memory rises out of lost homes and voices to populate a no-man's land with figures of the imagination.

Notes

1. Fiedler, "Some Notes on the Jewish Novel in English," in Sheps, ed., *Mordecai Richler*, p. 101. Fiedler echoes Edmund Wilson's remarks to the effect that the background of Canadian stories seems alien to England and the United States, but not strange enough to exercise the spell of the truly exotic. See Edmund Wilson, *O Canada*, pp. 10, 37, 41; see also Gerson, "Some Patterns of Exile in Jewish Writing of the Commonwealth," p. 104: Nadel, *Jewish Writers in North*

MICHAEL GREENSTEIN

America, xviii; Shechner, "Jewish Writers," in Hoffman, ed., *The Harvard Guide to American Writing,* p. 191 ff.

2. Lewisohn, "Forward," to Klein's *Hath Not a Jew* reprinted in Klein, *Collected Poems,* p. 350.

3. Quoted in Caplan, *Like One that Dreamed,* p. 113.

4. Ibid., p. 114.

5. Richler, "Their Canada and Mine," in Sinclair and Wolfe, ed., *The Spice Box,* p. 235. Several books on the New York Intellectuals have recently appeared and all of them overlap. For the most thorough history see Alexander Bloom, *Prodigal Sons.* See also Howe, *World of Our Fathers,* p. 588.

6. Kreisel, "Chassidic Song," *The Almost Meeting and Other Stories,* p. 35.

7. See Leonard Cohen, "Last Dance at the Four Penny," *Selected Poems 1956-1968,* 69; Mandel, "Snake Charmers," *Stony Plain,* p. 32; Gotlieb, *Ordinary, Moving,* pp. 1-8; and Gotlieb, "Hassidic Influences in the Work of A.M. Klein," in Mayne, ed., *The A.M. Klein Symposium,* pp. 47-64.

8. Layton, *The Pole -Vaulter,* p. 28.

9. Layton, *Collected Poems,* p. 330.

10. Waddington, *Say Yes,* p. 59.

11. Klein, *Collected Poems,* p. 234.

12. Kreisel, *The Almost Meeting,* p. 17.

13. Ibid., p. 21.

14. See Spiro, *Tapestry and Designs,* pp. 3-6; Fischer, *In Search of Jerusalem,* especially pp. 2-3, 207, for Klein's relationship to Spinoza, Hassidism, and Cabbala.

15. Quoted in Caplan, *Like One That Dreamed,* 197. See also Pollock, "From 'Pulver' to 'Portrait': A.M. Klein and the Dialectic."

16. Auerbach, *Mimesis,* pp. 1-20.

17. Adapted from Kafka, *The Basic Kafka,* p. 238.

DANIEL FRANCIS

THE IMAGINARY INDIAN: THE IMAGE OF THE INDIAN IN CANADIAN CULTURE

Part One: Taking the Image

One of the most famous historical paintings ever done on a Canadian theme is "The Death of General Wolfe" by Benjamin West. The huge canvas depicts the English general, James Wolfe, expiring on the Plains of Abraham outside the walls of Quebec City. In the background, his triumphant army is capturing Canada for British arms. Wolfe lies prostate in the arms of his grieving fellow officers. A messenger brings news of the victory, and with his last breath the general gives thanks. The eye is drawn to the left foreground where an Iroquois warrior squats, his chin resting contemplatively in his hand, watching as death claims his commander. The light shimmers on the Indian's bare torso, which looks as if it might be sculpted from marble.

From its unveiling in London in the spring of 1771, "The Death of Wolfe" was a sensation. It earned for its creator an official appointment as history painter to the King, and became one of the most enduring images of the British Empire, reproduced on tea trays, wall hangings and drinking mugs. West himself completed six versions of the painting. Today it still appears in history textbooks as an accurate representation of the past. Yet as an historical document, it is largely a work of fiction. In reality, Wolfe died apart from the field of battle and only one of the men seen in the painting was actually present. Other officers who were present at the death refused to be included in the painting because they disliked General Wolfe so much.

And the Indian? According to his biographers, Wolfe despised the Native people, all of whom fought on the side of the French,

BENJAMIN WEST, (1738-1820) *The Death of General Wolfe,* National Archives of Canada, C12248.

anyway. Certainly, none would have been present at his death. But that did not matter to Benjamin West. Unlike Wolfe, West admired the Noble Savage of the American forest. And so he included the image of a Mohawk warrior, posed as a muscular sage — a symbol of the natural virtue of the New World, a virtue for which Wolfe might be seen to have sacrificed his life.

II

When White Canadians of earlier generations asked themselves what is an Indian, how did they know what to respond? What information did they have on which to base an answer? By the end of the nineteenth century, there were about 127,000 officially designated Indians living in Canada. Non-Natives had little exposure to these people, most of whom lived on reserves isolated from the main centres of population. They were pretty much a forgotten people. When they gave Native people any thought at all, White Canadians

DANIEL FRANCIS

believed they were quickly disappearing in the face of disease, alcohol abuse and economic hardship.

For the vast majority of Whites, Indians existed only as images like that of the Mohawk warrior in Benjamin West's painting. These images originated with a handful of artists, writers and photographers who made the arduous journey into "Indian Country" and returned to exhibit what they had seen there. These image-makers to a large extent created the Imaginary Indian which Whites have believed in ever since.

Chapter Two: The Vanishing Canadian

...Paul Kane was the first artist in Canada to take the Native population as his subject. "The principal object of my undertaking," he later wrote, "was to sketch pictures of the principal chiefs and their original costumes, to illustrate their manners and customs, and to represent the scenery of an almost unknown country."[1] What made him decide to paint the Indians? Not even his biographer can say for sure. "There is no clear evidence to explain Kane's almost instant conversion at this time to the cause of painting Indians," writes Russell Harper. "A cynic might suggest that he saw a good thing and anticipated fame and fortune coming to him by means of a gallery of Canadian Indians."[2] Kane himself left no explanation for embarking on his great project.

Kane had had little personal exposure to Native people when he commenced his endeavour. As a youngster in Toronto, then the town of York, he saw a few Natives about the streets. But he did not take much interest in them until he travelled to Europe to study painting. There, in London, in 1843, Kane met the American artist George Catlin, whose canvases struck him with the force of a revelation. Catlin had ventured into the trans-Mississippi West during the 1830s to record the lifestyles of the Indians. After his return, he assembled six hundred paintings, along with a large collection of ethnological material, into a mobile display which toured the United States and Europe. In 1841, he published his first book about the Indians, the two-volume *Letter and Notes on the Manners, Customs and Condition of the North American Indians*. When Kane saw what Catlin had accomplished, he determined on the spot to give up portraiture, which had so far been his artistic bread and butter, return home, and do for Canada what Catlin had done so successfully south of the border.

Kane reached Red River by canoe in the middle of June, 1846, where he witnessed a Métis buffalo hunt. "The half-breeds are a very hardy race of men, capable of enduring the greatest hardships and fatigues," he wrote, "but their Indian propensities predominate, and consequently they make poor farmers, neglecting their land for the most exciting pleasures of the chase."[3] Kane crossed Lake Winnipeg to the trading post at Norway House where he remained for a month. Then he set off up the Saskatchewan River, the historic canoe route of the fur brigades, reaching Fort Edmonton towards the end of September. Travelling as he was in the company of Hudson's Bay Company men, Kane not unnaturally formed a positive impression of the company and its trading monopoly. Allowing free traders to enter the country to compete with the HBC would be akin to signing the death warrant of the Indians, he warned. "For while it is the interest of such a body as the Hudson's Bay Company to improve the Indians and encourage them to industry, according to their own native habits in hunting and the chase...it is as obviously the interest of small companies and private adventurers to draw as much wealth as they possibly can from the country in the shortest possible time, altho' in doing so the very source from which the wealth springs should be destroyed."[4] Kane was referring here to the debilitating effects of the liquor trade with the Natives, which he blamed on the free traders.

With winter fast approaching, Kane and his party hurried to cross the Rocky Mountains, then descended the Columbia River to Fort Vancouver where they arrived early in December. Fort Vancouver remained Kane's headquarters during his stay on the West Coast. He sketched several portraits of the local Flathead people, who were not quite sure how to interpret what they saw. "My power of portraying the features of individuals was attributed entirely to supernatural agency," reported Kane, "and I found that, in looking at my pictures, they always covered their eyes with their hands and looked through their fingers; this being also the invariable custom when looking at a dead person."[5] In the spring of 1847, Kane went on a three-month sketching trip to Vancouver Island. There would not be another artist interested in recording the Native people of the Pacific Northwest until Emily Carr over fifty years later.

That summer Kane left Fort Vancouver for the East. Travelling back up the Columbia River, he made an arduous crossing of the

DANIEL FRANCIS

Rockies and did not arrive at Fort Edmonton until December. He remained there for the next six months sketching on the prairie and waiting for the spring canoe brigade to depart with the season's trade of furs. Descending the Saskatchewan River, he crossed Lake Winnipeg and northern Ontario and reached Sault Ste. Marie on the first day of October. Two weeks later a steamboat carried him into Toronto harbour, home again after more than two years wandering the wild Northwest.

Kane's arrival home stirred up great interest. Within a month he mounted an exhibit much like Catlin's, including some of the five hundred sketches prepared on his travels and a selection of Indian "souvenirs." Response was enthusiastic. People flocked to the exhibit to see powerful portraits of Native hunters, scenes of the buffalo chase, and depictions of exotic pagan rituals. Critics remarked on the authenticity and exquisite detail of the work. "A striking characteristic of Mr. Kane's paintings...is their truthfulness," reported the *British Colonist* newspaper. "Nothing has been sacrificed to effect — no exaggerated examples of costumes — no incredible distortions of features — are permitted to move our wonder, or exalt our conceptions of what is sufficiently wild and striking without improvements."[6] The Ontario public was just beginning to wake up to the existence of the far Northwest, and was already predisposed to romanticize the western Native. In Kane's paintings of picturesque Indians in elaborate costumes of feathers and buffalo hide, his audience found confirmation of a fascinating wilderness world inhabited by fiercely independent, entirely mysterious people. Everyone agreed that Kane, their own local hero, had done even better than Catlin.

Kane's ambition was to complete a series of one hundred large canvases depicting the Northwest frontier from the Great Lakes to the Pacific Coast. After closing his one-man show in Toronto, he set to work on this task. As well, he had to prepare another fourteen paintings which he had promised George Simpson. In 1850, Kane asked the House of Assembly for financial help to complete his project and the next year the provincial government agreed to buy a dozen canvases. After much prompting, these were completed in 1856 and now reside with the National Gallery in Ottawa. Meanwhile, a wealthy Toronto lawyer, George W. Allan, purchased the entire set of one hundred paintings, which were by then almost finished. Together with Kane's Indian artifacts, Allan displayed the works for many years in his home, Moss Park. After his death in

1901, the paintings were sold to Sir Edmund Osler, who in turn donated them to the Royal Ontario Museum in Toronto, where they remain.

Kane was a documentary artist, but he worked within certain conventions and manipulated his images to suit the demands of these conventions. Though he was praised for his accuracy, he often added details of setting and landscape to highlight the romantic flavour of the scenes, and he sometimes "cheated" by adding clothing and artifacts foreign to the Indians in the paintings. His most famous "forgery" is a depiction of an Assiniboine buffalo hunt which was actually modelled on an Italian engraving of two young men on horseback chasing a bull. Recently Kane has been accused of exploiting the Indians by using them as "exotic curiosities" instead of painting them realistically.[7]

But I don't think Kane can be expected to have conveyed a realistic sense of the Native cultures he visited. He was essentially a tourist among the Indians. He spoke no Native languages; he had a superficial understanding of Native customs. Despite his sympathy for what he saw to be their plight, he showed little concern for Native people after his expedition and he was surprisingly narrow-minded about many aspects of their culture. Nonetheless, the power, the beauty and above all the uniqueness of his paintings established him as the pre-eminent artistic interpreter of the Indian for many years to come. Even today it is hard to find a history text-book that does not contain at least one of Kane's renderings of Indian life. For most of us, the Indian of nineteenth-century Canada is Paul Kane's Indian.

Like Catlin, Kane described his western adventures in a popular memoir. *Wanderings of an Artist among the Indians of North America* appeared in 1859 to laudatory reviews. A bestseller in English, it spawned French, Danish and German editions within four years. In the preface, Kane laments the inevitable disappearance of the Indian, and though the rest of the book does not deal with this subject in any detail, most reviewers took it as their theme. "One must make haste to visit the Red Men," said a typical review. "Their tribes, not long since still masters of a whole world, are disappearing rapidly, driven back and destroyed by the inroads of the white race. Their future is inevitable.... The Indians are doomed; their fate will be that of so many primitive races now gone."[8]

In their conviction that the Native people were doomed to disappear, Kane and his admirers were completely representative of their

DANIEL FRANCIS

PAUL KANE, (Canadian, 1810-1871) *Indian Encampment on Lake Huron*, c 1845-50, oil on canvas, 48.3 x 73.7 cm, Art Gallery of Ontario, Toronto.

age. If any single belief dominated the thinking about Canadian aboriginals during the last half of the nineteenth century, it was that they would not be around to see much of the twentieth. Anyone who paid any attention at all to the question agreed that Natives were disappearing from the face of the earth, victims of disease, starvation, alcohol and the remorseless ebb and flow of civilizations. "The Indian tribes are passing away, and what is done must be done quickly," wrote the missionary John Maclean, a noted Indian authority, in 1889. "On the western plains, native songs, wafted on the evening breezes, are the dying requiem of the departing savage."[9] Any number of other writers made the same point. Some believed that it was the Indian's traditional culture that was being eradicated by the spread of White settlement, while others believed the Indians themselves literally to be dying out. Some found the idea appalling; some found it regrettable; some found it desirable. But all were agreed that the Indian was doomed.

II

The "fact" that Indians were a vanishing breed made them especially attractive to artists. The pathos inherent in the subject appealed to White audiences. It also gave an urgency to the work. Artists like Paul Kane who chose to portray the Indian believed they were saving an entire people from extinction; not literally, of course, but in the sense that they were preserving on canvas, and later on film, a record of a dying culture before it expired forever.

This sense of urgent mission controlled the way Indians were portrayed in the work of White artists, who became amateur ethnographers seeking to record Indian life as it was lived before the arrival of White people. Artists ignored evidence of Native adaptation to White civilization and highlighted traditional lifestyles. Often the result was an idealized image of the Indian based on what the artist imagined aboriginal life to have been before contact....

V

At about the same time as Edmund Morris was recording the Plains Indian chiefs, Emily Carr was undertaking a similar project among the tribes on the coast of British Columbia. "I am a Canadian born and bred," she told the audience at a huge exhibit of her paintings in Vancouver in April, 1913. "I glory in our wonderful West and I hope to leave behind me some of the relics of its first primitive greatness."[10]

"These things," she continued, referring to the totem poles, house fronts and village scenes in her paintings, "should be to we Canadians what the ancient Briton's relics are to the English. Only a few more years and they will be gone forever, into silent nothingness, and I would gather my collections together before they are forever past."[11]

As these remarks reveal, Carr initially cast herself very much in the same mould as Paul Kane; that is, a documentary artist making a visual record of a condemned people. Carr conceived her Indian project in 1907 during a summer steamer excursion to Alaska with her sister. The two women spent a week at the Native settlement of Sitka where they visited the famous Totem Walk, a collection of poles erected as a tourist attraction. While she was at Sitka, Carr met the American artist, Theodore J. Richardson, who had been painting in the village every summer for many years. She viewed his work and showed him some of the watercolours she had done of the poles. Richardson praised her abilities and Carr decided on the spot to dedicate herself to recording the heritage of British Columbia's Native peoples before it vanished.

At this time Emily Carr had been studying painting for more than a decade, in California and London, and was teaching art in Vancouver as well as pursuing her own career as a painter. Her exposure to Native people was limited to the Indians she saw around Victoria when she was growing up, and to the visit she had made in 1898 to the Native villages near Ucluelet on the west coast of Vancouver Island. Yet even as a child, she felt a strong fascination for the Indian; "often I used to wish I had been born an Indian," she later wrote. Her biographers speculate that Carr, alienated from her own family and from polite Victorian society, was attracted by the apparent freedom and unconventionality of the Indians who inhabited the fringes of her world.[12] A bit of a misanthrope, she idealized Indians as outsiders, misfits like herself.

Having resolved to paint the Indian "like a camera" for posterity, Carr set about her project with great energy. Between 1907 and 1912, interrupted by a year of study in Paris, she visited Native villages all along the coast, from Campbell River and Alert Bay on Vancouver Island to the Haida settlements of the Queen Charlotte

Islands and the Tsimshian villages in the Skeena River Valley. These were arduous expeditions, especially for a woman travelling alone. They involved long voyages by steamship and open boat, toilsome hikes with heavy packs through dense forest, overnight camping in leaky tents in isolated villages. Through it all, her commitment to the project was total.

Carr's Indian painting came to a head in 1913 with the Vancouver exhibition. It contained almost two hundred pieces — oils, watercolours, sketches — covering fourteen years' worth of excursions. The long public lecture which she gave twice during the exhibition explained how totem poles were made and the role they played in the life of the Native people. In her talk, Carr revealed her strong affection and admiration for the Natives of the coast. Unlike Kane and the other artists who had set out to paint the Indian, Carr felt a deep personal bond with her subject. She was recording for posterity, but she was also striving for understanding.

Like many of her contemporaries, Carr interpreted contact between Native and non-Native in Christian terms. Before the White man came, she believed that the Indian lived in harmony with nature in something approaching a Garden of Eden. "In their own primitive state they were a moral people with a high ideal of right," she told her listeners. "I think they could teach us many things." When Whites arrived, they offered Indians the "apple" of a new way of life. But the apple had a worm in it. "They looked up to the whites, as a superior race whom they should try to copy. Alas, they could not discriminate between the good and bad, there was so much bad, and they copied it."[13] As a result, she believed, Indians had lost touch with their traditional culture which was speedily disappearing from the coast.

Carr's 1913 exhibition was well received, but she failed to win a hoped-for commission from the provincial government and had to return to Victoria where she assumed the life of a boarding-house keeper. Without encouragement, she could not afford to go on painting and eventually she abandoned her Indian project. Her "retirement" lasted until 1927, when a visit from Eric Brown, director of the National Gallery in Ottawa, suddenly elevated her and her Indian paintings into national prominence. Brown was looking for canvases to include in an upcoming show of West Coast Indian art at the National Museum. Stunned to discover the cache of paintings Carr had completed so many years before, he convinced her to contribute several to the exhibition. What followed — Carr's trip back east to the opening, her meeting with Lawren Harris, her discovery of the Group of Seven and their discovery of her — is one of the legends of Canadian art history.

The exhibition opened in Ottawa on December 2, 1927. A combination of Native art and modern paintings on Native themes, the show was hailed in the press as an historic occasion, the first of its kind anywhere in the world. "What a tremendous influence the vanishing civilization of the West Coast Indian is having on the minds of Canadian artists," reported the *Ottawa Citizen*. Carr received particular praise. "She is a real discovery," wrote the *Citizen* critic. Her work was "the greatest contribution of all time to historic art of the Pacific slope."[14] Early in January, the exhibition moved on to Toronto where the critic in the *Daily Star* described it as "a revelation" comparable to the discovery of a "Canadian tomb of Tutankaheman." The Native art and artifacts were among the country's greatest cultural treasures, he wrote, as important as the art of the Aztecs, the Mayans or the Incans.[15] It is noteworthy that he made the comparison not to a living tradition but to other vanished Americans.

A cynic might have taken a more jaundiced view of the exhibition. After all, the art seemed to be valued chiefly as examples of a Native tradition long dead. The death of that tradition was both the theme of the work and the necessary precondition of its sudden popularity. While artists like Emily Carr lamented the fate of the Indian, their success was predicated on it. Having first of all destroyed many aspects of Native culture, White society now turned around and admired its own recreations of what it had destroyed. To the extent that they suffered any guilt over what had happened to the Native people, Whites relieved it by preserving evidence of the supposedly dying culture. Whites convinced themselves that they were in this way saving the Indians. By a curious leap of logic, non-Natives became the saviours of the vanishing Indian.

Carr returned from the East with her confidence as an artist restored. She immediately resumed her painting career, and in the summer of 1928 made another excursion north to the villages of the Skeena and Nass rivers and the Queen Charlotte Islands. This trip resulted in some of her finest paintings, but it also marked an end to her Indian project. Under the encouragement of Lawren Harris, she began to feel that she had gone as far as she could as an interpreter of Native art and that it was time to concentrate on her own vision of the forest wilderness, unmediated by Native monuments.

But Carr's interest in Native people remained strong. As her health deteriorated in the late 1930s, she devoted more of her time to writing. She wrote stories about her odd assortment of pets, about her days as a landlady, about her childhood and about her early excursions to the coastal Indian villages. A group of the latter were collected and published in 1941 as *Klee Wyck*. The book received a warm critical reception — "there is nothing to be said in dispraise of her work," commented Robertson Davies — and the next year it won a Governor General's Award for non-fiction.

Carr's style in *Klee Wyck* is unique and charming, at its best when she describes her deep affection for the coastal forest, "the twisted trees and high tossed driftwood."[16] With few exceptions, though, her Indians lack individual character. They are noble figures, living in tune with forest and sea. But they are exotics — servants, street pedlars, subsistence fishermen who speak broken English — living outside White society and apparently having no place in it. Carr is never patronizing. She herself was alienated from mainstream Canadian society and her stories romanticize the poverty and dignity of the social outcast. She describes the harsh reality of life for the contemporary Native, but she is no social worker. Her stories ask the reader to admire the character of the Indian, just as her painting asks the viewer to admire the spirituality and art. Nowhere does she ask her audience to confront social reality. As a result, although she had great personal sympathy for the Indian, she nevertheless belongs to the tradition of artists who took for granted that Indians were vanishing and sought to preserve and idealized image of them, and not the reality of Native people.

Chapter Ten: Guns and Feathers

The last two decades have seen a revolution in public thinking about the Indian. Raised on *Howdy Doody* and *The Lone Ranger*, I have seen the Native peoples of the North defend their way of life against southern megaprojects which threaten their land. I have watched Elijah Harper change the constitutional direction of the country with a wave of his feather, and I have seen the tanks roll at Oka. It is a long way from Chief Thunderthud to the Mohawk Warriors.

DANIEL FRANCIS

In 1968, during the discussions leading up to his government's controversial White Paper on Indian policy, Prime Minister Pierre Trudeau wrote: "In terms of *realpolitik*, French and English are equal in Canada because each of these linguistic groups has the power to break the country. And this power cannot yet be claimed by the Iroquois, the Eskimos, or the Ukrainians."[17] In Canada, Trudeau was saying, political power depends on your ability to destroy the country: if you do not have that ability, you do not have real power. No one thought for a moment in 1968 that Native people had the ability, so why should they enjoy the power?

Now the country is twenty-five years older and we have learned how wrong we were. With the Meech Lake constitutional debacle, and the armed standoff at Oka, Native people proved that they, too, could break the country. If this is what it took — confrontation, roadblocks, constitutional impasse, threats of secession — Natives proved as adept at it as any White politician. The result? Now, suddenly, they enjoy unprecedented political power. Their representatives sit with the prime minister and the provincial premiers. Aboriginals are now recognized as one of the founding peoples of Canada. Constitutional talks are incomplete without Native people present.

All of this came about because Native people refused to live within the stereotypes White people fashioned for them. They would not disappear; they would not be obedient children and assimilate; they would not go away. But even as these events unfold before us, it is clear that our response to them, as non-Natives, is still conditioned by the image of the Imaginary Indian.

There is a simple test which people who study stereotyping like to perform. Ask a child to draw a picture of an Indian. Even though they can see Native people in ordinary clothes on the television news almost every night, youngsters invariably draw the Wild West Indian, in feathers and buckskin, usually holding a weapon. But then take the test yourself. When I did I discovered the first image that occurred to me was a photograph I remembered from the early 1970s of a young Ojibway man taking part in a roadblock at Kenora, Ontario, sitting on the hood of a car cradling a rifle. (Of course, for most of us this image was updated by the powerful photographs of Mohawks and soldiers confronting each other across the barricades at Oka.) And the second image that occurred to me was of Elijah Harper, seated at his desk in the Manitoba legislature, calmly twitching his eagle feather and bringing the process of constitutional change in the country to an abrupt halt. The warrior versus the wise elder; it turns out that the images of Indians we are offered today are not much different from what they have always been....

Sometimes we thought it was simply a matter of conquering the Indians, taking their territory and absorbing them out of existence. Then America would be ours. Sometimes we thought just the opposite, that we had to become Indians in order to be at home here. This myth of transformation lies at the heart of Canadian culture: Canadians need to transform themselves into Indians. In this sense, Grey Owl was the archetypal Canadian, shedding his European past and transforming himself into an Indian in order to connect through the wilderness with the New World. This is the impulse behind the appropriation by White society of so many aspects of Native culture, trivial as this cultural poaching often seems to be. It also explains the persistent desire by non-Natives to "play Indian," whether by dressing up in feathers and moccasins at summer camp, or by erecting another totem pole as a representative symbol of Canada, or by roaring an Indian chant from the bleachers at a baseball game. This behaviour, repeated over and over, reveals a profound need on the part of non-Natives to connect to North America by associating with one of its most durable symbols, the Imaginary Indian.

There is an ambivalence at the heart of our understanding of what Canadian civilization is all about. On the one hand, the national dream has always been about not being Indian. Since the days of the earliest colonists, non-Natives have struggled to impose their culture on the continent. Indians were always thought of as the Other, threatening to overwhelm this enterprise. Noble or ignoble, it didn't really matter. There was no place for the "savage" in the world the newcomers were building. Canadian history, as Stephen Leacock said, was the struggle of civilization against savagery. There was never any question on which side Indians stood.

On the other hand, as a study of the Imaginary Indian reveals, Euro-Canadian civilization has always had second thoughts. We have always been uncomfortable with our treatment of the Native peoples. But more than that, we have also suspected that we could never be at home in America because we were not Indians, not indigenous to the place. Newcomers did not often admit this anxiety, but Native people recognized it. "The white man does not

DANIEL FRANCIS

understand the Indian for the reason he does not understand America," said the Sioux Chief Standing Bear. "The roots of the tree of his life have not yet grasped the rock and soil. The white man is still troubled with primitive fears; he still has in his consciousness the perils of this frontier continent..."[18] As we have seen, one way non-Natives choose to resolve this anxiety is to somehow become Indian.

In the jargon of the day, Canadians are conflicted in their attitudes toward Indians. And we will continue to be so long as the Indian remains imaginary. Non-Native Canadians can hardly hope to work out a successful relationship with Native people who exist largely in fantasy. Chief Thunderthud did not prepare us to be equal partners with Native people. The fantasies we told ourselves about the Indian are not really adequate to the task of understanding the reality of Native people. The distance between the two, between fantasy and reality, is the distance between Indian and Native. It is also the distance non-native Canadians must travel before we can come to terms with the Imaginary Indian, which means coming to terms with ourselves as North Americans.

Notes

1. Paul Kane, *Wanderings of an Artist* in J. Russell Harper, ed., *Paul Kane's Frontier* (Toronto: University of Toronto Press, 1971), p. 14.
2. Ibid., p. 68.
3. Ibid., p. 74.
4. Ibid., p. 98.
5. Cited in ibid., p. 28.
6. Barry Lord, *The History of Painting in Canada* (Toronto: NC Press, 1974), p. 95.
7. Cited in Harper, p. 41.
8. John Maclean, *The Indians of Canada: Their Manners and Customs* (Toronto: William Briggs, 1889), p. 339.
9. The details of Verner's biography are from Joan Murray, *The Last Buffalo: The Story of Frederick Arthur Verner, Painter of the Canadian West* (Toronto: Pagurian Press, 1984).
10. A.Y. Jackson, *A Painter's Country* (Toronto: Clarke, Irwin and Co., 1958), p. 191.
11. Cited in Murray, p. 97.

12. Biographical details are from J. S. McGill, *Edmund Morris, Frontier Artist* (Toronto: Dundurn Press, 1984).
13. Cited in McGill, p. 110.
14. Toronto *Globe,* 10 April 1909.
15. Cited in Geoffrey Simmins and Michael Parke-Taylor, *Edmund Morris: "Kyaiyii" 1871-1913* (Regina: Norman Mackenzie Art Gallery, 1984), p. 51.
16. 21 July 1909, cited in Simmins and Parke-Taylor, p. 47.
17. Weaver, *Making Canadian Indian Policy*, p. 55.
18. Cited in Drinnon, *Facing West*, p. 230.

PART FOUR:
NATIONALISM

Sir Adolphe Basile Routhier & Robert Stanley Weir

Canada

O Canada! Our home and native land!
True patriot love in all thy sons command.
With glowing hearts we see thee rise,
The True North strong and free;
From far and wide, O Canada,
We stand on guard for thee.

God keep our land, Glorious and free!
O Canada! We stand on guard for thee,
O Canada! We stand on guard for thee.

O Canada! Where pines and maples grow,
Great prairies spread and lordly rivers flow,
How dear to us thy broad domain,
From East to Western sea!
Thou land of hope for all who toil!
Thou True North strong and free!

God keep our land, Glorious and free!
O Canada! We stand on guard for thee,
O Canada! We stand on guard for thee.

O Canada! Beneath thy shining skies
May stalwart sons and gentle maidens rise
To keep thee steadfast thro' the years
From East to Western sea,
Our own beloved native land,
Our True North strong and free!

God keep our land, Glorious and free!
O Canada! We stand on guard for thee,
O Canada! We stand on guard for thee.

Ruler Supreme, Who hearest humble pray'r,
Hold our Dominion in Thy loving care.
Help us to find, O God, in Thee
A lasting rich reward,
As waiting for the better day,
We ever stand on guard.

God keep our land, Glorious and free!
O Canada! We stand on guard for thee,
O Canada! We stand on guard for thee.

E. J. PRATT

TOWARDS THE LAST SPIKE

The Pre-Cambrian Shield

(i)

On the North Shore a reptile lay asleep—
A hybrid that the myths might have conceived,
But not delivered, as progenitor
Of crawling, gliding things upon the earth.
She lay snug in the folds of a huge boa
Whose tail had covered Labrador and swished
Atlantic tides, whose body coiled itself
Around the Hudson Bay, then curled up north
Through Manitoba and Saskatchewan
To Great Slave Lake. In continental reach
The neck went past the Great Bear Lake until
Its head was hidden in the Arctic Seas.
This folded reptile was asleep or dead:
So motionless, she seemed stone dead — just seemed:
She was too old for death, too old for life,
For as if jealous of all living forms
She had lain there before bivalves began
To catacomb their shells on western mountains.
Somewhere within this life-death zone she sprawled,
Torpid upon a rock-and-mineral mattress.
Ice-ages had passed by and over her,
But these, for all their motion, had but sheared
Her spotty carboniferous hair or made
Her ridges stand out like the spikes of molochs.
Her back grown stronger every million years,
She had shed water by the longer rivers

To Hudson Bay and by the shorter streams
To the great basins to the south, had filled
Them up, would keep them filled until the end
Of Time.

(ii)
Dynamite on the North Shore

The lizard was in sanguinary mood.
She had been waked again: she felt her sleep
Had lasted a few seconds of her time.
The insects had come back — the ants, if ants
They were — dragging *those* trees, *those* logs athwart
Her levels, driving in *those* spikes; and how
The long grey snakes unknown within her region
Wormed from the east, unstriped, sunning themselves
Uncoiled upon the logs and then moved on,
Growing each day, ever keeping abreast!
She watched them, waiting for a bloody moment,
Until the borers halted at a spot,
The most invulnerable of her whole column,
Drove in that iron, wrenched it in the holes,
Hitting, digging, twisting. Why that spot?
Not this the former itch. That sharp proboscis
Was out for more than self-sufficing blood
About the cuticle: 'twas out for business
In the deep layers and the arteries.
And this consistent punching at her belly
With fire and thunder slapped her like an insult,
As with the blasts the caches of her broods
Broke — nickel, copper, silver and fool's gold,
Burst from their immemorial dormitories
To sprawl indecent in the light of day.
Another warning — this time different.

Westward above her webs she had a trap —
A thing called muskeg, easy on the eyes
Stung with the dust of gravel. Cotton grass,
Its white spires blending with the orchids,
Peeked through green table-cloths of sphagnum moss.
Carnivorous bladder-wort studded the acres,

Passing the water-fleas through their digestion.
Sweet-gale and sundew edged the dwarf black spruce;
And herds of cariboo had left their hoof-marks,
Betraying visual solidity,
But like the thousands of the pitcher plants,
Their downward-pointing hairs alluring insects,
Deceptive — and the men were moving west!
Now was her time. She took three engines, sank them
With seven tracks down through the hidden lake
To the rock bed, then over them she spread
A counterpane of leather-leaf and slime.
A warning, that was all for now. 'Twas sleep
She wanted, sleep, for drowsing was her pastime
And waiting through eternities of seasons.

FRANK WATT

NATIONALISM IN CANADIAN LITERATURE

This is a topic you can take hold of from several sides, with rather different consequences. Most naturally, perhaps, you would begin by thinking of the extent to which nationalism has been, or is, a motive for the creation of literature, or at least an important factor conditioning the quality of writing in Canada. Obviously this approach requires an historical perspective. On the other hand, an outsider hearing this topic might first of all wonder whether the question was not, to what extent has Canadian literature been a motive for nationalism. An Englishman, I am sure, is all the more an Englishman and proud to be so when he numbers Shakespeare or Keats among his forbears. Anyone who has actually read a fair amount of Canadian literature is unlikely to imagine Canadians being nationalistic in this way out of satisfaction with their literature. Even so, one might conceive of Canadian writing as, in various ways, stimulating national pride and national awareness.

But pride and awareness are not necessarily the same thing. This brings me to a third way of approaching the subject, in which I am not sure whether nationalism, by whatever definition, does not come close to disappearing, leaving us with only Canadian literature, or more barely still, literature, to consider. In this approach we would be seeing nationalism, not as a direct encouragement to writers (one reason for writing), and not as an encouragement for readers (one reason for reading), but as an indirect product or by-product of literature. Literature is then seen as a force which, quite apart from its motives, contributes to the articulation and clarification of Canadians' consciousness of themselves and of the physical, social and moral context in which they live their lives. I say nationalism is an indirect product in this case, because the enlightened and articulate consciousness which literature helps to create might be related in many ways, even the way of outright opposition, to whatever people would generally call nationalism. For example, the poem entitled "From Colony to Nation" shows as strong a national feeling or sense of Canadian nationality as Arthur Lower's book by the same name, but the tone and direction seem to be a little different. Professor Lower hoped "that a careful reading of his pages [would] help Canadians to some of that self-knowledge so necessary if they are to take their rightful place in the world, and still more, if they are to be a happy people, at peace with themselves."[1] For Professor Lower, Canadian history is by and large a success story, and "Canada is a supreme act of faith."[2] For the poet Irving Layton, if Canadians are at peace with themselves their peace is complacency, and if there is a national faith it must be bad faith. This is the conclusion he sees for the triumphal progress from colony to nation:

> A dull people,
> but the rivers of this country
> are wide and beautiful
>
> A dull people
> enamoured of childish games,
> but food is easily come by
> and plentiful
>
> Some with a priest's voice
> in their cage of ribs: but
> on high mountain-tops and in thunderstorms
> the chirping is not heard
>
> Deferring to beadle and censor;
> not ashamed for this,
> but given over to horseplay,
> the making of money
>
> A dull people, without charm or ideas,
> settling into the clean empty look
> of a Mountie or dairy farmer
> as into a legacy.
>
> One can ignore them
> (the silences, the vast distances help)
> and suppose them at the bottom

        of one of the meaner lakes,
        their bones not even picked for souvenirs.[3]

A sophisticated reader might of course want to say that here
Layton is expressing a very familiar and recognizable variety of
Canadian nationalism. But before I go farther into this more atten-
uated aspect of my subject, the way in which Canadian writers help
to being alive the shared history, limitations, fulfilments, virtues
and depravities which make at least some Canadians feel related to
each other and to their land, before I go farther in this direction, I
must return to and develop the simpler approaches to my subject,
nationalism and literature in their historical perspective.

Using the historical approach I can avoid an objection some literary critics and many writers would immediately raise. There are
those who are inclined to distrust any approach to literature which
emphasizes a close relation with social forces. Both the so-called
New Critics who treat poems as self-contained verbal constructions, and artists who have their ears tuned to the Muses, to the subconscious, to the inner voice (or however they choose to describe
their inspiration), dislike the suggestion that writing may be conditioned or caused by social forces. They do not always equally dislike the notion that literature has or should have a social function,
though they usually object to being directed to any specific function. At one extreme is classical Marxist doctrine — the belief that
economic circumstances condition consciousness and artistry. At
the other extreme is pure creative imagination theory — that whatever materials he uses the artist brings to them a basic spontaneous
freedom of impulse, choice and form which is his essential creativity. Like wave and particle theory in physics, or free will and determinism in philosophy, these theories may seem irreconcilable, yet
each explains certain kinds of literary phenomena better than its
opposite.

In case this sounds like an excessive academic balancing of one
idea against its opposite, I should at once confess my bias
towards the romantic position. There does seem to me to be a
sort of indeterminacy principle in literature, whatever is true of
physics: artistic inspiration, like the most elusive forces in the
atom, apparently will not stay still to be charted accurately, and
the act of measurement itself can become an alien force distort-
ing the field of investigation. This is true whether you are dealing
with the motives of a living writer, or with the meaning of an

apparently stable monument of literary history. The approach to both must share some of their own nature, some of their own intuition and inspiration. Marxists, moralists and nationalists are usually reluctant to accept this conclusion.

The Literature of Nation-Building

Fortunately these subtleties can be set aside in any study of nineteenth century Canadian literary history. There the practice and theory of literature had a reassuring obviousness, and not much literary tact is required. Most writing in British North America before Confederation was "colonial," in A.J.M. Smith's sense of that word: "Colonialism is a spirit that gratefully accepts a place of subordination, that looks elsewhere for its standards of excellence and is content to imitate with a modest and timid conservatism the products of a parent tradition."[4] The chief fault of this writing, especially the poetry, was a tendency to abstraction, a fault which followed almost inevitably from the attempt to apply literary techniques and language fully formed in Europe to a largely different subject matter in the New World. Writers continued to see their native environment and experience through spectacles developed for a very different kind of world, and, therefore, not to see very clearly or intimately. Some steps, especially in the Maritimes, were being taken towards the acclimatization of the Muses, the founding of an indigenous literature, by the 1860s. But the Confederation movement intervened in this process with a new kind of force which ran, if not counter to, at least across the movement towards a localized and particularized regional literature.

Confederation was bound to have an impact on writing as on other aspects of British North American life; the effect was immediate, however superficial. The cry was raised by new nationalists that literature should serve the new nationality, and vice versa. "Now," H.J. Morgan, the biographer and bibliographer, wrote in 1867, "now more than any other time ought the literary life of the New Dominion develop itself unitedly. It becomes every patriotic subject who claims allegiance to this our new northern nation to extend a fostering care to the native plant, to guard it tenderly, to support and assist it by the warmest countenance and encouragement."[5] Three years earlier E.H. Dewart, the anthologist, had spelled out the social and political demands a Canadian nationality would make on its writers and the service writers would be asked to provide:

FRANK WATT

A national literature is an essential element in the formation of a national character. It is not merely the record of a nation's mental progress: it is the expression of its intellectual life, the bond of national unity, and the guide of national energy. It may be fairly questioned, whether the whole range of history presents the spectacle of a people firmly united politically, without the subtle but powerful cement of a patriotic literature.... It is to be regretted that the tendency to sectionalism and disintegration, which is the political weakness of Canada, meets no counterpoise in the literature of the country.[6]

Dewart then touched on a larger problem than he realized by adding that although "our French countrymen are more firmly united than the English colonists," "their literature is more French than Canadian, and their bond of union more religious than literary or political."[7] What he might have said more objectively is that French-Canadian writers had different aims from English-Canadian. A French-Canadian nationalism, reacting to the threat of assimilation implicit in the 1840 Union of the two provinces, and inspired by Garneau's historical account of the spiritual greatness of French Canada, was already a strong motive for literature. This nationalism, with its determination to keep pure and alive the language, laws and religion of French Canada, has of course continued to influence Canadian writers in French to the present day. I am unable to say to what extent the new and larger nationalism of Confederation has also been felt, but I would assume comparatively little.

Confederation created a new role for the writer, the role of nation-builder, and since that time few Canadian writers in English have been able to resist at least a few flourishes in this part. The role required enthusiastic involvement in the geography, history and future prospects of Canada. In the 1870s the Canada First Movement had its literary embodiment in Charles Mair, who was called the Keats of Canadian poetry, and who deliberately tried to load every rift of his poetry with Canadian ore. He indicated the programme for nation-building writers in this way: "Our romantic Canadian story is a mine of character and incident for the poet and the novelist, framed, too, in a matchless environment; and the Canadian author who seeks inspiration there is helping to create for a young people that decisive test of its intellectual faculties, an original and distinctive literature — a literature liberal in its range, but, in its highest forms, springing in a large measure from the soil, and 'tasting of the wood'."[8] Mair's historical poem "Tecumseh" was an attempt to follow this programme, and no doubt the plethora of nineteenth century historical novels exploiting the records and legends of early French and British North American life can be accounted for partly in the same way.

By the 1880s one detects a considerable growth in confidence among critics, at least, that the nation-building writer was in fact effectively at work. W.D. Lighthall prefaced his anthology *Songs of the Great Dominion* with spirited claims appropriate to his title: "You shall hear there," he said, "the chants of a new nationality...." "The poets whose songs fill this book," he continued, "are voices cheerful with the consciousness of young might, public wealth, and heroism." Lighthall saw the cultural life of Canada developing a grandeur comparable to that of her physical and political life, and here his enthusiasm was unbounded:

> Canada, Eldest Daughter of the Empire, is the Empire's completest type! She is the full-grown of the family, — the one first come of age and gone into life as a nation.... She is Imperial in herself, we sons of her think as the number, the extent, and the lavish natural wealth of her Provinces, each not less than some empire of Europe, rises in our minds.... Her Valley of the Saskatchewan alone, it has been scientifically computed, will support eight hundred millions. In losing the United States, Britain lost the *smaller* half of her American possessions....[9]

It is quite characteristic of writers like Lighthall, who see literature as serving and being nourished by the new nationality, that he should focus his ardour on the physical assets of the country. For of course the difficulties of knowing exactly what the new nation was and where it was heading were as great for the poets as for the politicians. Of the many poets who since 1867 have tried their hand at what might loosely be called the "Confederation ode," almost all have found the tangle of Canadian political involvements and affiliations too complex for simple enthusiasm, even when they were eager to provide it. A bemused poetaster in 1880 began his poem "Canada First" in this way: "Canada first! first, Canada we love! /Next glorious Britain, our most noble sire; /Next, our near

FRANK WATT

neighbour: let us brothers prove....,"[10] and so on. Another chose to spend a briefer time wrestling with political complexities ("Fair land of peace! to Britain's rule and throne /Adherent still, yet happier than alone..."), and went on quickly to the great natural simplicities: "But we who know thee, proudly point the hand /Where thy broad rivers roll serenely grand...", etc.[11] Prolonged meditation on Canada's political status and relations with Britain and the U.S. was more likely then, as it is today, to produce perplexity and debate than rapture, and writers aiming to arouse patriotic feeling would do better to dwell on the undeniable depth of the lakes, height of the mountains and breadth of the plains. The one safe common denominator of all nationalistic Canadian writing is the land itself.

During the 1880s and 1890s while Macdonald's National Policy was helping to establish the political and economic basis of the country, anthologists, critics and writers were showing an increasing patriotic interest in the growth of an indigenous literature. Bliss Carman wrote with pride of C.G.D. Roberts, "the acknowledged laureate of this vigorous young nation," and asserted revealingly, if not quite accurately, that "his poetry is in large measure the product of his enthusiasm and his patriotism."[12] In the journals of the day, critics were searching out and rewarding with praise signs of Canadianness among current writers. It would be an exaggeration to say that here we had in operation a *National Policy for literature*. But at least there was a strong awareness that nationalism and literature are intimately related; and in one direction this awareness led to the Canadian Authors' Association of the 1920s with its cultivation of home industries (Buy Canadian Books), and to the subsidized and protected cultural agencies that are making their contribution to national identity and independence today.

The dilemma of a patriotically conceived National Policy for culture is that only the worst writers seem willing and able to answer direct appeals that literature should serve the national cause, or if good writers respond, they do so with their poorest writing. I doubt if Roberts would have wanted to be remembered by stanzas like this from his poem called "Canada":

> O Child of Nations, giant-limbed,
>> Who stand'st among the nations now
> Unheeded, unadored, unhymned,
>> With unanointed brow....[13]

Looking at Canadian society in the 1880s and 1890s, Archibald Lampman was led to remark that what the country needed most was not panegyric but satire.[14] The only conclusion to be drawn from a study of post-Confederation literature is that the best writers at their best moments have similarly rejected, or simply let go by default, the public role of nation-builder which was created with the advent of Confederation.

Inventing Canada

But this brings me to the third and most difficult part of my paper: for nationalism may be influenced by writers who have no apparent interest in it and who would refuse to serve it if invited.

Vladimir Nabokov, in a note appended to his piquant American novel of unrequited love, *Lolita*, tells us how difficult he found it as an outsider in the United States to give his story a satisfactory substance and density. It could not have been the American language which held him up, for he was a master of the language; it must have been the vagueness and indistinctness of the social and atmospheric context, lack of the feel of the country. In order, he says, to write the novel, he had first of all to "invent America." For most readers of Nabokov, the invention of America was highly successful and his new America modifies their old image of the country. Aldous Huxley was obviously thinking along the same lines as Nabokov when he wrote, "Nations are to a very large extent invented by their poets and novelists." Other artists share in the job, as Huxley makes clear in the same discussion:

> How imperfectly did mountains exist before Wordsworth! How dim, before Constable, was English pastoral landscape! Yes, and how dim, for that matter, before the epoch-making discoveries of Falstaff and the Wife of Bath, were even English men and women!... The inadequacy of German drama and the German novel perhaps explains the curious uncertainty and artificiality of character displayed by so many of the Germans whom one meets in daily life. Thanks to a long succession of admirable dramatists and novelists, Frenchmen and Englishmen know exactly how they ought to behave. Lacking these, the Germans are at a loss.[15]

It is obvious that if the Germans are at a loss, Canadians are even more so. How should they behave? Should they be calm, urbane and ironical in the tradition of upper-class England, or should they be cheerful, lively and brash like the true North Americans; healthy peasants, or angry young men? Is their country "America's attic, an empty room," or "the big land" with "the big ale?" To what extent have writers succeeded in inventing Canada and Canadians? If one thinks first of all of geography, the physical environment, the Canadian terrain, the answer is that Canada has been very success- fully invented, but in a process as long and gradual as that by which this half-continent was explored, settled and mastered, both politi- cally and by technology and communications. It is easy to trace this process through the history of Canadian poetry. Pre-Confederation poetry shows the Canadian terrain as a vast, hostile, dimly seen, unpoetical mass, the poet often struggling ineffectually to catch and express its feeling in imitations of the clear, regular, elegant cou- plets and poetic diction which Pope and his school bred to civilized perfection in the gardens of England. By the 1880s poets are not any longer bemoaning the inhuman and unpoetical nature of Canadian landscape: they are recording its details and its moods with high fidelity. By the mid-twentieth century poets have gone a stage fur- ther: the terrain is no longer merely external, something to be observed closely and described accurately in appropriate language. If it is referred to at all it is used symbolically, or as an extension or manifestation of the human. The country may still appear vast, alien and forbidding at times, but the poet has it under greater imaginative control.

I said that the process of imaginative conquest paralleled that of political and physical conquest. An obvious landmark taken from a late stage in the process is, by a useful coincidence, a modern poem on the building of the transcontinental railway, E.J. Pratt's national epic, "Towards the Last Spike." Pratt has an easy grasp of the phys- ical sweep and immensity of northern North America which would have dazzled his Victorian predecessors, perched precariously on the fringes of their mysterious sprawling wilderness. In this he is helped greatly by a suggestive myth: he sees the northern continen- tal mass as a sort of vast prehistoric monster, a prostrate, somno- lent reptile or dragon, and, by an inevitable association, the states- men and engineers struggling to bridge the continent become drag- on-slayers. Because nature for Pratt is not merely external, the drag- on of the Canadian terrain becomes a visible manifestation of the monsters of fear and doubt and suspicion that lurked in the minds of many Canadians and nearly prevented them from building their railway and their nation from sea to sea. And because Pratt was a humanist and a Christian the dragon is related, as in most dragon-slaying stories, to the father of all dragons, the Devil, and to the forces of evil and chaos which human societies always struggle to master by imposing human order and civilization on nature. Pratt's poem could be seen as patriotic and nationalistic: it celebrates a central heroic event in Canadian history. But what value the poem has lies in the way it transcends nationalism and presents a national achievement as an instance of the universal archetypal human story. No mere nationalist would go so far in giving the devil or dragon its due as to suggest that the monster might still in the long run win the struggle:

> Some day perhaps when ice began to move,
> Or some convulsion ran fires through her tombs,
> She might stir in her sleep and far below
> The reach of steel and blast of dynamite,
> She'd claim their bones as her possessive right
> And wrap them cold in her pre-Cambrian folds.[16]

The process of inventing the Canadian terrain can also be traced in prose. One chain of examples would begin with Mrs. Frances Brooke's description of the St. Lawrence in the late eighteenth century: "On approaching the coast of America, I felt a kind of religious veneration, on seeing rocks which almost touch'd the clouds, cover'd with tall groves of pines that seemed coeval with the world itself: to which veneration the solemn silence not a little contributed; from Cap Rosières, up the River St. Lawrence, during a course of more than two hundred miles, there is not the least appearance of a human footstep; no objects meet the eye but mountains, woods, and numerous rivers, which seem to roll their waters in vain."[17] The last phrase, "in vain," particularly gives the lie to the conventional protestations of veneration, and points to the underlying baffled vagueness and sense of alienation. A century later William Kirby gives us this description of the St. Lawrence at Quebec: "The broad bay lay before them round as a shield, and glittering like a mirror as the mist blew off its surface. Behind the sunny slopes of Orléans, which the river circled in its arms like a giant lover his fair mistress, rose the bold, dark crests of the

Laurentides, lifting their bare summits far away along the course of the ancient river, leaving imagination to wander over the wild scenery in their midst — the woods, glens, unknown lakes and rivers that lay hid from human ken, or known only to rude savages, wild as the beasts of chase they hunted in those strange regions."[18] Here we have the fair mistress — giant lover image indicating an area of control which shades off into vast stretches of wilderness and chaos where the imagination is lost. Though the author's grasp is not entirely firm, there is a good deal of understanding and conviction in his character's enthusiasm for the landscape in general and for Quebec, "God's footstool," in particular.

Of the examples I would choose from the twentieth century, the best is the opening of Hugh MacLennan's *Two Solitudes*, focusing again on the St. Lawrence, but here the imaginative control of the material is assured and the descriptive detail is used to open up the essential subject matter of the novel, the French-Canadian, English-Canadian duality:

> Northwest of Montreal, through a valley always in sight of the low mountains of the Laurentian Shield, the Ottawa River flows out of Protestant Ontario into Catholic Quebec. It comes down broad and ale-coloured and joins the Saint Lawrence, the two streams embrace the pan of Montreal Island, the Ottawa merges and loses itself, and the mainstream moves northeastward a thousand miles to the sea.
>
> Nowhere has nature wasted herself as she has here. There is enough water in the Saint Lawrence alone to irrigate half of Europe, but the river pours right out of the continent into the sea. No amount of water can irrigate stones, and most of Quebec is solid rock. It is as though millions of years back in geologic time a sword has been plunged through the rock from the Atlantic to the Great lakes and savagely wrenched out again, and the pure water of the continental reservoir, unmuddied and almost useless to farmers, drains untouchably away. In summer the cloud packs pass over it in soft, cumulus, pacific towers, endlessly forming and dissolving to make a welter of movement about the sun. In winter when there is no storm the sky is generally empty, blue and glittering over the ice and snow, and the sun stares out of it like a cyclops' eye.
>
> All the narrow plain between the Saint Lawrence and the hills is worked hard. From the Ontario border down to the

beginning of the estuary, the farmland runs in two delicate bands along the shores, with roads like a pair of village main streets a thousand miles long, each parallel to the river. All the good land was broken long ago, occupied and divided among seigneurs and their sons, and then among tenants and their sons. Bleak wooden fences separate each strip of farm from its neighbour, running straight as rulers set at right angles to the river to form long narrow rectangles pointing inland. The ploughed land looks like the course of a gigantic and empty steeplechase where all motion has been frozen. Every inch of it is measured, and brooded over by notaries, and blessed by priests.

You can look north across the plain from the river and see the farms between their fences tilting towards the forest, and beyond them the line of trees crawling shaggily up the slope of the hills. The forest crosses the watershed into an evergreen bush that spreads far to the north, lake-dotted and mostly unknown, until it reaches the tundra. The tundra goes to the lower straits of the Arctic Ocean. Nothing lives on it but a few prospectors and hard-rock miners and Mounted Policemen and animals and the flies that brood over the barrens in summer like haze. Winters make it a universe of snow with a terrible wind keening over it, and beyond its horizons the northern lights flare into walls of shifting electric colours that crack and roar like the gods of a dead planet talking to each other out of the dark.

But down in the angle at Montreal, on the island about which the two rivers join, there is little of this sense of new and endless space. Two old races and religions meet here and live their separate legends, side by side. If this sprawling half-continent has a heart, here it is. Its pulse throbs out along the rivers and railroads; slow, reluctant and rarely simple, a double beat, a self-moved reciprocation.[19]

And finally there is Stephen Leacock who, despite his mordant criticism of Canadian life, felt the Canadian terrain to be his home. A misguided Englishman has asked him to go home to England, but he replied, I'll stay in Canada:

It's the great spaces that appeal. To all of us here, the vast unknown country of the North, reaching away to the polar seas, supplies a peculiar mental background. I like to think that in a few short hours in a train or car I can be in the primeval wilderness of the North; that if I like, from my summer home, an hour or two of flight will take me over the divide and down to the mournful shores of James Bay.... I never have gone to James Bay; I never go to it; I never shall. But somehow I'd feel lonely without it.... No, I don't think I can leave this country. There is something in its distances and its isolation and its climate that appeals forever. Outside my window as I write in the dark of early morning — for I rise like a farm hand — the rotary snow ploughs on the Côte des Neiges Road are whirling in the air the great blanket of snow that buried Montreal last night. To the north, behind the mountain, the Northern Lights blink on a thousand miles of snow-covered forest and frozen rivers.... We are 'sitting pretty' here in Canada. East and West are the two oceans far away; we are backed up against the ice cap of the pole; our feet rest on the fender of the American border, warm with a hundred years of friendship.... Thank you, Mother England, I don't think I'll 'come home'. I'm 'home' now.[20]

Discovering Canadians

So much for the invention of the Canadian terrain. But writers in this country, like painters, have had more success with landscape than with people. If Hugh Kenner is right, no one hearing this will take it amiss: "The surest way to the hearts of a Canadian audience," Kenner says, "is to inform them that their souls are to be identified with rock, rapids, wilderness, and virgin (but exploitable) forest," and, he adds, "this pathological craving for identification with the subhuman may be illustrated in every department of Canadian culture."[21] It is perhaps significant that the only memorable character produced in nineteenth century Canadian literature was an American, T.C. Haliburton's Sam Slick, the Yankee Clockmaker, whose travels through Nova Scotia clearly showed up the natives as apathetic and indistinct nonentities. In nineteenth century Canada there was apparently no actual or potential crystallization of national characteristics comparable to that which manifested itself, for example, in Henry James's *The American*.

By the twentieth century there is some indication that this very indistinctness, apathy, uncertainty of behaviour, this facelessness, is beginning to be recognized as a national characteristic. It is the Canadian type, one could argue, who is seen in Stephen Leacock's "My Financial Career," the confused and embarrassed little man whose efforts to open his first bank account end in ignominious flight.[22] Or he might be seen in a whole run of awkward, self-conscious, uncertain, priggish heroes populating Hugh MacLennan's novels, or in any of the series of helpless, confused, victimized figures created by Morley Callaghan. I sometimes think that Morley Callaghan himself is his most typically Canadian portrait: at a loss how to behave in front of a lukewarm, skeptical Canadian public, sometimes truculently advancing his claims as a great international writer and friend of the famous, and then withdrawing into self-doubts and despair and silence. Or the national type might be seen in the poet Raymond Souster's shadowy Toronto street-figures, standing at night in doorways smoking cigarettes, filled with desire and nostalgia, while the real energy and will of the world go about their business far away.

We might expect the feeling of passivity and helplessness, the sense of being on the periphery, to be part of the consciousness of a people accustomed to living on the fringes of the British and American spheres of power. Millar MacLure claims that this experience is the key to the Canadian sensibility: "this native sensibility, which I define, very badly I know," he says, "as an acute feeling of being at the edge of things, both in the sense of not being in the middle, where moods and modes are generated, but out where they can be felt, but observed tangentially and ironically, and in the other sense of being poised on the narrow line from which one may fall either in the smother of civilization where the mode is satire or into the wilderness where the mode is panegyric."[23] The poetry of George Johnston is full of the same sense of powerless and peripheral life, and he often speaks in similar tones of mild and affectionate irony. Here, for example, is his "War on the Periphery," which for the purposes of my theme I might sub-title, "portrait of the typical Canadian family:"

> Around the battlements go by
> Soldier men against the sky,
> Violent lovers, husbands, sons,
> Guarding my peaceful life with guns.

FRANK WATT

My pleasures, how discreet they are!
A little booze, a little car,
Two little children and a wife
Living a small suburban life.

My little children eat my heart;
At seven o'clock we kiss and part,
At seven o'clock we meet again;
They eat my heart and grow to men.

I watch their tenderness with fear
While on the battlements I hear
The violent, obedient ones
Guarding my family with guns.[24]

But Canada is a growing and changing country. Perhaps we may find clearer, more fully developed, more positive and powerful national types in current and coming literature, in the work of young writers like Mordecai Richler. Duddy Kravitz, for example, surely has an amount of energy unusual for Canadian fictional heroes. But it may be that he is typical in that he has doubts about what to do with it. He eagerly learns whatever his society has to teach him: to fornicate at every opportunity, to cheat anyone, when you can get away with it, and to make as much money as you can. Here Duddy Kravitz comes to share one of the traditional Canadian preoccupations, fascination with the land. Mordecai Richler has a stronger and clearer sense of the Canadian terrain than Mrs. Brooke or William Kirby, and he is more up-to-date than MacLennan. In Richler's novel, Duddy Kravitz gets possession at last of his portion of the Canadian terrain, a potentially valuable piece of resort real estate in rural Quebec; he visits it in winter and enjoys a brilliantly commercialized and vulgarized version of an old vision:

He had to walk the last three-quarters of a mile through deep snow. The drifts were soft and often, between rocks, he sunk to his knees. But it gave him quite a lift to see his land in winter. A thin scalp of ice protected the lake and all his fields glittered white and purple and gold under the setting sun. All except the pine trees were bare. It must be pretty in autumn, he thought, when all the leaves are changing colours. Duddy saw where he would put up the hotel and decided that he would not have to clear the wood all out in one shot. It's lovely, he thought, and lots of those pine trees I can peddle at Christmas-time.... He tried the thin ice on the lake with his foot. It cracked. He urinated into a snow bank, writing his name. It's my land, he thought.[25]

It may seem that I have come a long way from the subject of Nationalism in Canadian Literature, and perhaps I have. The movement has been from nationalism towards literature. Writing in this country which is done for the purpose of encouraging and advertising nationalism seems to me doomed to shallowness or hypocrisy. Canadian writers who choose to contemplate their country as a national social, political entity must do so, unless they are inconceivably simple-minded, with a highly critical eye; with affection and sympathy if they feel it, but strongly tempered by irony. Otherwise, their fate at best will be the one described by Mordecai Richler, to be world famous all over Canada. Canadian writers will go on with the job of inventing Canada, or holding up the mirror to their society. But a great deal that they create or reflect is likely to be unpleasing to the pious. They will show Canadians not reverently worshipping the beauties and mysteries of their vast homeland on God's footstool, but digging and exploiting and defacing, buying and selling the land, urinating and writing their names on pieces of real estate. And they are likely to show, not valiant Companies of Young Canadians idealistically setting out to fulfil a great national destiny, but weary and bemused intellectuals like Robertson Davies' innocuous young don, Solly Bridgetower, exasperated at the utter boredom of having to think about "Amcan..., particularly the Can half."

Why do countries have to have literatures? Why does a country like Canada so late upon the International scene, feel that it must rapidly acquire the trappings of older countries — music of its own, pictures of its own, books of its own — and why does it fuss and stew, and storm the heavens with its outcries when it does not have them? Solly pondered bitterly upon these problems, knowing full well how firmly he was caught in the strong, close mesh of his country's cultural ambitions.[26]

A country's best writers will often seem subversive, and it is a little difficult to know what the modern paternalistic state should do with a class of its citizenry who may at any time, like James Joyce's Stephen, say *non serviam* and fly by the nets of nationality. Perhaps the only answer, as hard for English Canada as for French Canada, is that a vital society is like a generous parent: it gives life to, supports and nourishes its writers as best it can, but it makes no demands and expects nothing in return except that they try to fulfil their potentialities. Its only reward is the chance to live a little more and to know itself better.

Notes

1. Arthur Lower, *From Colony to Nation*, Toronto, 1946, p. xiii.
2. Arthur Lower, as cited, p. 561.
3. Irving Layton, "From Colony to Nation," *Collected Poems*, Toronto & Montreal, 1965, pp. 159-160, reprinted by permission of McClelland and Stewart Ltd.
4. A.J.M. Smith, *Canadian Historical Association 1943-44, Report of Annual Meeting*, Toronto, 1944, p. 74.
5. H.J. Morgan, *Bibliotheca Canadiensis*, Ottawa, 1867, p. viii.
6. E.H. Dewart (ed.), *Selection from Canadian Poets*, Montreal, 1864, p. ix-x.
7. E.H. Dewart, as cited, p. x.
8. Charles Mair, *Tecumseh, A Drama, and Canadian Poems*, Toronto, 1901, p. 3.
9. W.D. Lighthall, *Songs of the Great Dominion*, London, 1889, pp. xxi-xxii.
10. "An Appeal to All Canadians by a Toronto Boy," pamphlet published in Toronto.
11. Pamela S. Vining, "Canada" in *Selections from Canadian Poets*, E.H. Dewart (ed.), Montreal, 1864, pp. 101 ff.
12. Quoted by E.M. Pomeroy, *Sir Charles G.D. Roberts*, Toronto, 1943, p. viii.
13. C.G.D. Roberts, "Canada" in *The Book of Canadian Poetry*, A.J.M. Smith (ed.), Toronto, 1957, p. 167.
14. *The Globe*, Toronto, November 19, 1892.
15. Aldous Huxley, *Texts and Pretexts*, New York & London, 1933, p. 52.
16. E.J. Pratt, "Towards the Last Spike" in *Collected Poems*, 2nd edition, Northrop Frye (ed.), Toronto, 1958, p. 379.

17. L.J. Burpee (ed.), *The History of Emily Montague (1769)*, Ottawa, 1931, p. 12.

18. W. Kirby, *The Golden Dog*, Boston, 1896, p. 4.

19. Hugh MacLennan, *Two Solitudes*, Toronto, 1945, pp. 3-4, reprinted by permission of the Author and the Macmillan Company of Canada Ltd.

20. Stephen Leacock, "I Will Stay in Canada" in *Canadian Anthology*, C.F. Klinck & R.E. Watters (eds.), Toronto, 1957, pp. 212-13.

21. Hugh Kenner, "The Case of the Missing Face" in *Our Sense of Identity*, Malcolm Ross (ed.), Toronto, 1954, p. 203.

22. Stephen Leacock, "My Financial Career" in *Literary Lapses*, Montreal, 1910, pp. 5-9.

23. Millar MacLure, "Smith's House of Fame" in *The Tamarak Review*, 17, Toronto, 1960, pp. 64-65.

24. George Johnston, "War on the Periphery" in *The Cruising Auk*, Toronto, 1959, p. 17.

25. Mordecai Richler, *The Apprenticeship of Duddy Kravitz*, London, Ont., 1959, p. 212.

26. Robertson Davies, *Leaven of Malice*, Toronto, 1954, p. 197.

PART FIVE:
INTERNATIONALISM

MAVIS GALLANT

HOME TRUTHS

AN INTRODUCTION

Only personal independence matters.
— Boris Pasternak

A Montreal collector once told me that he bought Canadian paintings in order to have a unifying theme in the decoration of his
house. It means — if anything so silly can have a meaning — that
art is neutral adornment, a slightly superior brand of chintz, and
that Canadian painters, because they are Canadian, work from a
single vision.

Like most of us, the collector probably has a defined range of
taste, and he is drawn to painting that happens to fall within its
scope. This will not prevent him from showing visitors art that can
be seen in good galleries all over Western Europe, not to speak of in
the United States, and calling it "typically" and even "uniquely"
Canadian. He has paid for an exclusive point of view; if art is universal, then he has been cheated.

To dissent would lead into hostile territory. It might be considered un-Canadian, an accusation to which the expatriate writer is
particularly susceptible, and will go to some lengths to avoid. I have
been rebuked by a consular official for remarking that Rome in winter is not as cold as Montreal; and it surely signifies more than light-
headedness about English that "expatriate" is regularly spelled in
Canadian newspapers "expatriot." Whether they know it or not,
Canadian artists are supposed to "paint Canadian."

Domestic embellishment, though of a slightly different nature, is
demanded, too, of Canadian writers, though only when their work
is concerned with Canada and Canadians; nobody cares what the
Canadian author thinks about Tibet. I often have the feeling with
Canadian readers that I am on trial. The accusation has nothing to

do with style or structure or content or imagination or control of subject and form — nothing that has any connection with literature in the usual sense — but with what are taken to be my concealed intentions. I am suspected of using language to screen a deep and disobliging meaning, or to perpetrate a fraud. I am asked if such and such a thing described "really happened," or, apparently more important, though entirely beside the point, "Did it actually happen to you?" The tone of the questioning suggests something more antagonistic than simple curiosity, and I wonder if there is not still somewhere a distrust of imagination. The writer, through whose work imagination speaks, has perhaps committed an act of intellectual deception, evidence of which will turn up in the work itself.

There is another question, asked, in my experience, only by Canadians: "Do you mean what you write?" Often the speaker will quote a passage that has offended him, not for what it says, which is plain, but for some unstated disparagement of Canada and Canadians he feels must be lurking behind it. He thinks there is more than meets the eye, and in a sense he is right: fiction, like painting, consists entirely of more than meets the eye; otherwise it is not worth a second's consideration. The interrogation is a settling of accounts with a Canadian who has failed to "paint Canadian." No division is allowed between the writer's citizenship, with its statutory and emotional ties, and his wider allegiance as an artist.

Unless he has rejected his native origin — and there may be many reasons for doing so — a citizen obviously owes more to his own country than to any other. In a democracy most of his obligations are moral and voluntary, and all the more to be observed on that account. But where his work is concerned, the writer, like any other artist, owes no more and no less to his compatriots than to people at large. This is by no means an original idea; it is an old-fashioned, liberal, and humanist one; but it is worth repeating in the present context of an introduction to Canadian stories.

I take it for granted that "Canadian stories" has a specific meaning. In contradiction to everything said above, I am constantly assured that Canadians no longer know what they are, or what to be Canadian should mean; for want of a satisfactory definition, a national identity has been mislaid. The most polite thing I can say about this is that I don't believe it. A Canadian who did not know what it was to be Canadian would not know anything else: he would have to be told his own name. It is as if a reassuring interpretation, a list of characteristics — the more rigid and confining the better — needed to be drawn up and offered for ratification. But ratified by what? A computer? A parliamentary committee? And what defines you will not define your closest relatives.

I suppose that a Canadian is someone who has a logical reason to think he is one. My logical reason is that I have never been anything else, nor has it occurred to me that I might be. I do not mean that traits that make me different from other people in places where I have lived and travelled are recognizably Canadian. I have lived in Paris for many years; when I travel in other parts of Europe I am often taken to be a Frenchwoman and addressed in French. The finest living writer of French prose, Marguerite Yourcenar, has lived in America for some thirty years. Although she writes only in French and, I would guess, thinks in French, I am sure that if I had never seen her picture and were to meet her in a train I would instinctively speak to her in English; there is a superficial coloration, an acquired surface, that reminds one more of — say — Willa Cather than Colette. And yet the essence of her mind, if one can judge from her writings, is wholly French. Except in rare cases of wilful destruction, the essence always remains undiluted.

I have sometimes felt more at odds in Canada than anywhere else, but I never supposed I was any the less Canadian. Feeling at odds is to be expected; no writer calls a truce. If he did, he would probably stop writing. I know that I could not suddenly turn myself into a Norwegian or a Pole or, to be reasonable, since I am English-speaking (and not, please, "Anglophone"), into an Australian or an American or an Englishwoman. (The persistent use of "English" in Quebec to designate me and people like me leaves me wondering if any amount of definitions will ever do. I have constantly to explain that if I were *Anglaise* I would hold a British passport and not a Canadian one.)

When in my American schools I refused to salute the flag, as I've described in *In Youth is Pleasure*, there was more to it than adolescent mulishness. I most certainly did not resent Americans; it was in New York, at fourteen, that I understood for the first time there was a possibility in life of being happy. It was simply that I was not an American, the Stars and Stripes was not my flag, and that was that. I resisted a change of citizenship when it was offered me because I knew the result would be fake: whatever I was called, I would continue to think of myself as Canadian. I believe it is a wholly respectable thing to be. Yet when I say this, it irritates Canadians. They take me to mean conformist, small-minded. I mean the word in its original sense of worthy of respect, the opposite of shameful and disreputable, and I have always made certain that respect was rendered that part of my identity on the few occasions when it had been slighted.

I am puzzled by those Canadians one occasionally meets abroad who seem reluctant to say what they are. (This, most emphatically, does not apply to French Canadians.) Sometimes they try to pass for British, not too successfully, or for someone vaguely chic and transatlantic. I have wondered, but not wanted to ask, how they replace the national sense of self. Once, in a Swiss hospital, emerging from a long anesthetic, I suffered a brief amnesia. I did not know where I was, why I was there, or what language I would be expected to speak. The first fact that floated to the surface was that I was Canadian and, almost simultaneously, that I was from Quebec. I supposed that I must be in a hospital somewhere in Quebec, and that I had been brought there after an automobile accident. I heard someone rustling pages and thought, They are tampering with my manuscripts: I was a writer. After that, the rest followed quickly.

What I am calling, most clumsily, the national sense of self is quite separate from nationalism, which I distrust and reject absolutely, and even patriotism, so often used as a stick to beat people with. Canada is one of the few countries that confers citizenship by birth, and we are apt to think that a national character automatically attaches itself to a birth certificate. The accident of birth does not give rise to a national consciousness, but I think the first years of schooling are indelible. They provide our center of gravity, our initial view of the world, the seed of our sense of culture. A deeper culture is contained in memory. Memory is something that cannot be subsidized or ordained. It can, however, be destroyed; and it is inseparable from language.

MAVIS GALLANT

2

As far back as I can remember, I read and spoke English and French, at about the same level. I had very young parents and they found it amusing to give me a simple text in English and have me rattle it off in French; it must have been like playing with a mechanical doll. At my first boarding school, in Montreal, I was the only English-speaking child. Toys were banned in this iron institution, but I had been allowed a few picture books from home. One was called *The Joyous Travellers*: a troupe of merry-looking animals adorned the cover; I do not remember what was inside.

In those days — the nineteen-twenties — it seemed to be mandatory for language teachers in both French and English schools in Canada to understand not a word of the language they set out to teach. The nun who taught English, and who might as well have been speaking Swahili for all I ever understood, held the book up to a class of docile little girls and announced that the title meant *Les Joyeux Travailleurs*, or *The Happy Workers*. My objection was taken to be insolence. Insolence was broken by deprivation of food. It is utterly confusing to a small child to be made to swear that black is white, particularly on a subject so vital as language and meaning. I owned up that "travellers" somehow meant the same thing as "workers," and received a dish of bread-and-milk. Children have fierce feelings about injustice and that is probably why the incident lodged in my mind. What interests me about it now is that a dead-lock could develop between a grown woman and a child over a word and its meaning. I knew the meaning; she was led astray by the sound.

A few years after this, when I was ten and at school in Ontario, I was stood before a class of children aged about thirteen and instructed to "say something in French" — an idiot request that plagued my school life until I became old enough to resist. I had just come from Montreal, where "saying something in French" had drawn only approval. If it was not a parlor trick many English-speakers could be bothered to learn, it was thought commendable in the intrepid and the young. And so it was with the confidence that rests on applause that I launched into my set recitation of *La cigale et la fourmi*. From the first words a black wave of hatred hit me; I feel it still. They cannot have hated Jean de La Fontaine, for they had never heard of him; nor can it have been disapproval of the rather nasty and ungenerous philosophy of the fable, for they had no idea what I was saying. It was hatred of an alien sound; and yet how alien those other children seemed to me, with their tiny blue eyes and little pug noses and large front teeth, and their flat, breathy way of "saying something in English."

I have never known anyone perfectly bilingual, and I wonder if such a phenomenon can exist this side of schizophrenia — leaving aside certain cases of genius: Samuel Beckett comes to mind. I wonder, even, if it is desirable: one needs a strong, complete language, fully understood, to anchor one's understanding. The rest is a luxury. What I do not understand is the hatred and fear of another sound, or even the lack of curiosity: how can one *not* want to know what other people think and feel, stated on their own terms?

For more than half my life I have heard and spoken more French than English. In the early nineteen-fifties, when I was moving round Europe, French was still the *lingua franca*. The people I see in Paris are for the most part either French or French-speaking; yet it has never occurred to me to write in French. In fact, I do not write it at all well; I spell it atrociously and deliberately refrain from improvement. I have to keep a strong writing wall in place or move to a different country. I think, write, and usually dream in English, and in thirty years have made only two idiomatic errors, one of which I caught: for "the house on the corner" I wrote "the house that makes the corner," a literal rendering of *"la maison qui fait le coin."* The other came back as a puzzled query on a proof: "Is this French?" I had written "a disaffected factory," which I changed to "an abandoned factory," though that is not the exact meaning of *"une usine désaffectée,"* the definition I wanted. There is no precise equivalent for much of anything between English and French, and that is why translations almost inevitably fall short. I cannot imagine any of my fiction in French, for it seems to me inextricably bound to English syntax, to the sound, resonance, and ambiguities of English vocabulary. If I were to write in French, not only would I put things differently, but I would never set out to say the same things. Words have an association that the primary, dictionary definitions cannot provide, and that are all translations usually offer. "It was the *best* butter" means nothing unless you know *Alice in Wonderland*. French conversation is totally different from exchange in English. (I mean by this conversation, not "Pass the salt.") The French taste for abstraction sails close to rhetoric and can sound false or insincere to an English-speaking listener, while a conversation in English, with its succession of illustrative anecdotes that

MAVIS GALLANT

take their departure from a point, rather than lead to one, soon bores a mind trained in French.

Gérard's hatred of English in "Saturday" is not blind and irrational. Deprived of the all-important first language, he is intellectually maimed. The most his mind can do is to hobble along. Like every story in this collection, "Saturday" needs to be read against its own time — the Montreal of about 1960. Rereading it, I see that it is not about a family or a society in conflict, but about language; or so it seems to me now. I could not write the same thing today; what loomed as cultural life-and-death a generation ago is now reduced to a much narrower preoccupation. Languages other than French and English are spoken in Montreal. I occasionally hear these referred to as "allophylian," with Greek, German, and Italian singled out for what I take to be arbitrary banishment from the Indo-European family. French and English occupy a stage designed to hold all the Aryan and Semitic tongues. It has the majesty of isolation, all right, but in the long run it may be lonely. The giddy misuse of "allophylian" is a good example of a word wrenched from its meaning to suit a transient need or, rather, transient wishful thinking. A writer stumbling over this and other linguistic taradiddles may feel like a grownup entering a nursery where politicians have been throwing blocks around: "Now then, this won't do at all. Put the alphabet back where you found it and try to be intelligible by suppertime."

3

Except for purely professional reasons, such as the writing of this introduction, I do not read my own work after it is in print. I had remembered "Jorinda and Jorindel" completely differently: I though it was a story about a summer weekend party of adults and that the children were only incidental. Of "Up North" I recalled a war bride and a train, of "Thank You for the Lovely Tea" that it had something to do with a school. All four were published in *The New Yorker* between 1954 and 1959 but are actually much older. I wrote "Tea" in New York, when I was eighteen, and the others in the forties, when I was working on *The Standard* in Montreal. Except for a few notebooks, I destroyed everything I had written when I left for Europe in 1950. Why I kept anything I do not recall. I did not open the notebooks for a long time. I typed "Up North" about eight years later, almost as I found it. Some pages had the wobbly look of having been written in a train, and I probably started it during a journey very like the one described while on assignment for *The Standard*.

I still fill scribblers and exercise books that remain unread for months and years and decades. Not long ago I came across a short novel I must have written twenty-nine years ago. The handwriting is so small that I had to use a magnifying glass. It is set in Spain: I have read so much twaddle written by foreigners about Spain that I was unable to judge it with the confidence I may have brought to writing it. I put it away for "later." "Later" is the imaginary, unhurried, idle future in which I intend to decipher, sort out, type, finish, save, or destroy "everything." I mention this because I know that readers sometimes believe fiction is composed, written, typed, and rushed into print without loss of time. The writer's preoccupations at the moment of publication — as much of these as may be visible — are thought to throw a light of some kind on the work. I am convinced that there is virtually no connection between mood and composition. "How I've fooled them!" Colette once said of critics who saw in one of her novels the mirror of her own life. The span between the germ of an idea and its maturation can be very long indeed, long enough for a writer's life to go through a good many upheavals and changes, particularly of the invisible and probably more devastating sort — intellectual, political. In my own case, the gap can be lengthened by a publishing delay in *The New Yorker* of anywhere from one to four years. By the time I finally read the work in proof, its origin has sunk out of recollection.

The third group of stories in this volume, set in Montreal, connected through a character named Linnet Muir who speaks in the first person, is an exception. I know exactly how the stories came to be written, and why. (Except for "With a Capital T," which appeared in *Canadian Fiction Magazine*, the stories were published in *The New Yorker* between 1975 and 1977, with unusual promptness, each appearing soon after it was received.)

It happened that by the mid-seventies I had been reading virtually nothing for two years except documents and books about the Dreyfus case. (Captain Alfred Dreyfus was a French Army officer, unjustly court-martialled for high treason in 1894, who spent four and a half years in solitary confinement on Devil's Island before being cleared. He was the first Jewish officer to serve at Staff Headquarters. The campaign to free him split French opinion into bitterly opposing factions; the breach has never quite healed.) If one can fix his personality through his letters and diaries and from the recollections of those who knew him, Dreyfus was a complex person, secretive and reserved. I once dreamed that we met and that he had nothing to say to me, which is probably how it might have been in real life. He was not overly interested in people outside his close family circle, and had next to nothing to say to civilians. He was a born soldier, an emotional nineteenth-century French patriot, identified mind and soul with French military attainments, the French military hierarchy, and the supremacy of French military tradition, none of which he ever questioned.

Nothing could be more remote from me than someone who deliberately could choose a life of rules and restrictions, of living by the book — and such a thin volume — with only a soldier's options: "I obey them" and "They obey me," both of which are to me totally abhorrent. Dreyfus came from a bourgeois and provincial family of cotton manufacturers. It was a background that bred good behavior but did nothing to foster imagination: there are no Dreyfus poets. His brand of impassioned patriotism was a flame of a kind; he lived to see it become murderous in the First World War, though he undoubtedly did not think of it that way; he lived to see Hitler come to power but died before discovering what the triumph of nationalism meant.

We — Dreyfus and I — were opposites in every sense, and had he been living he probably would have told me to leave his life alone. From beyond the grave he had the right to fairness. In writing about him, I could not say what I thought *might* be true, or would seem plausible if only life were tidy. I had to stand in his shoes, to assume, as best I could, an alien ambition (a soldier's career), an alien intelligence (he trained as an engineer and a mathematician before entering staff college), and to forget that I was a woman out of a twentieth-century North American society where women could vote and had the right to an education, where there was no such thing as peacetime conscription or penal transportation.

I used to wonder about the Paris Dreyfus saw — for instance, on the sunny October morning when he left his apartment near the Place de l'Alma to report to the War Ministry on Boulevard Saint-Germain, obeying a trumped-up order that was really a trap. I walked the route he followed many times, just as I often looked at all the paintings and photographs I could find of that particular Paris. Gradually, as I restored his Paris, his life, I discovered something in common with that tactiturn, reserved military figure: we had both resolved upon a way of life at an early age and had pursued our aims with overwhelming singlemindedness. He had been determined to become an officer in the French Army, over his family's advice and objections, just as I had been determined to write as a way of life in the face of an almost unanimous belief that I was foolish, would fail, would be sorry, and would creep back with defeat as a return ticket. ("Do you still have those nutty ideas of yours?" I was asked, not so many years ago.)

Once I had a point in common I moved with greater sureness into the book I wanted to write. I had thought of it sometimes as a river where I was drifting farther and farther from shore. At the same time — I suppose about then — there began to be restored in some underground river of the mind a lost Montreal. An image of Sherbrooke Street, at night, with the soft gaslight and leaf shadows on the sidewalk — so far back in childhood that it is more a sensation than a picture — was the starting point. Behind this image was a fictional structure of several stories, in the order in which they are presented here — three wartime stories, then the rest.

The character I called Linnet Muir is not an exact reflection. I saw her as quite another person, but it would be untrue to say that I invented everything. I can vouch for the city: my Montreal is as accurate as memory can make it. I looked nothing up, feeling that if I made a mistake with a street name it had to stand. Memory can spell a name wrong and still convey the truth. "*Je suis un mensonge qui dit la vérité.*" That was Jean Cocteau. It is not the last word about the writing of fiction, because no last word exists; but it says, briefly and plainly, what I might put with less grace.

MAVIS GALLANT

F.R. SCOTT

CREED

The world is my country
The human race is my race
The spirit of man is my God
The future of man is my heaven

EARLE BIRNEY

EL GRECO: ESPOLIO

The carpenter is intent on the pressure of his hand
on the awl, and the trick of pinpointing his strength
through the awl to the wood, which is tough.
He has no effort to spare for despoilings
nor to worry if he'll be cut in on the dice.
His skill is vital to the scene, and the safety of the state.
Anyone can perform the indignities; it is his hard arms
and craft that hold the eyes of the convict's women.
There is the problem of getting the holes straight
(in the middle of this shoving crowd)
and deep enough to hold the spikes
after they've sunk through those soft feet
and wrists waiting behind him.
The carpenter isn't aware that one of the hands
is held in a curious beseechment over him —
but what is besought, forgiveness or blessing? —
nor if he saw would he take the time to be puzzled.
Criminals come in all sorts, as anyone knows who makes crosses,
are as mad or sane as those who decide on their killings.
Our one at least has been quiet so far
though they say he has talked himself into this trouble —
a carpenter's son who got notions of preaching.
Well here's a carpenter's son who'll have carpenter's sons,
God willing, and build what's wanted, temples or tables,
mangers or crosses, and shape them decently,
working alone in that firm and profound abstraction
which blots out the bawling of rag-snatchers.
To construct with hands, knee-weight, braced thigh,
keeps the back turned from death.
But it's too late now for the other carpenter's boy
to return to this peace before the nails are hammered.

PIER GIORGIO DI CICCO

MALE RAGE POEM

Feminism, baby, feminism.
This is the anti-feminist poem.
It will get called the anti-
feminist poem. Like it or not.
Dedicated to all my friends who
can't get it up in the night,
accused of having male rage during the
day. This is for the poor buggers.
This is for me and the incredible boredom
of arguing about feminism, the right
arguments, the wrong arguments, the
circular argument, the arguments that stem
from one bad affair, from one
bad job, no job — whatever; fill in the
blanks _____ _____, fill in the ways
in which you have been hurt. Then I'll
fill in the blanks, and we'll send rosters
of hurt to each other, mail them, stock
them for the record, to say: *Giorgio Di Cicco*
has been hurt in this way x many times.
We will stock closets of Sarah's hurt,
Barbara's hurt, my hurt, Bobby's hurt.
This is where the poem peters out...oops! — that's
penis mentality, that's patriarchal bullshit,
sexist diction and *these line lengths are*
male oriented.
                    Where did he get so much male rage?
From standing out like a man for a bunch of
years, and being called the dirty word.
'When you are 21 you will become a Man.'
Christ! Doomed to enslave women ipso
facto, without even the right training for it.
Shouldn't have wasted ten years playing

baseball; should have practised
whipping, should have practised tying up the
girl next door, giving her cigarette burns...
oops! Male rage again! MALE RAGE — the words ring out —
worse than RING AROUND THE COLLAR, worse than
        KISSED
THE GIRLS AND MADE THEM CRY, jeesus, male rage
in kindergarten. MALE RAGE. You've got
male rage; I look inside myself and scrounge
for all this male rage. Must be there
somewhere. Must be repressing it. I write poems
faster and faster, therapeutically, to make sure
I get most of the rage out. But someone's
always there to say Male Rage — more Male Rage;
I don't leave the house, working on my male rage.

Things may lighten up. My friends may meet
fine women at a party someday and know
what to say to them, like: 'I'm not a Man and
you're not a Woman, but let's have dinner
anyway, let's fuck with our eyes closed and
swap roles for an hour.'

I'm tired of being a man.
Of having better opportunities,
better job offers,
too much money.
I'm tired of going to the YMCA and
talking jock in the locker room.
I'm tired of all the poems where
I used the word 'whore' inadvertently.
I'm tired of having secretaries type out
all my poems for me.
I'm tired of being a man.
I'm tired of being a sexist.
I'm afraid of male rage.
I'm afraid of *my* male rage,
this growing thing, this buddy, this
shadow, this new self, this stranger.
It's there. It's there! How could it have
happened? I ate the right things, said

yes to my mother, thought the good
thoughts.
      Doc — give it to me straight.
How long do I have before this male rage
takes over completely?
          The rest of your life.

Take it like a man.

PART SIX:
REGIONALISM

E.J. PRATT

NEWFOUNDLAND

Here the tides flow,
And here they ebb;
Not with that dull, unsinewed tread of waters
Held under bonds to move
Around unpeopled shores—
Moon-driven through a timeless circuit
Of invasion and retreat;
But with a lusty stroke of life
Pounding at stubborn gates,
That they might run
Within the sluices of men's hearts,
Leap under throb of pulse and nerve,
And teach the sea's strong voice
To learn the harmonies of new floods,
The peal of cataract,
And the soft wash of currents
Against resilient banks,
Or the broken rhythms from old chords
Along dark passages
That once were pathways of authentic fires.

Red is the sea-kelp on the beach,
Red as the heart's blood,
Nor is there power in tide or sun
To bleach its stain.
It lies there piled thick
Above the gulch-line.
It is rooted in the joints of rocks,
It is tangled around a spar,
It covers a broken rudder,
It is red as the heart's blood,
And salt as tears.

Here the winds blow,
And here they die,
Not with that wild, exotic rage
That vainly seeps untrodden shores,
But with familar breath
Holding a partnership with life,
Resonant with the hopes of spring,
Pungent with the airs of harvest.
They call with the silver fifes of the sea,
They breathe with the lungs of men,
They are one with the tides of the sea,
They are one with the tides of the heart,
They blow with the rising octaves of dawn,
They die with the largo of dusk,
Their hands are full to the overflow,
In their right is the bread of life,
In their left are the waters of death.

Scattered on boom
And rudder and weed
Are tangles of shells;
Some with backs of crusted bronze,
And faces of porcelain blue,
Some crushed by the beach stones
To chips of jade;
And some are spiral-cleft
Spreading their tracery on the sand
In the rich veining of an agate's heart;
And others remiain unscarred,
To babble of the passing of the winds.

Here the crags
Meet with winds and tides—
Not with that blind interchange
Of blow for blow
That spills the thunder of insentient seas;
But with the mind that reads assault
In crouch and leap and the quick stealth,
Stiffening the muscles of the waves.
Here they flank the harbours,
Keeping watch

On thresholds, altars and the fires of home,
Or, like mastiffs,
Over-zealous,
Guard too well.

Tide and wind and crag,
Sea-weed and sea-shell
And broken rudder—
And the story is told
Of human veins and pulses,
Of eternal pathways of fire,
Of dreams that survive the night,
Of doors held ajar in storms.

PAUL DUVAL

HIGH REALISM IN CANADA:
ALEX COLVILLE

Alex Colville, the signal figure in Canadian high realism, has won international acclaim for his hypnotic and superbly crafted paintings. As a pioneer contemporary realist, he remained steadfast to his creative commitment during a prolonged period when official art circles were under the spell of abstraction. As an educator, he spent seventeen years helping to inspire future painters in the disciplines of their craft. Such leading realists as Christopher Pratt, D.P. Brown, Hugh Mackenzie and Tom Forrestall have benefitted by his example, and the determined progress of his career has inspired Canadian painters who have never had occasion to meet him....

Between 1955 and 1960, Colville did a series of paintings which, perhaps unintentionally, celebrated domestic life around Sackville. These include *Family and Rainstorm* (1955 — National Gallery of Canada), *Woman at Clothesline* (1957 — National Gallery of Canada), *Child Skipping* (1958), *Boy, Dog and the Saint John River* (1958 — London Public Library and Art Museum)*Boy, Dog and School Bus* (1960) and *Mr. Wood in April* (1960). The fact that these paintings are universal in their creative power and human content, does not lessen the fact that they also remain, in a very real way, tributes to the specific domestic setting of their origin.

Colville had a real need for his teaching salary during his years at Mount Allison; his pictures found virtually no commercial market. From three one-man exhibitions (at the Hewitt Gallery, New York, in 1953 and 1955, and the Laing Gallery, Toronto, in 1958), he sold a total of four paintings. His determination and persistence with a demanding, time-consuming art in the face of such financial failure reflects his creative courage. His dedication finally paid off in February 1963, when his exhibition of twenty paintings at the Banfer Gallery in New York proved to be a sell-out. That success confirmed Colville's long-standing desire to leave teaching. It was followed in 1966 by international recognition when he was chosen

Canada's representative at the famed Biennale Internazionale d'Arte in Venice. In 1965 he won the open competition to design Canada's Centennial coins. In 1969 he was given an exhibition at the Kestner-Gesellschaft in Hanover, Germany. In 1970 twenty-three of his paintings were shown in a major one-man exhibit at the Marlborough Fine Art Gallery in London, England. And in 1971 he joined the Fischer Fine Art Gallery there as a regular exhibitor.

In 1963, at the time he left teaching to devote his full time to painting, Colville finally located a medium that met all of his creative requirements — acrylic polymer emulsion. Convenient, quick drying, mixable in water, and apparently permanent, acrylic colours (now universally popular) have remained his chosen medium. The restricted range of pigments available in acrylics is no limitation for Colville who uses only a small number of basic colours.

The acrylic paintings have caused unexpected and dramatic responses wherever they have been shown. European critics, in particular, have found in them "loneliness," "isolation" and "alienation." They find "devastation and the scent of death" in them. To this Colville says little. Typically, he remarked during a 1973 discussion about one of his small landscapes, *Snowstorm* (1971), "A painter is fundamentally a faker. If I say it is the sun in this painting, it is. If someone likes to see it as a moon, I have no quarrel." He has always insisted, "I paint almost always people and animals whom I consider to be wholly good, admirable and important." Certainly he constantly returns to favourite themes — his wife, animals, and the ever-present water which provides a firm horizon line for more than a quarter of his compositions.

Colville's working methods are governed by his slow, high-realist approach to art. He works in a small attic studio about twenty feet square on the third floor of his stucco home on Wolfville's main street. He normally paints for about four hours each morning, from 8:30 to 12:30, by the natural light of a west window, although he has no objection to artificial lighting. He does not use a mixing palette, but works directly from small china dishes, generally using a tiny sable brush. Unlike many realists, he keeps his picture panel almost vertical while he is painting on it.

Colville's acrylic polymer colours are limited to yellow ochre, burnt umber, burnt sienna, cadmium yellow light, cadmium red light, and cobalt blue, plus black and white. Until 1973 he used masonite panels as a painting surface, but then changed to K-3 board. He lays two coats of acrylic gesso to each side of the board.

DAVID ALEXANDER COLVILLE, 1920. Church and Horse, 1964. Acrylic on hardboard, 55.5 x 68.7 cm. Purchase, Horsley and Annie Townsend and anonymous donor. The Montreal Museum of Fine Arts, 1966.1529. © Alex Colville courtesy of Drabinsky & Friedland Galleries.

Although he usually makes about thirty preliminary drawings, Colville never prepares a full cartoon for a painting. He draws a geometric plan of his basic picture design in pencil, and then begins working directly with acrylics. On the average, it takes him four to six months to complete a painting.

Unlike many realists, Colville never uses the camera as an aid. During his years as a war artist, he constantly carried a camera to make detailed notes, but found that he could not use them when he came to compose a painting. On the other hand, he says that the motion picture may have affected his approach to art, particularly in relation to his sense of time.

The art of Alex Colville has survived some of the most pretentious verbiage and frantic footnoting ever visited upon a Canadian painter, but his own comments about art are fluent and unaffected. He shares with Jack Chambers the role of chief spokesman for Canadian realism. His comment, "I regard art not as a means of soliloquizing, but as a means of communication," could be applied to his own use of words.

In a talk at the Art Gallery of Hamilton in February 1973, Colville made a number of basic personal observations:

- Realists are primarily, or initially, concerned with content.

- A realist is fundamentally interested in experience and giving voice to experience.

- I don't think realists, by and large, are interested in art as play. The conception of art as puzzles and manipulations of shapes is not fundamental to artists who are called realists. This is not to say that realists do not have some formal preoccupation.

- I am concerned with space in a controlled way. I think I feel I am very much preoccupied with the problem of time. If you are concerned with the passage of time, you have to be concerned with space in a controlled way.

- My work has involved my wife to a considerable extent. Anyone working in art uses the life of other people, which is a humbling thought. [Colville's wife appears with him in a large percentage of his paintings.]

In 1963 Colville wrote in the introduction to a realist exhibition, *New Images From Canada*, held at the Banfer Gallery:

Many artists in a developing but essentially pioneer country like Canada have a tendency to want to prove that they can be conventionally *avant-garde*, and therefore not provincial. The artists in this exhibition have the courage and inner direction to be what they are and to do what they think they should do. This, of course, guarantees nothing but sincerity and good intentions; the real question is: "Are the paintings and drawings good?" I think they are, in various ways, the realist tradition being many-faceted, and to various degrees, some of the artists being more mature than others. All I can say in the end is that if they were horses, I would bet on them.

The evidence now in proves that Alex Colville would easily have won his bet. The high level of realism in Canada today owes much to him as spokesman and artist. His stubborn pursuit of realism and mastery of it has helped nourish the ambitions and talents of many of Canada's finest contemporary painters.

W. O. MITCHELL

A BOY'S PRAIRIE

Here was the least common denominator of nature, the skeleton requirements simply, of land and sky — Saskatchewan prairie. It lay wide around the town, stretching tan to the far line of the sky, shimmering under the June sun and waiting for the unfailing visitation of wind, gentle at first, barely stroking the long grasses and giving them life; later, a long hot gusting that would lift the black topsoil and pile it in barrow pits along the roads, or in deep banks against the fences.

Over the prairie, cattle stood listless beside the dried-up slough beds which held no water for them. Where the snow-white of alkali edged the course of the river, a thin trickle of water made its way towards the town low upon the horizon. Silver willow, heavy with dust, grew along the riverbanks, perfuming the air with its honey smell.

Just before the town the river took a wide loop and entered at the eastern edge. Inhabited now by some eighteen hundred souls, it had grown up on either side of the river from the seed of one homesteader's sod hut built in the spring of eighteen seventy-five. It was made up largely of frame buildings with high, peaked roofs, each with an expanse of lawn in front and a garden in the back; they lined avenues with prairie names: Bison, Riel, Qu'Appelle, Blackfoot, Fort. Cement sidewalks extended from First Street to Sixth Street at MacTaggart's Corner; from that point to the prairie a boardwalk ran.

Lawn sprinklers sparkled in the sun; Russian poplars stood along either side of Sixth Street. Five houses up from MacTaggart's Corner stood the O'Connal home, a three storeyed house lifting high above the white cottage to the left of it. Virginia creepers had almost smothered the veranda; honeysuckle and spirea grew on either side of the steps. A tricycle with its front wheel sharply turned stood in the middle of the walk.

Brian walked back towards his home. He did not turn down Bison Avenue where it crossed the street upon which the church was, but continued on, a dark wishbone of a child wrapped in reflection.

The wind was persistent now, a steady urgency upon his straight back, smoking up the dust from the road along the walk, lifting it and carrying it out to the prairie beyond. Several times Brian stopped: once to look up into the sun's unbearable radiance and then away with the lingering glow stubborn in his eyes; another time when he came upon a fox-red caterpillar making a procession of itself over a crack that snaked along the walk. He squashed it with his foot. Further on he paused at a spider that carried its bead of a body between hurrying thread-legs. Death came for the spider too.

He looked up to find that the street had stopped. Ahead lay the sudden emptiness of the prairie. For the first time in his four years of life he was alone on the prairie.

He had seen it often, from the veranda of his uncle's farmhouse, or at the end of a long street, but till now he had never heard it. The hum of telephone wires along the road, the ring of hidden crickets, the stitching sound of grasshoppers, the sudden relief of a meadow lark's song, were deliciously strange to him. Without hesitation he crossed the road and walked out through the hip-deep grass stirring in the steady wind; the grass clung at his legs; haloed fox-tails bowed before him; grasshoppers sprang from hidden places in the grass, clicketing ahead of him to disappear, then lift again.

A gopher squeaked questioningly as Brian sat down upon a rock warm to the backs of his thighs. He picked a pale blue flax-flower at his feet, stared long at the stripings in its shallow throat, then looked up to see a dragonfly hanging on shimmering wings directly in front of him. The gopher squeaked again, and he saw it a few yards away, sitting up, watching him from its pulpit hole. A suave-winged hawk chose that moment to slip its shadow over the face of the prairie.

And all about him was the wind now, a pervasive sighing through great emptiness, unhampered by the buildings of the town, warm and living against his face and in his hair.

Then for the second time that day he saw a strange boy — one who came from behind him soundlessly, who stood and stared at him with steady grey eyes in a face of remarkable broadness, with cheekbones circling high under a dark and freckled skin. He saw that the boy's hair, bleached as the dead prairie grass itself, lay across his forehead in an all-round cowlick curling under at the edge. His faded blue pants hung open in two tears just below the knees. He was barefooted.

W. O. MITCHELL

Brian was not startled; he simply accepted the boy's presence out here as he had accepted that of the gopher and the hawk and the dragonfly.

'This is your prairie,' Brian said.

The boy did not answer him. He turned and walked as silently as he had come, out over the prairie. His walk was smooth.

After the boy's figure had become just a speck in the distance, Brian looked into the sky, now filled with a soft expense of cloud, the higher edges luminous and startling against the blue. It stretched to the prairie's rim. As he stared, the grey underside carded out, and through the cloud's softness was revealed a blue well shot with sunlight. Almost as soon as it had cleared, a whisking of cloud stole over it.

For one moment no wind stirred. A butterfly went pelting past. God, Brian decided, must like the boy's prairie.

PAUL HIEBERT

SARAH BINKS

Introduction

Sarah Binks, the Sweet Songstress of Saskatchewan, as she is often called, no longer needs any introduction to her ever-growing list of admirers. In fact, it may be asked why another book should be added to the already voluminous and continually growing literature which deals with the work of this great Canadian. We already know about her life — we know about her tragic death. We know about her early struggles for recognition and her rise to fame. We know about the honours that were showered upon her, culminating finally in that highest award in the bestowal of the Saskatchewan people, the Wheat Pool Medal. But what is not known, or at least what is so often overlooked, is that quite apart from the Saskatchewan for which Sarah speaks, she was pre-eminently a poetess in her own right, that in a life so poor in incident and surrounded on all sides by the pastoral simplicity, if not actual severity, of the Municipality of Willows, she developed a character so rich and a personality so winsome and diverse. There is too, a profound personal philosophy which speaks to us quite apart from the sweep and beauty of the prairies with which she is associated. It is this theme which the Author has developed. It definitely strikes a new note.

From Shakespeare's "England, my England," to a Saskatchewan wheat farm may seem to be a far cry. But that same patriotism, that same confidence and joy in his native land which is the heritage of all poets, is also Sarah's. And when she cries out in a sudden awareness of her own gumbo stretch, "The Farmer is King!" or when she sings in full throat, *The Song of the Chore*, or hymns the joy of *Spreading Time*, or discusses with deep understanding but with impersonal detachment as in *To My Father, Jacob Binks*, the fine economic adjustment between the farmer and the cut-worm, we know that she speaks for the Canadian West in the language of all poets at all times. It is this which has given her the high place in the world of literature and in the hearts of her countrymen.

But there us much more to Sarah Binks than being the Laureate of Saskatchewan. Sarah was not only the expression of her day and age, she was also the product of her immediate environment. She was the product of her friends, of her books, and of the little incidents which shaped her life. She was the product of the Grade School, of her neighbours, of Mathilda Schwantzhacker, of Ole the hired man, of her grandfather the philosophical herbalist, of William Greenglow who taught her Geology, of Henry Welkin who took her to Regina. From all of these Sarah emerges as a character, as a personality, and above all, as a woman.

It has been no light task to gather together the many threads of personal and literary influence and to reconstruct from them, as in fine needlepoint, a truer, more intimate picture of Sarah Binks than we have hitherto known. Sarah, on the larger canvas, as a national figure, loses nothing thereby. But for those who like to look beyond the poetry to the poetess, for those who would see beyond the high achievement the unfolding and blossoming of the poetic spirit, this new life of Sarah Binks has been written.

There is an age in Western Canada which is fast disappearing before our very eyes; an age which began with the turn of the century and lasted at its best about thirty years. Sarah's dates, 1906 to 1929, practically define it. They were the halcyon days of Western Canada, the golden days of the dirt farmer. It was an age sandwiched between the romantic West of the "cow country" and the West of drought and relief and economic experiment. It was a prosperous age for Saskatchewan, and such periods of prosperity and commercial expansion are always accompanied by literary and artistic blossoming. On a small scale the Golden Age of Pericles in Greece, or the Elizabethan age of England, finds its counterpart in Canada's fairest and flattest province. Already in brief historical perspective that age is beginning to take on an aura of romance. Sarah Binks was its artistic expression.

Those most productive years of Sarah's also mark the high water mark of Saskatchewan's prosperity. The price of wheat rose to fabulous heights; clean eggs, not over three days old, sold in the general stores at prices ranging all the way from twenty to twenty-six cents a dozen, whilst at the Willows and Quagmire elevators the classifications of both screenings and Durum, No. 4, Smutty, were raised to No. 3, Smutty. Liver also showed signs of a rise.

PAUL HIEBERT

To the west the frontier had been rolled back; the tumble-weed had yielded to the sow-thistle, the coyote had vanished from the plains, and with the disappearance of these great herds, his last source of Vitamin B gone, disappeared also the prairie Indian, a proud and picturesque figure in overalls and plug hat — swept away before the ruthless march of civilization. The land was open for wheat. No economic cloud marked the Saskatchewan horizon; mortgage money could be had at any time for twelve percent, and the dry belt, which years later was to creep north and eastwards over a country already desiccated by prohibition laws, still lay in the heart of the Great American desert.

It is claimed by some writers that Sarah Binks sprang spontaneously from Saskatchewan's alkaline soil, that she was an isolated genius such as the ages have produced from time to time with no significance beyond her unparalleled talent. With this view the Author takes exception. Sarah Binks was the product of her soil and her roots go deep. But more than that, she was an expression of her environment and her age. Without Saskatchewan at its greatest, at its golden age, Sarah would have been just another poetess. Sarah was the daughter and the grand-daughter of a dirt farmer; she loved the soil and much of Jacob Binks' passion for another quarter section flowed in her veins. Her love for the paternal acres was a real love, she believed in the rotation of crops, and in the fall, after the plowing was done, she spread the fertilizer with a lavish hand. "The farmer is king!", she cries,

> The farmer is king of his packer and plow,
> Of his harrows and binders and breakers,
> He is lord of the pig, and Czar of the cow
> On his hundred and sixty-odd acres.
>
> The farmer is monarch in high estate,
> Of his barn and his back-house and byre,
> And all the buildings behind the gate
> Of his two-odd miles of barbed wire.
>
> The farmer is even Caesar of freight
> And tariff and tax, comes election,
> And from then until then he can abdicate,
> And be king on his own quarter section.

The farmer is king, oh, the farmer is king,
And except for his wife and his daughter,
Who boss him around, he runs the thing,
Come drought, come hell or high water.

It is significant, too, that Sarah Binks should have seized upon Warden and Rockbuster's *First Steps in Geology* and made it so singularly her own. Geology to her was the farm extended to the outer world, to the larger life. Any other book at that period of her life would have left her cold. It is undoubtedly true, to quote Principal Pinhole, "If the benign fates which rule the lives of men had passed William Greenglow in Geology II and had given him a supplemental in Maths II instead, Sarah's songs would not have been touched to the same extent. The binomial theorem as I understand it is by no means the same as the theory of crustal movements, and it is just because the one deals with rocks and the other has to do with figures without rocks, that the whole Neo-Geo-Literary school of literature is different by just that much. In fact some other province might have got the credit."

Sarah Binks has raised her home province of Saskatchewan to its highest prairie level. Unschooled, but unspoiled, this simple country girl has captured in her net of poesy the flatness of that great province. Like a sylph she wanders through its bluffs and coulees, across its haylands, its alkali flats, its gumbo stretches, its gopher meadows;

Hark! Like a mellow fiddle moaning,
Through the reed-grass sighing,
Through a gnarled branch groaning,
Comes the Poet —
Sylph-like,
Gaunt-like,
Poeming —
And his eyes are stars,
And his mouth is foaming.

Thus, Sarah herself, in the divine frenzy. No wonder she is called the Sweet Songstress of Saskatchewan. Indeed she could be called much more. No other poet has so expressed the Saskatchewan soul. No other poet has caught in deathless lines so much of its elusive

PAUL HIEBERT

spirit, the baldness of its prairies, the alkalinity of its soil, the richness of its insect life.

In presenting this new study of the life and works of the Sweet Songstress the Author feels that he is filling a long-felt want. Much has already been written, much more remains to be written, but hitherto no such complete study of the life and character of Sarah Binks has been published. The papers which have appeared from time to time have been fragmentary, generally critical studies dealing with one phase of her life or with a group of poems. Special mention must be made of the numerous papers of Horace P. Marrowfat, B.A., Professor Emeritus of English and Swimming, of St. Midget's College; of Dr. Taj Mahal, D.O., of British Columbia; and to the Proceedings of the Ladies' Literary League of Quagmire. These papers and publications have been of especial value in the preparation of this book, and proper acknowledgments have been made wherever it was considered absolutely necessary.

The Author also wishes to express his indebtedness to the recent work, *Great Lives and Great Loves*, by Miss Rosalind Drool, and to the publishers, Bunnybooks Ltd., for permission to quote therefrom. Miss Drool's intense and even introspective searchings into certain phases of Sarah Binks' life have been of great interest, more especially since her own personal offer to pursue further studies "at considerable lengths" has also heightened an interest in Miss Drool.

The great source of material for the student of Sarah Binks is, of course, the Binksian Collection in the Provincial Archives of Saskatchewan. This, together with the letters of Mathilda, has been the supply upon which all other students have hitherto drawn. But much inference has been published as fact. Many of the details of Sarah's life are still vague and have still to be filled in. There is, however, a great wealth of material still unturned and unexploited around Willows, Sarah's birthplace. The Author has not hesitated to make use of this material where it could be published.

It has been the aim of the Author at all times to give a deeper, truer meaning to the poetic heritage which belongs to Sarah, the unspoiled child of the soil. Sarah's lyrical poetry, small as it is in bulk, ranks among the rarest treasures of Canadian literature. The poems which have been included in this work are most of them well known, but no apology need be made for their repetition. Quite apart from their intrinsic beauty, they are significant in that they are expressions of facts and events in her life. Sarah, more than most poets, seizes upon the trivial, or what to lesser souls would appear trivial, incident and experience, for example the loss of Ole's ear by a duck, as an occasion for a lyrical outburst of pulsating beauty. These poems can only be understood within the context of Sarah's life, and free use has therefore been made of them. No one has ever wanted to copyright any of Sarah's poems, and they have therefore been quoted at length — wholly, partly, or just simply quoted.

In addition to the field work done in and around Willows the Author has made a special journey to Quorum, Sask., at which place Mrs. Steve Grizzlykick, (Mathilda) was interviewed, and to Vertigo, Manitoba, where Mrs. Pete Cattalo was questioned concerning Ole. Although the actual field data obtained in these investigations cannot be published, they have been of much value in giving atmosphere and in interpreting the scene around Willows and Quagmire during and immediately preceding the time when Sarah wrote *Wash Out on the Line*.

The Author is greatly indebted to the Editor of *The Horsebreeder's Gazette* for the opportunity of going through his files, and also, when he was out to lunch, his desk. Much interesting information was available here.

In the case of the Editor of *Swine and Kine* no files had been kept, but permission was given to interview the secretary and later on to take her out to the local dance. The information here was exceptionally good.

The Author in particular wishes to express his indebtedness to the Quagmire Malting and Brewing Company for much of the material embodied in this book, and to the Dominion Distillers, Limited, who so kindly read the proofs.

A.M. KLEIN

MONTREAL

O city metropole, isle riverain!
Your ancient pavages and sainted routs
Traverse my spirit's conjured avenues!
Splendour erablic of your promenades
Foliates there, and there your maisonry
Of pendant balcon and escalier'd march,
Unique midst English habitat,
Is vivid Normandy!

You populate the pupils of my eyes:
Thus, does the Indian, plumed, furtivate
Still through your painted autumns, Ville-Marie!
Though palisades have passes, though calumet
With tabac of your peace enfumes the air,
Still do I spy the phantom, aquiline,
Genuflect, moccasin'd, behind
His statue in the square!

Thus, costumed images before me pass,
Haunting your archives architectural:
Coureur de bois, in posts where pelts were portaged;
Seigneur within his candled manoir; Scot
Ambulant through his bank, pillar'd and vast.
Within your chapels, voyaged mariners
Still pray, and personage departed,
All present from your past!

Grand port of navigations, multiple
The lexicons uncargo'd at your quays,
Sonnant though strange to me; but chiefest, I,
Auditor of your music, cherish the
Joined double-melodied vocabulaire
Where English vocable and roll Ecossic,
Mollified by the parle of French
Bilinguefact your air!

Such your suaver voice, hushed Hochelaga!
But for me also sound your potencies,
Fortissimos of sirens fluvial,
Bruit of manufactory, and thunder
From foundry issuant, all puissant tone
Implenishing your hebdomad; and then
Sanct silence, and your argent belfries
Clamant in orison!

You are a part of me, O all your quartiers —
And of dire pauvrete and of richesse —
To finished time my homage loyal claim;
You are locale of infancy, milieu
Vital of institutes that formed my fate;
And you above the city, scintillant,
Mount Royal, are my spirit's mother,
Almative, poitrinate!

Never do I sojourn in alien place
But I do languish for your scenes and sounds,
City of reverie, nostalgic isle,
Pendant most brilliant on Laurentian cord!
The coigns of your boulevards — my signiory —
Your suburbs are my exile's verdure fresh,
Your parks, your fountain'd parks —
Pasture of memory!

A.M. KLEIN

City, O city, you are vision'd as
A parchemin roll of saecular exploit
Inked with the script of eterne souvenir!
You are in sound, chanson and instrument!
Mental, you rest forever edified
With tower and dome; and in these beating valves,
Here in these beating valves, you will
For all my mortal time reside!

MARYBELLE MYERS

THINGS MADE BY INUIT

Carving — The Stone

One of the biggest problems right now for carvers is finding suitable stone since easily accessible sites are rapidly being exhausted. We have talked for many years about getting help to find new sites and to mine the stone but this help has never materialized. For the most part, carvers continue to find their own stone. Some even consider the finding and extracting of the stone to be an integral part of the work of creation. This is expressed very well by Paulosie Kasadluak in an essay he wrote a few years ago, first published in the Winnipeg Art Gallery catalogue, Inoucdjouac-Port Harrison (1976). It is called Nothing Marvellous and we are repeating it below because it describes so eloquently the way carvers feel about their work and, especially, their feeling that obtaining the soapstone is one of the essential features of making a carving.

It is not only to make money that we carve. Nor do we carve make-believe things. What we show in our carvings is the life we have lived in the past right up to today. We show the truth.

We carve the animals because they are important to us as food. We carve Inuit figures because in that way we can show ourselves to the world as we were in the past and as we now are. That is why we carve men hunting and building igloos and women making something that they will use, maybe sewing kamiks or clothing or using an ulu. No matter what activity the carved figure is engaged in, something about it will be true. That is because we carve to show what we have done as people. There is nothing marvellous about it. It is there for everyone to see. It is just the truth.

It is the same with the work which the women do with their hands. We do not reveal ourselves only in stone. The work of the women shows the type of clothing which we as people had. That, too, contributes to the truth.

We Inuit have had many experiences. We have used just about everything for clothing: skins and furs and modern day cotton and wool. We have eaten all kinds of animals and, for our hunting gear, have used their bones, fur and skin. Our clothing also came from the animals we killed. So, these carvings we make of the animals and the Inuk in traditional clothing, engaged in his work, all of them reveal what we were or what we are now. Nothing marvellous about it.

Carving means many things to us. One has to find stone in order to make carvings. Summer or winter, each brings its own difficulty in obtaining the stone. This is something which I believe the people in the south do not understand. You have to think of where the stone comes from and the problems one goes through getting it out. The problem of locating it in the first place and the distance one has to carry it. I could write many words about all this.

Before one finds the stone, it is useless. It just exists. Maybe it is exposed on the surface of the earth. Maybe it is beneath the water. One thing I know is that the best kind of stone is usually the hardest for us to get.

It is hard in summer because you have to carry the stone to your canoe all the way from the quarry where you extracted it by hand. It is tedious work but the thought that this will enable you to feed your family and develop your Cooperative provides you with the initiative and stamina to survive this trouble. As does the thought that in this way, we will be able to communicate to the rest of the world about ourselves.

Even so, it is back breaking work. Even when you do not have to carry the stone so far to your canoe at the shore, there is always a certain amount of danger in transporting the heavy rock by canoe. And you cannot even eat it!

Getting the stone out of the ground, even in the summer when the ground is not frozen, is hard work because we do not have any fancy equipment. It is only because we help each other and work together to extract the stone that we are able to succeed.

In winter, it is particularly difficult to get at the stone. The snow can drift five to ten feet over the site so that you are unsure of the exact spot. You have to take a chance and when you shovel all that snow away you are still left to dig in the hard frozen earth.

The stone is never the same. Some is black and some is green. I really know the green stone because it is at a place where I grew up. The stone we are using now in Inoucdjouac is mined from a site about forty miles out of town. It costs a lot of money even to get to that place. You need proper equipment, skidoo or canoe, to go there and proper maintenance so you will not break down.

If you go by canoe, you go through huge swells and waves along the way because part of your journey is through the open Hudson's Bay where there are no little islands to shelter you. It is not much better in the winter because your snowmobile needs gas which costs $2.25 a gallon now and your route lies over the unevenly frozen sea ice. But some sites, I hear, are even farther away than that from the settlements.

It is unfortunate but the stone which is close to our village always seems to be of a poor quality and useless in our carvings. What I have said may be enough to convince you that making a carving is not play. It is man's work.

There is much that happens from the time the stone is found and the time the people in the south see it as a bird or anything. And everything is done with your hands. A man is dependent upon his hands when he wants to show what his life is.

Paulosie Kasadluak
Inoucdjouac, October 1976

(Translated by Ali Tulugak and reprinted with permission from *Port Harrison/ Inoucdjouac*, The Winnipeg Art Gallery, 1976)

Printmaking — An Old Technique Updated

Printmaking began in Povungnituk, in 1961, in one of the old stone houses which are still there. It was a cold place in which to work but that didn't stop people from gathering there to experiment with different printmaking techniques.

The first collection of Povungnituk prints was marketed in conjunction with the Cape Dorset collection in 1962. At that time, the marketing of Eskimo prints was handled by the Canadian Eskimo Arts Council. Now, the Arts Council acts only as advisor to the printmaking cooperatives and the prints are marketed by the appropriate distribution agency. The Council's approval of prints for marketing is indicated by a blind stamp in the lower right hand margin of each print.

Inuit printmakers follow international conventions concerning the production and handling of prints. Each print is numbered and signed and, after the prints are made, the stone block is defaced so that no more prints can be made from it. This is important because when someone buys a print which is numbered 5/50, he is entitled to assume that only fifty prints were made, of which he has number five. Generally speaking, prints from Arctic Quebec are published in editions of fifty with five artist's proofs.

Unlike those processed through a press, prints pulled from a stone block do not degenerate in quality as the successive images are made. There should, therefore, be no difference in value or "fineness" between a low edition number and the last print pulled from a particular stone. A slight colour tolerance is desirable in a hand pulled print but a careful printer keeps this to a minimum.

When a collection of prints is ready for marketing, they are catalogued, an expensive procedure but considered necessary for several reasons. Catalogues help to sell the prints but are even more important as an historical record and an authenticating tool.

Povungnituk has brought out fourteen catalogues, including the 1962 one they shared with Cape Dorset and a memorial collection of Davidialuk's last work in 1977. They have also contributed prints to two Arctic Quebec catalogues. The 1970 Povungnituk catalogue, a departure from normal practice, included all the prints on inventory up to that time as well as the entire 1969 collection.

In the early days, Povungnituk printmakers received some instruction from white artists, Gordon Yearsley and Viktor Tinkl, but from the fall of 1964 until 1972, they worked pretty much on their own. Although anyone in the community could make a stone and sell it to the print shop, a body of regular contributors developed — Syollie Arpatuk, Alasi Audla, Siasi Attitu, Annie Mikpigak, Leah Qumaluk, Juanisialuk, Paulosie Sivuak, Quananapik, Josie Paperk, Davidialuk, Joe Talirunili and Kanayook who was both artist and supervisor of the shop. For years, he was helped in this by Niali Timagiak who supervised the shop on her own from 1973 to 1977. Kanayook resumed his supervisory role in 1977.

The early Povungnituk prints did not sell very well even though they were offered at ridiculously low princes. Ironically, those early prints are now very much in demand and at very high prices. Because of their initial lack of success, as well as some unfortunate advice, the print shop undertook, in the late '60s, to produce "small prints" which were glued into a cardboard folder and retailed in the south for two dollars. Although this gave the printmakers some

MARYBELLE MYERS

work to do, it really didn't make that much sense when they had the talent to do more important work.

It was obvious that Povungnituk needed some help and, in 1972, a six week printmaking workshop was organized. All of the villages in Arctic Quebec were invited to send people to work with Bob Paterson, an artist-teacher now living in Ontario. Eighteen Inuit from nine communities in Arctic Quebec participated in the workshop and although most of these people had never made a print before, they produced an interesting collection of thirty-eight prints which were approved by the Council, catalogued, and sold very well.

There were two reason for this workshop — to locate new printmaking talent in other villages and to give some guidance to the Povungnituk artists who were no longer involved in serious printmaking. Some of the participants in that 1972 workshop attempted to set up small print workshops when they returned to their own communities, teaching what they had learned to others. In the early '70s, some of these people produced prints which were catalogued as "Arctic Quebec" collections.

No one ever expected that print shops would be established in every community. Obviously the market would not support mass production of prints. Nor would the medium benefit from a factory approach. The main print producing community in Arctic Quebec is still Povungnituk, although George River (on Ungava Bay) has a small print shop where Tivi Etook and his son-in-law, Peter Morgan, work. Great Whale River and Inoucdjouac had small print shops for a while, but in 1976, the Great Whale River shop was converted to a fabric screening centre and, two years ago, this activity was transferred to Inoucdjouac. There are some good printmakers in Inoucdjouac and it may be that they will one day return to printmaking. In the meantime, this printshop is producing original Eskimo T-shirts and tote bags designed for sale in northern communities.

In 1975, Ken Fitzpatrick, a white artist who was then living in Montreal, went to work with the Povungnituk printmakers. He established a good working rapport with the older printmakers particularly, and some very nice work was produced during his time there. Although he was there for less than a year, he helped revive interest in printmaking. After Fitzpatrick left, however, it seemed as if the print shop would never get back o its old level of production.

Some of the old-timers were going on to other things: Paulosie Sivuak wasn't making prints anymore. Kanayook gave up his supervisory position and stopped making prints. Syollie Arpatuk remarried and moved to Great Whale River after his wife's death. Annie Mikpigak got older. Davidialuk, Joe Talirunili and Juanisialuk died.

The obvious solution to the passing of old talent is the training of a new generation. This is being done. Werner Zimmerman, a young painter and printmaker, has been working with the Arctic Quebec print shops for two years and has succeeded in involving some of the younger people in printmaking.

A new generation means new things, hopefully, not just change but *growth*. The collection of prints in this exhibition is a record of development. From 1961 to 1979. From Joe Talirunili, an old man who lived the old life, to Sarah Putuguk, a young woman living the new life. From Leah Qumaluk's scenes of traditional life right up to Inoucdjouac's T-shirts. Although T-shirts are not in the same category as prints, we have included one in this exhibition because it, like printmaking, is an updated talent.

We have ended this section with a sealskin appliqué tapestry which nicely demonstrates the marrying of old skills and new concepts. The appliqué technique is very old. Once used to decorate skin clothing, it is used here with a pure graphic intent. It is a new use for an old skill and yet another example of *things made by Inuit*.

MARYBELLE MYERS

PART SEVEN:
BEAUTIFUL LOSERS

STEPHEN LEACOCK

MY FINANCIAL CAREER

When I go into a bank I get rattled. The clerks rattle me; the wickets rattle me; the sight of the money rattles me; everything rattles me.

The moment I cross the threshold of a bank and attempt to transact business there, I become an irresponsible idiot.

I knew this beforehand, but my salary had been raised to fifty dollars a month and I felt that the bank was the only place for it.

So I shambled in and looked timidly round at the clerks. I had an idea that a person about to open an account must needs consult the manager.

I went up to a wicket marked "Accountant." The accountant was a tall, cool devil. The very sight of him rattled me. My voice was sepulchral.

"Can I see the manager?" I said, and added solemnly, "alone." I don't know why I said "alone."

"Certainly," said the accountant, and fetched him.

The manager was a grave, calm man. I held my fifty-six dollars clutched in a crumpled ball in my pocket.

"Are you the manager?" I said. God knows I didn't doubt it.

"Yes," he said.

"Can I see you," I asked, "alone?" I didn't want to say "alone" again, but without it the thing seemed self-evident.

The manager looked at me in some alarm. He felt I had an awful secret to reveal.

"Come in here," he said, and led the way to a private room. He turned the key in the lock.

"We are safe from interruption here," he said. "Sit down."

We both sat down and looked at each other. I found no voice to speak.

"You are one of Pinkerton's men, I presume," he said.

He had gathered from my mysterious manner that I was a detective. I knew what he was thinking, and it made me worse.

"No, not from Pinkerton's," I said, seeming to imply that I came from a rival agency.

"To tell the truth," I went on, as if I had been prompted to lie about it, "I am not a detective at all. I have come to open an account. I intend to keep all my money in this bank."

The manager looked relieved but still serious; he concluded now that I was a son of Baron Rothschild or a young Gould.

"A large account, I suppose," he said.

"Fairly large," I whispered. "I propose to deposit fifty-six dollars now and fifty dollars a month regularly."

The manager got up and opened the door. He called to the accountant.

"Mr. Montgomery," he said unkindly loud, "this gentleman is opening an account, he will deposit fifty-six dollars. Good morning."

I rose.

A big iron door stood open at the side of the room.

"Good morning," I said, and stepped into the safe.

"Come out," said the manager coldly, and showed me the other way.

I went up to the accountant's wicket and poked the ball of money at him with a quick convulsive movement as if I were doing a conjuring trick.

My face was ghastly pale.

"Here," I said, "deposit it." The tone of the words seemed to mean, "Let us do this painful thing while the fit is on us."

He took the money and gave it to another clerk.

He made me write the sum on a slip and sign my name in a book. I no longer knew what I was doing. The bank swam before my eyes.

"Is it deposited?" I asked in a hollow, vibrating voice.

"It is," said the accountant.

"Then I want to draw a cheque."

My idea was to draw out six dollars of it for present use. Someone gave me a cheque-book through a wicket and someone else began telling me how to write it out. The people in the bank had the impression that I was an invalid millionaire. I wrote something on the cheque and thrust it in at the clerk. He looked at it.

"What! are you drawing it all out again?" he asked in surprise. Then I realised that I had written fifty-six instead of six. I was too far gone to reason now. I had a feeling that it was impossible to explain the thing. All the clerks had stopped writing to look at me.

STEPHEN LEACOCK

Reckless with misery, I made a plunge.

"Yes, the whole thing."

"You withdraw your money from the bank?"

"Every cent of it."

"Are you not going to deposit any more?" said the clerk, astonished.

"Never."

An idiot hope struck me that they might think something had insulted me while I was writing the cheque and that I had changed my mind. I made a wretched attempt to look like a man with a fearfully quick temper.

The clerk prepared to pay the money.

"How will you have it?" he said.

"What?"

"How will you have it?"

"Oh" — I caught his meaning and answered without even trying to think — "in fifties."

He gave me a fifty-dollar bill.

"And the six?" he asked dryly.

"In sixes," I said.

He gave it me and I rushed out.

As the big door swung behind me I caught the echo of a roar of laughter that went up to the ceiling of the bank. Since then I bank no more. I keep my money in cash in my trousers pocket and my savings in silver dollars in a sock.

CHARLES TAYLOR

SIX JOURNEYS:
A CANADIAN PATTERN

Introduction

> Canadians do not like heroes, and so they do not have them.
> They do not even have great men in the accepted sense of the
> word.
>
> George Woodcock

> If Canada does not often produce great artists, scientists and
> professional men, it is not because the material is not amongst
> us, but because we do not know how to handle it. The char-
> acteristics of genius too often arouse our suspicion and dis-
> trust, whence it comes that our prophets are so often without
> honour in their own country.
>
> B.K. Sandwell

More than most people, Canadians are prejudiced in favour of the
ordinary: it is a function of our history, our climate and our geography. In a harsh land, we still honour all those pioneering virtues
which impose restraint and engender mediocrity. If the work ethic
has become less compelling, if a variety of immigrants has weak-
ened the grip of our residual Calvinist rigidity, we are nevertheless
the creatures of our historic experience. Revolutions produce
heroes: it is one reason why the Americans have such an abundance
of exemplary figures. But we lack a revolution, and our rebellions
are notable mainly for their ineptitude. As Hugh Hood has pointed
out, we have never succumbed to the twin cults of Byronism and
Bonapartism, the personal and public versions of the Romantic
Hero. Even our constitution enshrines the resolutely unheroic goals
of peace, order and good government.

We are so uncertain in our response to greatness that an outside opinion can sway our judgment. It took the Chinese to make a hero out of Norman Bethune, and many Canadians accepted this verdict only when it was pointed out that our wheat sales might increase. Yet not even a Nobel Peace Prize could do the same for Lester Pearson, since Pearson was too much like the rest of us, with a basic Canadian diffidence. We found this reassuring: it seems we take a perverse pleasure in trivializing our public figures. When we look to the past, we need to see our heroes flawed: a drunken Macdonald or a lunatic Riel. This makes them less demanding, even dismissable. When a potential great man — a Diefenbaker perhaps — emerges among us, we are quick to cut him down to size, and to rejoice in his blunders. As Woodcock has also written, Canadians "suspect the sheer gigantic irrationalism of the heroic, for we like to consider ourselves a reasonable people." It might also be said that something in us hates a hero.

Despite this reluctance to acknowledge greatness in our midst, it is nevertheless clear that we have produced some remarkable people whose qualities often verge on the heroic. With a moment's reflection, any reader could suggest several Canadians, living or dead, whose attributes place them far above the ordinary run of their compatriots. It was never my intention to produce such a list, but for a long time the six subjects of this book have grappled my imagination. Apart from their specific virtues — especially their courage and panache — there was a tone or style to each life which struck me as quintessentially Canadian. At first it was hard to understand why this was so, since there was such an obvious diversity among them. But as I explored these lives, a curious pattern began to emerge.

At the start I could see one common link: my six characters represented British pioneer stock, rather than the contemporary mosaic. And while I chose them for themselves, and not to illustrate some sociological theory, this congruence seemed more appropriate than accidental. It has become fashionable in recent years to deplore our British heritage, but even this steady denigration of our traditions is a back-handed tribute to their potency. It is not only that British pioneers and their descendants were largely responsible for the creation of Canada, and are still dominant in our public affairs. It is also that British patterns become ingrained in our culture and have largely determined, for better or worse, the texture of our lives. Anyone who seeks to explore the deeper recesses of the Canadian spirit must eventually confront its basic Britishness.

CHARLES TAYLOR

Despite this British background, however, I soon realized there was no political or philosophical or religious persuasion which was common to all six characters. Indeed, there was apparently a world of difference between — for example — the Tory patriot, Sutherland Brown, and the liberal internationalist, Herbert Norman. In a similar way, some were Anglican, while others were Calvinist or Methodist: this was not merely a matter of church attendance, since it involved the essence of their sensibilities. Nor did they even belong to the same era: Bishop White and Emily Carr were fundamentally Victorian, while James Houston and Scott Symons are still among us.

Clearly there was no common tradition, yet the more I delved into each life, the more I discovered common themes. Despite the diversity of dates, each of my characters was in some manner a Victorian. Each had that exuberant spirit which animated the General Gordons, the Richard Burtons, the Hester Stanhopes and all those other Victorians who seem to have been born with a passion for the exotic, and with an appetite for more than their society had to offer them. Together with this craving for experience, each had some of that driving energy which impelled the Victorians to their best achievements. In a Canadian context, one thinks of the men who built the railway and opened up the West. Whatever their faults, these were men of substance; as we apprehend them in old photographs, they have a forceful presence which is rarely seen today. (Compare their portraits to those of any contemporary Canadian cabinet or board of directors.) Since Canada became a nation in the Victorian era, it is perhaps more than coincidental that this sort of energy and style has continued to prevail among the best of us.

Like the most exemplary of the Victorians, the subjects of this book felt a need to serve a larger cause. In their different ways, they appear as missionaries for something that is greater than themselves, something that transcends the narrow secularity of their time. Each was seeking a nobler and more spiritual way of being human than their Canadian society encouraged or even tolerated. They were believers and even visionaries; their lives were directed by an impulse which was basically religious, although hardly constrained by mere orthodoxy. Instead, some can be said to have created their own particular faiths, finding their inspiration in entities as remote as ancient Chinese temple paintings or the pre-historic Caves of Lascaux.

This religious impulse also made them conservative — not in a narrow political sense, but in the deeper sense of trying to enact traditions which are rooted in faith, and which rebuke the corroding cynicism of recent decades. Each was opposed to modernity, to what George Grant has called "the central fact of the North American dream — progress through technology." They steadfastly resisted the bland new world of the technocrats, although each chose a different form of opposition. There were those who wore masks: Herbert Norman guarding his sensitivity with the urbane guise of the scholar-diplomat; Bishop White exercising his spiritual intensity behind the facade of an extraverted man-of-affairs. And there were those, like Carr and Symons, who were much more blatant in confronting their compatriots, and who mounted their challenge with a showman's style. Their fortunes have been just as varied: in some cases there was compromise, in others an adamant refusal to capitulate. We are dealing, among other aspects, with four very particular deaths, and two lives whose outcomes are still in doubt.

Their society seldom heeded them. Sometimes it opposed them, although the opposition was almost always underhand. It was not so much a case of destroying these disturbing visionaries, as making them seem irrelevant. When Sutherland Brown began to embarrass his political and military masters, they avoided an open confrontation, and dispatched him with a flurry of memos. Perhaps this technique is particularly Canadian in its furtiveness: the only sustained example of overt opposition in this book is Norman's persecution by Americans.

More often, however, these six Canadians met with a bland acceptance which rarely hid a fundamental indifference. Carr was almost suffocated by a tolerance which ignored the deeper meaning of her work. We are pleased to have White's Chinese treasures in the Royal Ontario Museum, and we regard the Eskimo art which Houston fostered as part of our culture — but we hardly allow either to touch our lives. If Symons is also tolerated — and even subsidized by a government which once sent foreign police to hunt him down — the heritage he champions is still officially and systematically denigrated. If Norman is honoured, it is mainly as a victim of the McCarthy era, while the real implications of his suicide are conveniently overlooked. With each life there is a sense of enormous waste: how much *more* there might have been, if only their compatriots had been less fearful and begrudging. But our indifference to our prophets is also essentially Canadian: we seem incapable of using them.

CHARLES TAYLOR

Faced with such a strange mixture of opposition and indifference, each of these Canadians was forced into a life of loneliness and isolation. They felt compelled to escape their Canadian society, and to sharpen the edges of their identities in different forms of exile. For it was not only that each had a deeper, richer vision which demanded to be lived, and which Canada-as-modernity denied. It was also that to live that vision, each sought fulfillment in the older values of another civilization. This seems the most striking of their common traits: more than derivatively Victorian, it suggests a pattern which could be quintessentially Canadian.

In some cases (Brown, Houston, Symons), the "alien" culture was an authentic Canadian tradition which had been betrayed by the proponents of modernity, and thus made unnaturally foreign. In other cases (Carr and Houston again), it was our native peoples who offered the fuller vision — just as they themselves were being so strenuously modernized. For Bishop White, it was a matter of finding sustenance in the rich heritage of Chinese art and thought — at a time when his own Christian traditions had long been perverted, and when even those Chinese traditions were giving way to modernity in the form of Communism. With Norman, there was a reliance on another Oriental culture, and a stubborn adherence to an older humanism which had been debased by its modern followers. Going beyond his immediate Canadian and European background, Symons finds his life-giving vision in the incarnational worlds of Mexico and Morocco.

This is not to state that Canadians can achieve authenticity only by undertaking odysseys to distant lands, by going native, or by losing themselves in a foreign creed. But it is to suggest that to flourish as Canadians we need to be more than contemporary Canadians: good technocrats and complacent taxpayers, mere victims or survivors. All the subjects of this book explored the life-enhancing insights which older cultures have embodied so emphatically and which comprise our human heritage. They journeyed into spiritual realms which modern Canada ignores or denigrates, yet none was an escapist: each was concerned to formulate a vision which could work in Canada, for Canadians.

A.W. Purdy

Lament for the Dorsets

(Eskimos extinct in the 14th century A.D.)

Animal bones and some mossy tent rings
scrapers and spearheads carved ivory swans
all that remains of the Dorset giants
who drove the Vikings back to their long ships
talked to spirits of earth and water
— a picture of terrifying old men
so large they broke the backs of bears
so small they lurk behind bone rafters
in the brain of modern hunters
among good thoughts and warm things
and come out at night
to spit on the stars

The big men with clever fingers
who had no dogs and hauled their sleds
over the frozen northern oceans
awkward giants
               killers of seal
they couldn't compete with little men
who came from the west with dogs
Or else in a warm climatic cycle
the seals went back to cold waters
and the puzzled Dorsets scratched their heads
with hairy thumbs around 1350 A.D.
— couldn't figure it out
went around saying to each other
plaintively
       'What's wrong? What happened?"
       Where are the seals gone?'
And died

Twentieth century people
apartment dwellers
executives of neon death
warmakers with things that explode
— they have never imagined us in their future
how could we imagine them in the past
squatting among the moving glaciers
six hundred years ago
with glowing lamps?
As remote or nearly
as the trilobites and swamps
when coal became
or the last great reptile hissed
at a mammal the size of a mouse
that squeaked and fled

Did they ever realize at all
what was happening to them?
Some old hunter with one lame leg
a bear had chewed
sitting in a caribou skin tent
— the last Dorset?
Let's say his name was Kudluk
carving 2-inch ivory swans
for a dead grand-daughter
taking them out of his mind
the places in his mind
where pictures are
He selects a sharp stone tool
to gouge a parallel pattern of lines
on both sides of the swan
holding it with his left hand
bearing down and transmitting
his body's weight
from brain to arm and right hand
and one of his thoughts
turns to ivory
The carving is laid aside
in beginning darkness
at the end of hunger

A.W. PURDY

after a while wind
blows down the tent and snow
begins to cover him
After 600 years
the ivory thought
is still warm

MARGARET ATWOOD

THE ANIMALS IN THAT COUNTRY

In that country the animals
have the faces of people:

the ceremonial
cats possessing the streets

the fox run
politely to earth, the huntsmen
standing around him, fixed
in their tapestry of manners

the bull, embroidered
with blood and given
an elegant death, trumpets, his name
stamped on him, heraldic brand
because

(when he rolled
on the sand, sword in his heart, the teeth
in his blue mouth were human)

he is really a man

even the wolves, holding resonant
conversations in their
forests thickened with legend.

       In this country the animals
       have the faces of
       animals.

Their eyes
flash once in car headlights
and are gone.

Their deaths are not elegant.

They have the faces of
no-one.

TIMOTHY FINDLEY

FOXES

The face is only the thing to write.
— Roland Barthes

All the appropriate people had been forewarned: Morris Glendenning would be coming to the Royal Ontario Museum to do some private research in the Far Eastern Department. He was not to be approached; he was not to be disturbed.

Glendenning's reclusiveness was legendary, made doubly curious by the fact he was the world's best-known communications expert — a man whose public stances and pronouncements had put him at centre stage as long ago as 1965. The thing was, Morris Glendenning could not bear to be seen.

But, as with most eccentric beings, part of what was eccentric in him seemed determined to thwart whatever else was eccentric. In Morris Glendenning's case, his passion for privacy was undone by his need for warmth — which led to a passion for things made of wool and, as well, to what some considered to be the most eccentric habit of dress in the whole community of North American intellectuals.

He wore old-fashioned galoshes — the kind made of sailcloth and rubber, sporting metal fasteners shaped like little ladders lying on their sides. He was also given to wearing a multiplicity of woollen garments layered across his chest: scarves, sweaters, undervests — each of a prescribed colour. He wore, as well, a navy blue beret, pulled down over the tops of his prominent ears. He was six feet, six inches tall and was made, it seemed, almost entirely of bone. His skin was pale, translucent and shining — as if he polished it at night with a chamois cloth. Glendenning's overcoat was blue and had a military cut — naval, perhaps. It was pinched at the waist and almost reached his ankles. In magazine photographs — taken always on the run — Morris Glendenning had the look of Greta Garbo, heading for doorways and ducking into elevators: "COMMUNICATIONS EXPERT ESCAPES YET AGAIN!"

Mrs Elston, in charge of secretarial work for the Far Eastern Department at the Royal Ontario Museum, had been told by her boss that Glendenning would be turning up on the Friday morning, last week in February. She was quite looking forward to meeting the famous man. Dr Dime, the curator, had instructed her to offer all available assistance without stint and without question. On no account, she was told, was he to be approached by staff. "Whatever help he requires, he will solicit: probably by note...." By mid-afternoon, however, on the day of the visit, Mrs Elston said: "it doesn't take much to guarantee the privacy of someone who doesn't even bother to show up."

At which point Myrna Stovich, her assistant, said: "but he is here, Mrs Elston. Or — *someone* is. His overcoat and galoshes are sitting right there...." And she pointed out a huddled, navy blue shape on a chair and a pair of sailcloth overshoes squatting in a large brown puddle.

"For heaven's sake," said Mrs Elston. "How can that have happened when I've been sitting here all day?"

"You haven't been sitting here all day," said Myrna Stovich. "You took a coffee break and you went to lunch."

The night before, and all that morning, it had snowed. The clouds were a shade of charcoal flannel peculiar to clouds that lower above Toronto at the dirty end of winter. Merely looking at them made you cough. Morris Glendenning had supplemented his already overprotective array of woollen garments with one more scarf, which he pulled down crossways over his radiator ribs and tied against the small of his back. Even before he departed his Rosedale home, he pulled his beret over his ears and bowed his head beneath the elements.

Walking across the Sherbourne Street bridge, Morris set his mind on his destination and, thereby, shut out the presence of his fellow pedestrians. His destination at large was the Royal Ontario Museum but his absolute destination was its collection of Japanese theatre masks.

Long after midnight, Morris Glendenning had sat up watching the snow eradicate the garden and the trees beyond his windows. Now, he was tired. And reflective. Progress with his current work had stalled, partly due to the residue of sorrow over his wife's midsum-

TIMOTHY FINDLEY

mer death and partly due to the fact he had published a book two months later, in September. The work itself — the massing of materials, the culling of ideas — had been passing through an arid stage and it was only in the last few days that he'd begun to feel remotely creative again. Not that he hadn't traversed this particular desert before. Far from it. After every piece of exploration — after every publication of his findings — after every attempt at articulating the theories rising from his findings, Morris Glendenning — not unlike every other kind of writer — found himself, as if by some sinister miracle of transportation, not at the edge but at the very centre of a wasteland from which he could extract not a single living thought. For days — sometimes for weeks — his mind had all the symptoms of dehydration and starvation: desiccated and paralyzed almost to the point of catatonia. Five days ago it had been in that state. But, now, it was reviving — feeding again, but gently. And all because of a chance encounter with a photograph.

The photograph had appeared in a magazine called *Rotunda*, published by the Royal Ontario Museum; and it showed a Japanese theatre mask recently purchased and brought from the Orient. "Fox," the caption read. But it wasn't quite a fox. It was a *human fox*, alarming in its subtle implications. Reading about it, Morris Glendenning discovered it was one of three or four others — a series of masks created for a seventeenth-century Japanese drama in which a fox becomes a man. Each of the masks, so the article informed him, displayed a separate stage in the transformation of a quintessential fox into a quintessential human being. Glendenning's curiosity was piqued — and more than piqued; a trigger was pulled in the deeps of his consciousness. Something had been recognized, he realized, and he felt the reverberations rising like bubbles to the surface: signals, perhaps — or warnings.

He very well remembered reading David Garnett's horror story *Lady Into Fox* — that masterful, witty morality tale in which the English "hunting class" is put in its place when one of its wives becomes a fox. But here, in these Japanese masks, the process had been reversed. It was the fox who took on human form. On the other hand, this was more or less standard procedure when it came to balancing the myths and customs of the Orient against the myths and customs of the West. Almost inevitably, the icons and symbols employed by custom and by myth were opposites: white in the Orient, black in the West for mourning; respect for, not the arrogation of nature; death, not birth as access to immortality.

Whose fate, Glendenning had written in the margin next to the provocative photograph, *is being fulfilled within this mask? The fox's? Or the man's?*

Clipping the whole page out of the magazine, he slipped it into a file marked *Personae*, and five minutes later, he retrieved it — held it up in the snow-white light from the windows and stared at it, mesmerized. The question became an obsession. Looking into the lacquered face of the mask he imagined stripping off the layers of the human face. Not to the bone, but to the being.

The blooming of this image took its time. It occurred to him slowly that under the weight of all his personal masks, there was a being he had never seen. Not a creature hidden by design — but something buried alive that wanted to live and that had a right to life.

"Foxes into humans," he said out loud as he watched the photograph. *Their choice, not ours.*

Standing in the bathroom, later that afternoon, something sent a shudder through his shoulders and down his back when, in the very instant of switching on the light, he caught the image of his unmasked self in the mirror. And he noted, in that prodding, ever-observant part of his brain — where even the death of his wife had been observed with the keenest objectivity — that what had been unmasked had not been human. What he had seen — and all he had seen — was a pair of pale gold eyes that stared from a surround of darkness he could not identify.

Half an hour later, Morris picked up the telephone and placed a call to the Curator of the Far Eastern Collection at the Royal Ontario Museum, who happened to be his old acquaintance, Harry Dime. What privileges could Harry Dime afford him? Could he inspect the Japanese masks alone?

Privately, Harry Dime would later conclude he should have said no. For all his own awareness of intellectual curiosity, he had no sense at all of the dangerous threshold at which Glendenning stood. Dime had forgotten that, when he returned with these treasures from another time, he brought them with all their magic intact. Not with ancient spells, of course, since all such things are nonsense — but the magic they released in others: in those who beheld them without the impediment of superstition.

TIMOTHY FINDLEY

On the snowy Friday morning, Morris Glendenning debated whether to walk or to chance the subway. Chancing the subway might mean recognition, and given the loss of time that recognition inevitably produced, he decided to walk. Walking, he was certain no one would see him — let alone recognize him. *How many eyes*, he once had said to Nora, his wife, *meet yours on a crowded avenue?*

Bloor Street on a Friday is always massed with shoppers, most of whom, Glendenning noted, like to give the appearance of worldly indifference. *I could go in and buy that coat if I wanted to*, they seemed to be telling themselves. *But I won't do that today, I'll do that on Monday. Maybe Tuesday...* Their impassivity was almost eerie and it troubled Morris Glendenning.

The street, for all its people and all its motor traffic, was silent beneath the falling snow. Morris could see his own and everyone else's breath. If he paused, he could count the breaths and he could take the pulse of where he stood — each breath embracing so many heart beats — all the heart beats racing, lagging — all the secret rhythms of all the people visible in the frosted air. Even the motor traffic gave the appearance of being alive; as much an appearance of life as the people gave with their wisps and plumes of vapours. In behind the windows of these vehicles, the faces peering out of the silence were reflected in the clouds of glass that fronted Harry Rosen's; Cartier's; Bemelmans; Eddie Bauer's. Holt Renfrew...moon phases; passing on Bloor Street.

Morris Glendenning could feel the subway tumbling beneath him, not like an earthquake — merely an indication that something was there, alive and at work, whose underground voice made no more sound than voices make in dreams. Morris paused at the corner of Bellair Street and watched a man he had intimately known in boyhood wander past him with his eyes averted. Later on, both of them would say: *I saw old so-and-so out on Bloor Street, today. He looked appalling; dead...*

I saw old so-and-so today. We passed.

Here, Morris thought, was a kind of debilitating apartness — an apartness that once had been entirely foreign to all these people: the ones who were perfect strangers and the ones who were intimate friends.

We needed each other. That was why we looked each other in the eye. We needed each other. Morris clenched his jaw, afraid that perhaps his lips had been moving over the words. *We've always shared this dreadful place — these awful storms — this appalling climate*

— and we knew we couldn't afford to be alone. But now...

Now he was approaching the final stretch of Bloor Street before the stop at Avenue Road, where he would wait for the light to change, the way he had waited there for over forty years.

Beyond the veils of snow he could see the vaguest hint of neon, red in the air above him: *Park Plaza Hotel* — though all he could see was part of the *z* and part of the final *a*.

A small crowd of people formed near the curb and Morris Glendenning was aware, all at once, how many of them wore fur hats. A dozen fur hats and fifteen heads.

Not one person was looking at any other; only Morris Glendenning, counting. Why were they so unconcerned with one another? When had they all become collectively impassive?

Probably last Tuesday.

Morris smiled. Rhetorical questions formed the backbone of his profession, but he delighted in providing stupid, banal and irritating answers. It was a form of private entertainment.

Still, it affected everything they did — this intractable indifference. It affected the way they walked, he observed — the speed with which they walked — their gait, as they made their way along the street. They moved, Morris thought — gazing at them through the falling snow — with the kind of apathy acquired by those whom something — bitterness? — has taught that nothing waits for those who hurry home. It came to him slowly, standing on the curb at Avenue Road and Bloor, that, when he rode on the subway and was recognized, it was not their recognition of him that mattered: but their hope that he — in all his ballyhooed wisdom and fame — might recognize them and tell them who they were. *I know you from somewhere*: that's what they yearned for him to say. *I know — I recognize who you are.*

In the cellars at the ROM, there is a labyrinth of halls and passageways that leads, through various degrees of light and temperature, to various sequestered rooms where various treasures lie in wait for someone to come and give them back their meaning. Bits and pieces, shards and corners of time — numbered, catalogued, guessed at.

Morris Glendenning stood in one of these rooms — perspiring, it so happened — holding in his fingers, his fingers encased in white cotton gloves — the very mask he had encountered first in its photographed image.

TIMOTHY FINDLEY

The door behind him was closed.

The room — effectively — was sound-proofed by its very depth in the cellars and its distance from the active centre of the building. A dread, white light was all he had to see by: "daylight" shining from computered bulbs.

The mask's companions — three in number — were set out, sterile on a sterile tray: the fox on its way to becoming a man.

He thought of surgery.

He thought of layers.

How small, he thought: *the face is.*

Looking down at the others, beyond the mask he held, he counted over the variations and degrees of change — the fox in his hands at one extreme and the trio of variations, lying on their tray, burgeoning feature by feature into a close proximity of Oriental human beauty. The widely tilted, oval eyes of the fox became the evenly centered, almond eyes of a man. Of *a priest*, so the collection's catalogue had told him.

A priest. So apt a designation, it could only be amusing. Though amusing, of course, in a sinister way.

Morris felt like a marauding and possibly destructive child bent on mischief. A vandal, perhaps. Most certainly, he knew he was trespassing here, the victim of an irresistible impulse: *put it on....*

He had spent over three hours standing there, touching — lifting — contemplating the masks. Around him, resting on shelves and laid out, numbered in other sterile trays was the department's whole collection of Japanese theatre masks. Each mask was hidden: slung in a silk and sometimes quite elaborate bag, the drawstrings tied in neat, fastidious bows.

Heads, he thought. *The victims of some revolution.*

The truth was — he dared not open the bags to look.

Some of the bags were darkly stained. And, even though he fully recognized the stains were merely of time and of mildew, he could not bring himself to touch them.

Put it on. Don't be afraid.

Go on.

He held the mask up gently before his face.

He could smell its...what? Its mustiness?

Or was it muskiness?

He closed his eyes and fitted the moulded inner surface over the contours of his bones.

He waited fully fifteen seconds before he dared to open his eyes.

The masks below him, sitting on their tray, were smiling.

Had they smiled before?

He waited, knowing he must not give up until the whole sensation of the mask had been experienced — no matter how long it took.

He though he heard a noise somewhere out in the corridor. The voice of someone calling.

He held his breath, in order to hear.

Nothing.

And then, as he began to breathe again, he felt the vibrations of a sound between his face and the mask.

Another voice. But whose?

He was a long way off inside himself and standing in another light. A pattern of leaves threw shadows over what he saw, perhaps the verge of a clearing somewhere.

Creatures — not human — moved before him.

Foxes.

How elegant they were. How delicate: precise and knowing.

Why was he so unconcerned and unafraid?

He began to receive the scent of earth as he had never smelled the earth before: a safe, green, sun-warmed scent.

He looked at his hands. He held them out as far as he could. Human hands — in white gloves. Whose were they?

He tried to speak, but could not.

What emerged, instead of speech, was an inarticulate and strangled sound he had never heard before.

Down below him, where the earth replaced the floor, one of the foxes came and sat at his feet and stared up into his face. It seemed, almost, to know who he was.

Never in all of Morris's life had he been so close to anything wild. He was mesmerized.

Other foxes came, as if to greet him, and they leaned so close against his legs that he could feel their bones against his shins.

The fox that had been the first to come and sit before him narrowed its gaze. It stared so intently, Morris felt that something must be going to happen.

Say something to us, the fox appeared to be saying. Tell us something. Speak to us....

Yes — but how?

TIMOTHY FINDLEY

Morris was bereft of words. But the impulse to speak was over-
whelming. He could feel the sound of something rising through his
bowels — and the force of the sound was so alarming that Morris
pulled the mask away from his face and thrust it from him — down
into the tray from which he had lifted it. When?

How much time had passed. An hour? A day? How far away had
he been? Who was he, now? Or what?

He looked — afraid — at the backs of his hands, but they were
covered still with the gloves.

The creatures in the tray appeared to stir.

Morris closed his eyes against the notion he was not alone. He
did not want to see the floor — for fear the floor was still the sun-
warmed ground it had been a moment before.

And yet...

He wanted them back. Their breath and their eyes already haunt-
ed him. He waited for their voices — but no voices came.

Morris removed the white cotton gloves. He took a long, deep
breath and let it very slowly out between his teeth.

His fingers dipped towards the tray and even before they reached
the mask, he smiled — because he could feel the head rising up as
sure and real as the sun itself. And when the mask he had chosen
was in place, he paused only for seconds before he dared to breathe
again; one deep breath, and he found his voice — which was not his
human voice but another voice from another time.

Now — at last — he was not alone.

Just before five that afternoon, Mrs Elston was putting the cover on
her IBM Selectric and preparing to leave, when she became aware all
at once of someone standing behind her.

"Oh," she said — recovering as best she could. "We thought you
were not here, Professor Glendenning."

She smiled — but he did not reply.

His enormous height was bending to the task of pulling on his
galoshes.

"Shall we be seeing you tomorrow?" Mrs Elston asked.

With his back to her, he shook his head.

"Monday, perhaps?"

But he was buckling his galoshes; silent.

He drew his many scarves about him, buttoned his greatcoat,
took up his leather bag and started away.

"Professor Glendenning... It was such a great pleasure..."

But Mrs Elston could not reach him. He was gone and the door swung to and fro.

Mrs Elston sniffed the air.

"Myrna?" she said. "Do you smell something?"

Myrna Stovich needed no prompting.

"Sure," she said. "Dog."

"But there *can't* be a dog!" said Mrs Elston.

"Yeah, well," said Myrna. "We also thought there wasn't no Professor Glendenning, didn't we."

"True," Mrs Elston laughed. "You're quite right, my dear. But... goodness! What a day!" she said. "And now we have to go out into all that snow."

"Yeah," said Myrna Stovich. "Sure. But I like the snow."

"Yes," said Mrs Elston, and she sighed. "I like it, too, I guess." And then she gave a smile. "I suppose I have to, don't I — seeing it's what we've got."

'BOB & DOUG MACKENZIE'

THE TWELVE DAYS OF CHRISTMAS

On the first day of Christmas, my true love gave to me:

	A Beer
Second	2 Turtlenecks
Third	3 French Toast
Fourth	4 lbs. of Back Bacon
Fifth	5 Golden Touques
Sixth	6 Packs of 2, 4
Seventh	7 Packs of Smokes
Eighth	8 Comic Books

Good day and welcome to day 12.

PART EIGHT:

MULTICULTURALISM

Joy Kogawa

Obasan

Chapter Twelve

It is around this time that mother disappears. I hardly dare to think, let alone ask, why she has to leave. Questions are meaningless. What matters to my five-year-old mind is not the reason that she is required to leave, but the stillness of waiting for her to return. After a while, the stillness is so much with me that it takes the form of a shadow which grows and surrounds me like air. Time solidifies, ossifies the waiting into molecules of stone, dark microscopic planets that swirl through the universe of my body waiting for light and the morning.

September 1941.
The harbour is crowded with people. It is altogether bewildering. Aunt Emily is here and Aya Obasan, Grandpa Kato, Uncle, Father and his friend Uncle Dan, Grandma and Grandpa Nakane. The whole family. Stephen is wearing his short grey pants and grey suit top and grey knee socks and I am wearing the blue woollen knit dress that mother made and likes best. It has delicate five-petalled white flowers with red-dot centres stitched in wool and spaced all around the border of the skirt. I have short white socks and shiny black shoes with a single strap.

Father is holding my hand and asking foolishly if I can see my mother. There is nothing to be seen but legs and legs. All I know is that Mother and Grandma are at the other end of a long paper streamer I clutch in my fist. Father picks me up in his arms and points but I can see nothing except thousands of colourful paper streamers stretched between the people below and the railing of the ship. Stephen is gathering spools of streamers that lie here and there unused on the ground.

"She'll be back soon," my father says.

I do not doubt this.

Uncle Dan winks at me and smiles. Uncle Dan is almost always smiling or laughing, his mouth wide open and his head thrown back like the junkman's horse, showing his large straight teeth.

"Obaa-chan [the old grandmother] only needs to see their faces," Aya Obasan says, "then they will come back." She tells me that though Mother was born in Canada she was raised in Japan by her grandmother. "Obaa-chan is very ill," Aya Obasan says. My great-grandmother has need of my mother. Does my mother have need of me? In what market-place of the universe are the bargains made that have traded my need for my great-grandmother's?

The boat pulls away and I cannot see my mother's face, though Father keeps pointing and waves.

When we get home, Stephen gives me three of the spools he's retrieved, and I put them in the top left-hand drawer of my mother's sewing-machine cabinet for a surprise homecoming present for her. I put my fluffy Easter chicks in there as well, their feet three wire prongs. Last Easter I found them in a wicker basket sitting on top of candy and chocolate eggs.

There is a scene I imagine, in which I am my mother come home and am sitting at the treadle machine. My hand is poised at the round wooden knob carved into the ornate drawer, my fingers feeling around the smooth curves. With my eyes averted, I am my mother pulling the drawer open to look for the black darning knob, or a spool of thread, or scissors. To my mother's surprise, she finds the colourful paper streamer rolls and her fingers touch the soft fluff of the Easter chicks. She lifts them up one at a time. "Ah," I say in my mother's voice. Two small Easter chicks. Who would not cry out?

Everything we have ever done we do again and again in my mind. We take the streetcar to Kitsilano beach and buy potato chips in cardboard baskets. We go with Aunt Emily and Grandpa Kato in his shiny black car, across the Lions' Gate Bridge and along the Dollarton highway to visit Uncle Dan who is staying in the small house that Grandma and Grandpa Kato own. Or to New Westminster and the island where Aya Obasan and Uncle Isamu live in their beautiful house full of plants by the sea. I play with the dog they call "Puppy" though he is not a puppy at all, romping around the pond full of goldfish with the waterfall and the rock garden surrounding it. We go to the zoo at Stanley Park and sit on the grass by the dome of the outdoor theatre, listening to the symphony concerts in the dusk. I rehearse the past faithfully in preparation for her return.

Aya Obasan is in the house every day now. She is gentle and quiet like Mother. She sleeps in my room on an extra bed that has been brought upstairs from the basement. The first morning she is here, I am surprised to see her long black hair, a thick braid thinning out to a few tassels that reach to her buttocks. Normally her hair is coiled around and around in a braided bun at the back of her head.

Stephen and I watch her as she sticks countless hairpins in to keep the bun in place above the nape of her neck.

"Long legs, crooked thighs, no head, and no eyes," Stephen chants.

Obasan takes a while to understand the hairpin riddle.

She has an ivory brush with soft useless bristles and a comb with teeth as thick as chopsticks. I hold the matching hand mirror with its curved edges as she powders her face. A fold of her long velvet dressing-gown rests on my arms, soft and fluid and heavy as dry water. Many of Aya Obasan's things are soft against my cheek. Her fur coat, the fluffy quilt on her bed, and especially Obasan herself. She is plump, unlike Grandma Kato, whose knees are like bed knobs.

But even with Obasan's warmth and constant presence, there is an ominous sense of cold and absence — a darkness that has crept into the house as stealthily as Mrs. Sugimoto's dead animal fur piece she sometimes leaves on the living-room sofa.

One night I waken frightened. There is no light anywhere — in the hallway, in the streets, in the neighbours' houses. This night I remember we are not to turn on any lights. We are doing what Stephen calls a "blackout." I feel my way along the walls into the living-room where there are voices.

Old Man Gower is here. He has never come into our house before and it is strange that he should be sitting in the darkness with Father.

"Yes, yes," he is saying, his large soft hands rubbing together. The light from his pipe glares and fades. I don't know what he is agreeing to as he sits in the armchair. Even in the darkness, I can tell that Father's eyes are not at ease.

"I'll keep them for you, Mark. Sure thing." Old Man Gower's voice is unlike the low gurgling sound I am used to when he talks to me alone. "The piano. Books. Garden tools. What else?"

Although I am in the room, he acts as if I am not here. He seems more powerful that Father, larger and more at home even though this is our house. He sounds as if he is trying to comfort my father, but there is a falseness in the tone. The voice is too sure — too strong.

Father is as if he is not here. If my mother were back, she would move aside all the darkness with her hands and we would be safe and at home in our home.

I am relieved when Old Man Gower leaves but when I turn to my father, the safety has not returned to him. I clamber onto his lap and put my arms around his neck.

"Naomi-chan," he whispers, "could you not sleep?"

I understand later what it is about. The darkness is everywhere, in the day as well as the night. It threatens us as it always has, in the streetcars, in the stores, on the streets, in all public places. It covers the entire city and causes all the lights to be turned out. It drones overhead in the sounds of airplanes. It rushes unbidden from the mouths of strangers and in the taunts of children. It happens to Stephen even more terrifyingly than it does to me.

One day he comes home from school, his glasses broken, black tear stains on his face. Obasan is hanging up clothes on the line from the back porch. When she sees him, she does not cry out but continues hanging up the laundry, removing the pegs from her mouth one at a time.

"What happened?" I whisper as Stephen comes up the stairs.

He doesn't answer me. Is he ashamed, as I was in Old Man Gower's bathroom? Should I go away?

"What happened?" It is Obasan asking this time and her voice is soft.

He still does not reply and Obasan takes him by the hand into the kitchen and wipes his face. I stand hesitantly in the doorway, watching.

"I told you," Stephen says at last.

I am encouraged that he is speaking to me. "Oh," I say wishing to show that I understand, but I do not.

"You know, Nomi."

Stephen is in grade three at David Lloyd George School. There are "air raid drills" at school, he tells me, which means that when a loud alarm sounds, all the children line up and file out of the classrooms as quickly as possible. They lie flat on the ground, crouch by hedges or in ditches, to hide from the bombs which may drop on us all — not just on the school, but anywhere at any time out of enemy aircraft overhead. We may be killed or maimed, blinded for life or burnt. We may lose an arm, or a finger even. To be safe, we must hide and be still so they will not see us.

The girl with the long ringlets who sits in front of Stephen said to him, "All the Jap kids at school are going to be sent away and they're bad and you're a Jap." And so, Stephen tells me, am I.

"Are we?" I ask Father.

"No," Father says. "We're Canadian."

It is a riddle, Stephen tells me. We are both the enemy and not the enemy.

JOAN MURRAY

KURELEK'S VISION OF CANADA

Picture Making by the Seat of His Pants

Kurelek was one of the really important landscape painters in Canada but his work, perhaps because of its message, has remained outside the mainstream of Canadian art history. J. Russell Harper mentioned him briefly in *Painting in Canada* (1966); Dennis Reid not at all in *A Concise History of Canadian Painting* (1973). Early critics found his work "sombre," "menacing," "grotesque," and "macabre." His landscapes were "lonely and hostile," they said. There was a "frightening hint of madness" to his work, a sense of lurking terror, chaos and doom — a maniacal quality, as Elizabeth Kilbourn wrote in *Canadian Art* in the early 1960s. All conceded he was unique in Canadian painting.

Among important Canadian artists of recent times, William Kurelek (1927-77) was the only one to believe his ability to make art was literally a gift from God, and must be used in God's service. If this unfashionable conviction set him apart from his contemporaries, so did almost every other circumstance of his creative life, including his attitude to conventional aesthetics and his choice of subject matter. In the midst of Canada's love affair with abstract art, he remained sturdily representational, alternating anecdotal scenes from his prairie boyhood with savagely realistic depictions of the sin and corruption he saw everywhere around him. Far from scorning propaganda, he perceived it as his artistic duty. The winsome documents of immigrant farm life were, as he saw it, the catch-words for his urgent message that Armageddon was at hand. In 1976, at the height of his success, he told a reporter, "I have to stay popular."[1]

And he *was* popular. He was a master of book illustration; in the last four years of his life he either wrote or illustrated fourteen books, twice winning the award for the Best Illustrated Children's Book of the Year from *The New York Times*. When he illustrated

Ivan Franko's Ukrainian classic *Fox Mykyta* (published in English in 1978 by Tundra Press), Kurelek identified with Fox Mykyta who, summoned to King Lion to be punished, cleverly outwits the challenger, Wolf the Hungry, and becomes a member of the Royal Council. Curiously, Kurelek's career has a strange similarity to Mykyta's: from his first one-man show in 1960 at the Isaacs Gallery in Toronto, until his untimely death from cancer in 1977 at the age of fifty, he found an enthusiastic and evergrowing group of admirers and collectors; the painter who existed as an outsider in Canadian art created a body of work that has made him today the favourite of a diverse range of people, from the man-on-the-street to Premier Richard Hatfield of New Brunswick.

He was a favourite with the mass media, not only because his paintings told stories and took well to reproduction but because he himself was good copy. He was a Canadian-born Ukrainian farmboy who celebrated his heritage at the very moment that Canadians were congratulating themselves on their multiculturalism. Furthermore, anxious to bring his other message — the religious one — to anyone who would listen, he was searingly candid about his harsh, difficult childhood, his torments as a young adult, his suicide attempts, the four years in a British mental institution, the shock therapy ("fourteen treatments in all...like being executed fourteen times over"[2]) and the redeeming and transforming conversion to Roman Catholicism. By the time he died he was easily the most interviewed and written about of all living Canadian artists.

As a result he risked being dismissed by critics and academics as a mere crowd-pleaser, an author of painted rhetoric, a celebrity illustrator, rather than a serious artist. (And indeed his literalism sometimes evoked unwanted echoes of *Saturday Evening Post* covers.) But contemporary art historians now tend to agree that Kurelek's art transcends his didactic subject matter.

At its best, his work possesses the passionate intensity of a Bosch or a Bruegel. His compositional sense is singular and arresting. His pictorial surfaces are muscular. And there is something else. Kurelek almost never painted landscape as such, but during his lifetime he painted the length and breadth of the country and Canada's physical presence informs almost everything he did. This landscape element, its descriptive power and precision, its authenticity, its use as both compositional armature and conveyor of emotional content, unifies his work — and is the subject of the present collection.

WILLIAM KURELEK, *The Painter*, 1974. Mixed media, 121.92 x 91.44 cm. The Isaacs Gallery, Toronto, Ontario.

William Kurelek was born in Whitford, Alberta, seventy-five miles northeast of Edmonton. To outsiders, Whitford might look bleak — two grain elevators and three buildings huddled under a vast sky. But to Kurelek, even as a small child, the austere emptiness had its own charm. He responded in the same way to Stonewall, Manitoba, where he moved when he was seven and where his father ran a dairy farm: he loved the "great, free, flat bogland to the east" he said of it.[3]

But his home life was difficult. His father, Metro, was an old-fashioned Ukrainian patriarch (he had come from the village of Borivtsi, in the province of Bukovina) who was harsh and strict, contemptuous of his high-strung, imaginative oldest son. He thought William weak, "not like the other kids." "Wake up and be a boy," Kurelek recalled his father saying one night as he went to sleep. "Don't be a girl."[4] Neither of his parents seemed satisfied with him. And he felt starved for affection.

Painting was the only thing at which he excelled. From Grade One, he knew he was an artist. Encouragement came from the teacher in his one-room school in Stonewall who asked him to do a series of drawings of Canadian history. "It was then that I conceived the idea of some day illustrating the whole of Canadian history," he later recalled.[5] At the same time, a Greek Orthodox priest first aroused his interest in his ethnic heritage.

Kurelek often sat in the kitchen corner after the day's work, listening to his father yarning with the hired hands. His father was a spell-binding spinner of tales; Kurelek dreamed that he himself would someday be such a storyteller. Later, when he moved to a city high school, he envisioned himself surrounded by fellow students listening in admiration to his stories of farm adventures. Instead, he discovered that no one wanted to hear what he had to say. In his paintings, much later, he would find a way to fulfil his dream.

Secretly, Kurelek saw himself as a "shrewd" and "cagey peasant"; however his parents' contempt had already turned him tongue-tied and deeply shy. He was full of baffled pain mingled with fury, arrogance mixed with self-doubt as well as the need for approval. He sought father figures during his entire adult life. In art, the absence of any strong master-craftsman relationship left him dissatisfied with Toronto's Ontario College of Art, which he attended in 1949 and 1959 after graduating from the University of Manitoba with his Bachelor of Arts degree. Hoping to learn from the Mexican Social Realists such as Siqueiros, Orozco, or Diego Rivera, he hitch-hiked

JOAN MURRAY

to Mexico in 1950, but found no one of sufficient calibre to help him at the school he joined in San Miguel de Allende. He renewed his quest for a mentor in England, after his nervous breakdown and the sojourn in the mental institution. In 1956 and again in 1957 he wrote for an interview to Stanley Spencer, the well-known British figure painter. Spencer never replied. Meanwhile, though, Kurelek had found one satisfactory teacher — in a book. The book was Kimon Nicolaïdes' standard text, *The Natural Way to Draw* (1941), which Kurelek began to devour on his own in Montreal while waiting to sail for Europe. The exercises at the end of each chapter were the making of him as an artist, he said. Nicolaïdes "helped me break into the essence of art as I understand it."[6] Gesture and contour were emphasized in the master's lessons. Kurelek accomplished the whole course, which was supposed to take a year, in three months, using his own body as the model for anatomy assignments and sketching surreptitiously in restaurants and railway stations to master gesture.

The weakness of most of his figurative work — the way in which his figures sometimes seem to have no bones — seems to indicate that, aside from this course, he never drew much from life. He also seems to have been heavily influenced by the way he felt about his subjects. Children, perhaps because his own childhood was grotesque, are always thin, spindly, stick figures.

By the time Kurelek reached England in the mid-1950s, his self-hatred and self-pity had reached a crisis. The outcome was the nervous breakdown of 1957, then hospitalization, and shock therapy. He never stopped painting and produced through this period some remarkable expressions of personal anguish, nightmare phobia, and utter desolation. He titled one canvas *Help Me Please Help Me Please Help Me — Please Help.*

His conversion to the Roman Catholic faith the same year as his breakdown marked the turning point. He returned to Toronto in 1959, and his considerable commercial success can be dated from 1960 with his first one-man show at the Isaacs Gallery. (He was one of the few realists in the Isaacs group of artists, which included Michael Snow, Graham Coughtry, and Gordon Rayner.) Add to this a happily married life and Kurelek finally began feeling that "everything is going my way."[7] He found perhaps even the father he needed in his dealer, Avrom Isaacs. "Tell my father you think my paintings are good," he asked Isaacs on the occasion of his first show.[8]

Kurelek was, both as a person and as a painter, amazed by reality. He responded with wholehearted wonder to the natural world, and this quality appears in his art, making it fresh, direct, and authentic. His work is largely based on first-hand observation. He could paint tellingly the nuances of weather, the bright blue prairie sky (or the sky in its varying moods of darkness or storm), the shiny golden light, and the charm of the spareness and spaciousness of the western landscape.

From the beginning, Kurelek favoured the panorama — a distant, high horizon, a limitless expanse. Man is never lost in the luminous land, but engulfment threatens as he travels from the foreground into the distance, usually on a deliberate, carefully laid out, curving path, as in *Hauling Sheaves to the Threshing Machine* (1961). The dwarfed figure may traverse the featureless whiteness of snow, as in *Winter North of Winnipeg* (1962), or the figures — Kurelek himself as a young boy with his family — may confront the night landscape at the end of the journey, as in his 1964 recreation of his family's arrival on their Manitoba farm.

Always, monumental grandeur is inherent in the structure — a sense that the long perspectives meet only somewhere beyond, in infinity. "I work more in world terms," Kurelek once said.[9]

Kurelek had felt no different in his early world — almost overwhelmed by the setting but fascinated by the power of natural forces. Nature was "beautiful but heartless," implacable and often hostile. He'd seen his father's barn burn down, a memory he often recalled later, as in *A Ukrainian Canadian Prairie Tragedy* (1974). Against the panoramic background, the foreground often chronicles suffering, or frantic movement — mourners grieving the death of a child in *Lest We Repent* (1966) or farm workers outpacing a coming storm, as in *Thunder Driven* (1970).

Still, the mood is not always tragic. Just as often, Kurelek strikes a note of awed wonder. "The single outstanding feature of prairie landscape, just as of the ocean, is *expanse*," he wrote in 1970.[10] When in 1974 he painted the Atlantic lobster fisherman looking across the sea to a distant boat, he found himself recalling "the warm glow a prairie farmer gets from seeing a far-off neighbour's farmhouse lights come on in the evenings."[11]

Kurelek brought to his landscape painting both his own sense of doom and his own redemptive rapture. In his heart, he believed a holocaust was inevitable: "... retribution will catch up with us soon."[12] Hence, he used the atomic bomb in the background of some of his works like *Not Going Back to Pick up a Cloak...*(1971). "I am not made gloomy by the prospect of the end, by the approaching of nuclear annihilation, by destruction of the world.... I am ready for it. It will be a beginning... of the salvation of man."[13]

The wind in particular seemed to Kurelek to convey the breath of God's spirit. In Ireland in 1974, he'd been impressed by the high wind: "The lush valley with the hills...seemed in paroxysm. The trees...were like blown heads of hair."[14] It remained for him a moment of supreme religious insight. Later, the vision of a mystical union with nature came back to him in the form of his own self-portrait, *By The Breath of The Spirit II* (1975). The inspiration came from John 3:8, "the wind breathes where it will, and thou canst hear the sound of it, but knowest nothing of the way it came or the way it goes; so it is, when a man is born by the breath of the Spirit."

By The Breath of The Spirit II is not Kurelek's most accomplished work. It reflects a feature of his paintings at their worse: somehow it lacks focus, or has only a weak centre. However, it also possesses a quality inherent in Kurelek's work at its best: the whole pictorial surface is involved in writhing movement. When this kind of musculature is anchored by a firm composition, the results are fresh and grand. It is this quality that interested artists as disparate as Ivan Eyre and Dennis Burton, Kurelek's peers in the Isaacs group of artists.

Both Eyre and Burton are, of course, western artists. Eyre found that Kurelek was the only painter to depict accurately the prairie landscape, particularly a view down the centre of the fence-lines, which he himself had often studied in the area around his home outside Winnipeg. For Burton, Kurelek's prairie landscape was the only authentic one he knew.

From the beginning, Kurelek painted night scenes. Around 1970 he began to work outside, studying the sky and different kinds of weather. "The most magnificent feature of the prairies is the panorama of the sky, awesomely grand and varied," he wrote in 1975.[15] From high school, he had loved Wordsworth; now in Nature's innocence and beauty, he found God. "Nature of itself is nothing but a blind set of chemical and physical laws.... But it *is* a person, an infinitely wise and powerful Designer and Provider who created Nature," he said, and he noted the "beautiful design God put into Nature."[16] "Only a Creator who is beauty itself can create beauty — only those who are made in His image can appreciate that beauty," he said.[17] With beauty, he wished to distract viewers from his moralizing.[18] *Glimmering Tapers 'Round the Day's Dead Sanctities* (1970), in which he depicted the Northern Lights, is perhaps his masterpiece.

Also around 1970 his painting began to depict fewer western subjects and more of the Ontario countryside or urbanscape. His book *O Toronto* — paintings of, and notes about, the city — was published in 1973 and symbolized his new viewpoint. At the same time, he decided to travel the distance of Canada — to make "the whole country mine."[19] His landscape art was a way of appropriating the country, beautiful and picturesque even when interlaced with evidence of human use.

His difficult personal life, with its wistful searching and its violent transitions, is reflected in the dualism of his work: innocent nostalgia, apocalyptic vision. But many of the more than two thousand paintings he left are unified by the landscape. Kurelek's sense of Canada's physical reality is the most consistent, powerful, and characteristic feature of his work. It is almost as though his native talent had found its own subconscious retort to the wilful subject-orientation of his canvases.

The extraordinary fact of Kurelek's life is that he was so nearly not an artist at all. The forty-eight colour works in this book reveal that, for him, painting was an incredibly difficult activity, and the results were often out of kilter.

Kurelek always carefully documented his sources. He had studied art history at university, and thus had a wide base from which to draw. Though he admired Leonardo, Michelangelo, and Van Gogh, it was the great moralists and illustrators of northern Europe, Bosch and Bruegel, who seized his imagination. Later in his work, he drew inspiration from them, quoting subjects or copying figures. He admired Rouault's *Miserere* series. And he loved American painting. He recalled the work of Thomas Eakins in *Indian Summer on the Humber* (1972). More important were the realists of his own day, like Andrew Wyeth (he had seen a show of his work in Buffalo in the early 1960s and liked his symbolic equivalents of the country, his use of mood and locales).[20] Kurelek liked Edward Hopper, Ben Shahn, and the Canadian Alex Colville. He loved poetry, and drew upon a poem by the English mystical poet Frances Thompson for the titles of the paintings of a show in 1970.

At the Ontario College of Art, he met Graham Coughtry, later

JOAN MURRAY

one of the artists with whom he showed at the Isaacs Gallery. He was always interested by the work of his peers in the gallery, and not only the realists, like Jack Chambers, whose *401 Towards London No. 1* (1968-69, Norcen Energy Resources Limited, Toronto) inspired Kurelek's own *Don Valley on a Grey Day* (1972). He also admired the abstract painters in the Isaacs stable, especially those with an interest in landscape, like Gordon Rayner, to whom he wrote a frank fan-letter about his first collage show in 1975: "I really love this show," he wrote (fig. 4). He may have thought of the imagery in Rayner's *The Lamp* (Magnetawan Series) (1964, The Robert McLaughlin Gallery, Oshawa), a glowing blue canvas with a yellow "lamp," or that work's loose painting and largeness of scale, when he painted his own Northern Lights painting. In *Thunder Driven* (1970), the sky looks extraordinarily like a Rayner. (The field itself recalls more an Antoni Tapies.) In *Plane Watchers at Malton* (1972), the freedom of handling of the clouds seems to owe much to Rayner's lessons in pouring paint onto absorbent canvas.

Perhaps the influence of Kurelek's Isaacs Gallery peers can be sensed only in retrospect. From Rayner and others like him in the Isaacs Gallery, he may have assimilated his abstract way of composing and his keen decorative sense. His use of an all-over composition in which every inch was important was common to abstract painters of the day as well as to many folk artists. Kurelek loved Ukrainian vernacular art. He filled his canvases even to the frame (he'd begun with the Isaacs Gallery as a frame-maker, as well as an artist). Sometimes his frames extend the meaning of his canvases. He had a strong sense of central image, around which he discreetly wove his compositions. "I tend to flout artistic rules by doing taboo things like dividing a composition exactly in half," he once said. "I believe aesthetics can take care of themselves."[21] The use of the strong central vertical created a symmetry of design, one which other painters, in particular Ivan Eyre, noticed.

Kurelek had an almost rudimentary sense of composition. He saw painting as a way of disposing simple geometric blocks in space. In the earliest work in this book, *Hauling Sheaves to the Threshing Machine* (1961), a haywagon sits in the foreground, a square block over which we must look to seek the expansive landscape, the prairie Kurelek dearly loved. Kurelek's idea of picture making was stark: the land was never more nor less than a flat table top from his earliest work to the paintings he did in 1975 for his book *Fields*. The grass often looks like a mat you can roll up.

From an early date in his work, he had tilted the ground plane, often fields in his barren land, towards the picture's surface to exaggerate the distances. But his use of depth could be mechanical. And his usual painting technique was almost preposterously simple and rough: he applied a gesso ground to masonite board, then either oil or acrylic (sometimes in the form of spray), then outlined the composition with a ballpoint pen. For texture, he used coloured pencils; for fine details, he scratched, scrubbed, or brushed the surface. He finished by adding details in pen. This method of fill-in-the-shapes inclined to flat areas. The airbrush helped a little. In *Glimmering Tapers 'Round the Day's Dead Sanctities* (1971), he found it useful to express the melting, shimmering screen of the Northern Lights. However, without his spacious vision of the landscape, a two-dimensional surface would invariably have been the result.

Kurelek had other difficulties. His colour sense varied between too garish and too plain. In *The Atheist* (1963), for instance, Cerulean blue — always a difficult colour — is brushed across the top of the canvas to indicate sky. The habit of a solid sky colour remained with him all of his life. For one period in the early 1970s all his barns were the same shade of red. And Kurelek's sense of form was deficient. There is never a doubt that Kurelek's paintings are painful, laborious *constructs*. His bushes sometimes look remarkably like hedgehogs, the expressions on his faces are phony — as in *Pastoral Symphony* (1974) — and his figures are often lumpy, or stick-like. His best figure work, as the illustrations for *Fox Mykyta* prove, are of animals. In the present selection, the best figures are dogs, especially in a 1976 painting used to illustrate a new edition of W.O. Mitchell's classic, *Who Has Seen the Wind*.

Like other artists of his day, Kurelek often used photographs as reference. Much has been made of his camera-like vision. In fact, his paintings are less camera conscious than theatrical. His scenes seem more like dramatic stage-sets in which figures act out a preordained narrative.

For Kurelek, of course, had a different idea at the heart of his work: for him it was the Christian message that counted. Christ crucified appears dead centre in his *Dinnertime on the Prairies* (1963), and at front left in a tree in *In the Autumn of Life* (1964). Kurelek was at his best painting parables like *The Parable of the Sower* (1963), or the holocaust he fiercely expected, as in *And They Were Taken Unawares...* (1971) and *Not Going Back to Pick up a Cloak...* (1971). From first to last, his thoughts were on his message.

JOAN MURRAY

In *Trustees Meeting on the Barber Farm, Regina* (1976), two pieces of wood on the ground form a cross. The initials Kurelek used to sign his work also featured a cross.

Emotional intensity is a keynote of his painting. Occasionally, he said, the painting took over and dictated to him, although this occurred only when he was under heavy pressure.[22] Things occurred then which he hadn't planned, and which pleased him. In a way, he needed the pressure.[23] It was "need" — the enthusiastic response of the public — which released in him the floodgates of his creativity, and proved always potent later in his life.

What salvages Kurelek's work for us today is not only his distant view — marvellously appropriate to landscape — but his curiously elusive details: the entrancing white horse gazing out from behind a silo in *Satan Sowing Weeds in the Church* (1963), or, in the same picture, the man in bed with his work-boots on the floor beside him, the garden by the house in *In the Autumn of Life*, the half-emerald, half-olive pine tree by the path in *Suburban Church* (1965), the houses on the horizon in his masterpiece *The Painter* (1974), the foreground weeds in *Abandoned Goulettes* (1976). After a while, you forget the clumsiness of Kurelek's way of painting and concentrate on surprises like these. On the other hand, sometimes Kurelek seemed possessed to put in *every* detail, like the police stopping a car in *Don Valley on a Grey Day* (1972). Occasionally a detail destroys a work, like the touch of scratched away snow in the background of *B.C. Seen through Sunglasses* (1973).

These examples of over-finishing suggest that picture making was like a game for him. Or perhaps Kurelek didn't know when to stop. Certainly his greatest difficulty lay in making his details combine with his abstracted backgrounds. Sometimes he managed it successfully, as in *Indian Summer on the Humber* (1972), light tonalities all the way through, *Plane Watchers at Malton*, and in part of *Newfie Jokes* (1974). (The rock in *Newfie Jokes* is an example of what did work: pencil dusted with colours.)

By the time Kurelek died, at fifty, he had just barely improved as a painter. The table-top composition remained, but by 1975 he could achieve small miracles of colour and mood (as in *Stooking*). A big show of his landscape paintings teaches you to hate the finicky detail and ever-present green grass. In his work, in fact, there's much to hate — an unformed sense of picture making, for instance.

But William Kurelek had a larger vision of Canada, and his

struggle was not in vain. He contributed to Canadian art a special kind of awareness of what a symbol means. William Kurelek is the only Canadian artist who can, by showing us a path leading into the distance (as in his 1977 *Piotr Jarosz*), make us think of our impending death.

Notes

1. Joe Sornberger, "The Two Faces of Kurelek — Chronicler and Prophet," *Edmonton Journal*, October 30, 1976.
2. William Kurelek, *Someone with Me, The Autobiography of William Kurelek* (New York: Cornell University, Center for Improvement of Undergraduate Education, 1973), p. 31.
3. William Kurelek, *Kurelek's Canada* (Toronto: Pagurian Press, 1975), p. 12.
4. Metro Kurelek quoted by Peter Sypnowich, "The Easter Story," *The Star Weekly*, April 13, 1963.
5. William Kurelek, *The Passion of Christ* (Niagara Falls: Niagara Falls Art Gallery and Museum, 1975), p. 7.
6. "A Prairie Boy on Canvas," *Windsor Star*, October 16, 1975.
7. Videotape Interview with William Kurelek by Phillip Earnshaw, Ray Konrad and Dell Wolfson, June 20, 1975.
8. Peter Sypnowich, "The Easter Story," *The Star Weekly*, April 13, 1963, p. 7.
9. Videotape interview with William Kurelek by Phillip Earnshaw, Ray Konrad and Dell Wolfson, June 20, 1975.
10. Foreword to *Nature, Poor Step-Dame* (Toronto: The Isaacs Gallery, 11-13 November, 1970), The Isaacs Gallery, Toronto.
11. *Kurelek's Canada*, p. 29.
12. Agnes McKenna, "Kurelek: Artist in Torment," *Oakville Journal Record*, February 13, 1976.
13. Marq de Villiers, "The Agony and the Ecstasy of William Kurelek," *Weekend Magazine*, July 6, 1974, p. 8.
14 *Someone with Me*, p. 448.
15. *Kurelek's Canada*, p. 88.
16. William Kurelek, *The Last of the Arctic* (Toronto: Pagurian Press, 1976), p. 14.
17. William Kurelek, *A Northern Nativity* (Montreal: Tundra Books, 1976), no. 6.
18 William Kurelek quoted by Judith Sandiford, "Painting beauty — Kurelek's 'miracle,'" *Ottawa Citizen*, March 6, 1976.

JOAN MURRAY

19   William Kurelek, *O Toronto* (Toronto: New Press, 1973), p. 32.

20   *Someone with Me*, p. 115; conversation with Jean Kurelek, February 24, 1982; videotape interview with William Kurelek by Phillip Earnshaw, Ray Konrad and Dell Wolfson, June 20, 1975.

21   *O Toronto*, p. 14.

22   *Someone with Me*, p. 238.

23   Marq de Villiers, "The Agony and the Ecstasy of William Kurelek," *Weekend Magazine*, July 6, 1974, p. 2.

Marlene Nourbese Philip

Harriet's Daughter

3

My father is always telling me I should do my homework in my room so I can 'concentrate better.' I like the kitchen, it's warm (it's got a nice red tiled floor), and has a friendly feeling. My mother likes to iron there as well, not in the basement like my father would like her to, and I like to sit there and talk to her sometimes.

I was sitting in the kitchen one evening doing my homework and thinking about swearing, it must have been right after our swearing lesson. Why else would I have been thinking about swearing? My mother didn't think it was proper to swear, even words like damn and blasted which you hear on T.V. all the time — she says these words are too heavy for my tongue to lift up. So as I was sitting there thinking about this and figuring out my maths problem, I said to my mum: 'Look Mum — damn, blasted, shit, see — my tongue can lift them up. It's real easy too.' She got all righteous with me and sent me up to my room to finish my homework. That is what I don't understand about adults, how when you show them they're wrong they always punish you for their mistake. All I was doing was show-ing her I could use those words and the world wouldn't come to an end. Also I don't really think any word is good or bad — it's what you do with it and how you use it.

But my mother? She doesn't know any better, after all she does live with HIM. On a scale of one to ten I would give her a five, and maybe another three points for sympathy, for living with Him. Him, I would give a minus ten. A lot of the time I feel sorry for my mum; she lets my father push her around too much. She fights back some-times but not often enough. There are times when I want to take her and shake her and say: 'Stand up for yourself.' Like the Bob Marley song: *Get up, stand up, stand up for your rights.* I'm sure she would pretend she had never heard of Bob Marley; my father, of course, would say he was a disgrace to black people. No, he would never say black but Coloured People, capital C, capital P.

Some people — I don't know who, and don't care to know either — might say I had nothing to complain about, but I think I do. My mum thinks that because I am a girl, I should like to dress up and wear make-up, like my sister; that I should always be polite and not swear or curse. I say to her, 'Look Mum, if someone calls you a name like nigger, what d'you want me to do? Say excuse me, you shouldn't say that? No way, I tell them exactly where to go,' and when I tell her where that is, she gets pissed off with me and sends me to my room.

I discovered a word a few days ago — neurotic — I looked it up in the dictionary; and that's what I think my mother is — neurotic. My father, on the other hand, is a male chauvinist pig, no doubt about that. That's what I mean about having problems with parents: one a neurotic, the other a male chauvinist pig. I mean like why else would my mother always by buying things, we don't need half the things she buys but she still buys them. If you go in our basement you'll find three sewing machines, four electric irons, three toasters and on and on; and these aren't new things, she buys them all at second-hand stores, but we don't need them.

Sometimes she and my father fight about it, then she calls the Goodwill, or Salvation Army, and they come and pick up some of the things. And beds, beds she buys new; it seems like every year one of us gets a new one. She has this thing about beds; I think it must be because she was really poor when she was a child. She doesn't talk about it much but every so often my father, the MCP, brings it up to show HOW FAR WE HAVE COME. She just sits there and lets him go on and on about how she doesn't want to remember how poor she was; how she didn't have a bed to sleep on and would often only have sweetened water for lunch.

Sometimes though, especially when he's not around, she can be real nice; then I can get her to braid my hair. She really doesn't like to do it — braid my hair — she thinks it's kind of lower class. Only poor people, she says, would corn row their hair, and no matter how many *Essence* magazines I show her, with these super cool black women wearing braids, she just sucks her teeth and says it's all foolishness, that 'straightened hair is so much better.' Of course my sister, Jo-Ann, the Chub Queen herself, has *her* hair straightened with all kinds of gunk. One day though, I even got Mum to

MARLENE NOURBESE PHILIP

braid my hair *and* Zulma's — we were like two African princesses, except my skin wasn't dark enough. I wish I had Zulma's kind of dark black skin, it's just like velvet, and with her long braids — ooh she was beautiful...

I wish my mum would stick up for me more though, with my father. He's always trying to push me around — not physically, but he's always on at me about something: how I'm not like Jo-Ann (thank God); how I'm too rude; and how I need some Good West Indian Discipline, in capitals of course. There are a lot of capitals around my house — Rudeness, Coloured People, Punctuality, Respect for Adults, and on and on.

One day I got so fed up with him going on about Good West Indian Discipline, I said to him: 'Dad, you're always talking about Good West Indian Discipline, what is Bad West Indian Discipline?' He gave me this look, like he didn't know if I was being rude or not. Then he made a kind of noise that he makes in his throat — 'Harrumph!' — it's a real gross sound, and he continued eating. I could barely keep from smiling, for once I had shut him up. I took a quick glance at my sister and she was sniggering too.

My father is always going on about HOW IMPORTANT IT IS TO DO WELL AT SCHOOL, and get good grades and all that stuff, because being COLOURED PEOPLE we have to be twice as good to get anywhere — and I believe him. I just wish he wouldn't go on so about it. Once or twice a year would be enough; instead it's like every week we get this lecture. The funny thing is that although I get good marks and am at the top of the class, he still prefers Jo-Ann, who's lucky if she scrapes a fifty average.

Then there's my dear brother, Jonathon, the great Rib-Roast Prime Minister I call him. He's so perrrfect — not half as smart as me, but *he's* going to be a lawyer, my father says. Me, he says, my mouth will get me in trouble. I keep wishing my brother would scrape my father's car — he's just learning to drive — but no such luck. I really don't understand how girls can like him, they're always calling him. He's so lifeless, so perfect. I mean like he won't wear an Afro because that's too street — his words — and punk, of course, horrifies him. He wants his hair cut low like my father's, and he even chews like my father now — like a cow, slow and stupid.

I don't want to say my father is a bad man, he's not. It's just that he is a phoney in a lot of ways, and I can't stand phoneys. The only thing he's got going for him is that he's adult!

He's phoney because he goes on at my mother about how she won't keep her money in the bank — and she won't. She has this 'partners' saving scheme where she and her women friends pool their money and take turns getting it. Every month my mother puts one-hundred dollars into the kitty along with her friends (I think there were nine of them including my mother). One month my mother gets nine-hundred dollars; the next month Daisy gets it, the next month Dorcas, and so on until all nine of them have each got nine-hundred dollars. He, my father, says this is primitive; that she's losing interest; that she has 'got to move into the modern age and leave her past behind her.' He's an accountant with the government, so this really burns him up. But he plays dominoes — he and all these men from the West Indies sit around all day and play this real stupid game.

My mother doesn't like him playing; she says he wastes his Saturdays when he could be helping her. He likes the game, but wishes he didn't like it. I've heard him telling my mother that he has done the best of all the men he plays with; that he thinks it too lower class, but he still plays and goes on at my mum about her 'partners' saving scheme.

That's why I say he's a phoney. He's not leaving *his* past behind him, but he wants her to. And he's *so* concerned about being coloured, which as far as I can see means being stuffy and boring and not liking anything worth liking, like the Wailers or calypso, or even Caribana, our version of Carnival.

W. A. Spray

The Blacks in New Brunswick

Slavery in New Brunswick

The largest number of Black people ever to come to New Brunswick arrived in the years 1783-84 with the United Empire Loyalists. As a result of the loss of the American colonies 30,000 to 35,000 people, who remained loyal to Britain, came to Nova Scotia and New Brunswick. Shortly after the arrival of the loyalists, in 1784, the Province of New Brunswick was created to satisfy those loyalists who had moved to the St. John River and who did not wish to be governed from Halifax. With the loyalists were several thousand Black people. Some came as slaves or indentured servants, others as free Blacks or Black loyalists. In documents, the loyalists always preferred to refer to their slaves as "servants." However, the status of the majority of Blacks who were listed as "servants" was certainly no different than that of those listed as slaves. It is impossible to determine the exact number of Black people who came to New Brunswick with the loyalists as slaves. In a report of 1784 the number of servants listed as having come with the loyalists is 1,232.[1] A second list states that 1,578 servants came to New Brunswick and Nova Scotia with the loyalists.[2] It is safe to assume that the majority of these servants were Black people. W.O. Raymond claims that the loyalists who came to Saint John brought 441 servants with them.[3] T. Watson Smith says that 441 came to Saint John but that many more arrived later when a number of prominent loyalists moved from Nova Scotia to New Brunswick. There were probably at least 500 Black slaves in the Saint John area in 1784.

Many loyalist officers had one or two slaves, some had 4 or 5 and a few as many as 9 or 10. Many other loyalists who were not connected with the various regiments disbanded in New Brunswick also brought slaves with them. Among the prominent loyalists who brought slaves to New Brunswick were: Gabriel G. Ludlow, the first mayor of Saint John; Col. Isaac Allen, a judge of the Supreme Court; Col. Edward Winslow, a member of the Executive Council of New Brunswick and later a judge of the Supreme Court; and a number of ministers of the Anglican church such as the Rev. James Scovil, who brought two slaves with him to Kingston.

In the early years most slaves could be found in Saint John. As the loyalists moved up the St. John River and into other parts of the Province, slaves were soon found in almost all the prominent settlements such as Fredericton, Maugerville, Gagetown, Hampstead, Kingston, Hampton, Sussex, Westmorland, Kingsclear, Prince William, Woodstock and St. Andrews. At the time of the Province's first census, in 1824, there were Black people living in every county in the Province.

There was one settlement in New Brunswick where those who owned slaves found they were not welcome. This was the Quaker Settlement at Beaver Harbour in Charlotte County.⁴ The founders of this settlement, all members of the Quaker faith, banded together in 1783 and agreed to form a settlement where no slaveowners were to be allowed to settle. At the top of their agreement in large letters were the words, "No Slave Masters Admitted." Also, no person belonging to the settlement was allowed to traffic in slaves under any pretence. W.P. Ganong wrote, "No slave masters admitted to my mind makes that page one of the most magnificent in all our history."⁵ Unfortunately, this was only one small settlement and their policy certainly did not find acceptance in any other settlements in the Province. In 1784, this Quaker settlement was probably the only settlement in British North America where slaves were not allowed.

In addition to the large number of slaves or servants who came to this Province with the loyalists, there were also a number of Black indentured servants. These were people who had bound themselves to serve White masters not for life, but for a specific period of time as labourers and servants. These indentured servants were mostly Black people who had escaped from slavery during the American Revolutionary War and who had found themselves destitute in New York on the conclusion of the war. They were able to leave New York with the loyalists, but in order to obtain necessities not provided by the British, they signed away their newly acquired freedom for a period of time in return for wages or other concessions.

It is impossible to determine the number of indentured servants who came to New Brunswick with the loyalists. Occasionally the indentured servant found that his master had no intention of living

W . A .   S P R A Y

up to his obligations and there are cases where masters later sold their indentured servants as slaves. One unfortunate Black man, who came to Saint John as an indentured servant, petitioned the Lieutenant-Governor for assistance in 1785.[6] This man, Zimri Armstrong, claimed that he had agreed to serve Samuel Jarvis for a period of two years. In return, Jarvis had promised to purchase the freedom of Armstrong's family, who were slaves, and to pay Armstrong's passage to New Brunswick. At the end of the two year period, Jarvis was to set Armstrong up in his trade. Armstrong accused Samuel Jarvis of not living up to this agreement. Jarvis had returned to the United States and his brother John claimed Armstrong as his servant until the two years were up. Armstrong agreed to this only to find that Samuel Jarvis, after his return to the United States, had sold his wife and children as slaves. Armstrong asked the Lieutenant-Governor whether John Jarvis had the right to keep him as his servant. He mentioned his services in the loyalist forces during the war and asked about the possibility of his receiving land. Since Armstrong had served in one of the loyalist regiments, he was entitled to provisions and an allotment of land as was promised to all loyalists who had fought during the war. Armstrong's appeal to Lieutenant-Governor Thomas Carleton and his council was not apt to meet with much success. Carleton, unlike some later governors such as Smyth and Douglas, showed very little concern for the welfare of the Black people whether slaves or free. The majority of the members of his council were slaveowners who were no more sympathetic than Carleton. The council decided that they could do nothing and that Armstrong would have to take his case to the courts. Armstrong was barely able to write and had no money for a lawyer or for legal fees. He was not in a position to have his case presented to any court. There is no record of the fate of this unfortunate man who had lost both his freedom and his family.

Although there is little information concerning Black indentured servants, the county records offices contain ample evidence that slavery was widespread in New Brunswick, particularly in the last fifteen years of the eighteenth century. Since slaves were considered property like land, household furniture, tools and utensils, the transfer of slaves from one master to another was usually recorded. Also many wills record the fate of many slaves. In Saint John in 1799, Munson Jarvis, a leading merchant of the city, sold to Abraham DePeyster, "one negro man named Abraham and one negro woman names Lucy."[7] The same year George Harding of

Maugerville sold to his son John for the sum of £15 a Black boy named Sippio.

There was very little concern shown for the feelings of the slaves and often mothers were sold separately from their children and husbands were separated from their wives. The lack of concern of White masters can be seen in a letter dated October 29, 1787 from a prominent citizen of Brooklyn, New York, to the Hon. George Leonard, a member of the Executive Council of New Brunswick.[8] The letter concerned a mother and child, who were sent to Saint John to be sold. Leonard was to dispose of them, "to the best advantage." He was told to sell them separately, if it seemed to be the most profitable arrangement.

In New Brunswick, slaves were usually sold privately and advertisements like the following were very common:

JAMES HAYT HAS FOR SALE
A BLACK BOY, fourteen years of age, in full vigour of health, very active, has a pleasing countenance and every ability to render himself useful and agreeable in a family. The title for him is indisputable.[9]

However, slaves were occasionally sold at public auction when they were not disposed of privately and advertisements like the following are not uncommon:

TO BE SOLD
A likely healthy negro wench of about 17 years of age, is well calculated for the country, and sold for want of employ. The title is indisputable. If not sold within 8 days from the date hereof by private sale, she will be sold at public auction.
Enquire of
THOMAS MALLARD[10]

Slaves were often included in auction sales of cattle and household effects. At one auction held at the Exchange Coffee House in Saint John in 1786 the items for sale included various kinds of wine, furniture, kitchen tensils, "a NEGRO MAN and BOY; a sloop rigged vessel, with mast, bowsprit, sails, etc." a waggon, birch boards and "a variety of other articles too tedious to mention."[11]

Many slaves attempted to escape from their masters either because of cruel treatment or because of desire to be free. Some were successful but the majority were recaptured and returned to their masters. A number of slaveowners' homes had rooms in the basement equipped with chains, which were used to confine slaves who had attempted to run away. Some slaves made several attempts to escape. Capt. Caleb Jones, who lived near the mouth of the Nashwaaksis River, advertised for runaway slaves on several occasions. One man named Ben was mentioned frequently. Occasionally ship's captains in Saint John harbour would carry off runaway slaves. Some of these slaves worked aboard the vessels, others were sold back into slavery in other ports. The following advertisement is in many ways typical of those found often in early New Brunswick newspapers. The only difference in this advertisement is that a Black indentured servant is mentioned as well as two runaway slaves.

RUN-AWAY

In a BIRCH CANOE, from the subscriber two negro Men and one Wench, who have taken sundry things with them. SAM, between a black and dark mulatto 17 or 18 years old, middling tall and slim, quick spoken, attempts to play the VIOLIN, has a London brown coloured coat, ticking trousers, and other clothes.

BELLER, a sister to SAM, between black and mulatto, 16 years old, middling tall and slim, is rawboned, has a scar between her eye and temple, is slow in her speech, has a black covered hat with white lining, and lived formerly with Judge Peters at Saint John.

TONY SMITH, some call him JOE, a free fellow, but hired for a time, he is tall and slim, speaks broken, wears a blue or brown coat, ticking trousers, and has other clothing with him. Two of the above mentioned servants were raised in the family. Any person apprehending them or giving information to Mr. Ezra Scofield in King Street, St. John, or the subscriber, shall have one GUINEA for each, and if taken out of St. John, reasonable charges paid — if taken out of the province, it is requested that they may be confined in jail until called for. All masters of vessels and every other person is forewarned not to carry any of these said negroes off or from harbouring or concealing them, or they will answer for it at their peril.

THOMAS LESTER
Waterborough, 19 June 1787[12]

The last advertisement for a runaway slave in New Brunswick appeared in a newspaper of September 5, 1818, when John Mount of Musquash advertised for a runaway "Negro Boy named Samuel Hutchings".[13]

Some slaves were granted their freedom in the latter part of the eighteenth century. Occasionally this was done in a will or by the drawing up of a legal manumission document, which was often recorded in the County Court House. One such document recorded in the records of Saint John County reads in part as follows:

> Frederick William Hecht, for himself, his Heirs, Executors, Administrators, hath renounced and disclaimed, relinquished and by these presents doth clearly and absolutely renounce relinquish, disclaim and release unto the said Molatto Joshua Moore all the Estate, Dominion, Right, Title, Interest, Claim and Demand whatsoever of him the said Frederick William Hecht in Law or Equity of in over and to the Person and Services of the said Molatto Joshua Moore, hereby desolving and making the said Molatto Joshua Moore to all intents and purposes whatever manumitted and discharged from a state of slavery and the service of the said Frederick William Hecht, his Heirs, Executors, and Administrators forever, as if free-born.[14]

A number of documents similar to this are recorded in other county record offices.

Although no laws were ever passed in New Brunswick which legalized slavery, it was considered legal simply because it was recognized in other British colonies. However, by the beginning of the nineteenth century there were a number of people in New Brunswick who began to work toward the abolition of slavery. Because of this, an attempt was made in 1800 to test the legality of slavery in the New Brunswick courts.[15] The case involved Capt. Caleb Jones, one of the most prominent slaveowners in the Province, and a Black woman named Nancy. The best legal council in the province was employed in this case. Capt. Jones was represented by four of the most prominent lawyers in the Province, including the Attorney General and two men who were later to serve as Attorney Generals of the Province. Nancy was represented by Ward Chipman, who was later Chief Justice of the Province, and by Samual Denny Street, a fiery former loyalist officer. Chipman and Street were not paid for their services. They volunteered to defend the slave because of their opposition to slavery and as "volunteers for the rights of humanity."[16] In later years, Chipman was to attempt on a number of occasions to aid Black settlers in New Brunswick.

The trial was long and tedious as all six lawyers prepared detailed briefs which they presented to the judges. Every trial and legal decision on slavery which had taken place in Britain or the British colonies, and which could in any way strengthen the case of either side, was searched out and cited in their briefs.

The case was presented to the full bench of the Supreme Court of New Brunswick. The judges present were: Chief Justice George Duncan Ludlow, a brother of the first mayor of Saint John and a slaveowner; Judge Joshua Upham, a slaveowner; Judge Isaac Allen, a slaveowner; and Judge John Saunders, the only opponent of slavery on the bench at that time. After lengthy and heated discussions, the judges were left to attempt to reach some decisions. They were unable to agree. The Chief Justice and Judge Upham found for the slaveowner and gave as their reason their opinion that Black people could be held as slaves under the existing laws of the Province. Although no law stating that slavery was legal had ever been passed in New Brunswick, there were bills passed which allowed immigrants to bring their slaves into the Province. According to the two judges this was evidence that slavery was legal.

Judge Saunders and Allen held that slavery could not be legal in New Brunswick since slavery was not recognized by law in Great Britain. Since the bench was evenly divided, no judgement was entered. The slave was returned to her master. Several years later, when Capt. Jones decided to return to Maryland, a number of his slaves escaped rather than be carried back to the United States where they could be sold.

As a consequence of his decisions, Judge Allen had to decide what to do about his own slaves. He decided to give them their freedom. A number of slaveowners in the Province followed his good example, but many others considered the trial a victory for the slaveowners and continued to hold their slaves.

The trial sparked a number of quarrels between prominent loyalists and resulted in Judge Allen being challenged to a duel by Stair Agnew, a quick-tempered loyalist officer who lived at the mouth of the Nashwaak. Judge Allen refused to accept the challenge. Two of the lawyers involved in the case had come to blows during one heated argument and the result was a duel between John Murray Bliss and Samuel Denny Street. No one was hurt as a result of the first exchange and the two men were persuaded not to continue the duel.

The supporters of slavery reacted to this trial by attempting to have slavery legalized once and for all by an Act of Parliament. In 1801 they had two bills introduced into the House of Assembly.[17] These bills were supposedly designed to insure that masters provided proper care for old and infirm slaves. However, there were sections of the bills which, if passed, would have made slavery legal. One such clause read "all sales or bargains for the sale of any Negro or Negroes shall be registered in the Registry Office in the several and respective counties in the same manner and under the same regulations and restrictions as deeds of conveyance of Real Estate." Another clause would provide fines for anyone concealing or harbouring negro "servants." Because of opposition, these bills were withdrawn from the House before they became law and they were never reintroduced. Slavery then, seems never to have been given recognition by any law passed by the New Brunswick government. There is also no record of a law or court decision that made slavery illegal. However, slavery existed in the American colonies before the American Revolution and, as one judge involved in the 1800 case claimed, "if it existed in the old colonies it certainly remains in the present ones."[18]

In the early decades of the nineteenth century there were many legal battles in the courts over the legality of slavery. This happened in New Brunswick, as well as in other parts of British North America. Many presiding judges were opposed to slavery and many slaveowners found that whenever any doubt could be raised as to the master's right to hold a slave, the courts tended to rule in favour of the slave. The result was that more and more slaves refused to serve their masters and ran away. Slaves therefore began to depreciate in value and were not easily sold unless an unquestioned title of ownership could be produced. In some cases of questionable titles masters entered into agreements with their slaves whereby the slaves agreed to serve the master for a number of years in return for their freedom. Many slaves therefore became indentured servants and were eventually free of all obligations.

W.O. Raymond states that slavery in New Brunswick was generally of a mild type. The master, he says, had no control over the life of his slaves.

If he killed him he was liable to the same punishment as if he had killed a free man. The master was liable to have an action brought against him for beating or wounding, or for immoderate chastisement of his slave. The slave had the same right of life and property as an apprentice; and the practical difference between a slave and an apprentice in early days was that the apprentice was a servant for a limited time while a slave was a servant for life.[19]

This sounds very comforting but in fact it was not so. No white man was ever tried for killing a slave in New Brunswick and if one had, the chances of his being convicted of murder were as remote in New Brunswick as they were in any other place in America. Also I have been unable to locate any records that show that masters who mistreated their slaves were ever brought before the New Brunswick courts. There are many cases of slaves being treated with kindness and in some households the slaves were made to feel almost like one of the family. Nevertheless, after announcing that slavery was of a "mild type" in New Brunswick, Raymond tells this story of one slave master in Woodstock. The slave master was a former loyalist officer, who rode up to the local tavern every day for a glass of liquor. He was followed by his slave on foot who had to get his glass and then return it after it was empty. In the process the slave was made to perform "lively movements worthy of an acrobat, in order to avoid the blow from his master's whip which invariably accompanied the return of the glass."[20] Another slaveowner in Maugerville is reported to have had the habit of tying his slaves up in the barn and whipping them on the slightest pretext. There are also a number of stories of slave quarters in old loyalist homes where chains were used to lock up slaves who might attempt to run away. Other examples can be given which hardly illustrate a "mild type" of slavery. However, regardless of how the slaves were treated they were still slaves, deprived of freedom and subject to the whims of their owners who could punish or sell them whenever they pleased. Joseph Drummond writes: "Telling anyone that any form of slavery is mild is, in my thinking, tantamount to a doctor telling a woman she has a mild form of pregnancy; to hold any human being in servitude no matter how kind the owner is or was, is a gross denial of all that is Godly and decent. Slavery and discrimination have no varying degree of severity."[21]

It is impossible to determine when the last slave was given freedom in New Brunswick. The New Brunswick government reported in 1822 that there were no slaves in the Province.[22] It is difficult to prove or disprove this statement. When the bill calling for the abolition of slavery within the British Empire was discussed in the New Brunswick newspapers, there was no mention made of slaves in New Brunswick. But there was considerable comment on the effects abolition would have on the British possessions in the West Indies. When the bill was given royal assent on August 8, 1833, there were probably no slaves in New Brunswick. The date set for emancipation was April 1, 1834. Local legislatures in the colonies were given the opportunity of accepting or rejecting an apprenticeship plan which provided that slaves should serve as apprentices for a period of six years after their emancipation. This system was not put into practice in any of the British North American colonies. The plan was never discussed by the government of New Brunswick. Two slaves in Upper Canada demanded and received their freedom as a result of the abolition of slavery but there is no record of slaves in New Brunswick having demanded their freedom. It is very probable that if there had been slaves in the Province they or the opponents of slavery would have demanded their freedom.

Notes

1. N.B. Museum, "United Empire Loyalists," cb. article unsigned; also T. Watson Smith, *The Slave in Canada*, p. 32.
2. N.B. Archives, Fredericton, "Return of Loyalists gone from New York to Nova Scotia per returns in the Commissary General's Office."
3. Raymond, W.O., "The Negro in New Brunswick," p. 30.
4. Information on this settlement can be found in "The Pennfield Records," ed. J. Vroom, *Collection of the New Brunswick Historical Society*, No. 4, 1899, pp. 73-80.
5. N.B. Museum, F. 61, Book 3, "History of Charlotte County," by J. Vroom, p. 294.
6. N.B. Archives, Land Petitions, St. John County, No. 78.
7. Smith, *The Slave in Canada*, p. 63.
8. Raymond, W.O., "The Negro in New Brunswick," p. 31; also *The New Brunswick Magazine*, November 1899, Saint John, N.B., pp. 221-24.
9. *The Royal Gazette*, Saint John, N.B., September 19, 1786.

W. A. S P R A Y

10. Ibid, September 11, 1787.
11. *The Royal Gazette*, Saint John, N.B., July 4, 1786.
12. *The Royal Gazette*, Saint John, N.B., July 17, 1787.
13. *New Brunswick Courier*, Saint John, N.B., September 5, 1818.
14. Smith, *The Slave in Canada*, p. 60.
15. A copy of the court transcript of this trial can be seen in the University of New Brunswick Archives. Much information about this trial can also be found in Jack, I. Allen, "The Loyalists and Slavery in New Brunswick." Proceedings of the Royal Society of Canada, 1898, Section II, No. 9.
16. Smith, *The Slave in Canada*, p. 103.
17. N.B. Archives, Fredericton, RLE/802/A/bi/7a and 7b.
18. *The Royal Gazette*, July 28, 1801, also quoted in Smith, *The Slave in Canada*, p. 112.
19. Raymond, "The Negro in New Brunswick," p. 28.
20. Raymond, "The Negro in New Brunswick," p. 33.
21. Drummond, Joseph, "Bibliography of the History of Black People in New Brunswick and Maritimes in General," p. 4. (manuscript in author's possession).
22. N.B. Archives, C.O. 193/5 Reel B-1265 New Brunswick Blue Book, 1822, p. 37.

PART NINE:
IDEOLOGY IN CULTURE

John Ross Matheson

Canada's Flag

The Flag Committee, 1964

On Thursday, 10 September 1964 at 2:00 p.m. the prime minister announced to the House all party agreement respecting a flag committee of 15 members: 7 Liberals, 5 Conservatives, 1 New Democrat, 1 Social Crediter and 1 Créditiste. It was agreed that the committee would report back to the House in the normal way within six weeks, and that committee meetings, or at least most of them, would be confidential.[1]

The prime minister called me to his office and alluding to my experience and success as chairman of the Standing Committee on External Affairs that had successfully completed an exhaustive study of the Columbia River Treaty, he invited me to chair this committee. I told Mr. Pearson that I thought I would be a disastrous choice to resolve the present flag impasse, and that any role that I might play should be active rather than judicial. He then requested me to draw up a list of possible members from our party to serve on the committee. Pearson knew that I was terribly disheartened and fearful of our prospects in the special flag committee. He agreed with my recommendation of Herman Batten (Humber-St. George), solid as English oak, from Corner Brook, Newfoundland, as chairman. He accepted five of my suggestions for Liberal committee members and added two names of his own. It was generally understood that the prime minister's choice of a flag had failed and that we should now start afresh.

By the middle of the month the composition of the committee had been agreed upon. Late in the evening of 15 September James Walker (York Centre) moved:

> That the special committee on a Canadian flag appointed September 10, 1964, be composed of Messrs: Batten, Cadieux (Terrebonne), Deachman, Dubé, Flemming (Victoria-

Carleton), Mrs. Konantz, Langlois, Lessard (Lake St. John), Macaluso, Matheson, Monteith, Pugh, Rapp, Ricard and Scott.

The motion received immediate and unanimous consent.[2]

At this stage I despaired of political solutions, thinking that nothing very aesthetic was likely to be produced by a committee. In yielding to the demand for a committee, the government tacitly acknowledged its inability to rule in the Commons. Now, in the worst possible circumstances of acrimony and mistrust, the government members of the committee (in minority) were expected to produce a result which had theretofore defied Canadian statesmanship for nearly a century. Deifenbaker believed that he would be able to use the committee's failure to rout a wobbly government, so with a gun at our heads we were asked to produce a flag for Canada and in six weeks!

Generally in a parliamentary committee the chairman and his government supporters are aided by a minister, and even more important by a deputy minister equipped with a full complement of experts and with a developed policy. In this contentious matter the government was relying upon me, a member of the committee, to fill this role. Independent of my efforts no really serious research or study had been undertaken so that outside of the speeches of the prime minister and myself we had no policy.[3]

Mr. Pearson had been responsible for starting the all-party committee system in the Canadian Parliament and he entertained an unbounded confidence in its contribution to the legislative process. Although he believed in cooperation, frankness and goodwill, personally as a member of Parliament he had never had any committee experience and therefore did not understand its limitations. In this very worst of times, this perennial optimist sent us out to do our best, and to his everlasting credit, he left us entirely to our own devices and did not interfere. This is one point that I must stress because it is noteworthy, and so very characteristic of the man. It was agreed that our meetings would be conducted in camera. Not once did the prime minister question me directly or indirectly as to what transpired in our deliberations and not once did I communicate with him. I do not believe that he communicated with anyone else on the committee. He must have been brimful of curiosity for each day he looked at our anxious faces with a smile that spelled encouragement, affection, and absolute trust.

JOHN ROSS MATHESON

Each person on the committee had been hand-picked. Collectively they were no doubt a fine lot. But would we be able to work effectively together or would we pull in opposite directions? Théogène Ricard, a French Canadian Conservative, had delivered a particularly opaque speech on 20 August, which in its way was quite a memorable speech, if only because it was quite impossible to deduce from it what he thought about the flag other than that the prime minister had been acting like a dictator.[4]

Peter Newman had given us one clue as to the thinking of this French Canadian Conservative in his report in the *Montreal Star* on 31 August:

> In his dealings with the Quebec members, Diefenbaker seems to believe that the main trouble has been a failure to proselytize what he has called "the real meaning of the Red Ensign" in French Canada. When Théogène Ricard (St. Hyacinthe-Bagot), one of the remaining Diefenbaker supporters from Quebec, rose at a recent caucus to advocate a Canadian flag which would consist of a Red Ensign with some fleur-de-lis in the fly, the Opposition leader turned to his other French Canadian members, and said: "You see, that's what I mean. You go and sell it in your constituencies. It can be done."[5]

As far as the English-speaking Conservatives Flemming, Monteith, Pugh, and Rapp were concerned, there was absolutely no doubt at all as to where they stood. Each of these men had already committed himself unequivocally in the House to the retention of a Red Ensign so on these four loyalists Mr. Diefenbaker could now rely with the utmost confidence that "virtual unanimity" would never be achieved except by a choice of some variant of the Red Ensign. Unlike Pearson, who did not interfere with the committee, Diefenbaker was believed to be in constant communication with the Conservative members.

This flag struggle was above all an exercise in loyalty. The phlegmatic Canadian was not really phlegmatic at all. His concern and his passion were just beneath the surface and the debate had disturbed that surface sufficiently to show loyalty in all its blazing anger, an anger close to tears. John Diefenbaker had recognized that passion, that immense caring, that utter fidelity in his respected former cabinet colleagues Hugh John Flemming and Waldo Monteith; and as well in David Pugh, a Legionnaire and veteran of the First Canadian Division; and in Reynold Rapp, a gallant little Lutheran from the Crimea, who had become a Canadian Citizen in 1936 and was now more British than the British. Four finer Tory patriots could not be found in the Commons, nor four men more determined never to yield.

But loyalty speaks in different voices and my determination now was to improve upon the government design, to produce a flag which was aesthetic, and which, by colors, design and proportions signalled "Canada." I caused a sketch of the original government proposal, strikingly reproportioned and redesigned, to be placed in a prominent position in the committee room. It became a model, something of a challenge to any rival. My secondary purpose, as firm as the first, was to obstruct by all possible means the selection of a compromise Red Ensign flag for I believed that such a flag would constitute a national disaster at this moment in Canadian history.

It was expected that within committee I would provide leadership, but I knew that my powers of persuasion were well nigh exhausted. I had hoped that through two witnesses whose credentials were unimpeachable the committee would at least understand some of the important considerations implicit in the government thinking. Of the many witnesses who appeared before the flag committee, these two are deserving of particular mention for quite different reasons. Col. Archer Fortescue Duguid was the Canadian who over the years was most responsible for keeping Canada on the correct heraldic track. Prof. Arthur Reginald Marsden Lower was the historian who best articulated Pearson's own feelings respecting the importance of an early resolution of the flag question to Canada — a nation in crisis. Many witnesses appeared on their own initiative; but both Duguid and Lower appeared on the invitation of the committee. Without hesitation each has authorized me to use any or all parts of his evidence without further consultation. Each of these witnesses quickly got to the very heart of the matter. Each, however, was controversial.

Colonial Duguid had served between 1921 and 1947 as director of the Historical Section of the General Staff at National Defence Headquarters. He was a thrice-decorated and a wounded gunner in World War I, a counter battery officer on the staff of Gen. A.G.L. McNaughton. Duguid, born in 1887, in Aberdeenshire and a cousin to the Right Honourable Sir Thomas Innes of Learney, long-time Lord Lyon King of Arms, was a simple and direct Scottish gentleman with no taste nor gift for politics or diplomacy. With him there was no equivocation and no subterfuge and his utter candor and his contempt for rhetoric render his testimony noteworthy. He was exactly the kind of witness that parliamentarians occasionally need to remind them of human quality and dignity. The colonel's brief opening statement provides the key to all his later advice. He can be faulted only for being too purist, too consistent, and too rigid. A tiny man with the pride, bearing, and mien of a Skye terrier, this fierce little patriot walked into a parliamentary snake pit, but proud and unscathed he emerged with only a few sharp bites.

In view of the importance of his evidence it is quoted here at length. His own words are more enlightening than any summary I might prepare. He began by pointing out that Canada had its own colors and its own symbols:[6]

I have not seen everything everybody has written nor have I seen everything which has been published in the newspapers. I would have liked to have commented on and contradicted some of the falsehoods which have been printed but I simply have not done anything. I stood back and read most of these statements that our fellow Canadians have made on the matter of the flag and it is perfectly astonishing. They still persist in it although 40 years ago Canada was given a complete outfit of colours, designs, augmentations and everything; everything was put right on the line there. Canada asked for it. The King was consulted and the King in turn consulted the College of Heraldry and these colours, designs and augmentations were approved for Canada. That is what Canada should be using on all proper and appropriate occasions. This was issued by a royal proclamation. I think I am right in saying that that Royal Proclamation is the law of Canada; it states that these designs and devices will be used in future on all proper occasions. That has been done. You have only to look at any Government publication or any piece of Government stationery; there it is. It is on the back of a 50 cent piece; it is ready for convenient reference. Everything is there. The result is, of course, that everybody outside Canada knows all about Canadian colours, devices, augmentations, and so on, but an astonishing number of Canadians simply do not know anything about it at all; it is news to them. About eight persons out of every ten I have spoken to say "Oh, I did not know that; nobody told me." But it is everywhere.

Another point about this is that the deed is registered. These devices and arms are registered and copyrighted at the patent office here in the Dominion of Canada; that is a definite specific statement that these devices belong to the Dominion of Canada. That is a legal document. Registration of this is highly important; it makes that the property of the Government of Canada in the same way that a deed of property makes a person the owner of that property. It is there registered.

There is one other thing which I think I might give you. I do not think you will find this in any law book, although I think you will find this statement is correct. In Canada anyone can fly any flag he pleases, provided he does not thereby convey false information and further does not infringe upon the rights of anybody else. That, I think, is quite important.

After this short initial statement the committee members began their questions. Duguid's answers were short and to the point, sometimes on the sharp side when he considered the answers to be obvious. When one member remarked, "Someone mentioned to me that it is not customary for people to put national emblems on flags, and I wonder if I could get your comment on that. Can you tell me if there is any validity in that statement?" Duguid replied, "My suggestion is that you should look at the flags of the nations and you will very soon arrive at your answer," and he went on to explain:

Let me give you a specific case. Take the flag of Lebanon, take the flag of Russia, there are many flags, particularly the central American flags, which group the whole heraldic achievement in the centre of the flag. Then there is the Austrian flag; they have an achievement of arms in the centre — and Albania, China and Brazil. Cambodia has its building in the centre and Ceylon has the lion holding a sword in the centre....

Perhaps we might go back to the meaning of the national flag; a flag is essentially the flag of national colours — displaying a national design, pattern, device or devices of a nation. As far as Canada is concerned, there is no question that the national colours of Canada are white and red....

The national flag should be distinctive and it should not infringe upon the rights of any other party or persons.

It was inevitable that the question of Canada's colors should be raised by the committee. One member, drawing attention to a design by A.J. Casson of the Group of Seven artists, asked Duguin if "a device like that on a blue field would not be proper?" "Proper for what?" replied the witness. "As a national flag" was the answer. "Not for Canada," said Duguid. Then, in answer to further questions he pointed out that the Canadian national colors were red and white and that they derived from the proclamation of 1921. When pressed by the committee about the possibility of using green maple leaves or a blue background, he stubbornly maintained that these might be used on a flag designed for a special purpose but not for a national flag. A national flag could correctly only carry the national colors: and those colors were red and white only. From this stand he could not be pushed. One committee member gave him some assistance by asking:

> If we value our armorial bearings, granted and proclaimed in 1921 and refined, I believe, in 1957, and if we value the integrity of those arms and those national colours, and if we as the Parliament of Canada should ultimately decide on a flag which denotes an emblem or colours which are different from those in the arms, would it not be sensible and reasonable that we should make application to change the armourial device so that it is in conformity with our flag?

Duguid replied:

> The national device on the armorial bearing in many other countries conforms to those shown on the flag. In one case you are putting it on paper and in another case you are putting it on a piece of cloth, but it is the same and they ought not to conflict....
>
> If you look up the definition in the dictionary under national flag, you will find that a national flag is a flag of the national colours displaying the national design or emblems and devices, and you can add these at will.

The question of Canada's emblem was also discussed and Duguid pointed out that by the proclamation of 1921 the emblem was "three maple leaves conjoined on one stem." The question came at once: "Was a single leaf acceptable?" To this Colonel Duguid replied:

Yes, a single leaf is very, very general; it is not exclusive to the Government of the Dominion of Canada. That is why it is perfectly all right for vendors of anything be it gasoline or bacon; they have a perfect right if they wish to use one maple leaf and they do. The use of a single maple leaf by the Dominion of Canada is not sufficiently distinctive.

Colonel Duguid remained the heraldic purist, preferring that the colors and the emblem of the arms be repeated intact on the flag. He was undoubtedly influenced by his contribution to the First Canadian Division in creating the "battle flag" in 1939. Speaking of this flag, he told the committee:

In the second world war, Canadian units did not carry flags or colours. Just before they proceeded overseas I was ordered to produce a suitable flag for the First Canadian Division. I first decided that the most important thing was to make sure of the national colours of Canada and the national device because it seemed to me that they were obviously the main items for any such flag. On looking at the armorial bearings of Canada, the other obvious item was that there were two flags showing, one of which was the Union Jack and the other a blue flag with three fleur-de-lis. So I placed on the white flag with the three red maple leaves, a union jack on the upper corner next to the staff, which was one seventh of the area of the whole flag. Then I wondered how to include the three fleur-de-lis on the blue ground and I found that a proper heraldic method of introducing such a device was to put a circle in the fly. So I put a blue circle in the upper fly with three gold fleur-de-lis. I had that made and I handed it to General McNaughton just as he was boarding the train to go overseas with the First Division. That flag was flown, so the record has it, from the merchant ship on which the headquarters of the First Division proceeded overseas. While on board it was blessed and consecrated. On the other side, it was flown in the Headquarters of the First Canadian Division.

When His Majesty the King came to review the First Canadian Division, that flag was flying and the General Officer Commanding the First Canadian Division had a small flag on the cap of his radiator on his car. He had one made very similar to that, a small flag, and presented it to the King who accepted it and I think expressed approval.

There followed a sharp exchange for Duguid did not suffer fools gladly; he had covered the matter of colors and emblems thoroughly only to have one committee member remark, just a little belligerently, "I want to ask a question. The three red maple leaves are considered to be the emblem of Canada?' Quickly Duguid replied, "They are not only considered to be, they are registered and proclaimed; everybody knows it." The official committee report records the exchange:

AN HON. MEMBER: Everybody does not; that is the problem.
THE WITNESS: Well, that is the fault of the individual if he does not know it.
AN HON. MEMBER: If that is your attitude, we are not going to get very far. We want some information from you and not a lot of high-handed answers.
AN HON. MEMBER: I am sure the Hon. Member does not intend to say what he has in fact said.
AN HON. MEMBER: I interpreted the answer in that way. It was a very cavalier response.
THE WITNESS: I am very sorry; there was never any thought in my mind or intention of being cavalier or anything like that.

If the raison d'être of a Canadian flag was to contribute to national unity, an important question had to be faced. What message was in fact, as well as in theory, being signalled with one leaf and with three leaves? One leaf was clear-cut and unequivocal. To the Canadian public at large, what would a trilogy of leaves denote? Duguid, in reply, referred to the Christian concept of the Trinity. "I was interested in your explanation of the Christian trilogy, the use of three of anything," said one member. Then he asked, "I take it that the colour and also the three can mean almost anything that you care to attach to it?" To which the witness answered, "Certainly." Pursuing this matter the questioner continued:

Each person in Canada might see something different. If there were three leaves, one leaf might stand only for British origin, while another might stand for French origin, and a third might stand for any other origin; that is, it could stand for a third ethnic group, you see. Someone might say this really belongs to the first, and it excludes the two founding races.

Again, Duguid replied:

> A military man might say that the three stand for the army, navy and air force. But you can apply it to anything that you happen to have in mind which strikes you personally. You are using a signal of three red maple leaves, and you can make what you like of it.

Though not particularly surprising this was a disturbing answer. If the three leaves had a veiled religious significance alluding to the Holy Trinity, as undoubtedly it did in medieval heraldic parlance, then was it appropriate on a national flag for Canada, a country wherein not all persons are Christians? In any event, why confuse the signal. Should one be free to interpret the cluster of three to stand for British, French, and other ethnic stock? Was this not of itself a divisive device denying the oneness that the flag purported to represent? This honest and realistic answer provoked a rethinking on the question. Ultimately was message not far more important than copyright?

Most controversial was Colonel Duguid's reply to questions relating to the use of an ensign, and, in particular, the Red Ensign which for so many years had represented Canada at home and abroad. Here is how this issue was dealt with:

> AN HON. MEMBER: I would like to ask one question here. I am asking for a personal opinion and I would not want the witness to think I am trying in any way to go into sentiments. With your knowledge and background of this whole set-up, is your frank opinion of this situation that the Canadian Red Ensign, or any kind of red ensign used today such as in South Africa and Bermuda and for the British Fleet, could properly be called a distinctive flag to one country?
> A: It is not distinctive, is it? You cannot say it is distinctive; it is almost the same as Bermuda's.
> AN HON. MEMBER: Do you not think that distinctive is a matter of interpretation on behalf of the beholder?
> A: I do not think it is.

Q: Well, I happen to think it is and I trust I am entitled to an opinion.

A: You have to examine it pretty closely because the only part of the Red Ensign that is Canada *per se* is the bottom of the shield, which is one forty-eighth of the whole. If you want to proclaim Canada, just enlarge that area and enlarge the leaves, and that is Canada and Canada alone, no background, no history, nothing; it is Canada only.

AN HON. MEMBER: That comment was in reference to what?

A: The Red Ensign. The Red Ensign gives you England, Scotland and Ireland in the Union Jack and gives you those and France in the shield. If you want Canada, you do not pay any attention to these other countries, you put up Canada alone. The way to give that message is by the white field and three red maple leaves; and that means Canada and it means nothing else.

Q: Do you disagree with the suggestion that following the battle of St. Julien and the first gas attack when six thousand Canadians were either killed or wounded, that an artist in Punch depicted a Canadian soldier in the mire and mud carrying a rifle in one hand and a Canadian Red Ensign in the other? You would not agree that this could easily be recognized as a Canadian soldier?

A: Yes, I would suggest that that is artistic licence. He wanted to put in a flag. He put in the flag of the Canadian merchant service because it was the only Canadian flag that he knew.

AN HON. MEMBER: What message does the Red Ensign, which we now fly as our national flag, send?

A: British merchant men of Canadian register.

AN HON. MEMBER: Which is pursuant to the warrant of 1892, when it was first granted.

Q: Does the Order-in-Council of 1945 not give it an extra status? The Order-in-Council said it would be Canada's flag until Canada otherwise decided. Does that not give any extra status?

A: I do not think a Canadian Order-in-Council supersedes the Royal Proclamation, and I think any flag used at sea, which has the Union Jack on it, is considered by the British Admiralty, which issues the instructions in respect of whom, when and where this flag would be flown.

Q: At the present time, do they issue these instructions in respect of anyone flying the Red Ensign at sea?

A: I do not know.

Q: But they did in the first instance.

A: Yes, they did, and the reason why this colonial significance has been printed on the Red Ensign is that so many of the colonists had just that to fly on their ships, the Red Ensign with their own device.

Q: I would like to follow up along that line of questioning. Could you define a flag and an ensign? What is the proper definition of a flag and what is the proper definition of an ensign?

A: You ought to be more descriptive of the flag. What kind of flag?

Q: Let us start with a national flag.

A: The ensign is a modification of the national flag which brings it down one level. If you put another badge in the flag, then you are bringing it down to another level and into a different group.

Q: Let us deal now with the Red Ensign. Does the Red Ensign belong to Great Britain, does it belong to the crown vested in Great Britain?

A: The regulations governing the flying of the British white, blue and red ensigns are a matter for the Admiralty.

Q: The British Admiralty?

A: Yes.

Q: They come under their jurisdiction?

A: Exactly.

Q: So that if anybody wants to use the Red Ensign, this is granted by Admiralty authority?

A: Yes.

Q: I want to pursue that question. What I meant to ask is whether all the ensigns granted today are granted under Admiralty authority?

A: Yes. In the United Kingdom there are many modifications of the Union Jack. For instance, the Queen's representative in all colonies at one time — and some remain — had the Union Jack upon which is placed the device of the particular colony or country, in a circle in the centre. Similarly, you can treat the blue ensign; you modify the Union Jack by putting this blue on the flag and you modify it still further by putting on the circle with the device of the colony.

Q: The device of the colony? I want to start just from there. This flag, which was designed in the 1800s, shows the device of the colony. When a country decides on a flag which incorporates the Union Jack, such as Canada did with the Canadian Red Ensign which incorporates the Union Jack, is there any sign of subservience?

A: There is exactly the same subservience as there is between a colony and the parent government, I would say. That is the kind of message you are sending, it is what you are conveying to the beholder, the person receiving the signal.

AN HON. MEMBER: I have a very strong attachment for the Red Ensign and when I look at it to me it means Canada, our Canadian flag. It would be the observer who would have to decide. But, suppose we had such a flag and it was in existence for 15 to 25 years; would you then feel it might have attached to it the word "Canada" so that most people when they looked at it, would say "Canadian"?

A: Well, so far as I am concerned, when I look at it — that is, a Red Ensign — I note that a quarter of it is the Union Jack, which is a British flag, so far as I am concerned. It is a British Admiralty flag, no matter what you put in the fly.

Throughout the whole of this evidence Colonel Duguid never deviated from his view that the only message that should be telegraphed by the flag of Canada was the signal "Canada."

Dr. Arthur Lower, the second invited witness, was born at Barrie, Ontario, in 1889. He was a renowned authority on Canadian history and, like Duguid, a veteran of World War I. In his incredibly productive life, every academic honor had been showered upon him. The committee had been treated to a series of witnesses, some of them academics, several of whom were not ashamed to display their raw emotions and at times their racial bigotry. One valuable lesson learned by the committee members was that intolerance and prejudice look very much alike in both languages. This shaggy, shortsighted scholar, like Duguid, was simple and direct and he emerged as somehow monumental. Dr. Lower understood as few others what this complex parliamentary exercise was all about — the search for a country, the desire for a better Canada. His concerns were far larger than the mere symbol.

Unlike Duguid, Lower was not an expert in heraldry flags or banners and did not pretend to know more than any well-informed citizen would know. But he was at home in his own field of history, as he showed in replying to the question, "What do you feel history should teach?"

I heard a wise man define education as initiation into the habits and customs of the tribe. Well, what tribe? You ask the question "What Tribe?" and then we get into the centre of our Canadian dilemma right there — what tribe is the student to be introduced to; whose habits and customs is he to become familiar with?

From there he went on to talk about the appeal of the national idea to young Canadians:

As I cast my mind back over my lifetime, things have changed very greatly. But the idea of Canadianism has come very much more to the front...the other day, just after your Chairman called me, I said that these young people — I thought to myself that this Committee might be interested in having a piece of evidence. So I just scribbled down two questions: Are you in favour of a distinctive national flag, and do you approve of omitting from it the traditional jack? These are the scribbled answers. There are no names. I will pass them around and you may look at them. There are only two of them, I think, or perhaps three, which are a bit out of line; the rest are practically identical.

The answer is in the affirmative in each case except for those two or three. So you see that I think that little test in itself would suggest how strongly the tide of Canadianism is flowing among our students.

It was only a short step from the development of Canadian nationalism among students to the question: "May we deduce from that that we are on our way to develop a real Canadian nation as such?" To which Lower answered, surprisingly, "I am not sure that we can." Asked to elaborate his reply, Dr. Lower remarked:

I say that I am not sure that we can. There we get into very difficult and dangerous ground, you see, because immediately the fact of facts comes up: How far are we a nation, and how far are we two nations? I do not know. Insofar as the young people that I know are concerned, yes, they are enthusiastic and eager young Canadians.

A flag, he thought, "should aid greatly, there is no question about it; it should aid greatly." Then he continued:

The question is whether we can all make this great jump. Is the thing big enough to bring us all together? I think we have all to realize that there are many many enemies to this idea of making a large family out of two separate ones....I am refer-ring to extremists generally on both sides, people who for some reason or other do not welcome the idea of unity, who do not welcome the idea of autonomy and who, not out of sheer wickedness entirely, but from some kind of knots in their mentality do not see life in terms of a unified country, who are so determined apparently to maintain their own spe-cial identity that they cannot surrender it to the larger identi-ty.

You have a very self-conscious group, particularly in Montreal, and also I should imagine, in Manitoba, and they are very conscious of English attitudes....There is a vast dif-ference, I know from my own experience, between the University of Montreal and the University of Laval. Laval is open and free. The French people are at home in Laval; they are masters of their own houses. Montreal seem to be on edge all the time. Of course you understand that I am speaking as an English-speaking Canadian and consequently I may be rather hard on my own people. I think that if we are going to have this change of heart, it has got to come on both sides. Can we get these various groups in Montreal to pipe down? How can we get them to take a different attitude? I do not know, but I suppose that it is for the stronger group to lead the way.

Interestingly enough in view of Dr. Lower's long-time reputation as a liberal democrat, he did not favor holding a plebiscite on the flag question:

I would imagine, whatever the result of a plebiscite was, it would be misinterpreted. I would fear very much that it would divide people rather than unite them. Suppose you have, we will say, a 48-52 vote. You would not decide anything on that. The people would be given to examining the vote by sections and by provinces.

During Dr. Lower's evidence a committee member commented not only on the variety of opinions he had received in his correspondence, but also on the bigotry displayed in some of the letters by people of good education. "In fact, I have started a file called bigotry," he said, "It has got to be quite bulky, and it will certainly make most interesting reading in a little book some day. I marvel at the intensity of feelings shown by some people who by letter indicate that they have academic education, and a great number of them are teachers." Dr. Lower shared this committee member's views and was not surprised at bigotry on the part of teachers or educated men:

When I first went to the west 35 years ago, to Winnipeg to teach, I was surprised to find that meetings there began with "O Canada" because I had never heard it in the east. When I came back to the east — about half way along in that period — I found that it was very generally used. There are extremists. I addressed a club in Kingston once, quite a large meeting. We closed with "O Canada." I did not notice this, but there was a man there whom I had known many years before. He came up to me and said, "You may have noticed that I did not stand up for 'O Canada'." I told him that I had not noticed but I said, "I certainly have no sympathy with that silly point of view at all." I think people of that sort are becoming very much less common than they were.

Despite the prevalence of bigotry, Lower felt there was some hope for Canada for after all, Canadians — French and English — shared a common love of their country. Enlarging upon this theme he said:

I made that statement when I was doing my *From Colony to Nation*; I put that in my concluding chapter. I had a peculiar experience in winding up that book. I do not think that any-

368   JOHN ROSS MATHESON

one can live with an essential piece of creative work for very long without having some such experience. I thought I was experiencing a vision which was the land about which I was writing. I am so familiar with the elements which divide us. I have lived with them for so long, I mean the elements which divide Canadians from Canadians, such as language, religion, tradition, and that sort of thing. I was groping all the time for what we had to give which would bring us together. As I say, I thought I had a little clue in something in the land. Now, the land of Canada is not, let us say, the land of Scotland, where you can see the whole thing from an airplane. Canada is a vast entity itself on the earth's surface. It is hard to grasp it as a whole. There are very few people indeed who have seen the out of the way parts of Canada. Probably there are very few people who have lived in more than one province. Distance makes us pretty provincial. But it has been my lot to move about a great deal and to live in various places and to meet a great variety of men. Particularly I come back to my students because wherever I have taught — and I have taught on the Atlantic coast, on the Pacific coast, and in various areas in between, I have found the same people. They have been produced from something; they have been produced, I think, from the land, just as many people have been.

I mentioned in that brief a few examples, bonnie Scotland and merry England. Also la belle France, la belle province, indeed, God's country. All these expressions suggest that men very rapidly get themselves and their affections rooted in the land. *Dulce est pro patria mori.* All these things focus on the land, whatever it may be. The physical identity which lies behind human institutions, behind the state; and I have another bit of evidence in that direction, and a very interesting one too. Some years ago — a good many years ago — I went across the ocean on a students' ship. There were some 1,500 students aboard. Most of them were Americans. All but about 100 of them were American students. The Canadians were going to attend a seminar or conference or something which has been held every year since somewhere in Europe, and they meet with an equal number of foreign students. They were, of course, of both races. There were fewer French-speaking than there were English-speaking Canadians, but there was quite a number.

Now, two things: The presence of so many American students and the fact that they could, as it were, see the shores of Canada receding, brought them together very quickly. They found out that they were all Canadians before we got over there. In fact the Americans were beginning to call them clannish. You see, it was not a matter of English Canadians going and becoming part of an American group at all. English Canadians and French Canadians came together as one group.

What is it that ties people up like that? I suggest for one thing it is the land, the physical entity, suitably organized, of course, with institutions. You see what I mean. You asked me to enlarge upon this subject, and I have enlarged upon it in that way.

When asked if he had in mind "a symbol or an image that would represent the land and which could perhaps go on a flag," Dr. Lower replied:

Like everyone else, I am puzzled on that point. There are so many questions of judgment which come into this. Personally I do not see why the traditional symbol could not be the maple leaf; it is one that was carried in the first world war. When I was a child I was brought up to sing "The Maple Leaf, our emblem dear" and we sang it with gusto. I think it comes about as close to a national symbol as we can get. If one begins inventing new ones we will have so much difference of opinion, as everyone knows, that there will not be much possibility of agreement. What others can I think of? The beaver? I do not like the beaver very much. He is very representative of English Canada rather than French; that is to say he is a pretty intelligent animal on a rather low level who is very fond of work and has not much idea beyond that. We are very safe and sane, we English Canadians, in a lot of ways and I think it represents us very well, but I do not like to be represented too much by the beaver, I must say. I would like an animal that gets his nose off the ground a little farther.

At this point one of the French Canadian committee members interjected:

In Quebec we have had French Canadians there for a longer period — we go back centuries. For a long time we have had the sentiment of being Canadian. I think we can be happy today to see that that same sentiment is developing in the English part of Canada. It explains why we have this upsurge of the separatist movement in Quebec; it is developing among people who are fed up waiting for you people to become Canadian. I believe the best aspect we can give to the situation in Quebec is to realize that the sooner we become Canadians all together, I am sure in a good proportion the problems we have will fade away. Do you think there is some base for that?

To which remark Dr. Lower replied:

I can quite understand that. I do not think the people of Quebec understand the English Canadian situation nearly as well. I grew up as a colonial, I suppose, having great pride in Canada. But Canada was just a department of the Empire. That was the dominant spirit in Ontario when I grew up. I think one of the things which in so far as my personal story goes which swung me over a bit was my service in the first world war. I was in a British force in the navy and I received nothing but the finest treatment. There was no distinction made between Canadians and Englishmen. But I got the impression that Englishmen were not very much interested in the empire. They were interested in England. So I could not say that I should not be interested in Canada, but I could go on indefinitely in that direction. However, my experience must have been pretty typical, I would think. I have often heard it said that Canadian nationalism came home in the baggage of the soldiers from the first world war. I think it certainly received very considerable impetus from the first world war. Ever since I have taken to teaching I have found a ready response on the part of young people and a recognition that their country is here and not somewhere else. I think the second world war had an even greater effect, certainly on English Canadian thinking. I felt very strongly in the midst of the second world war that I could feel the English Canadian people emerging. We never had a people in English Canada before of any validity. What we had was a collection of individuals, but that is not a people. We had millions of immigrants who had no roots, and who were here today and gone tomorrow. But we never had a Canadian people.

I felt strongly during the second world war that there was an English Canadian people emerging, and the tragedy that I could see emerging would be that if this occurred, we would have a counterpart to the French Canadian people and very likely would go back to the situation which Lord Durham pictured, that of two nations warring in the bosom of a single state. We all come back to the same dilemma; everything in Canada comes back to this point of two nations warring in the bosom of a single state. That is the tragic element in our history.... This is a country of ingrown prejudices and always has been, of the most miserable kind of ingrown prejudice. It seems to me, such as unthinking, irrational, and mean. I do not know how to get over it.

There would have to be some kind of general recognition throughout the country that we have been going in very dangerous and diverse directions and that here is an opportunity for us all to come together under the badge of a common loyalty — loyalty to Canada.

Dr. Lower was gloomy about the future, about the difficulty of getting rid of long-standing prejudices, and specifically of persuading Canadians to agree to a flag:

I am afraid it is going to need a greater machinery even than it would have required to evangelize China, because of the deep seated prejudices in all of Canada. I see a good deal of work in what other people write too. Somehow or other this tremendous effort has to be made.... There could not have been a more tragic experience for the Americans than their civil war. I have something of the same feeling today. How can we avoid it? I wish you could tell me. I have done my humble best in every possible way by preaching the virtues of tolerance, good neighbourliness, understanding, and specifically by suggesting an extension of bilingualism is possible, and the breaking down of barriers. You will be pleased to hear of the withdrawal of the discrimination against French schools, and things of that sort. I have spoken, in season and out, year after year, in those terms. I do not know how far I have got....

...there is a sense of urgency.... We are at some kind of parting of the ways. If you read American history of the 1850s, you will see just what everybody's feeling was then, that there was a sense of tragedy in the air, and that unless the opportunity could be grasped, the nation might founder. We all know what happened at the end of the 1850s, and it is still going on in a sense, that is, the American civil war. In some respects we feel that that is where we are today, that is, we are in our 1850s.

It is difficult to say how the committee members reacted to Dr. Lower's Cassandra-like observations. One member did, however, ask Lower, whether, "if we were to abandon all symbols of the past and come out with one flag with the strictly Canadian emblem, these divisions would tend to disappear" and whether people who were actually hostile to the idea "would come around to it and help promote that flag in view of the necessity for Canadian unity?" Dr. Lower's reply was lengthy but interesting:

I think the only answer I can give to that is that I personally would be willing to take the risk.

The only thing that will replace the old sentiments is a powerful new sentiment, a sentiment for the county as a whole, which I have been trying to describe. It is something I have stood for all my life. There is no reason at all why I should not be in exactly the same position as the people I describe because I have nothing in my past that would require me to seek new symbols, nothing whatsoever. My whole identity is English. From my childhood I have been soaked in English and English institutions, and there is nothing that would require me to seek a change in them except this simple fact, that if we are going to make the country united we have to get together and we have to find things on which we can agree and, in the interests of this greater goal I am ready to abandon my past. I quite recognize there are any number of English speaking people who are not ready to go that far.

You ask me whether I think they would eventually go that far. Well, I am inclined to think they would. The little sheet that I passed around is very significant; it is the voice of youth, and it is the voice of very intelligent youth.

There is another point there which I think should be made. French Canada was separated from France first by the English conquest and secondly, and perhaps more vitally, by the

French revolution. France became atheistic, republican and democratic to a considerable degree. French Canada was none of the three. So, its relations with its mother country were practically terminated by the French revolution.

Now, the relations between English Canada and Great Britain never have been terminated by any revolution and I guess are not likely to be. I think we have to be very practical in these matters. You cannot expect any people to get rid of themselves, as it were; a leopard cannot change its spots. Every English Canadian knows very well, without having to be told, that he is a member of a group which he can find throughout the world in free communities. He knows that the Australian is very close to himself, even if he never sees an Australian; he know that. You cannot expect English Canada to turn right around and repudiate everything in its tradition. That is asking more than you could expect from human nature. Do you see my point? Somehow or other the past and current situations have to be reconciled. I do not think many people in English Canada today, at any rate, expect the French in French Canada to repudiate or abandon their past; the past is there, it is vital. The past is not dead; it cannot be dead. If you like, we are prisoners of our past. Somehow or other reconciliation with the past and the present has to be made....

A symbol is important. I must say that until relatively recent years I did not pay much attention to this business of symbolism because my own nature does not call for symbolism, my psychology does not call for it. However, I can see that a symbol is a very important thing; it sums up, somehow or other, a people's experiences, hopes and aspirations.

I can see that a symbol is a very important thing and therefore I would put very considerable emphasis indeed on the flag. I have come to that.

Dr. Lower's sober testimony confirmed the worst fears entertained by Canadians that profound national divisions actually plagued the body politic in 1964 to the point of danger. He suggested the laying aside of older loyalties in favor of a deeper commitment to Canada. He reiterated the importance of a national symbol in the struggle to survive — Canada's need for a flag was real and not contrived. It remained to be seen whether his remarks had made any real impact upon the flag committee. Although the expertise and high credentials of these two witnesses had been acknowledged by all, I had the despairing feeling that it didn't much matter what the witnesses said, minds already had been made up. Dr. Lower may have made an impression but Duguid's impact had been as slight on our committee as it had on the Joint Senate and Commons Committee of 1945-1946.

On Tuesday, 29 September, I suggested summoning two other witnesses, Dr. Conrad Swan of the College of Arms, London, and Dr. George F.G. Stanley, dean of arts and head of the Department of History at the Royal Military College of Canada.

I had been satisfied from the printed testimony of Colonel Duguid in the 1945-1946 committee hearings that heraldry and flags were indeed aspects of the same science and art. It would be reasonable, therefore, that the English authority, the College of Arms, which had acted for Canada in the obtaining of her ensigns armorial in 1921, would have some quite useful contribution to make respecting the production of a flag in 1964. This, however, was a sensitive constitutional question. Equipped with a letter of introduction from the prime minister, I made a preliminary courtesy visit to the College of Arms in 1963 where I was received graciously by the Garter Principal King of Arms, Sir Anthony Wagner. Sir Anthony, a great authority on medieval heraldry, had served the college in several capacities and was finally elevated to its head in 1961.

When I informed him of Canada's interest in a flag, a subject whereof he appeared to be fully aware, Sir Anthony advanced the startling proposition that this was a subject over which he himself was vested by the Queen with complete jurisdiction and authority. I pointed out that this was a question which successive prime ministers of Canada had undertaken to place before the Parliament of Canada before a decision was finalized. Garter expressed visible annoyance at any such proposition, noting that intervention by Canada's Parliament was entirely unnecessary. A flag should constitute a grant from himself, the Queen's Principal King of Arms, to the Canadian people. Of course, he would seek to please the government but, ultimately, he believed the decision was for himself to make. This easy solution to our problem, I felt, was not politically possible. Garter was living too much in the past.

I discussed our flag problem on several subsequent occasions with Dr. Conrad Swan, then Rouge Dragon at the College of Arms. Swan, a native of Vancouver Island, had pursued his studies in history in Canada prior to attending Cambridge University where he obtained his doctorate degree. He was the first Canadian to be appointed an officer-of-arms to Her Majesty. Swan shared my understanding that while there were certain heraldic proprieties that one should observe — certain international heraldic rules of good taste — Her Majesty in right of Canada could act independently of Her Majesty's officer-of-arms in any other realm. We both agreed that Canada enjoyed full executive as well as legislative and judicial autonomy, which would include any decisions to be taken respecting the flag. Upon my return to Canada I did not apprise Mr. Pearson fully concerning the comments of Her Majesty's senior herald, the Garter King as I feared that the prime minister might discount entirely the importance of heraldry, and in his wrath opt for a paddy-green flag for Canada. After this interview with Sir Anthony, Swan and I agreed that we would thereafter cooperate closely with one another. We would join forces against the Philistines on all sides.

It occurred to me that Colonel Duguid needed support from some qualified heraldic authority and that perhaps the Conservatives in our committee might be persuaded more readily with testimony from London. There was brief discussion concerning the possibility of us hearing evidence abroad. Then I learned by a personal communication that Swan intended to come to Ottawa on some private matter. On 29 September I caused the committee to wire the College of Arms, praying permission for Swan to appear as our committee witness. I did not see the final wording of our request but I have wondered since whether it may have been indelicately worded. Indeed, I do not know to whom precisely the message was dispatched. Certainly no slight or discourtesy was intended to Garter. To the considerable consternation of our committee, a curt reply by cable was received from Sir Anthony Wagner on Monday, 5 October denying permission to Rouge Dragon to appear. Garter stated that he alone would appear for the college. The shocked reaction of the committee when this communication was studied destroyed utterly the influence in Canada of this historic heraldic authority. It was not helpful, at this vital and delicate juncture, to be instructed from London whom we should and should not hear. Thereafter no member of the committee was interested in any advice from the London source, and Canada was completely on her own.

As for Conrad Swan, he did come to Ottawa but for his own reasons. Although he did not appear before the committee, as a friend of Canada and as my friend, he spent considerable time privately in the committee room. He was most generous and entirely uninhibited in his advice and unreservedly endorsed the design which was ultimately selected. With professional thought and considerable care he composed the blazon which was later embodied in the royal proclamation.

As a final parenthesis, it was not altogether surprising to committee members that after Her Majesty herself, as Queen of Canada, had finally approved and proclaimed the new Canadian flag, Sir Anthony saw fit to express himself publicly in criticism.

I must swell upon the signal contribution and influence of Lt. Col. G.F.G. Stanley, Ph.D., then dean of arts at the Royal Military College since his suggestion became the basis for the flag ultimately chose. Dr. Stanley and I had been friends for some years, sharing a mutual enthusiasm for the Scottish arts. I had visited with him at different times in Kingston, in Cape Breton, and in Ottawa. I solicited his interest and help early in my researches and received from him a memorandum on Canadian symbols and the recommendation that Canada's flag should consist of three pales, or bars, red-white-red, with a red maple leaf on the center pale. I particularly recall standing beside George Stanley and looking up at the Royal Military College flag flapping furiously from the Mackenzie Building, one of the college's buildings in Kingston. This flag had three vertical pales, red-white-red, with the college crest (a mailed fist holding three maple leaves) on the white center pale. We had just emerged from the college mess and Dr. Stanley remarked "There, John, is your flag." Interpreting him literally I remarked that Canadians would not accept a mailed fist symbol. He said, "No, I mean with a red maple leaf in the place of the College Crest." It was an interesting proposal that I kept very much to myself, but pondered it from time to time.

To many Canadians, Royal Military College was just a name but to me it was a hall of honor. In the early months of the war, I had taken military lectures and training there as a Queen's University officer cadet. I was later commissioned in the First Field Brigade of the Royal Canadian Artillery in Kingston. Thereafter, I served overseas with many Royal Military College graduates in the three batteries of the Royal Canadian Horse Artillery. Inevitably, I was powerfully predisposed to this small elite institution which for so many years had upheld the motto: "Truth, Duty, Valour." The alumni of that place were a nonvocal lot, who had been unstinting in their personal service to country and in their sacrifice.

The most renowned living alumnus of Royal Military College was Lt. Gen. Guy Simonds who initially had been much distressed over the government's plans for a Canadian flag and therefore complained bitterly to his long-time friend "Mike" Pearson. The prime minister referred the general to me. After I had been exposed to a searching cross-examination, the general (under whom I had the honor of serving in Britain and in the Mediterranean) appeared to undergo a most comforting change of heart. Simonds had commanded my own regiment in 1940, where he was affectionately known behind his back as "the great God Guy." Possibly my unrestrained admiration for him was a factor in keeping Royal Military College, its colors, and its traditions uppermost in my mind when thinking of Canada's standard. I referred to the college again and again in my flag speeches in the House.

Dr. Stanley presented impressive credentials of his own, among them numerous academic honors. In addition, he had served Canada as an infantry officer and later as deputy-director of the Army Historical Section. A former president of the prestigious Canadian Historical Association, Stanley was now firmly established as an author. Although he made no pretensions to heraldic expertise, he appeared to grasp instantly any technical points that were advanced. Moreover, this soldier-intellectual sensed exactly what the flag question was all about for he was British in his background, generously sympathetic to French culture, and competently bilingual. Here was a Rhodes Scholar from Alberta with a doctorate from Oxford University who nevertheless was first and foremost a Canadian. Personally, I rejoiced in the fact that George Stanley appeared to trust the sincerity of my own motives. Such friends as he, in those days, were precious and rather hard to come by.

Dr. Stanley agreed with my emphasis on the importance of colors. What I at first found disturbing was his declared preference for a single red maple leaf over the triad appearing in the arms. Incidentally, this opinion was beginning to express itself with increasing regularity in correspondence to the prime minister and in press comments. The major thrust of my research had been to establish the historical emphasis upon the emblem, the three maple leaves conjoined. I thought I had developed an iron-clad case that any professor of history would seize upon and support. Early coinage, army and other service badges, the Arms of Ontario, Quebec and Canada, the First Canadian Army Division Flag of 1939, the Canada Medal, the Queen's Flag of 1962 — indeed, there

JOHN ROSS MATHESON

appeared to be no limit to this long list. Dr. Stanley understood my technical argument, but he remained unimpressed with its importance. He believed that simplicity was of the essence in a flag and that a single leaf would serve the purpose better than the three. I was troubled by his views. They echoed doubts which had been expressed by the prime minister quite early when he wondered whether one red leaf might not proclaim Canadian unity more clearly than three.

My initial recommendation of flying the Canadian element of the Arms of Canada, namely three red leaves on white, had become badly beclouded by the Beddoe blue bars. These bars destroyed the heraldic integrity of the concept. If we were now to start afresh and create a flag, then the Stanley suggestion had considerable merit. While there was evidence to the effect that with advances in technology, modern flags could be cleaned readily, and, while British naval experts advised that washing had no appreciable effect on the life of their White Ensign, nevertheless, it was indisputable that a predominantly white flag must get dirty. The Stanley proposal shifted the color weight dramatically from white to red. This seemed a happy emphasis for a country long accustomed to a red ensign. What compelled me to seriously ponder his recommendation was how completely this proposal answered the experts' definition of a national flag — "a piece of textile displaying national colours and/or national emblem."

I acknowledged to myself that my research efforts respecting the triad of leaves had been somewhat tendentious. Had I chosen, I might also have compiled an impressive list of the use of the one maple leaf as representative of Canada. A single red leaf on a white background appeared on the attire of Canadian athletes at successive Olympic Games, red and white being the official colors of the Canadian Olympic Association. In fact, a maple leaf had been consistently worn by Canadian Olympic contestants ever since Canada first entered the games at St. Louis in 1904. More impressive even and more eloquent was the single maple leaf carved in stone at the head of each overseas grave for Canada's fallen dead.

By the time that the battle for a flag was shifted from Commons to committee, I at least aspired to a more open mind. Discussions with Stanley and much reading of press clippings about the flag issue had caused me to wonder whether I had allowed myself to become too technical, too inflexible, too opinionated. I resolved to start afresh, to consider once more every suggestion that had been made.

Speaking in the House on the afternoon of 30 November I recounted:

I went to the Committee with a strong personal preference that the device accepted by the Queen (the three red leaves conjoined) should be recognized as the official emblem of the nation, but with the resolve that my personal preference would not impede the creative work of our committee. I prayed that I might forget my own heraldic notions and views and think only of Canada and her welfare.[8]

The more I studied the various options, the more the Stanley proposal seemed the obvious answer to that prayer. In the end, it truly changed my own preference.

In reviewing once again the pictures of the flags of the world I was anxious respecting the resemblance of the Stanley proposal to the flag and ensign of Peru. This initiated another consideration initially ignored in the original government recommendation — the use of proportions. Proportions were, manifestly, of enormous importance, not alone for aesthetic result but for the prime purpose of identity. Canada's flag required to be differenced in dramatic fashion from that of Peru or any other country. Moreover, to present adequately a large and striking red leaf, a square field of white appeared desirable. As I developed these refinements I was reminded of the suggestion of Major General Eugène Fiset to the arms committee in 1919, to the effect that Canada's national emblem should be a single red maple leaf on a white field. I thought, also, of the widely publicized misgivings of the Royal Canadian Legion in 1960 when the new Legion badge — a red maple leaf on a white field — was chosen. The irony of now presenting Canada's angry Legionnaires with their own badge on a flag appealed to my sense of mischief. It would be the perfect retort courteous!

In experimenting with proportions, I was assisted by a careful reading of the design study and recommendation of a war veteran, George Bist, who at considerable personal expense in May 1964 had adapted the original government proposal into his own attractive and striking one-leaf design. His widely circulated brief was enthusiastically endorsed by the New Democratic Party. It could be faulted, I believe, because of the use of blue bars and, indeed, in the choice of an air-force blue that literally faded into the sky. I felt, also, he had made an unfortunate selection of a round, five-fingered

JOHN ROSS MATHESON

maple leaf, a stylized version of the black maple. However, his flag proportions were excellent. In so effectively presenting his stylish recommendation, Mr. Bist illustrated the options that were available with respect to proportions and thereby contributed substantially to the ultimate flag result. Dr. Stanley's preference for one leaf, I found, was supported by visibility tests conducted by Bist which established that the single leaf (6' x 3') image became a bull's eye at 600 yards, whereas the three-leaf version became blurred and indistinguishable at 350 yards. George Bist's conclusions respecting visibility and legibility prompted a series of later studies on my own part calculated to improve the choice of our maple leaf design.

In committee I endeavored to maintain a low profile and said nothing respecting this and other design experiments which I was conducting. When at last I was satisfied with proportion modifications to the Stanley proposal, the sketch went on the wall — but secretly and without any suggestion of my interest or support. Surrounding it were a series of other quite attractive designs.

On Tuesday, 29 September 1964, I offered the name of George Stanley as a prospective witness to be heard. I did so with some trepidation inasmuch as Colonel Duguid and Dr. Lower had been summoned at my request. Not all members of the committee were likely to share my enthusiasm for the Royal Military College. I was anxious lest my sponsorship of Stanley might prove the kiss of death to his proposal, so I did not press the point and took care never to mention his name again.

Only very much later did I learn that George Stanley had indeed been invited by the chairman to appear. Unfortunately, the then commandant at the Royal Military College, Air Commodore L.W. Birchall, O.B.E., D.F.C., desirous of protecting the college from political controversy, had forbidden his dean of arts to answer the committee summons. By the time Dr. Stanley's duty and right to appear had been cleared through the minister of national defence, a decision had already been reached.

We must accordingly acknowledge, with gratitude, the contribution made by Commodore Birchall to the flag of Canada. By acting as he did, he prevented George Stanley from appearing before the committee. Had Stanley appeared, I am persuaded that some opposition would have been generated to the suggestion advanced. Certainly unanimity would never have been achieved. Providence often works in mysterious ways.

There was no such thing as calm or reasoned discussion in committee. Such was impossible for the emotionalism and bitterness of the debates in the Commons had left their scarring imprint on us all. The presence of that gracious lady, Margaret Konantz, no doubt saved us from terrible scenes. As political enemies we had been quartered too closely for too long. Herman Batten, the most admirable of chairmen, knew he was sitting on a land mine for the Tories had everything to gain by delay and gave no indication of budging one inch. The days passed and we made no progress.

I was now convinced that if a good flag was to come out of committee, I would have to choose it. But choosing a flag was one thing and having it accepted with virtual unanimity was another. Such seemed impossible so the only way to proceed was by stealth.

Always held before us by the Anglophone Tories was the offer of a modified Red Ensign, purporting to honor "the two Founding Nations," but inevitably placing the Union Jack in the canton — the position of honor. It was to be either this kind of flag or no flag at all. That was the Conservative stand. Time was fast running out.

As each day passed, Grant Deachman, whom we had made responsible for government strategy, was becoming increasingly distraught for he felt that to return to the House without a recommendation would constitute a political catastrophe. I had long been aware that my firm views had been an embarrassment to the steering committee. At this stage one was prone to be hypersensitive and a little paranoiac. It was not easy to distinguish when one was acting upon important principle and when one was just self-opinionated and stubborn. I appreciated, of course, that as our Liberal member on the steering committee, Deachman had to be in constant touch with Reid Scott of the New Democratic Party and with Waldo Monteith of the Conservatives. I had not allowed, however, for the despair of Deachman and the persuasive powers of Monteith.

One late afternoon, I was confronted by Deachman and Scott, who advised me that I was, in fact, isolated. In order to produce some unanimous result, it had been thought best, and decided upon, to "go along" with something acceptable to Monteith. I listened with horror in stunned silence. Concealing my fury I replied that I had long abandoned any thought of a unanimous report, and that whatever report the others on the committee might choose to produce would be followed by my own minority report. I stated that thereafter I would marshall all possible opposition against a compromise ensign, that being now reconciled to not achieving a good result I would most resolutely oppose a bad one, and that I felt I might rely confidently upon the support of "all the experts." I somewhat pompously asserted that my responsibility was to Canada — not to any party.

Deachman, not reckoning on my intransigence, felt sure that my loyalty to Lester Pearson would compel me to be reasonable. Reid Scott indicated that for obvious political reasons the three-leaf design was now definitely out.

I protested that I was not committed to a three-leaf design, that long since I had been won over to the view that one leaf represented an improvement. I insisted, however, that we must choose a flag, not an ensign, that displayed Canada's colors and Canada's emblem. This design should, at least, match the aesthetic standards of the now stylish "Pearson Pennant" on the center of the wall.

When Deachman and Scott invited me to point out examples of designs that would meet such exacting criteria, I drew their attention to the refined proposal of George Stanley, dilating upon its characteristics without disclosing from whence it had originated. Almost instantly a consensus was reached and a bargain struck — that design was to become our choice. We agreed then that secretly we would select that flag while the tactics of the voting operation and the political strategy were to be left to Grant Deachman. In subsequent speeches no member of the Flag Committee was more angry or more distressed than Waldo Monteith. Did he believe perhaps that some arrangement had been made and that he had been betrayed? I do not know. All I know is that I personally was beholden to nobody and I felt enormously grateful to Mr. Pearson for my complete independence.

By way of reiteration on this matter of independence, on 30 November 1964 I told the House that during the period that we had sat as a flag committee, I had had no conversation on the subject of flag with my leader directly or indirectly.[9] My categoric declaration on this matter, I learned later, came as a very considerable surprise to my Tory friends.

Our story of the Canadian flag would remain incomplete without some digression to the A.Y. Jackson design energetically endorsed by Mr. Robert McMichael, the inspiration and donor of the Group of Seven art gallery at Kleinburg. The Committee was favored by the presence of representatives of both Jackson and Kleinburg on the afternoon of Thursday, 15 October 1964. I suspect that the Tories believed that their appearance as witnesses was simply a Liberal ploy to win support for a near "Pearson Pennant" result by associating it with the name and prestige of a man many considered as Canada's greatest artist.

To understand the subsequent events we must refer back to the original government proposal. On 14 February 1963 I had recommended by letter and by memoranda to the prime minister that three red maple leaves on a white background would form a distinctive and correct flag for Canada. This was, in effect, what Colonel Duguid had recommended before the Joint Committee of the Senate and House of Commons in 1945. Duguid's views had in no wise changed in the intervening nineteen years, and I had been persuaded by the expertise and the logic of Duguid. Mr. Pearson then authorized me to procure the service of my friend Alan Beddoe to illustrate some designs. Beddoe had indicated to me that he was in entire sympathy with the views of his friend and old employer, Colonel Duguid. One Saturday morning I was invited to the prime minister's residence to show Mr. Pearson several triad designs — three red leaves on white and I brought along Alan Beddoe with me. The prime minister studied the sketches produced. Then, without any prior advice or warning to me, Beddoe extracted from his brief case another design, with vertical blue bars, which he handed to the prime minister saying: "Perhaps you would prefer this flag which conveys the message: From Sea to Sea."

Pearson, whose entire purpose was to strengthen national unity, was enchanted. I spluttered my protests, but to no avail. Alan Beddoe was in his glory and it was quite useless at that stage for me to endeavor to urge that this flag had serious heraldic defects and that it constituted the creation of a flag, whereas the flying of arms did not. Very shortly afterwards when this model was publicly displayed informed critics seized upon the fact that in heraldic language vertical bars do not signalize water. Such a message is conveyed only by the use of a wavy fess, that is to say, a wavy horizontal bar. When confronted by this argument on a national television news program, Beddoe rejoined brightly: "Well, if you don't like the blue bars, you can take a pair of scissors and cut them off."

This merry interview marked the end of the influence of Lt. Comdr. Alan Beddoe on the Canadian flag. Thereafter he was a source of anxiety to the Liberals and to the Tories he was an enemy who had helped produce the "Pearson Pennant."

JOHN ROSS MATHESON

I have no doubt that Mr. Pearson fully appreciated my heraldic arguments.[10] Like another historian, George Stanley, he understood the argument, but was not convinced since he wanted a flag to serve Canadian unity and not something to impress a few heraldry buffs. His spirited reference to the old patriotic song "Hurray for the Red, White and Blue!" was no real argument, as he was well aware. He knew, too, that in spite of my intense disappointment I would continue to give him my unqualified support in all of his undertakings. Being the great gentleman that he was, he recognized later, once his own proposal had failed, that I was then on my own, with one objective only in mind — the finest flag possible for Canada. To me a good flag implied good heraldic taste for heraldry embodied the proven and internationally established principles of design.

Since Mr. Pearson's death, a thought has occurred and reoccurred to me. Is it within the wild realm of possibility that from the beginning Mike Pearson knew that his innocent, very amateurish pennant could never succeed? Did he nevertheless feel compelled to preach that simple message of unity, "from sea to sea"? His uncontrolled joy with the final flag result suggests to me that his sights were always upon something loftier, something far more fundamental to the nation than the mere design of a flag. He desired a better country.

On 2 July 1964 a Canadian Press story written by Stewart MacLeod startled the flag combatants on all sides. A.Y. Jackson himself had entered the flag war. His flag sketch and his comments were flashed across the nation. The story, in its entirety reads as follows:

> Among the 5900 odd flag designs submitted to the Government is one from A.Y. Jackson, whose color-conscious eyes were peering out at the Canadian landscape from behind an easel before most members of Parliament were born.
>
> His suggestion for a distinctive Canadian flag painted about three years ago, is similar to that now being proposed in Parliament by the Government.
>
> The design of the 81 year old painter, one of Canada's famed Group of Seven artists, has three red maple leaves joined on a single stem on a white background. But where the Government's design has a vertical blue bar at each side of the flag, Mr. Jackson proposes a wavy horizontal blue bar at the top and bottom.

This, to him, makes a big difference.

"You see," he said recently in his apartment-studio, "it was the rivers that opened up Canada. Every province has rivers, and all were explored that way. These wavy lines indicate that history."

Mr. Jackson has been "fooling around" with flag designs for years. About three years ago he turned out the design that was recently submitted to the Government by a friend.

The copies went to the Prime Minister's office and to State Secretary Lamontagne. The Government has carefully avoided commenting on individual designs, but Mr. Pearson has indicated he would like to talk to Mr. Jackson about his flag.

"I don't really want to push my design," said the artist. "The Government has apparently decided on a flag — although it's not a very good one."

Besides the vertical bars, Mr. Jackson doesn't like the stylized maple leaves.

"They look like they were cut out of leather, and a stylized maple leaf is not a maple leaf at all. I don't like the stems either: they are just like tree branches."

But he's all in favor of the maple leaf motif.

"We had to decide either on an emblem or an abstract design such as a tri-color, and there's so many of those it's hard to get a distinctive flag. We have no animal — the beaver looks like a rat — and so the maple leaf seems best.

"Having decided that, the Government should have called for suggestions, and then made up some of the designs in full-sized flags and flown them in various parts of the country.

"You have to think how a flag will look through a telescope from three or four miles away. One maple leaf, from that distance, might look like a circle or something and the flag would not be distinctive. The three leaves would make it distinctive."

He said he would actually prefer green leaves to red on the grounds that a combination of green and blue would be more distinctive than red and blue, and "when leaves turn red they are ready to fall.

"But I don't think there is any chance of that being accepted."[11]

JOHN ROSS MATHESON

The Honorable Maurice Lamontagne, secretary of state, who was pleased to regard himself as a devotee of the arts, felt this to be a most timely and fortuitous intervention. What extraordinary luck that this great man of Canadian art "about three years ago" should have turned out a design which so nearly approximated the government proposal! How fortunate that he should now be available to save the government from heraldic error!

Personally, I was startled to learn that A.Y. Jackson had ever entertained even the slightest interest in the esoteric field of heraldic art. His proposition that our flag should incorporate any combination of green and blue was nothing short of incredible. I studied the press reports and smelled a hoax. What added to the intrigue was that the small piece of torn cardboard on which the Jackson flag design was sketched, had already been sold by bill of sale to a wealthy Ottawa art dealer. It was represented that this sketch, whose reverse side listed a series of telephone numbers, had only recently been discovered. I studied the sketch, examined and photographed this important piece of evidence, and was not unduly surprised to learn upon inquiry that some of the telephone numbers appearing thereon were quite new. I then had the pleasure of entertaining Dr. Jackson at lunch, at which time I questioned him alone. Behind those twinkling, merry eyes, I discovered the spirit of a mischievous boy. Dr. Jackson knew Canada's north country and the bush. He revelled in the ways of some of our prospecting fraternity. I deduced that the Jackson flag design was of rather recent manufacture.

When, much later, on the afternoon of Thursday, 15 October 1964, the committee was favored by the testimony of Dr. A.Y. Jackson, preceded by his sponsor, Robert McMichael, the Liberal committee members were gracious but, I think, under no illusions. I treated Dr. Jackson with great warmth and courtesy. The old gentleman proved to be a delightful, if a somewhat vague witness.

The indirect result, entirely unpremeditated and unintended, was to reinforce Conservative convictions that the members of the government flag committee were still committed to the "Pearson Pennant" or an A.Y. Jackson variant thereof. My own very cordial relationship with this famous elderly genius tended to confirm the worse Conservative fears — Dr. Jackson was a devious part of a Liberal conspiracy.

Indeed, in retrospect, and after careful reading of the remarks of Donald MacInnis (Cape Breton South) appearing in *Hansard* on 29

October, it does appear clear that the efforts of certain art enthusiasts to promote this Jackson design and the testimony of Dr. Jackson at such a very late date tended to deceive the Tory committee members and even to arouse the worse suspicions of the Conservative caucus.[12]

Today, this costly little piece of cardboard with the A.Y. Jackson sketch is included in the Firestone Art Collection at Minto Place in Rocklitte, the property of the Province of Ontario. It is displayed to visitors by the curator, Dr. O. John Firestone, as the flag Canada might have had, had Philistine tastes not prevailed.

On 13 October 1964 each member of the committee was asked to post on the back wall his choices of flag design as a first sorting. I was most careful not to telegraph my choice. On Tuesday, 20 October, each member of the committee selected one flag design. By secret agreement among themselves, the Stanley proposal kept moving forward. By that evening the number of designs was reduced to thirty. It was then agreed that the final eliminative voting procedure would be left to the steering committee.

The Subcommittee on Agenda and Procedure met in camera on 21 October 1964 and arrived unanimously at a whole series of important procedural decisions. In particular, they decided that all votes would be taken in camera and that the results would not be disclosed but would be recorded in the minutes of proceedings as carried, without any revealing figures. For obviously quite different reasons, these rules appealed to different members of the steering committee. The degree to which these rules served the common purpose of Deachman and Scott will become obvious.

The flag designs were divided into three groups. No individual results of votes were to be disclosed before the voting on the groups was completed. Deachman's strategy was to have every member of the committee, except the Tories, voting in accordance with Deachman's own secret directions. Because the votes were recorded but never disclosed the Tory members continued voting blind as to results. The strategy required that they must at all times vote in fear of an ultimate victory for the "Pearson Pennant." They must on no account suspect that a decision had been made by all the others to support the Stanley design. The dreaded date of voting was set for Thursday, 22 October 1964.

The presentation by Herman Batten of the sixth committee report on 29 October 1964 reveals what decisions were taken

JOHN ROSS MATHESON

pursuant to the foregoing rules — it being understood always that as chairman, Batten himself, did not vote. *Hansard*, in part, reports:

5. Your committee considered the following motions:
(a) For a national plebiscite — motion defeated by a vote of nine to five (9 to 5);
(b) The adoption of only one national flag — motion carried fourteen to zero (14 to 0);
(c) That the Canadian Red Ensign be the national flag for Canada — motion defeated ten to four (10 to 4).
6. The designs received by the Committee, together with those previously submitted, were grouped into three categories, namely:
Class A — those containing three maple leaves;
Class B — those containing one maple leaf;
Class C — those containing the Union Jack and/or fleur-de-lys.
Elimination by an agreed procedure left only one design in each category. A vote for the retention of each finalist was then taken with the following results:
A — The three maple leaf design was retained by a vote of — eight to six (8 to 6);
B — The single maple leaf design was retained by a vote of — thirteen to one (13 to 1);
C — The design containing the Union Jack and/or the fleur-de-lys was rejected by a vote of nine to five (9 to 5).
A vote was then taken to determine the Committee's preference between the design containing three maple leaves and the design containing one maple leaf. The single maple leaf design was retained by a vote of fourteen to zero (14 to 0).
As previously agreed, a vote was taken to determine whether or not the final selection was acceptable as a national flag for Canada. The result of this vote was in favour, ten to four (10 to 4).
7. Your Committee, therefore, recommends that the flag to be designated as the national flag of Canada be a red flag of the proportions two by length and one by width, containing it its centre a white square, the width of the flag, bearing a single red maple, or in heraldic terms, described as gules on a Canadian pale argent a maple leaf of the first.[13]

Deachman's generalship had accomplished an altogether extraordinary result. For a moment he had won unanimity of support for the proposed new flag with a vote of 14 to 0, a result which, when announced, produced consternation and dismay among the four Anglophone Tory members. One may safely conclude that Théogène Ricard had been divided in two votes from his fellow Conservative fellows.

The technical description of the new flag was dictated by myself after the vote. I was happy to report that Dr. Conrad Swan had recommended that we could, on this great occasion, bring a new technical term into the lexicon of heraldry, "a Canadian pale"; for, of course, as I have explained, the flag blazon had been drafted earlier by himself. The members were amazed and greatly reassured by the information that such an authority as Swan had lent a critical professional eye to our undertakings. I took the occasion to emphasize that our choice characterized Canada in three important ways; colors, emblem, and finally — proportions.

There were then in existence seven national flags composed only of the colors red and white while nineteen national flags consisted of perfect pales. Our proportions were thus of the utmost importance as an additional mode of recognition, and, in particular, as a means of differentiating Canada's flag from the national flag and the ensign of Peru. The peculiar width of Canada's center white field rendered her flag unique in all the world. This information was well received by the members of the committee after they had studied my copy of the Admiralty publication *Flags of All Nations*.[14] There was not one comment of adverse criticism and not one expression of anxiety respecting the flags of Peru.

The full committee then repaired to "The Farm" at Kingsmere, Quebec, where a banquet appropriate to the great occasion was provided by the Speaker of the House. After adequate dining and much wining we persuaded Margaret Konantz to remove one of the dark curtains from the window and costume herself as a medium. We then besought, with the aid of her crystal ball, the spirit of Mackenzie King and his revered mother. We invoked a series of blessing by the spirits upon our efforts. We felt like battle veterans, well bloodied. With the sweat of the Liberals and the tears of the Tories, something truly immense had been accomplished. That night the freemasonry of our flag enfolded us all and we were truly fond together. I think Mackenzie King smiled.

On Thursday, 22 October, we concluded our decision respecting the Canadian flag and then considered the second important question — whether the Union Jack or the Red Ensign should be retained to show Canada's membership in the commonwealth. It was decided that no vote on this matter should be taken before Tuesday morning, 27 October 1964. Prior to taking the decision that we recommend the adoption of only one national flag, a decision which was carried by a vote of 14 to 0, I had stressed and belabored the word "national." The national flag was our flag alone — Canada's only. The Union Jack was a flag we shared with many others in our loyalty to commonwealth and our devotion to sovereign. I myself moved an amendment in committee substituting the words "royal union flag generally known as the Union Jack" for the Tory words "Canadian Red Ensign," which amendment carried by a vote of 7 yeas to 2 nays with 5 abstentions. The Tory members, as they reported later, abstained. The motion as then amended carried 8 to 1. Had we yielded to a Tory wish to recommend a continued permissive use of the "Canadian Red Ensign" to express old loyalties, we would have in effect established two national flags in Canada.

The committee report thus recommended continued permissive usage of the Union Jack "as a symbol of Canada's membership in the Commonwealth of Nations and of her allegiance to the Crown." It was argued by some members that such a recommendation was inconsistent with our earlier decision for the recommended adoption of "only one national flag." Personally, I found no such inconsistency for as I later explained in a speech to the House on 16 December 1964, this question had been hammered out as Liberal party policy prior to the election of 1963. In my own riding of Leeds, I had distributed party literature which said under the heading of "Positive Canadianism":

> The new Liberal Government will submit to Parliament a design for a flag which cannot be mistaken for the emblem of any other country.
> The Union Jack will be flown on appropriate occasions as a symbol of our membership in the Commonwealth.[15]

Thus, in some incredible fashion, the Special Committee on a Canadian Flag had fulfilled the prime minister's fullest hopes. This committee continued to exist legally and in camera, until the moment of the presentation by its chairman to the House of its sixth and seventh final reports some few minutes after the House opened at 2:30 P.M. on the afternoon of Thursday, 29 October 1964.

Two extraordinary and vexatious events occurred, however, before the tabling of these reports while the special committee continued in being and therefore in camera. Late on the evening of 28 October, over national CBC television, John Diefenbaker, leader of the opposition, was interviewed by Geoffrey Scott and to the shocked amazement of many observers, he prematurely discussed the flag which had already been chosen in secrecy by the committee, indicating that he would not accept "that type of flag." His words, in part, were:

> All I have to say about that, aside entirely altogether from the fact that it shows nothing of our heritage, is that it would be far from being distinctive. As a matter of fact, it would be the Peruvian flag.... If we ever get that flag, we would have the Peruvians saluting it anyway.

In this way Diefenbaker brought the political cease-fire to an end and the warfare resumed. Someone had leaked the proceedings of a secret committee. The anger in the government lobby upon hearing this Diefenbaker broadcast was indescribable. Now it was "go for broke."

A disturbing consequent event, with most unpleasant overtones, occurred immediately after opening prayers the following afternoon. Just prior to the tabling by Herman Batten of the sixth, seventh and final reports, Donald MacInnis (Cape Breton South) arose on a question of privilege to protest a front page press release in an early edition of the *Ottawa Citizen*.[16] This was no less than a copyrighted interview given by Grant Deachman respecting the strategy employed by himself in committee to obtain support for the Canadian flag. It was a truly shabby account, however accurate, showing the Conservative members in the very worst possible light. Deachman, thereafter called Grant Leakman, arose at once and assumed entire responsibility. This unkind story, which cast its baneful shadow over all the subsequent debates, was quite uncharacteristic of Grant Deachman. On the basis of his service as a member of the Press Gallery apparently Deachman had expected the normal later distribution of the newspaper. It was an inexcusable account of events obviously delivered in hot anger after an exhausting ordeal. The story was a disgrace that all of us bitterly regretted. Because of the sensational nature of the story, the *Citizen* had rushed to press and prematurely pushed their papers onto the streets.

The Tories on committee had suffered and had agonized just as surely as we had and I believe that, privately, they were not altogether unhappy in the final result. Conservative obstinacy had given Parliament a much needed opportunity for a long, sober, second thought. It gave Canada an in-depth consideration of the meaning of nationhood.

Ultimately all the warriors, and in particular the committee warriors, shared in the common victory.

Notes

1. *Debates of the House of Commons,* Ottawa, 1964, vol. 7, p. 7817.
2. Ibid., vol. 8, p. 8067.
3. The reader cannot readily imagine the acute sense of dread experienced in moving into special flag committee after our stalemate, or defeat, in the House. I recall feeling too depressed to attend the first organizational meeting on the morning of Thursday, 17 September 1964. During the period of writing this chapter, more than a decade after the event, I had a nightmare. I dreamt that Mr. Pearson and I were at a swimming pool. He took a straight pin and tossed it into the water. He told me to recover it. I swam down to the bottom of the pool and then proceeded to sweep the surfaces of the bottom with my hands in a desperate effort to recover his pin. After exhausting all the air in my lungs in vain I found I could not make my way back to the surface.
4. *Debates of the House of Commons,* Ottawa, 1964, vol. 7, p. 7091.
5. *Montreal Star,* 31 August 1964.
6. Extracted from my copy of the unpublished Flag Committee Evidence for Thursday, 23 September 1964.
7. Ibid.
8. *Debates of the House of Commons,* Ottawa, 1964, vol. 10, p. 10700.
9. Ibid., p. 10701.
10. Following the surprise production by Alan Beddoe of the design with blue borders I begged permission of the prime minister to prepare a memorandum setting out the advantages of maintaining rigidly to the basic design, that is red leaves on a white field. Within hours I had available for cabinet the document shown in Appendix A. I understand that my views were considered but did not prevail.

Thereafter I supported the decision of the government and, next to the prime minister, became the principal parliamentary spokesman.

11. *Brockville Recorder and Times,* 2 July 1964.
12. *Debates of the House of Commons,* Ottawa, 1964, vol. 9, p. 9545.
13. Ibid., p. 9546.
14. *Flags of all Nations,* Admiralty rev. ed. (London: H.M.S.O., 1955), 2 vols. illus. (col).
15. *Debates of the House of Commons,* Ottawa, 1964, vol. 10, p. 11249.
16. Ibid., vol. 9, p. 9545.
17. *Debates of the House of Commons,* Ottawa, 1964, vol. 10, p. 10690.
18. Ibid.
19. Ibid., p. 10696.
20. Ibid., pp. 10698-10703.
21. Ibid., p. 10723.
22. Ibid., p. 10718.
23. Nicholson, *Vision and Indecision,* p. 348.
24. Ibid.
25. *Debates of the House of Commons,* Ottawa, 1964, vol. 10, pp. 10741-10744.
26. Ibid., p. 10719.
27. Ibid., p. 10723.
28. Ibid., p. 10725.
29. Ibid., p. 10747.
30. Ibid., p. 10782.
31. Ibid., p. 10783.
32. Ibid., p. 10784.
33. Ibid., p. 10824.
34. Ibid., p. 10841.
35. Ibid., p. 10925.
36. Ibid., p. 10965.
37. Ibid., p. 10967.
38. Ibid., p. 10969.
39. Ibid., p. 10971.
40. Ibid., p. 10990.
41. Ibid., p. 10992.
42. Ibid., p. 10994.
43. Ibid., p. 11004.
44. Ibid., pp. 11030-11038.
45. Ibid., p. 11038.
46. Ibid.
47. Ibid., p. 11046.

48. Ibid., p. 11075.
49. Ibid.
50. Nicholson, *Vision and Indecision,* p. 240.
51. *Debates of the House of Commons,* Ottawa, 1964, vol. 10, p. 11080.
52. Peter C. Newman, *The Distemper of Our Times* (Toronto, 1968), p. 261.
53. Nicholson, *Vision and Indecision,* p. 206.
54. *Debates of the House of Commons,* Ottawa, 1964, vol. 10, p. 11132.
55. Ibid., p. 11135.
56. Ibid., p. 11142.
57. Ibid., p. 11144.
58. Ibid., p. 11145.
59. Ibid., p. 11149.
60. Ibid., p. 11150.
61. Ibid.
62. Ibid., p. 11167.
64. Ibid., p. 11170
65. Ibid., p. 11298.
66. Ibid.

CANADIAN CULTURE